D0759370

GREED, LUST & GENDER

GREED, LUST & GENDER

A HISTORY OF ECONOMIC IDEAS

NANCY FOLBRE

OXFORD
UNIVERSITY PRESS

OXFORD
UNIVERSITY PRESS

Great Clarendon Street, Oxford OX2 6DP

Oxford University Press is a department of the University of Oxford.
It furthers the University's objective of excellence in research, scholarship,
and education by publishing worldwide in

Oxford New York

Auckland Cape Town Dar es Salaam Hong Kong Karachi
Kuala Lumpur Madrid Melbourne Mexico City Nairobi
New Delhi Shanghai Taipei Toronto

With offices in

Argentina Austria Brazil Chile Czech Republic France Greece
Guatemala Hungary Italy Japan Poland Portugal Singapore
South Korea Switzerland Thailand Turkey Ukraine Vietnam

Oxford is a registered trade mark of Oxford University Press
in the UK and in certain other countries

Published in the United States
by Oxford University Press Inc., New York

British Library Cataloguing in Publication Data

Data available

Library of Congress Cataloging in Publication Data

Data available

Typeset by SPI Publisher Services, Pondicherry, India
Printed in Great Britain
on acid-free paper by
Clays Ltd., St Ives Plc

ISBN 978–0–19–923842–2

1 3 5 7 9 10 8 6 4 2

To A. M. C. W.,
open-minded economist with a smattering of divinity

ACKNOWLEDGMENTS

The ideas developed here grew, in a topsy turvy way, out of an article I co-authored with Heidi Hartmann, entitled "The Rhetoric of Self-Interest: Ideology of Gender in Economic Theory," presented at a conference memorably attended by Robert Coats, Arjo Klamer, Donald McCloskey, and Robert Solow, and published in the conference volume *The Consequences of Economic Rhetoric* in 1988. I cannot accurately remember or adequately thank all those who have helped me over the last twenty years, but offer a brief chronology of gratitude that begins with institutional thanks.

A generous fellowship from the French American Foundation that sent me to Paris in 1995–1996 offered me the opportunity to learn more about French history. Jean Heffer of the École des Hautes Études en Sciences Sociales served as a superb host and Linda Koike as logistical problem-solver par excellence. A five-year Fellowship from the McArthur Foundation in 1998 gave me the luxury of devoting time to the history of economic ideas. A position as visiting Adjunct Professor at the Social and Political Theory Program Research School of Social Sciences at Australian National University widened my disciplinary horizons. A fellowship at the Russell Sage Foundation in 2005–2006 helped me expand my ideas. A Samuel F. Conti Fellowship from my own institution, the University of Massachusetts Amherst, facilitated my final revisions.

My friendship with Anthony Waterman, to whom this book is dedicated, has proved one of the most rewarding aspects of this adventure. Despite strong disagreement with many of my specific arguments, Anthony consistently provided warm, supportive, detailed, and extremely knowledgeable feedback. His efforts improved my own intellectual capabilities, as well as the manuscript, in profound ways. Deirdre McCloskey also offered generous encouragement and assistance animated by her love of bourgeois virtues. Thank you, friends, for strengthening my faith in the virtues of academic debate.

The International Association for Feminist Economics (IAFFE) and its journal, *Feminist Economics*, created a rich new intellectual space for the development of my ideas. I greatly appreciate the largely anonymous efforts of members, officers, editors, and contributors. My close personal and professional relationships with feminist scholars Paula England and Julie Nelson informs everything I write. I'm grateful for their direct and indirect contributions to this final product. Robert Goodin of the Research School of Social Sciences at Australian National University also gave me invaluable feedback and encouragement.

I thank Robert Dimand, Evelyn Forget, and Janet Seiz for attending a meeting (along with Anthony Waterman) to discuss an earlier version of this manuscript in San Antonio, Texas in 2002. Conversations with Ulla Grapard and Edith Kuiper—as well as their pioneering work in the history of feminist economics, contributed to the development of my ideas. My friend and colleague in Economics at the University of Massachusetts, Carol Heim, gave me the benefit of her broad knowledge of economic history and careful attention to detail. My colleague in English at this university, Nicholas Bromell, offered many discerning comments and suggestions. Others who offered comments and criticisms on specific chapters include Elisabetta Addis, Gerald Friedman, Susan Himmelweit, and Wally Seccombe.

Over the last two years I have used this manuscript in a writing course on the History of Economic Thought, asking students for feedback on my work in return for mine on theirs. I hope we are all better writers as a result. Thanks to my students in Spring 2007: Dalyah Assil, Scott Babineau, John Barrington, Rick Bihrle, Alex Brotschi, Whitney Dorin, Charles Forsyth, Jacob Gordon, Daniel Kelly, Samir Khan, Nathan Kollett, Andrew Mackay, Mitchell Markowitz, Paul Piquette, Tomer Radbil, Michael Sullivan, and Nicholas Swaim. Thanks to those in Fall 2007: James Burbidge, Matthew Donalds, Matthew Greenstein, Sami Korna, Betty Mac, Ali McGuirk, Greg Michalopoulos, Sean Monroe, Michael Monsegur, Huy Nguyen, Matthew Radowicz, Mark Rovenskiy, Alexis Santiago, Christina Shuker, Zach Simmons, Matthew Spurlock, Thien Tran, Alex Weinstein, and Amanda Wong.

My editor at Oxford University Press, Sarah Caro, always responded smartly to my questions and concerns and nudged me in the right directions. The memory of my good friend Helen Smith, superb writer, editor, and independent intellectual, sustained my efforts. My husband Robert Dworak indulged many of my sins. Thanks to all.

While every effort was made to contact the copyright holders of material in this book, there are instances where we have been unable to do so. If the copyright holders contact the author or publisher we will be pleased to rectify any omission at the earliest opportunity.

TABLE OF CONTENTS

EPIGRAPH

Myth
by Muriel Rukeyser

Long afterward, Oedipus, old and blinded, walked the roads. He smelled a familiar smell. It was the Sphinx. Oedipus said, "I want to ask you one question. Why didn't I recognize my mother?" "You gave the wrong answer," said the Sphinx. "But that was what made everything possible," said Oedipus. "No," she said. "When I asked, What walks on four legs in the morning, two at noon, and three in the evening, you answered, Man. You didn't say anything about woman." "When you say Man," said Oedipus, "you include women too. Everyone knows that." She said, "That's what you think."

INTRODUCTION

The point is, ladies and gentlemen, that greed—for lack of a better word—is good. Greed is right. Greed works.

Gordon Gekko, *Wall Street*

Fictional characters are not the only ones to argue that greed redeems itself by motivating economic growth. Over the last three hundred years, our cultural spokesmen have expressed increased confidence in the pursuit of economic self-interest even when it might lapse into greed. Our fear of lust, another of the Seven Deadly Sins, also seems to have receded over time. Still, during periods of war and economic depression, moral anxiety sometimes intensifies. We worry more about the difficulties of balancing the satisfaction of our immediate desires, our long-term needs, and the needs of others.

Michael Douglas played the ruthless takeover capitalist Gordon Gekko in Oliver Stone's 1987 film, *Wall Street*, with arrogant style.[1] His "greed is good" speech mirrored the spirit of the decade, echoing the words of William Safire in a *New York Times* column the previous year.[2] But the film, unlike the column, set the capitalist up for a fall. Gekko successfully uses both money and sex (provided by his ex-girlfriend, who has herself been bought) to corrupt Bud Fox, a young up-and-coming stockholder. Gekko's dishonesty eventually backfires, undermining Bud's allegiance. With the support of his irascible but lovable working-class father, Bud provides the evidence and testimony that will send Gekko to jail.

In the second half of 2008, a financial crisis rocked the U.S., and then the world, resulting in the threat of bankruptcy for banks and insurance companies deemed too big too fail. The Bush administration and the Congress enacted a government bailout of unprecedented size and scope, at a huge cost to taxpayers. Confidence in both the self-regulation of the market and in corporate management suddenly collapsed. The ideological basis of free-market capitalism came into question. As it happens, a Hollywood remake of *Wall Street* was already underway. The conservative British magazine *The Economist* suggested a rewrite of Gordon Gekko's famous speech: "Greed, provided it is sufficiently regulated, is tolerable."[3]

The new concerns about economic vice echoed those heard less than a decade earlier, in the wake of the so-called dot-com bust of 2001. At that time the chair of the U.S. Federal Reserve Bank, Alan Greenspan, laid blame on an "infectious greed" within the business community. "It is not," he explained, "that humans have become any more greedy than in generations past. It is that the avenues to express greed had grown so enormously."[4] Many great thinkers have worried about the size of those avenues and the speed with which we travel on them. The pursuit of individual self-interest can be a positive force. Under what circumstances does it become a vice?

Most efforts to answer this question dwell on the vice of most obvious economic relevance—greed. Alan Greenspan has never expressed concern about infectious lust, though some political figures have met their downfall from it. Lust, like greed, represents the pursuit of self-interest beyond virtuous bounds. Sexual self-interest may seem distinct from economic self-interest, but it can have important economic consequences for gender inequality, family formation, and population growth. The avenues to express lust as well as greed seem wider than they once were, especially for women. Lust is to feminist theory what greed is to economic theory—a marker of contested moral boundaries.[5]

Gender, Vice, and Virtue

Feminist theory offers important insights into the discourse of economic and sexual self-interest. It helps explain forms of gender inequality that long predated capitalist relations of production, and were, in some respects, weakened by them. Attention to gender inequality reveals a moral double standard that regulated women's economic and sexual behavior more forcefully than men's. Attention to ideologies of inequality based on gender as well as class and race enriches our understanding of the links between economic, political, and cultural change.

Some critics of capitalism describe it as a system that displaced more virtuous and egalitarian societies, Gardens of Eden in which individuals were free of economic sin.[6] But the historical record shows that the individual and collective pursuit of gain shaped the evolution of human societies long before money was invented or labor paid a money wage.[7] The patriarchal family-based economies that often emerged in agrarian societies gave males considerable control over the labor of women and children, creating incentives for coercive pronatalism.[8] The emergence of individual wage employment gave women and young adults new opportunities outside the home that gradually weakened patriarchal power.

Still, the notion that capitalism represented a purely liberating force seems far-fetched. One can agree that capitalists can be virtuous but disagree that they have "improved our souls".[9] New forms of collective power counterbalanced new opportunities for individual autonomy, and the benefits of economic growth were unequally distributed. Over the course of capitalist development women gained "self ownership" but remained subordinate to men in large part because they continued to specialize in producing something that could not be easily bought and sold—the next generation of citizens and workers.

The net effects of capitalist development depend in part upon its social context—capitalism compared to what? They also depend on political details like democratic governance, civil rights, and social safety nets. Karl Marx and Friedrich Engels famously declared capitalism a progressive force for change up to some point at which it would, they believed, inevitably collapse. Modern critics are more likely to emphasize adverse effects on families, communities, and the global ecosystem. In the early twentieth century, competition with state socialist regimes created pressures for regulation and an expanded welfare state. When those regimes collapsed (like the Soviet Union) or morphed into more capitalist forms (like China) global competition led to deregulation and efforts to cut back on public spending that have backfired.

All societies face a problem that is simultaneously moral and economic: how to balance individual interests against those of family, friends, and other beings. Robert Nelson describes the particular challenge of market societies as follows:

> The requisite normative foundation for the market requires a dual attitude with respect to self-interest—strong cultural inhibitions against the expression of self-interest (of opportunistic motives) in many areas of society, but at the same time strong encouragement for another powerful form of "opportunism", the individual pursuit of profit within the specific confines of the market.[10]

Capitalist societies have typically glorified the pursuit of individual self-interest, especially for men. Yet markets depend on civility, trust, and the rule of law. The pursuit of short-term self-interest can lead to long-run losses, especially when individuals can't coordinate their efforts. Markets operate within a complex matrix of other crucial institutions, including the family and the state. Competition among groups requires cooperation within them: social identities shape individual interests. Perhaps because they emerged from patriarchal antecedents, capitalist societies have typically relied on much stricter regulation of women than of men. Restrictions on women's freedom to compete have been accompanied by normative encouragement for women to devote themselves primarily to the care of others.

It is small wonder, then, that conservatives bemoan the decline of the traditional family and sometimes describe feminism as a threat to western civilization itself.[11] As women have gradually gained individual rights comparable to those of men, the relative weights we place on individual rights and social obligations seem to have shifted. The pursuit of individual self-interest has gained more cultural power. In many affluent countries around the world today considerable numbers of women as well as men opt out of parenthood. Our inertial reluctance to address global environmental problems suggests that we may overly discount the future.

Gender differences have shaped ideologies of self-interest, including concepts of greed and lust. Following many other historians of economic thought, I define ideology as a set of rationalizations produced by powerful groups to glorify their own importance and advance their interests.[12] I do not believe that such rationalizations are imposed unilaterally from above. Rather, they represent forms of social regulation that evolve over time, reflecting conflict and negotiation among groups with varying degrees of power.[13] Collective interests based on gender are particularly relevant to the persistence of a moral double standard for men and women that gradually proved susceptible to women's individual and collective efforts to reconfigure it.

Intersections between gender, vice, and virtue help to explain the moral regulation of economic life and, therefore, the process of economic growth itself. If ideologies are key, so too are the ideas that underlie them. One way to study these ideas is to ask how other thinkers have confronted them.

The Dimensions of Desire

The first principle of conventional economic theory, which I have taught introductory students for many years, is that we all benefit if everyone pursues their own self-interest. The next principle is that there are many exceptions to this rule. Yet this pedagogical sequence usually unfolds without much discussion of the distinction between self-interest, which most people today view in positive terms, and selfishness, which still carries negative connotations.

I first became interested in this issue when I noticed that many economists have praised men for pursuing their self-interest, but criticized women for being selfish. This apparent inconsistency derives in part from the fact that women have traditionally been assigned greater responsibility for the care of family members, particularly children. Selfish women seem to pose a greater threat to society than selfish men. Tracing the history of anxiety about this threat, I found that selfishness included two more colorful specific vices: greed and lust. Both have been traditionally considered less acceptable in women than in men.

Both vices are characterized by a dangerous intensity. In an early dictionary of the English language, Samuel Johnson defined the adjective *greedy* as "eager, vehemently desirous", and the verb *lust* as "to desire vehemently".[14] He located both vices in the body. Greediness began with food; its synonyms were "ravenousness", "voracity", and "hunger". *Lust* included carnal desire. Today the meaning of greed comes closer to avarice, a desire for money, with which, of course, food can be purchased. The meaning of lust now implies animal urge. Both greed and lust are still defined by adjectives such as "inordinate", "insatiate", "excessive", and "unrestrained".[15] They invoke moral categories: wanting more than one needs or deserves.

However, the effort to define greed or lust in quantitative terms—as wanting "too much" or going "too far"—leads us astray. Most people use these pejorative terms to describe behavior that is either harmful to others or to one's own future health and happiness. Making a lot of money every day does not imply that you are greedy, and having a lot of sex every night does not imply that you are lustful. What matters is how you treat others along the way. John Stuart Mill (admittedly one of the heroes of the following chapters) argued in his classic essay "On Liberty" that individuals should be allowed to pursue their own interests so long as they do not infringe on the rights of others to pursue theirs.

Another misleading convention lies in the putative contrast between self-interest and altruism, which are often described as if they represent extreme ends of a spectrum. But self-interest is not the opposite of altruism, because it can be altruistic. If you love someone else, their interests can become your own. If you have altruistic preferences, making other people happy can increase your own happiness. Consider a different picture of the motivational spectrum, with one end representing perfect selfishness or lack of concern for anyone else and the other perfect selflessness, complete lack of concern for one's own welfare. In between lie complex combinations of self-regarding and other-regarding preferences—the motivational terrain which most of us inhabit.

Another useful way to unpack the term "self-interest" lies in separate attention to the meaning of the "self". If we think of the "self" as an entity entirely separate from others, literally coinciding with the physical body, and defined largely in terms of its physical desires for food or rest or sex, then self-interest will seem predominantly selfish. But if we think of the "self" as an entity connected to others through ties of affection and obligation, its boundaries become less clear. Christian theology describes married couples as "one flesh". Loved ones become a part of us. Under these conditions, to act in one's self-interest is hardly selfish. On the other hand, one can identify with a group that pursues collective interests at the expense of others. Altruism is not necessarily virtuous.

The terminology of neoclassical economics also helps clarify these issues. When introductory microeconomic textbooks specify that an idealized consumer has no "interdependent preferences" what they mean is that he or she is entirely selfish. Introducing concerns for others in the form of interdependent preferences complicates the story: positive interdependence implies altruism; negative interdependence implies taking pleasure in other people's pain. Since preferences are largely unobservable, many economists would like to minimize their influence on the argument.

Interdependent preferences are key. If people are never selfish, it may seem less risky to encourage them to pursue their own self-interest, because they will always take the welfare of others into account. Adam Smith offered a related version of this argument, based on his confidence in natural moral sentiments. However, much depends on *which* others people care about. Individuals who care only about their own family members pursue dynastic interests. Individuals who care more about others with the same skin color as their own pursue racist interests. Individuals who care more about others of the same sex pursue sexist interests, and so on. Altruistic motivation helps to explain group solidarity and collective conflict.

Standard neoclassical models assume that individuals know exactly what their preferences are. But we often don't know exactly how much we care for other people. We may adore someone in the morning and be aggravated by them in the afternoon. Many personal relationships, including marriage, come undone. Feelings of identification with groups of other people also wax and wane. Moral values and cultural norms provide more stable and consistent guidelines for behavior than personal preferences, which helps explain why we often comfortably conform to them. Rather than taking values, norms, and preferences as a given, we can explore the ways they co-evolve in different economic environments over time.

Ideological Evolution

The following chapters explore debates over greed and lust in Britain, France, and the United States, over a period of three centuries of capitalist development. They show how cultural constraints on the pursuit of individual self-interest have been loosened in different ways for different groups in different economic realms. Rather than providing a continuous or comprehensive history, I single out the episodes and ideas that best illustrate the arguments above. I write with a "presentist" orientation, more interested in the retrospective significance of historical debates than their meaning for those who participated in them at the time.[16]

Long before the emergence of capitalism the patriarchal feudal and household-based economies of Britain and France enforced obedience to real and symbolic fathers. The pursuit of economic self-interest elicited moral disapproval only when it threatened principles of hierarchical authority based on inherited privileges of family status, age, and gender. There was no evidence that such systems were any less greedy than our own. Greed did, however, take a different economic form, with different economic consequences.

The transition to capitalism did not magically liberate women, or anyone else for that matter. It did contribute to significant improvements in living standards and advancements in human knowledge and technology. But the expansion of markets for labor delivered enormous power to those best positioned to take advantage of them. Early capitalism weakened but did not eliminate patriarchal rules, relying on the subordination of daughters, wives, and mothers both in the home and in the factory. While women gradually gained new rights and opportunities to compete with men, their continued specialization in the care of dependents often left them with little bargaining power, dependent on support from the fathers of their children.

Capitalist societies have never been pure market societies. They have always relied on families for the production and care of their workers. They have always engaged in collective action, including use of military force to advance or defend their collective interests. Over time, most capitalist societies have gradually developed democratic rules of governance, outlawed property rights in people (slavery), established strict forms of regulation (such as laws against child labor), invested in the human capital of the younger generation (through mandatory public schooling), and developed extensive systems of social insurance. In other words, they have regulated the pursuit of individual self-interest.

Moral discourse plays an important role in the process of regulation. Christian theology listed greed and lust among the Seven Deadly Sins that would be accounted for by the Last Four Things: death and judgment, heaven or hell. By Augustine's account, God in his goodness and mercy uses our vices both as a punishment and a remedy for sin. But the pursuit of economic self-interest—once easily labeled greed—was partially redeemed by the prospect that it would please God and benefit others by promoting economic growth. The motives underlying the search for gain began to matter less than its happy consequences. Economists gained in cultural and moral influence.

From the eighteenth century to the present, political economy has careened back and forth between the moral poles without much explicit attention to women, their work, or their special concerns. But gender marked the social construction of self-interest, revealing apprehensions about a purely selfish economy (absent the "natural" altruism of the mother). Men constructed a theory of interests that, with poetic circularity, served their own. Early political theorists largely excluded women from their theories of the polity; early political economists largely excluded them from their theories of the economy. Feminists, contesting these exclusions, differed on how underlying asymmetries should be redressed: Liberal feminists argued that women should become more self-interested, while socialist feminists demanded that men should become more altruistic.

Liberal political theory built upon Thomas Hobbes's claim, in *Leviathan*, that self-interested men forge a social contract for their mutual benefit. The masculine noun was hardly incidental. Most liberal individualists confined their enthusiasm for the pursuit of individual self-interest to men. From their vantage point, women and children inhabited a realm of natural instinct and moral duty. In retrospect, the inconsistency of an ideology asserting obligations for women but not for men seems transparent. But early critics of this moral double standard—and there were some, including Mary Astell and Poulain de la Barre—could not gain a hearing until new economic circumstances gave women more space for cultural and political maneuver.

In the early eighteenth century, Bernard de Mandeville gave "Greed is Good" a comic treatment in his *Fable of the Bees*. Another of his tracts, advocating public support for prostitution, could have been titled Lust is Good (for young men). But conceptual buffers against both greed and lust proved indispensable to the new science of political economy. Like most other famous thinkers of the Enlightenment, Adam Smith was confident that moral sentiments came naturally to men: the wealth of nations could but strengthen them. However, as Jean-Jacques Rousseau and other skeptics pointed out, one could as easily assume the opposite: wealth could bring corruption.

The early mercantilists recognized that much of a country's wealth lay in the capabilities of a healthy population. Treating families as units of production, they tallied wives and mothers as productive workers. With the rise of political economy that convention was overturned. Thomas Robert Malthus treated population growth as an unfortunate consequence of unregulated lust.

David Ricardo and others who believed that labor was the most important input into the production of commodities—a common denominator that could help explain relative prices—ignored the fact that labor was also the output of non-market work that lacked an explicit price.

Early political economists—Malthus is the best case in point—worried more about the disruptive effects of lust than greed. With a few notable and entertaining exceptions (such as Jeremy Bentham's secret defense of homosexuality) they favored conventional morality and strict social regulation of the pursuit of sexual self-interest. Here again, a double standard based on gender came into play: prostitution, an institution that enhanced men's opportunities for self-indulgence, was widely tolerated. Dissemination of contraceptive information that women might effectively deploy was, however, considered dangerous.

French thinkers like Montesquieu and Voltaire tended to worry more about greed, but less about lust than their British counterparts. In the United States, both democracy and mobility strengthened the ideology of individualism. In the early nineteenth century there concerns about economic morality began to coalesce around the condemnation of slavery as an institution. Abolitionists mobilized considerable outrage against extreme inequalities that created opportunities for greedy and lustful abuse of slaves. Debates over slavery's moral and economic meaning informed the early development of the feminist ideas and shaped the trajectory of capitalist economic development.

Early socialist feminists such as Owen, Saint Simon, and Fourier, dismissed as utopians, flouted conventional norms of appropriate economic and sexual self-interest and denounced arbitrary inequalities based on both class and gender. Not all of their ideas were far-fetched; their advocacy for democratic governance, public education, social insurance, and gender equality proved at least partially prophetic. Other early socialists such as William Thompson developed theories of collective interests based on both class and gender. Marx and Engels largely sidestepped issues of gender inequality in their efforts to construct a more "scientific" socialism. The end result was a simplistic model of convergence between individual and working-class interests that was not borne out by historical events.

John Stuart Mill hybridized socialist feminism with liberal political theory, insisting that women and men should be free to act upon their interests so long as they did no harm to others. Early feminist activists in the U.S., including Elizabeth Cady Stanton, were thrilled to cite a British authority in support of their cause but also made distinctive contributions of their own, calling attention to the undervalued contributions of family work and the economic significance of family law.

The British neoclassical economists Stanley Jevons and Alfred Marshall emphasized individual choices rather than group interests. They hoped to focus the gaze of their discipline on the forces of supply and demand within competitive markets. Yet they believed that women should be prohibited from competition, lest they neglect their moral duties to their families. The neoclassical assumption that non-market work, however morally indispensable, was economically unproductive exerted long-lasting influence on census categories and national income accounts. Economic growth came to be defined narrowly as growth in the number and size of transactions passing through the market.

In the early twentieth century, the cumulative impact of increased female labor forced participation, fertility decline, and gender-based collective action became evident. Beyond obvious victories such as the right to vote, women gained something that might be termed the right to sex. Openly advocating contraception, Margaret Sanger and Marie Stopes celebrated application of the concept of self-interest to the sexual sphere. They challenged fears of lust in much the same terms that an earlier generation of economists had challenged fears of greed.

Fertility decline stoked pronatalist concerns, expressed by men as influential as President Theodore Roosevelt. Those concerns provoked serious thinking regarding the limits of a wage-based economy. Individuals unencumbered by responsibilities for dependents would always be able to get by on a lower wage than those with children to support. If parents were to be paid a wage based only on the forces of supply and demand, how would they bear the costs of raising children? Patriarchal tradition and Catholic doctrine supported a so-called family wage for men; those who hoped to more directly support the work of mothers, like Eleanor Rathbone, made the case for family allowances. By the mid-twentieth century the United States, United Kingdom, and France all provided substantial public support for childrearing, either directly or through tax subsidies.

In the twentieth century, debates over the virtues of capitalism versus socialism echoed debates over self-interest versus altruism. The emergence of a welfare state—a public sector providing education and a social safety net—represented a compelling compromise. Yet those on either side continued to push, pull, and wrestle with one another. During periods of war or economic dislocation, those who advocated state intervention, like John Maynard Keynes, won adherents. During periods of economic prosperity, militant individualists like Milton Friedman gained ideological advantage. Yet both economists deployed moral concepts in their analysis of economic outcomes.

After the 1960s, neoclassical economics directly confronted issues such as family decision-making and the development of human capital. In some ways, this theoretical expansion represented the culmination of confidence in the pursuit of individual self-interest. But in the models developed by Gary Becker, the most famous proponent of this view, a moral division of labor remained in place. While perfect selfishness reigns within the market, perfect altruism reigns within the home. No wonder that women must earn less money, on average, than men do; they prefer to specialize in family care. In this model, the instability of the boundaries between the market and the family—exemplified, for instance, by the high probability of divorce—goes largely unexplored. The realms of the environment, the community, and the polity are also nudged out of the picture. These are realms in which individuals might need to coordinate their actions rather than making all their choices on their own.

Efforts to explain persistent economic inequalities between men and women have gradually engendered the new field of feminist economics. The stylized model of rational economic man has been dismembered, replaced by an androgynous decision maker with a complex range of motivations intermediate between the selfish and the selfless. New research in behavioral and institutional economics highlights the economic relevance of social norms as well as the limited influence of market income on measures of reported happiness. It also reveals the significance of efforts to renegotiate the meanings of masculinity and femininity, rather than taking them as a given.

What Should We Want?

It is difficult to know how intellectual debates bear upon the attitudes and desires of ordinary people. Whatever we may learn about the social construction of vice and virtue may be approximate and crude. Still, hindsight makes it easier to examine the past than the present, and yesterday's discourse defines today's dilemmas. The relationship between economic and ideological transformation cannot be squeezed into simple cause and effect. The development of new economic institutions weakened some aspects of patriarchal authority and promoted the uneven growth of individualism. But concepts of self-interest embedded in notions of appropriate behavior for men and women shaped the way markets themselves were structured. Concepts of right and wrong, good and bad, virtue and vice inevitably influence the design and regulation of economic institutions—as well they should.

Greed and lust have often been described as natural aspects of human desire. Since at least the eighteenth century, the claim that something is "natural" has implied that it need not and should not be changed. Scientific discourse has reinforced the notion that selfishness is the driving force of biological and social evolution. Ironically, science has also shown us that human nature is more malleable than it once seemed. As we begin the twenty-first century, we have less confidence in nature and more power over it. Genetic engineering and behavior-altering drugs, not to mention more subtle tools such as advertising and media control, have increased the potential to program human desire.

What should we want? If the answer to that question were inscribed in our genes, there would be little point in asking it. But part of what we want is determined by our cultural context. Social norms shape individual preferences, telling us how to feel as well as how to act. This programming is decentralized, approximate, and contradictory, which is why we are at least partially aware of it. The physicist Werner Heisenberg, founder of quantum mechanics, pointed out that attempts to measure the location and speed of an electron would modify its location and speed. The same could be said of selfishness. Our very discussion of it may alter its dimensions.

As the intellectual historian Quentin Skinner observed, "It is commonplace—we are all Marxists to this extent—that our own society places unrecognized constraints upon our imagination...To learn from the past—and we cannot otherwise learn at all—the distinction between what it necessary and what is the product of our own contingent arrangements, is to learn the key to self-awareness itself."[7] Economists have never argued that greed and lust are good: but they have not tried hard enough to figure out how to discourage both. If we want to care for others, we need to build social institutions that encourage that care, rather than taking moral sentiments as a given. The intellectual history of greed and lust offers some discouraging insights into the relationship between ideals and reality. However, it also reveals useful efforts to set boundaries on selfish behavior. Tracing the movement of these boundaries over time might help us decide where we think they should be placed. Whether we will ever be able to move them where we want them is, of course, another question.

NOTES TO INTRODUCTION

[1] A video clip can be viewed at http://www.americanrhetoric.com/MovieSpeeches/moviespeechwallstreet.html, accessed January 2008.

[2] William Safire, "Ode to Greed," *New York Times*, January 5, 1986, section 4, p. 19.

[3] *The Economist*, October 18, 2008.

[4] Floyd Norris, "Greenspan Coins a New Phrase," *New York Times*, July 17, 2002.

[5] Mary Daly, *Pure Lust. Elemental Feminist Philosophy* (New York: HarperCollins, 1992); Lisa Duggan and Nan D. Hunter, *Sex Wars: Sexual Dissent and Political Culture* (New York: Routledge, 1995).

[6] Bill McKibben, *Deep Economy, The Wealth of Communities and the Durable Future* (New York: Times Books, 2007).

[7] Jared Diamond, *Guns, Germs and Steel. The Fates of Human Societies* (New York: W.W. Norton, 2005).

[8] Nancy Folbre, "Chicks, Hawks, and Patriarchal Institutions," 499–516 in *Handbook of Behavioral Economics*, ed. Morris Altman (Armonk, N.Y.: M. E. Sharpe, 2006).

[9] Deirdre McCloskey, *The Bourgeois Virtues: Ethics for an Age of Commerce* (Chicago: University of Chicago Press, 2006), pp. 1, 23.

[10] Robert H. Nelson, *Economics as Religion. From Samuelson to Chicago and Beyond* (University Park, PA: Pennsylvania State University Press, 2001), p. 3.

[11] For more on this theme see my *The Invisible Heart. Economics and Family Values* (New York: The New Press, 2001).

[12] A. M. C. Waterman, *Revolution, Economics, and Religion. Christian Political Economy, 1798–1833* (New York: Cambridge University Press, 1991), p. 8.

[13] My emphasis on the discourse of self-interest may reflect the influence of Michel Foucault, but I draw few specific insights from his radically decentered approach in *History of Sexuality: An Introduction*, vol. 1 (New York: Vintage, 1990).

[14] Samuel Johnson, *A Dictionary of the English Language* (London: W. Strahan, 1755).

[15] See *Oxford English Dictionary*, 2nd edn (Oxford: Clarendon Press, 1989), and *The American Heritage Dictionary of the English Language*, 3rd edn (New York: Houghton Mifflin, 1992).

[16] Quentin Skinner, "Meaning and Understanding in the History of Ideas," 29–67 in *Meaning and Context. Quentin Skinner and His Critics*, ed. James Tully (Princeton, NJ: Princeton University Press, 1988), p. 49.

[17] Ibid., p. 67.

CHAPTER I

The Eye of the Needle

Thus it came to pass that every womanly function was considered as the private interest of husbands and fathers, bearing no relation to the life of the State, and therefore demanding from the community as a whole no special care or provision.   Alice Clark

Once upon a time, it is said, our ancestors didn't care very much about making money. They lived miserable lives and consoled themselves with a religious faith that offered them the hope of eternal life. Then something happened, we are not exactly sure what. Maybe some of them figured out better ways of doing things, which changed the way they thought about themselves. Maybe some of them decided they wanted something better in this world rather than the next and changed their behavior as a result. In any case, European society began to undergo a series of related but distinctive transitions: from production for use to production for exchange, from kin- to non-kin-based units of production, from strict patriarchal control over women and children to greater scope for individual choice. At approximately the same time, concepts of appropriate human behavior began to shift along a series of related but distinctive spectra: from solidarity to self-interest, from authoritarianism to democracy, from patriarchy towards gender equality.

This is the basic story we like to tell our children about the origins of our prosperity, with titles like *The Protestant Ethic and the Spirit of Capitalism,*

The Rise of the Western World and *How the West Grew Rich*.[1] On its moral implications, however, we are profoundly divided. Some argue that women have become more virtuous as well as more prosperous over time.[2] Men have less power to order women about than they once had. On the other hand, some argue that the weakening of religious values—and a new-found faith in the purchase of happiness—have corrupted us. In *Religion and the Rise of Capitalism*, R. H. Tawney warned that unbridled pursuit of self-interest would lead to moral bankruptcy.[3] Tawney's contemporary, the English historian Alice Clark believed that the growth of individualism had adverse effects on wives and mothers because it weakened recognition of work that was not conducted for individual gain.[4]

In this debate over moral progress versus regress much hinges on the interpretation of economic systems in place before capitalism got fully underway. Consider the most extreme possibilities: If these were moral economies shaped largely by obligations to care for others, the growth of individualism could have enabled more selfish behavior. If these were authoritarian economies shaped largely by inherited authority, the growth of individualism could have weakened selfish forms of arbitrary power. A careful look at changing ideologies of gender paints a more complex picture. Women only gradually gained new rights because they found it difficult to reassign their traditional obligations.

Liberation

Modern economic historians, situated for the most part in the advanced capitalist countries, tend to describe the growth of capitalism as a liberating force. Individualism is modernity: it is associated with adjectives rational, economic, or secular, contrasted with the emotional, spiritual, or religious. At first glance it might seem inconsistent with Christian injunctions to love our neighbors as we love ourselves. Jesus warns men not to store up treasure on earth, warning that it is "easier for a camel to pass through the eye of a needle than for a rich man to enter the kingdom of God."[5] But perhaps the "eye of the needle" was actually a narrow gate in the city wall of Jerusalem that a camel could squeeze through on its knees.[6]

Max Weber's influential writings insisted that capitalism was not associated with any weakening of religion, but rather with a new Protestant ethic that promoted savings and investment: Economic success could reflect God's favor. Weber argued that traditional societies were not self-interested enough.[7] In the absence of cultural values urging them toward personal advancement, men might be satisfied by the comfortable indulgence of habit. Such would always tempt women. Weber described young girls as particularly inefficient workers, because they lacked the energetic capitalist spirit.[8]

The concept of a Protestant ethic soon lost its sacred undertones. By the twentieth century, Weber acknowledged, the pursuit of wealth had been "stripped of its religious and ethical meaning" (especially in the United States).[9] Economists began to preach that prosperity promised happiness.[10] In the late twentieth century, ethical concerns that conflicted with economic growth were often derogated as timidity. In *The Rise of the Western World*, Douglass C. North and Robert Paul Thomas announced that, "the acquisitive spirit triumphed over moral qualms".[11] In his authoritative history of the family, sex, and marriage in England from the sixteenth to the nineteenth century, Lawrence Stone warbled that "Man was now freed to seek his own personal pleasure here and now, no longer hedged in by the narrow boundaries laid down by moral theology or traditional custom."[12]

The triumphalist view that economic development represents a shining path to freedom is not confined to the United States. Fernand Braudel, the highly respected French historian, inverts the religious metaphor by claiming that a widening of the needle's eye can lead men back to a world not unlike Eden:

> The market spells liberation, openness, access to another world. It means coming up for air. Men's activities, the surpluses they exchange, gradually pass through this narrow channel to the other world with as much difficulty at first as the camel of the scriptures passing through the eye of a needle. Then the breaches grow wider and more frequent, as society finally becomes a "generalized market society".[13]

Braudel mentions men's activities and the surpluses they exchange. Women engage less in labor markets than do men, even in the most advanced capitalist countries in the world. They cross over to the "other world" in rather different ways.

Damnation

Where some historians have seen liberation, others, like the English historian and Christian socialist R. H. Tawney, have seen damnation. Tawney argued that concern for the welfare of others was the basis of social cohesion. The rhetoric of free choice, in his view, obscured the weakening of social obligation: capitalism delivered greater benefits to the strong than to the weak and social divisions further reduced solidarity. The search for personal pleasure, in Tawney's view, was a source of energy that should be confined to its proper sphere, harnessed and controlled. Economic ambitions might serve as "good servants", but they were "bad masters".[14] He feared that the decline of religious influence would unleash a sorcerer's apprentice.

Alice Clark prefigured many of Tawney's concerns in her classic account of the lives of seventeenth-century English women.[15] She singled out the effects of the transition to capitalism on women. In her view, the shift from family-based production to an individual wage system reduced social recognition of those aspects of women's work that took place outside the market, such as the care of children and other dependent family members.[16] Families in which men and women once combined productive and reproductive effort were divided—men moved into the new market economy leaving women behind with responsibilities for work that was inevitably less empowering.

Clark was among the first of many to describe the growth of wage employment as a wedge driven between the production of things and the reproduction of people.[17] Joseph Schumpeter, an historian of economic ideas, warned that the transition to capitalism would undermine family life:

> As soon as men and women learn the utilitarian lesson and refuse to take for granted the traditional arrangements that their social environment makes for them, as soon as they acquire the habit of weighing the individual advantages and disadvantages of any prospective course of action-or, as we might also put it, as soon as they introduce into their private life a sort of inarticulate system of cost accounting—they cannot fail to become aware of the heavy personal sacrifices that family ties and especially parenthood entail under modern conditions.[18]

The economic historian Karl Polanyi drew from both Tawney and Clark to argue that what he called the "great transformation" could weaken values, norms, and preferences central to the functioning of the families and communities on which market-based societies depend.[19] More recently, Marxist feminist scholar Sylvia Federici has argued that capitalist development increased the incentives for male control over women's reproductive capacities, including the persecution of women as witches.[20] All these arguments imply that the ideology of individual self-interest undermines forms of social solidarity beneficial to women in their roles as caregivers.

Patriarchal Feudalism

The historical record is complicated by fierce debates over how the transition to capitalism should be defined and when it actually took place—for men. Attention to changing relationships between men and women has been tenuous and intermittent. Still, recent research details the patriarchal aspects of Western Europe's feudal economies, providing a picture of precapitalist— or at least largely non-capitalist—societies inconsistent with the rosy picture painted by many of capitalism's strongest critics.[21]

Patriarchal feudalism could be described as a set of implicit exchanges in which the subordinated parties (whether serfs, women, or children) received protection and security in return for working long hours in the service of their superiors—relations between lords and serfs have been described in these amicable terms.[22] But these exchanges were enforced by threat of violence as well as weight of political and military power. A variety of collective interests were at work: lords benefited from the extraction of labor dues from serfs; men benefited from a division of labor that assigned women the least remunerative forms of work; and parents benefited from their children's labor and support.

None of these relationships left much scope for individual choice. Feudal lords, for the most part, inherited their land and privilege. Men, having chosen a wife, were legally bound for life. Parents, having borne their children, could not exchange them for a new set. The relative permanence of these social relations made the strong at least somewhat dependent upon the weak; oppression implied at least some obligation. Secular hierarchies were modeled upon religious principles. The power and the glory of the heavenly Father were metaphorically shared by the lord, and on a smaller scale, the male head of household.

The internal organization of the lowest level of society, the peasant family, replicated the hierarchical organization of the whole. Its divergent individual interests were coordinated in part by a cosmology that urged solidarity among true believers. The Church mobilized significant quantities of wealth partly by promising salvation in return. Religious precepts also reinforced the authority of men over their wives and children, enhancing incentives to high fertility within marriage. The exclusion of women from access to education within the church or to apprenticeships in trade or commerce constricted their alternatives to marriage. Only relatively wealthy families could place their daughters in convents and nunneries. Within marriage, women had no right to refuse intercourse or to avert conception. The resulting pressures created what twentieth century demographers would call "coercive pronatalism".[23]

Western Europe enjoyed geographical advantages that were conducive to the rapid spread of agricultural innovation. Its political diversity left room for healthy competition among emerging nation-states.[24] But patriarchal religious doctrines also played a role, encouraging high birth rates and sanctions against infanticide that probably contributed to demographic expansion. The brutal repression of women through witchcraft trials may have been intensified by economic insecurities, but it served patriarchal interests more directly than the interests of any nascent capitalist class.

Sustained levels of high fertility in Europe contributed to slow but persistent population growth, interrupted and reversed by recurrent plagues such as the Black Death of the fourteenth century. In some areas at some times, population pressure contributed to economic stress, even famine. But over the long term, it encouraged technical innovation and increased the density of settlements, promoting commerce.[25] In Northwestern Europe, a distinctive pattern of delayed marriage came into play: Parents pressured their children to marry at a later date, or not to marry at all, a factor that probably contributed to the gradual empowerment of women.[26] In sum, patriarchal power influenced family formation and fertility, which, in turn, influenced patriarchal power.

The Growth of Markets

Cracks and weaknesses in the feudal system allowed labor markets to gradually expand. These, in turn, reduced both feudal and patriarchal privilege. Landowners lost some of their leverage over peasants, parents lost some of their leverage over sons and daughters, and skilled artisans became more vulnerable to competition. Many official policies, including punishment of vagrants and denial of any assistance to the poor born outside the parish, aimed to discourage labor mobility. Towns and cities, new epicenters of commerce based on urban labor markets, often grew up in the interstices between feudal domains.[27]

In the wake of plagues, peasants and serfs renegotiated relationships with large land owners, expanding systems of money rent accompanied by guarantees of continued access to land. Monetization of rents proceeded more rapidly and extensively in most areas of Britain than in France. England was an island nation in an age of war, when commerce rode more happily on sea than land.[28] Markets in general—labor markets in particular—expanded more rapidly there. When they actually came into prominence is less important than their gradual expansion over time. By the sixteenth century, according to one estimate, over a half of all households received at least a part of their income in wages.[29] Also significant were differences in the type of labor markets that emerged in the two countries, related, in turn, to different rules for family bequests.

As both the technological and military potential for expanding the margins of cultivation declined, inheritance of existing land loomed larger in significance. Primogeniture (the practice of leaving the bulk of family property to the eldest son) averted the parceling of family property, and therefore protected the relative economic position of the lineage. The practice also weakened family solidarity by increasing inequality among male children. In England, where primogeniture was widely practiced, younger sons often set off alone in search of wage employment. In France, on the other hand, many sons inherited plots of land too small to support themselves and their families, but sufficient to provide them with a means of subsistence that could be combined with occasional or part-time wage employment in rural areas.[30]

Early wage employment was modeled on family labor. Young men and women worked as servants in households other than their own, often provided with board and lodging as well as modest pay.[31] Guilds of skilled workers stipulated that new entrants to their trade serve many years as underpaid apprentices and journeymen before being allowed to go into business on their own. In 1563, the English Statute of Artificers restricted entry and specified long training periods for most trades, in addition to setting maximum wages.[32] The same system provided a convenient means of limiting women's access to most skilled occupations in both England and France.[33] Widows who had worked alongside their husbands were sometimes, but not always, allowed dispensations. The Paris guild of pastry bakers forbade women to sell any product of their trade.[34]

As more individuals fanned out in search of work, many aspects of guild regulation gave way. In 1685 English courts absolved most wage earners of apprenticeship requirements; French guilds lost much of their influence after the Revolution of 1789.[35] Yet explicit rules and strong social norms restricting women's access to education and skilled employment remained in force. The spatial organization of markets made it easier for men to circumvent the localized power of feudal lords than for women to circumvent the more decentralized power of male employers, workers and family members.

Patriarchal Ideology

Christianity defined greed and lust explicitly with lists of carnal, venal, and mortal sins. It condemned sinful desire as well as behavior, encouraging believers to resist their inner devils. In modern economic parlance, it encouraged sinners to bring their personal preferences into conformity with the prescriptions of the Holy Catholic Church. In return it offered promises of paradise. The gospels of the New Testament warned against preoccupation with the pleasures of this world. Beyond camels and needles, the gospel of Matthew tells us not to store up treasures on earth, lest they grow rusty and moth-eaten. The gospel of Luke encourages us to love our enemies, to do good, and to lend money without expecting any return.[36] The Jesus described in scripture did not conform to classical standards of masculine behavior, and never sought to exclude women from his church.

Yet the most influential apostles agreed that Christianity should be preached by men alone. The burden of Eve's sin weighed heavily on her daughters. In general, Christian doctrine held that women were more prone to wickedness than men because they were more likely to be consumed by sexual passion.[37] Both the Jewish tradition and its Christian offshoot venerated maternal love, often using it as a metaphor for God's love of his children. At the same time, scriptural authority justified strict forms of social control over women, including restrictions on their economic opportunities.[38]

Many early Christians warned against the corrupting influence of wealth. St. Jerome explained that opulence was always the result of theft, if not by the actual possessor, then by his predecessors.[39] The Greek father St. John Chrystostom called for voluntary communism, while St. Basil preached charity as a solution to earthly woes: "For if each one, after having taken from his wealth whatever would satisfy his personal needs, left what was superfluous to him who lacks every necessity, there would be neither rich nor poor."[40] The early Christian emphasis on obligations to family and community may have discouraged economic growth.

However, significant doctrinal changes came early, as Christianity became the official ideology of the Roman empire.[41] The fourth-century writings of St. Augustine described social equality as impractical and disruptive. He spoke favorably of merchants and narrowed definitions of charitable obligation. Augustine also elaborated at length on female susceptibility to lust, equating masculinity with rationality and femininity with sensuality. As the father of a child born out of wedlock, he could not argue that men were invulnerable to lust, but he could blame women for their seduction. His *Soliloquia* idealized celibacy: "I feel there is nothing which so degrades the high intelligence of a man than the embraces of a woman and the contact with her body."[42]

Thomas Aquinas, whose thirteenth century *Summa Theologica* codified Catholic doctrine, held that commerce, though riddled with temptations, was no sin in and of itself. He systematized the concept of a just price, explaining that it was morally wrong to sell a thing for more than it was worth. Since worth itself was difficult to define independently of price (as the classical political economists would later emphasize), this explanation left ample room for an interest charge and a profit margin.

Like Augustine, Aquinas offered women's lack of sexual self control as justification for their subordination, stipulating that sexual intercourse was permissible only for the conception of children within marriage.[43] Both men viewed prostitution as a necessary means of channeling male lust.[44] Just as God creates sin, he also creates a partial remedy for it. Aquinas famously linked prostitutes to sewers that drained unhealthy substances, protecting the public from worse contamination.[45]

Women other than prostitutes were held to high standards of chastity or fidelity enforced by a father, a brother, or a husband. The economic disruption and depopulation wrought by the plagues and wars of the later Middle Ages periodically weakened patriarchal authority, but led to new means of reinforcing it. The concatenation of femininity, sexuality, and sin reached its height in the *Malleus Malificarum*, the influential witch hunters' manual published in 1486 that helped rationalize the murder, over the next two and a half centuries, of about one hundred and sixty thousand women and forty thousand men.[46]

Most women and men married, but women's sexual desires were compressed more tightly into one small arena—intercourse for the purpose of procreation within marriage. (No estimates exist of the number of prostitutes and nuns compared to the number of men who became monks or priests). Thomas Aquinas lumped masturbation, intercourse with animals, homosexual intercourse, and non-procreative heterosexual intercourse into one category—vices against nature.[47] Church authorities condemned the Manichean and Cathar heresies that encouraged avoidance of births within marriage, and approved the brutal extirpation of those who clung to them.[48] Between 1250 and 1300, homosexual activities once considered legal in most of Europe were redefined as capital crimes.[49]

More positive reinforcement for fertility within marriage came in the form of idealized images of motherhood, exemplified by veneration of the Virgin Mary. As the Mother of God, she is free of sin, promising to serve as a feminine intercessor for divine mercy as well as a role model for every woman. Religious icons and statuary typically portray her caring for the baby Christ with extraordinary tenderness.

With the gradual growth of commerce in the later Middle Ages, greed became more prominent in the pantheon of sins. Visual representations often featured a wicked man holding coins or a money bag.[50] In 1275 a

French monk ventured the opinion that "avarice is worse than debauchery, which does not prevent people from loving their neighbor or from spending generously."[51] Catholic interpretations of scripture held that it was sinful to charge interest to fellow Christians.[52] But money lending, like prostitution, was discouraged more in principle than in practice. Bans on charging interest were never completely effective, but they did increase the difficulty, and therefore the costs, of borrowing money.

Markets and Mentalités

We cannot say which came first, the "more" or the greater permission to pursue it. We can, however, explore the ways permission and reality intertwined. Commercial freedom came far more quickly to men than to women. Martin Luther's rebellion against the Pope in the sixteenth century went beyond a challenge to centralized authority and institutional corruption. The new Protestant sects widened the eye of the needle, preaching that a wealthy man could squeeze through as long as he was Godly in his pursuit of manly goals. As Luther's most influential successor, John Calvin, put it:

> We shall not rush forward to seize wealth or honors by unlawful actions, by deceitful and criminal acts, by rapacity and injury of our neighbors, but shall confine ourselves to the pursuit of those interests which will not seduce us from the path of innocence.[53]

The Calvinists preached hard work, frugality, and savings, and were happy to borrow or to lend at virtuous rates of interest.

The Reformation itself should not be given too much credit for the waves of commercialization associated with its spread. Catholic Italian cities had once been the centers of European trade. Jews, as well as Protestants, were innovators in trade and banking. In fact, many different minority ethnic and religious groups were in the economic vanguard, perhaps because they combined solidarity among themselves with a more calculating attitude towards their clients.[54] Still, Protestantism was kind to merchants, and vice versa. By the seventeenth century, the map of Europe revealed a distinct correlation between economic and ideological predispositions. Protestant Holland, England, and Scotland were, rich in port facilities, prospering with trade. France, with fewer maritime resources, and a large and less integrated economic hinterland, remained predominantly Catholic, with a Protestant population just large enough to excite religious tension. In the late sixteenth century, the most prosperous and successful French Protestants were driven into exile.

The growth of trade required the growth of credit. Even Catholic rules began to be interpreted with greater latitude. It became allowable to charge interest if the client was not a Christian, if the money was needed to fight a Christian war, if the lender was running a risk, or if the borrower's goal was to make a profit. Usury was effectively redefined as charging an excessively high interest rate. Calvin confidently stated that it was acceptable for merchants to lend money to one another at rates no higher than 5 percent.[55]

After 1640, denunciations of money lenders dwindled in Britain, lingering a bit longer in France.[56] The weakening of moral sanctions against interest almost certainly contributed to the development of a more efficient capital market, with rates determined by the forces of supply and demand. The reins loosened, the horses of trade galloped on. They did not, however, run roughshod over all ethical constraints or traditional customs. Their highway was carefully fenced by restrictions on women in particular.

In agriculture, differences in men's and women's wages could be partially explained by differences in their physical strength. But women were less "productive" at commerce and trade only because such pursuits were labeled inappropriate and unfeminine. Women who flouted those labels faced cultural as well as economic sanctions. Women lacked any official voice within the Church, and religious views continued to emphasize women's susceptibility to sin.

Men could not be completely absolved. Officially, at least, the market for sexual services became more restricted. In the sixteenth century, municipal brothels in France were shut down, and public disapproval intensified.[57] Early Protestants strongly disapproved of sexual self-indulgence. But the moral double standard remained in place. Martin Luther waxed eloquent on the subject of women's insatiable lust.[58] When Oliver Cromwell and his Puritan fellows gained control of the English state in the 1640s they made adultery a capital crime, carefully stipulating that men (only) could escape execution if they could prove they did not know that their fellow-fornicator was a married woman.[59]

At least some of the Protestant sects that emerged in England created new opportunities for women to contest their subordinate position in the church. The Quakers became explicit advocates of women's rights to education. On the whole, however, Protestantism had more favorable consequences for commerce than for women. Buying cheap and selling dear could be considered a divine occupation for a man, his wife, or his widow, but not for a single woman. A successful businessman could point to commercial success as evidence of his own virtue. A wife could point to her family's success, but not her own.

The morality tale remained the central narrative of human existence. John Bunyan's popular *Pilgrim's Progress*, published in 1678, told the story of Christian struggling to stay on the path to salvation. His tempters include Mr. Money-Love and Sir Having Greedily, as well as Mrs. Love-the-Flesh and Madame Wanton.[60] In the story, Christian prevails with the help of others such as Goodwill. After considerable delay his wife Christiana and their four sons, accompanied by a neighbor, Mercy, also make the journey.

Regulation

The regulation of markets often requires the regulation of self-interest. Listening to what people said about the one tells us something about the other. In order to listen effectively, though, we need to reject the view that markets automatically either represent progress or decline, sin or salvation. Their effects cannot be disembedded from the social institutions that create the environment in which they operate. Markets require not merely the rule of law and regulation of the state, but also the economic infrastructure of families and communities.

Both Alice Clark and R. H. Tawney cautioned against an overly triumphalist vision of the transition to capitalism. We do not have to accept their idealized description of medieval society to appreciate their point: Changes in the regulation of self-interest have very different implications for strong and weak, rich and poor, men and women, old and young. Some changes may be liberating, as Weber emphasized. But the liberation of some individuals can lead to the neglect of others. If its eye becomes too large, the needle itself can fall apart.

Alice Clark urged us to consider how the growth of a market economy might weaken the family economy. The homemaker's needle and its thread became a metaphor for the process of repairing and maintaining the social fabric of early capitalist society. That fabric itself was oppressive, more strongly binding women than men. However, as the following chapters will show, the fear that it might unravel may have exerted even greater disciplinary force on women than the direct exercise of patriarchal power.

NOTES TO CHAPTER I

[1] Max Weber, *The Protestant Ethic and the Spirit of Capitalism,* first published 1930 (New York: Charles Scribner's Sons, 1956); Douglas North and R. P. Thomas, *The Rise of the Western World: A New Economic History* (Cambridge: Cambridge University Press, 1973); Nathan Rosenberg and L. E. Birdzall, Jr., *How the West Grew Rich. The Economic Transformation of the Industrial World* (New York: Basic Books, 1986).

[2] Deirdre McCloskey, *The Bourgeois Virtues: Ethics for an Age of Commerce* (Chicago: University of Chicago Press, 2007); Benjamin M. Friedman, *The Moral Consequences of Economic Growth* (New York: Knopf, 2005).

[3] R. H. Tawney, *Religion and the Rise of Capitalism* (London: John Murray, 1926).

[4] Alice Clark, *Working Life of Women in the Seventeenth Century*, first published in 1919 (New York: Augustus Kelley, 1967).

[5] *The New English Bible* (Oxford University Press and Cambridge University Press, 1970); Matthew 19:23. Note that versions of the same warning also appear in the gospels of Mark and Luke.

[6] See the interesting discussion of this issue in Hugh Nibley, *Approaching Zion, The Collected Works of Hugh Nibley*, Vol. 9 (Salt Lake City: Deseret Books, 1989).

[7] Weber, *Protestant Ethic*, p. 57.

[8] Weber, *Protestant Ethic*, p. 61.

[9] Weber, *Protestant Ethic*, p. 182.

[10] Robert H. Nelson, *Economics as Religion. From Samuelson to Chicago and Beyond* (University Park, PA: Pennsylvania State University Press, 2001).

[11] North and Thomas, p. 140.

[12] Lawrence Stone, *The Family, Sex, and Marriage in England, 1500–1800* (New York: Harper and Row, 1977), p. 233.

[13] Fernand Braudel, *The Wheels of Commerce,* (Berkeley, CA: University of California Press, 1992) p. 26.

[14] Tawney, *Religion and the Rise of Capitalism*, p. 282.

[15] For a fine brief description, see the entry by Amy Louise Erickson on Alice Clark in *Encyclopedia of Historians and Historical Writing* (Chicago: Fitzroy Dearborn Publishers, 1999), p. 233, and her introduction to Clark's *Working Life of Women in the Seventeenth Century* (New York: Routledge, 1992).

[16] Alice Clark, *Working Life of Women in the Seventeenth Century,* first published 1919 (New York: Augustus Kelley, 1967), p. 307.

[17] Ivy Pinchbeck, *Women Workers and the Industrial Revolution 1750–1850* (New York: Augustus M. Kelley, 1969); Bridget Hill, *Women, Work, and Sexual Politics in Eighteenth-Century England* (New York: Basil Blackwell, 1989); Wally Seccombe, *Weathering the Storm. Working-Class Families from the Industrial Revolution to the Fertility Decline* (New York: Verso, 1993); Deborah Valenze, *The First Industrial Woman* (New York: Oxford University Press, 1995).

[18] Joseph A. Schumpeter, *Capitalism, Socialism and Democracy*, 3rd edn, first published 1942 (New York: Harper Torchbooks, 1950), p. 157.

[19] Karl Polanyi, *The Great Transformation* (Boston: Beacon Press, 1944).

[20] Silvia Federici, *Caliban and the Witch: Women, The Body, and Primitive Accumulation* (Brooklyn: Autonomedia, 2004).

[21] Wally Seccombe, *A Millenium of Family Change: Feudalism to Capitalism in North-western Europe* (New York: Verso, 1992); Mary S. Hartman, *The Household and the Making of History: A Subversive View of the Western Past* (New York: Cambridge University Press, 2004).

[22] North and Thomas, *Rise of the Western World;* Nancy Folbre, *Who Pays for the Kids? Gender and the Structures of Constraint* (New York: Routledge, 1994).

[23] Judith Blake, "Coercive Pronatalism and American Population Policy, in 85–108 in *Aspects of Population Growth Policy*, ed. Robert Parke and Charles E. Westoff (Washington, D.C.: Government Printing Office, 1974).

[24] Jared Diamond, *Guns, Germs, and Steel: The Fates of Human Societies* (New York: W.W. Norton, 1999).

[25] J. Komlos, "Thinking About the Industrial Revolution," *The Journal of European Economic History* 18:1 (1989), 191–206; Ester Boserup, *The Conditions of Agricultural Growth* (New York: Aldine, 1965); D.B. Grigg, *Population Growth and Agrarian Change: An Historical Perspective* (Cambridge: Cambridge University Press, 1980).

[26] Hartman, *The Household and the Making of History.*

[27] Perry Anderson, *Passages from Antiquity to Feudalism* (London: New Left Books, 1974) and *Lineages of the Absolutist State* (London: Verso, 1979).

[28] Christopher Hill, *Century of Revolution, 1603–1714* (New York: W.W. Norton, 1982), p. 15.

[29] Peter Laslett, *The World We Have Lost. England Before the Industrial Age* (New York: Charles Scribner's Sons, 1965), p. 50.

[30] Ralph Davis, *The Rise of the Atlantic Economies* (Ithaca, New York: Cornell University Press, 1973), p. 197.

[31] Ann Kussmaul, *Servants in Husbandry in Early Modern England* (New York: Cambridge University Press, 1981), p. 3.

[32] Christopher Hill, *The Pelican History of Britain, Vol. 2: Reformation to Industrial Revolution* (Harmondsworth, England: Penguin Books, 1969), p. 92.

[33] See Hill, *Women, Work and Sexual Politics*, and Deborah Simonton, *A History of European Women's Work. 1700 to the Present* (New York: Routledge, 1998).

[34] David Herlihy, *Opera Muliebra. Women and Work in Medieval Europe* (Philadelphia: Temple University Press, 1990), p. 177.

[35] Hill, *Century of Revolution*, p. 205.

[36] *The New English Bible*, Matthew 6:19, Luke 6:35.

[37] Nancy Tuana, *The Less Noble Sex. Scientific, Religious, and Philosophical Conceptions of Women's Nature* (Bloomington: Indiana University Press, 1993), 79–81.

[38] Elizabeth A. Johnson, *She Who Is. The Mystery of God in Feminist Theological Discourse* (New York: Crossroad, 1992).

[39] Joseph F. Flubacher, *The Concept of Ethics in the History of Economics* (New York: Vantage Press, 1950), p. 39.

[40] Barry Gordon, *The Economic Problem in Biblical and Patristic Thought* (New York: E. J. Brill, 1989), p. 106.

[41] Gordon, *The Economic Problem*, p. 132. See also Rosemay Radford Reuther, "The Liberation of Christology from Patriarchy," 138–148 in *Feminist Theology: A Reader*, ed. Ann Wages (SPCK, 1990).

[42] Kari Borresen, *Subordination and Equivalence. The Nature and Role of Woman in Augustine and Thomas Aquinas* (Washington, D.C.: University Press of America, 1981).

[43] David F. Noble, *A World Without Women. The Christian Clerical Culture of Western Science.* (New York: Alfred A. Knopf, 1922), p. 157. See also Borresen, *Subordination and Equivalence.*

[44] Jacques Rossiaud, *Medieval Prostitution*, translated by Lydia G. Cochrane (New York: Basil Blackwell, 1988), p. 80.

[45] See On Faith, *Summa Theologiae*, Part 2-2, Questions 1–16 of St. Thomas Aquinas, trans. Mark D. Jordan, vol. 1 (Notre Dame, IN: University of Notre Dame Press, 1990), p. 207.

[46] N. Ben Yehuda, "The European Witch Craze of the 14th to the 17th Centuries: A Sociologist's Perspective," *American Journal of Sociology* 86:1 (1980), 1–31; Margaret Murray, *The Witch Cult in Western Europe* (Oxford: Clarendon Press, 1971).

[47] J. T. Noonan, *Contraception. A History of its Treatment by the Catholic Theologians and Canonists* (Cambridge: Harvard University Press, 1965).

[48] Jonathan Sumption, *The Albigensian Crusade* (London: Faber, 1978).

[49] John Boswell, *Christianity, Social Tolerance and Homosexuality. Gay People in Western Europe from the Beginning of the Christian Era to the Fourteenth Century* (Chicago: University of Chicago Press, 1980).

[50] Huizinga, *The Waning of the Middle Ages*, trans. F. Hopman (New York, 1954); Richard Newhauser, *The Early History of Greed. The Sin of Avarice in Early Medieval Thought* and Literature (New York: Cambridge University Press, 2000).

[51] Ibid., p. 74.

[52] Jacques Le Goff, *Your Money or Your Life. Economy and Religion in the Middle Ages* (New York, Basic Books, 1988).

[53] Cited in Rosenberg and Birdzell, *How the West Grew Rich*, p. 130.

[54] Fernand Braudel, *Civilization and Capitalism, 15th–18th Century. Vol. II. The Wheels of Commerce*, trans. Sian Reynolds (New York: Harper and Row, 1979), p. 165.

[55] Braudel, *Wheels of Commerce*, p. 568.

[56] William Letwin, *The Origins of Scientific Economics. English Economic Thought 1660–1776* (Westport, CT: Greenwood Press Publishers, 1963), p. 81; Braudel, *Wheels of Commerce*, p. 560.

[57] Jean-Louis Flandrin, *Sex in the Western World. The Development of Attitudes and Behavior* (Philadelphia: Harwood Academic Publishers, 1991), p. 8. See also Rossiaud, *Medieval Prostitution*.

[58] G. R. Quaife, *Wanton Wenches and Wayward Wives: Peasants and Illicit Sex in Early Seventeenth Century England* (New Brunswick, NJ: Rutgers University Press, 1979), p. 93.

[59] Antonia Fraser, *The Weaker Vessel* (Reading, Berks, England: Cox and Wyman, 1995), p. 262.

[60] John Bunyan, *The Pilgrim's Progress*, with an afterword by R.F. Leavis, first published 1678 (New York: Signet, 1981).

CHAPTER 2

The Springs of Desire

Why may we not say that all Automata (Engines that move themselves by springs and wheeles as doth a watch) have an artificiall life? For what is the Heart, but a Spring; and the Nerves, but so many Strings; and the Joynts, but so many Wheeles, giving motion to the whole Body, such as was intended by the Artificer?

Thomas Hobbes

Of all the inventions put to metaphor in early political economy, none seems more appropriate than the clock. It was a major technological accomplishment of the pre-industrial era.[1] Once designed and set in motion, a clock operates in an orderly way under its own power, much as we would like societies to behave. Its very purpose is social: to coordinate the activities of individuals seeking to find one another at the same place at the same time. One could describe the agreement to observe a common demarcation of time as one of the first and most important social contracts. The concept of a contract, a set of explicit rules more formal than the traditional covenant was as much a product of mercantile society as the clock itself. Like clocks, contracts are driven by a spring—the pursuit of mutual self-interest.

When used to describe the origin of political governance, the word "contract" itself is a metaphor. No state was ever formed by individuals signing on a dotted line, but the concept of a social contract was an appealing one for critics of the patriarchal feudal order, because it evoked the role of rational negotiation. This role was initially restricted to adult men.[2] Women had no natural rights, only natural obligations. Both Thomas Hobbes and John Locke bolstered this view by minimizing the importance of male relationships that might have fostered obligation, "as if a man were author of himself and knew no other kin."[3]

Contention between pioneers of individualism and conservative defenders of feudal patriarchy was complicated by feminist critics who rejected both. Mary Astell in Britain and Poulain de la Barre in France eloquently insisted that women's care for children and family should be considered a form of social labor. Early proponents of political economy viewed the family as a unit of production and population growth as a source of wealth. William Petty, John Grant, and Gregory King were less concerned with women's rights than with mothers' fertility. But their fascination with the rules of monogamy and threat of adultery revealed the sexual dimensions of their contractual logic. They believed that societies could and should control the springs of female desire.

The Commonwealth of Fathers

By the beginning of the seventeenth century, Britain was enjoying an economic boom stimulated by international trade. New businesses were slowly but steadily providing alternatives to family-based production. Still, King James I hoped to create a Great Britain, uniting both countries under a Catholic banner and familial obligation. He pronounced himself the father of his people, commissioning a book to this effect to be read by all students and purchased by all householders.[4] The book was not entirely persuasive, and James's son and heir, Charles I, proved unpopular with Parliament. The civil war that ensued prompted a famous reconsideration of the origins of polity itself.

The liberal political theorist Thomas Hobbes inverted the religious narrative of an idyllic Garden of Eden before the Fall. In the original State of Nature, he argued, it was every man for himself. The war of all against all made economic progress impossible: "In such condition, there is no place for Industry; because the fruit thereof is uncertain; and consequently no Culture of the Earth."[5] Political initiative saved the day. Men (at least those inhabiting civilized countries such as England) agreed to subject themselves to a sovereign power that would offer them protection from one another in return for obedience. This Leviathan could take the form of a single man or an assembly of men, but its authority must be permanent and absolute, else the war of all against all resume.

This fear was not unwarranted. After four years of fighting between 1642 and 1646, Charles lost both the war and his head. A Republic was declared, and Oliver Cromwell, Protestant leader of the Parliamentarian cause, came to power. The many warring factions could not agree on a constitution, and two years after Cromwell's death in 1658, the son of the executed king was invited to resume the monarchy. Most of those unhappy with the restoration of Charles II agreed that he was, nonetheless, preferable to anarchy. Yet royalists scoffed at the notion of a social contract. To agree that ordinary men consented to subjection would be to concede the relevance of their consent.

Despite his many references to the Artificer as divine watchmaker, Hobbes denied the Deity any direct role in choice of the secular Sovereign. As a result, his account of the social contract was deemed heretical. His individualism also came under attack. Oxford Dons denounced the notion that "self-preservation, being the fundamental law of nature, supersedes the obligation of all others."[6] The new political science emphasized the force of self-interest. Leviathan was not created by struggle between right and wrong but by the tension between short-run and long-run advantage. Men should sacrifice some freedom in order to pursue the promise of prosperity, a trade-off over which political economists—and others—would haggle for centuries to come.

Hobbes assumed rough equality among men negotiating a mutually beneficial social contract. Others were more inclined to emphasize its uneven benefits. As the protesters labeled Levellers and Diggers pointed out, laws such as primogeniture had been imposed by Norman conquerors.[7] Hobbes avoided consideration of such inconvenient details. But he did refer, in passing, to civil laws that gave fathers rather than mothers authority over children. In his view this was a natural result of the fact that men rather than women had formed the state.[8]

Like most of his contemporaries, Hobbes located women in a separate world. His image of the war of all against all evoked individuals who had neither collective interests nor family ties, men "sprung out of the earth, and suddenly, like mushrooms, come to full maturity, without all kind of engagement to each other."[9] Men, acting intentionally and out of self-interest, chose a sovereign. Women and children, though subject to this sovereign, had no choice. Hobbes's ideas reflected seventeenth-century realities: men ruled their wives and children.[10] Not even the Levellers proposed to give women the vote.

Patriarchy Defended

An implicit patriarchalism based on religious scripture pervaded the English polity from its inception.[11] In the late sixteenth century, the French philosopher Jean Bodin had emphasized the parallel authority of fathers and kings.[12] But nothing clarifies a theory more than direct attack. The political theory of patriarchalism was most systematically developed in response to Hobbesian apostasy and the Civil War. Sir Robert Filmer's *Patriarcha,* published in 1680, was welcomed as an eloquent defense of the divine right of kings.[13] Even if it became "the most refuted theory in the history of politics" it offered a clear and consistent justification of inequalities based on lineage, age, and gender.[14]

Filmer's defense of patriarchy glorified the hierarchies inscribed in Holy Scripture. All men were children of a heavenly father ruled by his representatives in the flesh. The King of England derived his authority by direct descent from Adam (Filmer traced the genealogy in some detail). Likewise, men derived their authority over women and children from the original dominion God gave Adam over Eve. The very idea that men might have joined together to negotiate their own social contract was preposterous. They were placed upon earth by God to fulfill his purpose, not their own.[15]

Filmer did more than reiterate religious doctrine. He ridiculed Hobbes's account of how men and society came to be:

> I cannot understand how this right of nature can be conceived without imagining a company of men at the very first to have been all created together without any dependency, one of another, or as mushrooms (*fungorum more*) they all of a sudden were sprung out of the earth without any obligation one to another.[16]

In reality men begin their lives as children. They must be nurtured before they can begin to fight. In Filmer's cosmology, God took more credit than parents who presumably acted out the Father's will. Even if a father implanted a tiny homunculus in the mother's womb—as Aristotle confidently explained—a mother's care was indispensable.[17] Hobbes conceded this point as a basis for maternal authority within the state of nature (before fathers framed the Commonwealth). Filmer simply insisted that God gave authority over children to the father as the "nobler and principle agent" in generation.[18]

Logic played a lesser role in Filmer's account than his oft-reiterated parallel between the divine rights of kings and those of men. The two sets of rights sometimes conflicted, as when kings or their aristocratic minions laid claim to the daughters or wives of ordinary men. More often they constituted a patriarchal quid pro quo: Defend my authority as your master and I will defend your authority as master of your wife and children. Filmer warned liberals that if men gained the right to vote, women would soon begin to clamor for it. If men designed their own social contract, women would soon begin to revise it. These warnings proved prophetic, if somewhat premature.

Patriarchy Modified

In his thoughtful critique of Filmer's *Patriarcha*, John Locke proclaimed that men not only had the right to choose their rulers but also to replace them anytime they wished. His *Treatises of Civil Government* became the foundation of liberal political theory, helping justify virtually every democratic revolution that was to come. They also helped justify women's exclusion from the polity.

Locke offered an attractive model to the English, who seemed unable to follow Hobbes's advice to stick with one sovereign through thick and thin. Charles II provided the stability his influential countrymen demanded, but his brother, James II, was a devout Catholic stubbornly reluctant to cooperate with Parliament. A powerful opposition hoped to place his Protestant daughter Mary, wife of the Dutch ruler William of Orange, on the throne. In the year Locke's *Treatises* were published, 1688, they succeeded. James II fled the country in a bloodless and therefore glorious revolution. The notion of monarchy based on divine right receded as democracy gained force.

As a dissident, Locke had been forced into exile in Holland between 1683 and 1689. He published his *Treatises on Government* anonymously, concentrating much of his effort on a critique of Filmer's most patriarchal principles.[19]

"Honour thy father," he maintained, did not dictate political power. Sons owed their fathers obedience until they came of age. Past that point, they owed only respect and love. Like Filmer, Locke believed in a certain parallel between the family and the state. He hoped to reform both by giving sons more independence from their fathers.

Locke also challenged Filmer's depiction of women as guilty descendants of Eve, departing from the opinions of many of his peers.[20] He defended maternal authority. He asserted that men and women had similar mental capacities and should receive similar educations. He owned a copy of an anonymous tract entitled *An Essay in Defense of the Female Sex* and may even have coauthored a tract with a woman of letters.[21]

Still, he carefully defended male authority, extolling the natural character of a wife's subjection to her husband, "the power that every husband hath to order the things of private concernment to his family, as proprietor of the goods and land there, and to have his will take place before that of his wife in all things of their common concernment."[22] He explained that husbands had dominion over wives not because they had greater faculties of reason but simply because they were the "abler and the stronger".[23] It was an odd argument for someone who despised the claim that abler and stronger men should have dominion over weaker ones.

Why should a husband's authority within the home create an obstacle to women's political representation? Locke simply avoided the question. Some of his political allies were less diplomatic. James Tyrell rebutted Filmer's claim that the enfranchisement of men would lead to the enfranchisement of women by labeling it a *reductio ad absurdum*:

> There never was any government where all the promiscuous rabble of women and children had votes, as not being capable of it, yet it does not for all that prove that all legal civil government does not owe its origin to the consent of the people, since the fathers of families, or freemen at their own dispose, were really and indeed are all the people that needed to have votes.[24]

Locke's defense of male property rights followed much the same pattern as his defense of male voting rights. He despised restrictions on so-called usury, and published a book in 1691 arguing that interest rates should be left to the forces of supply and demand.[25] The right to trade in markets was based, in his view, on rights to ownership. Individuals owned themselves and should therefore own the products of their labor. Such rights were grounded (like Hobbes's theory of Leviathan) in their positive economic consequences. Men who own and control the products of their labor will work hard and accumulate wealth. Those who don't won't.

Locke's theory of self ownership, however, was limited. He believed that men had a right not only to their own labor, but that of their hired servants. He proposed a constitution for the state of South Carolina giving freemen absolute control over slaves.[26]

What about women's incentives to work? In some of his writing, Locke hinted that women should enjoy at least limited property rights.[27] But he considered the question of little relevance to the primary aspect of women's work, the provision of domestic services for family members.[28] Principles of ownership could not easily be applied to this form of labor. They certainly could not be applied to motherhood. If children are the product of mothers' labor, they should own their children and whatever they in turn produce. But this implies that children do not own themselves or the products of their own labor.

The solution to this conundrum lies in the assumption that care and nurturance are not forms of labor. Reproduction is not production. Domestic services lie outside the economy, in the realm of natural, god-given instincts. Locke took great pains to explain that parents should not be considered producers of their own children, but vehicles for God's procreative will. Indeed, he invoked religion to challenge Filmer's primary justification of paternal authority: "I made thee, therefore I will rule over thee." Locke insisted that fathers did not actually make their sons.

> God in his infinite wisdom has put strong desires of Copulation into the Constitution of Men, thereby to continue the race of Mankind, which he doth most commonly without the intention, and often against the Consent and Will of the Begetter. And indeed those who desire and design Children, are but the occasions of their being, and when they design and wish to beget them, do little more towards their making, than Ducalion and his Wife in the Fable did towards the making of Mankind, by throwing Pebbles over their Heads.[29]

Perhaps Locke wanted to reserve property rights for those forms of labor that required rational design and concerted effort. However, one of his most famous examples concerned the collection of acorns and apples in the forest (you pick them, they're yours).[30] Surely God deserved at least as much credit for fruit collection as for procreation (having put strong desires to eat into the Constitution of Men). Why should fruits belong to the men who picked them, but children only to themselves?

Locke emphasized that mothers harbored and nourished their children, who therefore owed obedience to both parents until they reached maturity. Indeed, he argued that the rules of monogamous marriage served children's interests.[31] Still, he pictured childcare as the fulfillment of a natural proclivity rather than a form of work, God having "woven into the Principles of Humane Nature such a tenderness for their Off-spring".[32] No need, then, to worry about incentives, rights, or recompense in the reproductive realm.

The economic devaluation of family care supported the early liberal defense of male superiority. What women produce is not sold in the market, and therefore has no exchange value. Men, in addition to being stronger, provide the superior productive contribution.[33] Locke believed that individual rights and private property were male prerogatives because he believed that only men made choices and responded to incentives. If this view reflected his social reality, it also shaped it: men should lay claim to natural rights, but women should remain subject to divine responsibilities. This prescription was greeted almost immediately by protests that would, in retrospect, be labeled feminist.

A Supremacy to Themselves

Barred from formal education, most women in seventeenth century England also lacked the economic resources required to indulge their intellect. Yet they were aware that a new social contract could either help or harm them relative to men. Many of the dissenting religious sects that became increasingly prominent before and during the Civil War questioned the sexist precepts of traditional religious doctrine.[34] Women of the aristocracy enjoyed privileges that occasionally allowed them to criticize the existing order. As early as 1655 a wayward duchess named Margaret Cavendish claimed, contra Hobbes, that, women were men's equals in the State of Nature, and that men had "usurped a Supremacy to themselves".[35]

In France, a cleric who preferred Descartes to the Bible announced that conventional views of women's inferiority were preposterous. In *A Physical and Moral Discourse on the Equality of the Sexes, Which Shows the Importance of Getting Rid of One's Prejudices*, published in 1673, Poulain de la Barre argued that lack of access to education made it difficult for women to realize their full potential.[36] Women were just as virtuous and just as rational as men, and even more charitable. Furthermore, their economic contribution to society was unfairly depreciated:

> A man who tamed a tiger would be rewarded generously. Those who know how to train horses, monkeys or elephants are highly valued; a man who writes a little book, which hardly takes any time or effort, is spoken highly of. Women, however, are neglected although they spend many years in nourishing and educating children.[37]

Such arguments found little audience, in part because they were repressed. Even Descartes's writings were included in the Index of Forbidden Books.

In Britain, the emergence of a prosperous middle class created more space for debates over women's place. Mary Astell, a largely self-educated merchants' daughter, managed to eke out a living for herself as a writer. Her most famous salvo, *A Serious Proposal to the Ladies for the Advancement of Their True and Greatest Interest* was published in 1694. It accused the new individualism of inconsistencies, pointing out that absolute sovereignty was no more necessary in a family than in the state. If men were born free, were women born slaves?

Interestingly, Astell was no individualist. She believed that hierarchies of both church and state served the useful purpose of enforcing social obligation.[38] She rejected the notions of original war and the social contract for the same reasons Filmer did: Men were children. She poked delicate fun at Hobbesian mushrooms:

> How I lament my stars that it was not my Good Fortune to live in Those Happy Days when Men sprung up like so many Mushrooms or Terraie Filii, without Father or Mother or any sort of dependency.[39]

Astell explained why she preferred the Kingdom of God to a contract forged by men seeking their own self-interest: the former, unlike the latter, was designed to protect the weak.[40] Christian doctrine persuaded Astell that a married woman should obey her husband and fulfill her wifely duties.

But she also felt that marriage, in its contemporary form, was tantamount to slavery. Applying Locke's reasoning, she pointed out that wives held no rights to the free use of their intellect and abilities, much less their own money.[41] Why, she protested, should all women be excluded from most remunerative employments, and therefore forced into marriage?

Astell also complained, like Poulain de la Barre, that family labor had been devalued. She observed that men seemed to consider the nursing of children as something low and despicable even though no activity deserved more honor, or greater thanks and rewards.[42] She located the source of women's subordination in their caring responsibilities:

> Our more generous souls are bias'd only by the good we do to the children we breed and nurture: Daily experience reminding us, that all the gratification we can hope for from the unnatural creatures, for the almost infinite pains, anxieties, care, and assiduities to which we subject ourselves on their account, and which cannot be matched in any other state of civil society, is an ungrateful treatment of our persons, and the basest contempt of our sex in general. Such the generous offices we do them: Such the ungenerous returns they make us.[43]

The exchange of care was inherently unequal, because genuine care would be offered even if unreciprocated. Maternal altruism could be taken for granted—and therefore, it was. Both Poulain de la Barre and Mary Astell anticipated arguments that twentieth century feminist economists would develop further in analysis of the costs of caring labor (see discussion in Chapter 20).

(Re)production

In the seventeenth century reproduction was not relegated entirely to the realm of nature. Aristotle set the classical precedent for analyzing families in economic terms. His first piece of advice to men who wanted to prosper was to acquire slaves. His second was to capture the economic benefits of raising children. He described an implicit contract between the generations:

> Nor do mankind beget children merely to pay the Service they owe to Nature, but also that they may themselves receive a benefit; for the toil they undergo while they are strong and their offspring weak is repaid by that offspring when it in turn is grown strong and the parents by reason of age are weak.[44]

Children were valuable to nations as well as families as future farmers, taxpayers, and army conscripts. In 1669, French Minister of Finance Colbert explicitly invoked the patriarchal power of the state, outlawing emigration on the grounds that anyone born in France assumed a lifelong obligation to remain there.[45] In the 1680s, Sir Josiah Child pronounced that the riches of cities and nations consisted in the "multitude of their Inhabitants" and that emigration would, therefore, impoverish the Kingdom.[46]

The English mercantilists believed that the country should export as much as possible and minimize its overseas purchases. They insisted that population growth could become a fountain of income, as well as of soldiers.[47] Gregory King bragged that England was "better peopled" than Europe in general.[48] Sir William Petty observed that families nurtured the homunculus of capitalism: "Hands being the Father, as Lands are the Mother and Womb of Wealth."[49] Petty considered human beings themselves a store of wealth. His calculations of the value of the English people emphasized losses incurred when they were killed, mutilated, or imprisoned, or subjected to epidemics such as the Plague.[50]

Petty assumed that all family members other than young children were productive (he cited specific evidence that the children of Norwich between the ages of six and sixteen produced considerably more than they consumed).[51] He tallied married women alongside their husbands as co-workers: "For the tillage of 500,000 Acres of land for Corn, Men and their Wives, 100,000 . . . Taylors and their Wives, 45,000, Millers and their Wives, 1,600, and so on."[52] Likewise, Gregory King, tallying the British labor force a few years later, counted married women. In his view, the only persons who decreased rather than increased the wealth of the nation were seamen, soldiers, paupers, and personal servants.[53]

Such implicit definitions of productive labor provided a rationale for greater public assistance to the needy. An anonymous eighteenth century tract urged that, "every poor man that has a numerous family be looked on as a great benefactor to his country; and all that have more children than they can comfortably maintain, be allowed sufficient to assist them."[54] But positive valuations of childrearing would soon fall out of fashion, along with other aspects of mercantilist theory. The vigorous expansion of the market economy, combined with declines in mortality, shifted attention from human labor to financial capital as a factor of production. Trade itself came to be seen as the driving force of capitalist development, even if it led to deficits, loss of gold, or fertility decline.

Sexual Efficiency

Those who favored population growth in the seventeenth century were fascinated by the sexual aspects of the social contract. They favored rules that would promote high fertility and were convinced that monogamy combined with a sexual double standard served this end. A tract entitled *Natural and Political Observations Upon the Bills of Mortality* explained the low birth rates typical in London as a result, in part, of the low number of "breeders" there, including men who had moved to the city without their wives and apprentices who were forbidden to marry. The more serious problem, however, was barrenness attributable to female immorality:

> The intemperance in feeding, and especially the Adulteries and For-
> nications, supposed more frequent in London than elsewhere, do
> certainly hinder Breedings. For a Woman, admitting ten Men, is so
> far from having ten times as many Children, that she hath none at all.[55]

The theory that female immorality lowered fertility was elaborated by an explanation of the low fertility of foxes and wolves compared to sheep: Canine vixens were promiscuous, while ewes typically shared the services of a single ram.[56] Another seventeenth century observer assumed that African women experienced low fertility as a result of promiscuity.[57] Once a woman had lost her virtue, her reproductive capacity was compromised. Better for men to fornicate with prostitutes than to ruin maidens who would otherwise become wives and mothers.[58]

Such theories shaped a distinctly asymmetric sexual contract: Promote marriage and require men to help support their children. Enforce female but not male chastity, punish female but not male adultery. Encourage prostitution within limits. Such rules would serve the greater good, because "if there were universal liberty, the Increase of Mankind would be but like that of Foxes at best."[59] The ram/ewe model of polygamy might deliver even higher fertility, but it would leave many men without partners of their own. In 1696 Gregory King warned that low fertility rates in London were due to more frequent Fornications and Adulteries, as well as Greater

Luxury and Intemperance.[60] Private vices, he observed, could lead to public problems.

Contractual Power

A social contract binds individuals in an agreement that presumably serves the greater good. The greater good, however, is seldom evenly distributed. Capitalist development destabilized the power of a feudal aristocracy, forcing renegotiation of the rules of state.[61] It also destabilized the power of patriarchal households, weakening the power of fathers over sons and daughters. The individualism that emerged took a fraternal form: men were to be brothers on an equal footing in the polity, but the sisters were to stay at home.[62]

Liberal political theorists sought to design property rights that could harness the individual pursuit of self-interest to the welfare of the commonwealth. But the property rights they prescribed applied only to white men engaged in production for exchange. Later liberal theorists would bring slaves and women into the picture, insisting that they should be treated just like white men. The boundaries of acceptable self-interest reflected the boundaries of political power: but they were also shaped by a problem that Poulain de la Barre and Mary Astell (as well as Clark and Tawney) worried about—the limits of the market. The most important product of women's labor was labor itself. Women could be brought into the market, but the market itself could not reward the tasks of family care unless children could be bought and sold.

NOTES TO CHAPTER 2

[1] David Landes, *Revolution in Time. Clocks and the Making of the Modern World* (Cambridge: The Belknap Press, 1983). See also Tawney, *Religion and the Rise of Capitalism*, p. 177.

[2] Teresa Brennan and Carole Pateman, "'Mere Auxiliaries to the Commonwealth': Women and the Origins of Liberalism," *Political Studies*, XXVII:2 (1979), 183–200; Carol Pateman, *The Sexual Contract* (Stanford, CA: Stanford University Press, 1988); *The Disorder*

of Women. Democracy, Feminism, and Political Theory (Stanford, CA: Stanford University Press, 1989); Christine DiStefano, *Configurations of Masculinity. A Feminist Perspective on Modern Political Theory* (Ithaca: Cornell University Press, 1991).

³ William Shakespeare, *Coriolanus*, ed. Philip Brockbank (New York: Harper and Row, 1976), V, iii, lines 34–37.

⁴ Lawrence Stone, *The Family, Sex, and Marriage in England, 1500–1800* (New York: Harper and Row, 1977), p. 152.

⁵ Thomas Hobbes, *Leviathan*, ed. C. B. MacPherson (Harmondsworth, England, Penguin, 1986), p. 186.

⁶ C. B. MacPherson, Introduction to Hobbes, *Leviathan*, p. 21.

⁷ Gerard Winstanley asked, "If the common people have no more freedom in England, but only to live among their elder brothers and work for them for hire, what freedom then have they in England more than we have in Turkey or France?" Christopher Hill, *Century of Revolution, 1603–1714* (New York: W.W. Norton, 1982) p. 311.

⁸ Hobbes, *Leviathan*, p. 253.

⁹ Thomas Hobbes, *Man and Citizen*, ed. Bernard Gert (Gloucester, MA: Peter Smith, 1978), p. 83.

¹⁰ Antonia Fraser, *The Weaker Vessel.* (New York: Vintage, 1985).

11. Gordon J. Schochet, *Patriarchalism in Political Thought: The Authoritarian Family and Political Speculation and Attitudes, Especially in 17th Century England* (Oxford: Blackwell, 1975).

¹² Jean Bodin, *The Six Books of a Commonwealth.* A facsimile reprint of the English translation of 1606, ed. Kenneth Douglas McRae (Cambridge: Harvard University Press, 1962), pp. 20–30.

¹³ F. L. Carsten, ed. *The New Cambridge Modern History.* Vol. V. *The Ascendancy of France, 1648–88* (Cambridge: Cambridge University Press, 1961), p. 105.

¹⁴ Peter Laslett, *The World We Have Lost* (New York: Routledge, 1989).

¹⁵ Sir Robert Filmer, "Observations Upon Aristotle's Politics," in *Patriarcha and Other Political Works*, ed. Peter Laslett (Oxford: Basil Blackwell, 1949).

¹⁶ Filmer, *Patriarcha*, p. 241.

¹⁷ David F. Noble, *A World Without Women. The Christian Clerical Culture of Western Science* (New York: Oxford University Press, 1993), p. 286.

¹⁸ Ibid., p. 245.

¹⁹ Richard Ashcroft, *Revolutionary Politics and Locke's Two Treatises of Government* (Princeton: Princeton University Press, 1986), p. 600.

²⁰ George Savile, Marquis of Halifax, from the Lady's New Year's Gift: or, Advice to a Daughter, 1688, in *Women in the Eighteenth Century. Constructions of Femininity*, ed. Vivien Jones (New York: Routledge, 1990), p. 18.

[21] Chris Nyland, "John Locke and the Social Position of Women," *History of Political Economy* 25:1 (1993), 39–63.

[22] Brennan and Pateman, "Mere Auxiliaries;" Mary O'Brien, *The Politics of Reproduction* (Boston: Routledge and Kegan Paul, 1981); Lorenne M. G. Clark and Lynda Lange, *The Sexism of Social and Political Theory: Women and Reproduction from Plato to Nietzche* (Toronto: University of Toronto Press, 1979); John Locke, *Two Treatises of Government*, ed. Peter Laslett, (Cambridge: Cambridge University Press, 1967), p. 192.

[23] Locke, *Two Treatises*, II, section 82, p. 339.

[24] Cited in Laslett, *World We Have Lost*, p. 190.

[25] William S. Sahakian and Mabel Lewis Sahakian, *John Locke* (Boston: Twayne Publishers, 1975), p. 22.

[26] A. Leon Higginbotham, *In the Matter of Color* (New York: Oxford University Press, 1980), p. 163.

[27] Chris Nyland, "John Locke and the Social Position of Women," *History of Political Economy* 25:1 (1993), 39–63; Melissa Butler, "Early Liberal Roots of Feminism: John Locke and the Attack on Patriarchy," *American Political Science Review* 72 (1978), 135–50.

[28] Brennan and Pateman, "Mere Auxiliaries," p. 192.

[29] John Locke, *Two Treatises of Government*, Book 1, section 54, p. 197.

[30] Ibid., section 28, p. 306.

[31] Ibid., section 82, p. 339.

[32] Ibid., section 67, p. 330.

[33] In an interpretation that would certainly have pleased Locke himself, Chris Nyland argues that men's dominion in marriage is perfectly reasonable in an economy in which physical capacities count for a great deal: "Greater strength is a property that belongs to the man and the benefits of which belong to him. If wives wish to share the material rewards this capacity enables them to generate, Locke considered it reasonable that men ask a price for this concession." Nyland, "John Locke," p. 47.

[34] Keith Thomas, "Women and the Civil War Sects," *Past and Present* 13 (1958), 42–62.

[35] Margaret Cavendish, cited in Jerome Nadelhaft, "The Englishwoman's Sexual Civil War, 1650–1740," *Journal of the History of Ideas* 43:4 (1982), p. 564.

[36] Chris Nyland, "Poulain de la Barre and the Rationalist Analysis of the Status of Women," *History of Economics Review* 19 (1993), 18–33.

[37] François Poulain de la Barre, *The Equality of the Sexes,* trans. Desmond M. Clarke (New York: Manchester University Press, 1990), p. 80.

[38] Ruth Perry, *The Celebrated Mary Astell. An Early English Feminist* (Chicago: The University of Chicago Press, 1986), p. 165; Joan Kinnaird, "Mary Astell and the Conservative Contribution to English Feminism," *The Journal of British Studies* 19:1 (1979), 53–75.

THE SPRINGS OF DESIRE 33

[39] Mary Astell, "A Prefatory Discourse to Dr. D'Avenant," in *Moderation Truly Stated* (London: Printed by J. L. for Rich. Wilkin at the King's Head in St. Paul's Church-Yard, MDCCIV), p. xii.

[40] Astell, "The Hardships of the English Laws in Relation to Wives," in Jones, ed. *Women in the Eighteenth Century*, p. 217.

[41] Ibid., p. 220.

[42] Ibid., p. 225.

[43] Ibid.

[44] Aristotle, *Metaphysics, Books X-XIV, Oeconomica and Magna Moralia*, trans. G. Cyril Armstrong (Cambridge: Harvard University Press, 1935), p. 331.

[45] Joseph Spengler, *French Predecessors of Malthus. A Study in Eighteenth Century Wage and Population Theory* (New York: Octagon, 1965), p. 23.

[46] Eli Hecksher, *Mercantilism* (New York: Macmillan, 1931), p. 159; E. P. Hutchinson, *The Population Debate. The Development of Conflicting Theories Up to 1900* (Boston: Houghton Mifflin Company, 1967), p. 51.

[47] E. A. J. Johnson, *Predecessors of Adam Smith* (New York: Augustus Kelley, 1965), p. 247. See also A. W. Coats, "The Relief of Poverty, Attitudes to Labor, and Economic Change in England, 1660–1782," *International Review of Social History* 21 (1976), p. 104.

[48] Gregory King, *Two Tracts. Natural and Political Observations and Conclusions Upon the State and Condition of England: Of the Naval Trade of England Around 1688 and the National Profit then Arising Thereby,* ed. George E. Barnett (Baltimore: Johns Hopkins Press, 1936), p. 19.

[49] Sir William Petty, *The Economic Writings of Sir William Petty Together with the Observations Upon the Bills of Mortality more probably by Captain John Graunt* (New York: Augustus M. Kelley, 1963), p. 377.

[50] Petty, *Economic Writings*, p. 109.

[51] Ibid., pp. 144, 307, 308.

[52] Ibid., p. 145.

[53] King, *Two Tracts*, p. 31.

[54] Cited in Deborah Valenze, *The First Industrial Woman* (New York: Oxford University Press, 1995), p. 128.

[55] Petty (or Graunt), *Observations Upon the Bills of Mortality*, p. 373.

[56] Ibid., p. 375.

[57] John Ogilby, *Africa* (London, 1670), cited in Jennifer L. Morgan, *Laboring Women, Reproduction and Gender in New World Slavery* (Philadelphia: University of Pennsylvania Press, 2004), p. 66.

[58] Rossiaud, *Medieval Prostitution*, p. 124.

[59] Ibid., p. 377.

[60] King, *Two Tracts*, p. 28.

[61] C. B. McPherson, *The Political Theory of Possessive Individualism: Hobbes to Locke* (New York: Oxford University Press, 1962); E. K. Hunt, *History of Economic Thought: A Critical Perspective* (Belmont, CA: Wadsworth Publishing Company, 1979).

[62] Brennan and Pateman, "Mere Auxiliaries,"; Pateman, *The Sexual Contract*; Christopher Middleton, "The Sexual Division of Labor in Feudal England," *New Left Review*, No. 113–14 (1979), 105–154; Wally Seccombe, *A Millenium of Family Change: Feudalism to Capitalism in Northwestern Europe* (New York: Verso, 1992); Nancy Hartsock, *Money, Sex and Power: Toward a Feminist Historical Materialism* (New York: Longman, 1983); Lorenne Clark and Lynda Lange, *The Sexism of Social and Political Theory: Women and Reproduction from Plato to Nietzche* (Toronto: University of Toronto Press, 1979).

CHAPTER 3

Defining Virtues

Self-love is the instrument of our conservation. It resembles the instrument that perpetuates the species: it is necessary, it is dear to us, it gives us pleasure, and it must be hidden.   Voltaire

The notion that men could renegotiate a social contract, rather than taking it as a given, required a certain confidence in human reason. Such confidence could be weakened by uncertainties regarding both means and ends. Were men's desires selfish or beneficent? Addressing this question, many eighteenth-century thinkers replayed the Christian drama of the contest between vice and virtue. The spokesmen of the French Enlightenment were more likely than their British counterparts to worry that the pursuit of self-interest might lead men astray.

Different trajectories of economic development had unfolded. In France, the King had greater power and fathers more authority. Both wage employment and commodity trade were less widespread than in Britain. Still, a new generation of Parisian intellectuals, including Montesquieu, Voltaire, Saint Lambert, and Diderot, relentlessly disputed the relationship between moral virtue, human nature, and economic progress. Most were hopeful that self-interest—especially sexual self-interest—would be naturally tempered by natural benevolence. They were more tolerant of feminine lust than their British counterparts, even if their sympathy for women stopped short of any systematic critique of male authority.

The Ancient Regime

The patriarchal feudalism imprinted deeply on the French social order helped justify the centralization of authority under a single sovereign. Ironically such centralization became a source of instability. The very King who decided that women should not be allowed to wear the French crown, Phillip the Fair, died in 1328 without male heirs. It was largely his own fault. In 1314 he permanently imprisoned two daughters-in-law who had been accused by a third of adultery.[1] The recurring difficulties of generating an adequate supply of legitimate male successors intensified rival claims and generated political turmoil.

The French proscription against queens as sovereigns symbolized the larger tensions of a system based on overlapping inequalities of class, gender, age, and order of birth. The principle of obedience to one's superiors bound everyone but the King. In the late sixteenth century, the witch-hunter Jean Bodin defended slavery and urged re-enactment of an ancient Roman law that gave fathers the right of life and death over their offspring. Kings, after all, exercised such rights over their subjects. Neither fathers nor kings were likely to abuse such rights, Bodin continued, because of their natural love for those who they commanded.[2]

France was less susceptible than Britain to both markets and mobility. Its religious doctrines discouraged dissent.[3] Its capital city was not a port. The country was large, heterogeneous, and difficult to get around in. An archaic social and political structure neutralized the potential benefits of rich natural endowments and easy access to the rapidly expanding commercial markets of Northwestern Europe. Many peasants lacked control over the products of their labor. A royalty more interested in waging war than in building roads discouraged the development of trade.[4]

While the propertied men of England were getting rid of a sovereign whose brother they had themselves placed upon the throne, those of France were dining and dancing with the Sun King at Versailles. Louis XIV, an astute strategist and capable administrator, built effectively on the authority of his predecessors. The religious wars of earlier regimes had left Catholics in a dominant position and the King enjoyed the strong material and ideological support of a large religious establishment, which virtually guaranteed papal sanction for all his actions. His administrative efficiency was, however, undermined by costly military endeavors against the Spanish and Dutch, which would probably have been vetoed by taxpayers had anything resembling the English Parliament been in force.[5]

The common people of France seemed to respect Louis XIV despite the huge press of taxes he imposed upon them. He spoke of monarchy as an obligation as well as a privilege, and took at least some responsibility for meeting his subjects' subsistence needs. Master of the glorious gesture, he spent huge sums importing grain during the famines of the 1660s, describing himself as a father who provides for his children and his servants.[6] Such investments may have paid off better politically than his military adventures, but they too were expensive. The King's Minister of Finance, Colbert, sought to promote economic development in order to increase tax revenues. Determined to increase French silk production, he insisted that farmers plant mulberry trees rather than grape vines, even where agricultural conditions were far better suited to the latter. He offered monopolies to some new trading companies, but not to others. On one of the rare occasions on which he actually asked merchants themselves what he could do to help them, they answered, "leave us alone." The French expression "laissez faire" became a liberal catch phrase.

The tensions between paternalism and efficiency were particularly apparent in the regime's system for monitoring grain production. Bread was the basic stuff of subsistence in France. In ordinary times, most people spent about half of their income on it. When adverse weather conditions led to crop failures, regional famines could become disastrous. A weak transportation and communication infrastructure was clogged by tolls, taxes, and other impediments to trade. Local merchants or millers able to stockpile grain could exercise monopoly power, often sparking protests and riots.

The crown monitored and regulated the grain trade in Britain as well as France, but the French system was particularly centralized.[7] Louis XIV's successor forbade grain exports altogether. Grain merchants were required to register with the authorities. They could not conduct transactions anywhere except in the public market. They were sometimes required to sell any grain they had purchased within three days. Such rules were designed to discourage hoarding in anticipation of price increases, a self-interested practice that was considered distinctly anti-social. A vast bureaucracy emerged to monitor production and distribution, to watch for early signs of shortages, to plan imports and transportation of grain where necessary, and to slap limits on prices. Such policies discouraged grain production and probably slowed the progress of French agriculture. Their success in mitigating famines remains unclear. In bad years, however, official policies had a soothing effect. When the price of bread grew unattainably high and political unrest grew, municipal officials would often re-establish calm by fixing grain prices below market levels.[8]

The absolutist state may also have hindered the development of a *bourgeoisie* by stipulating that any noble who engaged in trade must relinquish his title. Such rules were not, however, particularly binding, and the lines between classes were difficult to draw. Members of the nobility were forced to invest money in order to maintain their standard of living, and wealthy merchants could buy themselves noble titles.[9] Positions in the government were routinely sold as a way of raising revenue. The potential to reap a high rate of return buying offices or tax exemptions discouraged riskier ventures; an entrepreneur who could simply buy into the established order was less likely to upset it.

Age and Gender, Love and Sex

Such blurry class distinctions amplified the influence of age and gender. French fathers did not enjoy the right to life and death over their offspring that Jean Bodin thought was their due, but they could prevent sons under age thirty and daughters under age twenty-five from marrying someone they considered unacceptable. They could also obtain a legal order to incarcerate their juvenile or adult children, just as the King could issue a *lettre de cachet* to imprison or exile anyone who, in his opinion, threatened public order.[10] At Versailles, important servants, such as the King's valet, passed their jobs on to their eldest sons just as their sovereign did. Women remained under their fathers' authority until they married, at which time their husbands assumed control. A legal text published in 1770 explained that a husband should expect from his wife all the forms of submission due from an inferior to a superior.[11]

Inferiors were entitled to something—but it was never clear exactly what. Protestants preached self-reliance and discouraged almsgiving. The French Catholic Counter-Reformation sought to "reinfuse society with a consciousness of its obligations".[12] Non-governmental assistance to the poor remained significant in France for far longer than in England, especially in the form of informal aid provided by local priests trusted to identify the deserving poor.[13] Women and children who came to Mass hungry might, for instance, be sent to an affluent parishioner's home with permission to ask for leftovers. Charitable giving, particularly private legacies and banquets for the poor designed to redeem the soul of the deceased, apparently began to decline after about 1720.[14] No one knows how transfers before or after that date compared to those effected by the formal British poor laws.

Traditions of equal inheritance in some regions, along with stagnant labor productivity, created local population pressures. Parents preferred a smaller number of prosperous children to the prospect of an overcrowded brood, and the French became adept at postponing and spacing births. *Coitus interruptus* and use of condoms made of animal intestines were risky for unmarried women, for whom a mistake could prove quite costly. French communities had traditionally pressured men to marry women who they impregnated, but the increased mobility associated with wage employment weakened efforts to enforce such obligations. Illegitimacy rates in France, as in England, rose throughout the eighteenth century.[15] Many children were abandoned at orphanages and churches.[16]

Mid-eighteenth century Paris was a cosmopolitan city, somewhat disconnected from its rural hinterland, supporting both a hereditary elite and a new generation of intellectuals able to eke a living from their pen. The philosopher Diderot's father was a cutler, Rousseau's a watchmaker.[17] Some families chose to educate their daughters and literate men preferred literate mistresses and wives. The critique of despotism that emerged in this environment was less individualistic and more moralistic than English political theory. It was also, at least initially, more critical of gender inequalities.

The Rebellion of the Harem

An anonymously written book entitled *Persian Letters* took Paris by storm in 1721, going through ten editions within the year.[18] The author, soon revealed as the Count of Montesquieu, posed as a prosperous, well-educated Persian named Uzbek traveling through Europe, writing home to his friends and wives. His letters are livened by reports of a rebellion in the harem that leads to infidelity, punishment, and suicide.

The narrative dramatizes a philosophical treatment of self-interest. Uzbek invents a history of the Troglodytes, a selfish tribe that seems to inhabit a Hobbesian state of nature. Its members are unable to enforce any social contract or to provide any of the mutual assistance upon which their collective survival depends. When floods destroy the crops of those living in the valley, those living in the mountains simply laugh. When drought destroys the crops of those living in the mountains, the survivors left in the valley shed no tears.

Their inability to collaborate almost leads to their extinction, but the last two surviving men (no mention of women here) are exceptionally virtuous as well as smart. They teach their children to subordinate themselves to civic virtue, explaining that "the individual's self interest is always to be found in the common interest; that wanting to cut oneself off from it is the same as wanting to ruin oneself; that virtue is not such as to cost us anything, and should not be considered as a wearisome exercise."[9] The next generation of Troglodytes takes heed and prospers ever after.

The moral of the tale seems clear. But Montesquieu soon pokes fun at his own piety. Uzbek explains to his friend Rhedi that men sometimes act unjustly, though they know that God is just. They are only one step above tigers and bears.[20] Uzbek himself bares his teeth, forbidding his wives to set eyes on any other man with genitals. The Chief Eunuch's letters recount a minor mishap. The wives, while being carried by porters to the country estate, accidentally see a man bathing naked in the river. The man is immediately put to death. Uzbek's hypocrisy could be interpreted by official censors as a comment on Persian culture. But sophisticated readers could recognize a thinly disguised caricature of a French aristocrat. Uzbek's friend Rica relays a discussion with a Frenchman on whether a law of nature makes women subject to men:

> "No," a very chivalrous philosopher said to me the other day, "nature has laid down no such law. Our authority over women is absolutely tyrannical; they have allowed us to impose it only because they are more gentle than we are, and consequently more humane and

reasonable...If our upbringing were similar, our strength would be also. Judge them on the kinds of ability that their upbringing has not impaired, and we shall soon see if we are so superior."[21]

The text refers to a chivalrous philosopher who has already made this point—almost certainly Poulain de la Barre. Uzbek's friend Rica chuckles at the argument, concluding that the Prophet Mohammed has settled the issue: husbands should honor their wives but have one degree of advantage over them (the measure of one degree remains unspecified).

Montesquieu's Persians consistently treat the patriarchal family as a model for society. They leave mothers out of the picture, but do not take adult men as a given. In a direct criticism of English debates over the social contract, Rica ridicules the notion that men come together as adults to form society. Men begin their lives as children, in families that presuppose society.[22] A bit of irony intrudes when Uzbek writes to his wife Roxana that she would be outraged by the freedom European women have. She has, meanwhile rebelled by taking a lover of her own.[23] The book ends with her letter explaining how she has swallowed fatal poison to defy his punishment, preferring death to subjugation.[24]

The *Persian Letters* often allude to the need to encourage population growth, criticizing both the Muslim practice of polygamy and the Christian emphasis on celibacy as obstacles to a higher birth rate. Unlike the English mercantilists who blame female promiscuity, Montesquieu argues that poor government and poverty play a larger role.[25] He offers a rational, if entirely male-oriented, picture of reproductive decision-making: Men will not marry and have children if they fear this will ruin them financially, or leave their families destitute. The miserable poor are the exception, because they already have so little that they have nothing to lose. Peasant children will, however, do the country little good unless they manage to survive to adulthood. Greater equality and democratic governance will promote economic growth because they will lower infant mortality and encourage population growth.

The Climate of Reason

Montesquieu presented his political theories more systematically in *The Spirit of the Laws*, which soberly explains differences among republics, monarchies, and despotic regimes, relates these to the forms of male tyranny over women, and prescribes appropriate designs for government. He was convinced that climate largely determined the relative strength of the passions. Men living in colder climes (or descended, like the French, from men of the north) were bolder, braver, more patient, and more reasonable than those living in the south.[26]*The Spirit of the Laws* would have been more aptly named *The Spirit of the North*. It puts Montesquieu's condescending image of the Persian seraglio in context:

> If we draw near the south, we fancy ourselves entirely removed from the verge of morality; here the strongest passions are productive of all manner of crimes, each man endeavoring, let the means be what they will, to indulge his inordinate desires.[27]

The virtually inevitable results, he explained, were despotism, polygamy, and domestic slavery. In the North, on the other hand, Montesquieu observed republics, monogamy, and greater equality in marriage. There is less need to control and isolate northern women in seraglios, because their passions are subdued.[28]

That Montesquieu deprecated Asians, Africans, and Peruvians alike is less surprising than his lack of concern for religious apostasy. He suggested that the forms of government they developed were an appropriate response to local conditions, and that efforts to change them might therefore be futile. Christians should not try to impose monogamy on Asians, because it was not suited to their circumstances. At the same time, he felt compelled to deplore polygamy because it lowered fertility and could lead to homosexuality, the "passion which nature disallows."[29]

Catholic doctrine based on Augustine and Aquinas emphasized women's greater susceptibility to passion; Montesquieu displaced this susceptibility onto the national and racial "other". Not surprisingly, this led to an assessment of European female character that was more generous than that of many of his predecessors. How gallant to insist that the most virtuous countries are those who treat their women the best. His gallantry did not extend, however, to advocacy on their behalf.[30] Adopting his character Uzbek's stance, he pronounced it "contrary to reason and nature that women should reign in families."[31] He noted that women occasionally became queens in other countries, but did not criticize the Salic law that explicitly denied them that right in France.

Montesquieu's dislike of the passions helps explain his affection for the spirit of commerce based on "frugality, economy, moderation, labor, prudence, tranquility, order, and rule."[32] But the motivating force he praised, unlike Weber's spirit of capitalism, was one that he believed would actually be destroyed by excessive wealth. Only a passionate, primitive society would encourage individuals to pursue their own self-interest without regard for others. The republic, and along with it the successful conduct of commerce, depends on civic virtue. Hence the need, argued Montesquieu, to eliminate slavery and to tax the rich to help support the poor.[33] *The Spirit of the Laws* praises the state, not the market.[34] The state represents an abstract embodiment of the procreative forces of the father, and its indebted citizens owe it full allegiance.[35] Civic virtue is a responsibility, and the political scientist's task is to design the institutions that can reinforce it. Montesquieu's prescription of checks and balances in government later shaped the Constitution of the United States. His prescriptions for ending slavery and gross inequalities of wealth proved far less influential.

Self, Love, God, and Nature

Among other French intellectuals of the early eighteenth century, Voltaire stood out for his playful yet thoughtful approach to greed and lust. In his *Philosophical Letters*, published in 1734, he repeated the standard condemnation of selfishness as a source of disorder, but described self-interest as happily benevolent.[36] After all, if men were wicked, they could hardly be trusted to govern themselves.[37] "What is virtue?" he asked rhetorically. Religious orthodoxy replied, "Doing God's will"; his own reply was both secular and specific: "Doing good to one's neighbor."[38] The two answers were not inconsistent, but the latter required no obeisance to a spiritual master.

As a young man, Voltaire had fallen in love with a woman of whom his family did not approve. His father promptly applied for a *lettre de cachet* authorizing his son's imprisonment or exile to the West Indies.[39] The threat sufficed in that instance, but later disagreements with the King resulted in brief stays in jail. Such punishments left Voltaire's good spirits untouched, and in his old age he putatively enjoyed a delightful love affair with his niece. Perhaps this helps explain why he believed that sensual pleasure was necessary, rather than inimical to economic and demographic success. As the epigraph to this chapter shows, he expressed his views in mischievously phallic terms.

Commerce and Virtue

Most Enlightenment philosophers believed the growth of commerce would have a civilizing influence. But they remained convinced that virtue was necessary in its own right, and they liked the idea that men might increasingly be motivated by interests, rather than by passions. Interests require cognitive attention, even calculation. Passions, on the other hand, connote impulse and emotion, femininity and heat. The distinction between the interests and the passions became the basis for a new concept of stages of development, the secular pilgrim's progress. Man was climbing an historical ladder beyond the feudal pursuit of power and glory to the commercial pursuit of pecuniary gain.[40] As Saint Lambert put it, "I believe it is better for a people to obey frivolous epicureans than fierce warriors, and to feed the luxury of voluptuous and enlightened rascals rather than the luxury of heroic and ignorant robbers."[41] Better still, many economists would later argue, to obey noble and innovative capitalists.

The distinction between interests and passions was somewhat overdrawn. The term "interest" conveys calm consideration. When attached to the word "self", however, its meaning shifts. Self-interest arises from self-love, or *amour-propre*, a term the French particularly liked. Love implies not only interest and commitment but also emotion. Self-interest is susceptible to self regulation. But self-love threatens greed and lust. Confidence in a society based on the pursuit of interests, therefore, requires that self-interest is not carried to passionate extremes.

Such was the consensus of most contributors to the remarkable compendium of eighteenth century French thought edited by Diderot and D'Alembert, the *Encyclopédie,* the first volumes of which appeared in 1765. The entry on "commerce" could hardly have been more enthusiastic about the civilizing effects of trade, portraying it as an advantageous alternative to war: "The Supreme Being forged the bonds of commerce in order to incline the peoples of the earth to keep peace with each other and to love each other."[42]

Commerce was good if men were good, and men were good if they were wise. Why fuss over the possibility of conflict between individuals and society, instead of hoping for the best?

Saint Lambert even published a catechism for children, an alternative to what the local priest might recommend. "Question: Who are those that love themselves aright? Answer: Those who seek to know one another and who do not separate their own happiness from the happiness of others."[43] The wisest of men (philosophers, of course) were not tormented by greed; they merely desired the basic comforts of life. In his essay on need, Diderot distinguished between real needs and those created by society and fashion. He defined the duties of men as making themselves *and* their fellows happy.[44]

Human Nature

Questioning of religious authority required some consideration of what might take its place. What limits should be imposed on the pursuit of individual self-interest? Most French Enlightenment thinkers offered a functionalist response—those limits which serve the interests of human society. The specification of these limits proved more difficult, though more interesting, than traditional Christian proscriptions.

Rational economic man knew where his gender interests lay. Most French Enlightenment thinkers defended the authority of men in general and husbands in particular. Montesquieu suggested that families could never be egalitarian: French wives who considered themselves oppressed should recognize how much better off they were than women of the South. Voltaire endorsed the conventional notion that women were physically and mentally weaker than men, more naturally predisposed to virtue because they had stayed home while men had gone to war.[45] Other French writers described women as less rational, more emotional, mysterious, and passionate than men.[46] Among thinkers of the period widely recognized today, only Diderot insisted that such intrinsic differences did not justify the unfair treatment of women by society and law.[47]

The French may have invented the term *laissez-faire*, but their leading eighteenth century thinkers emphasized the role of enlightened self-interest and the long-term benefits of cooperation. True, they viewed self-interest in masculine terms, as a force of nature (and an instrument of pleasure). But in a sense they welcomed its domestication in a marriage of commerce and the rule of law, a marriage in which small infidelities on either side might be permitted. Passion could, after all, be a unifying force. Voltaire put it this way: "If it is true that bees are governed by a queen with whom all her subjects make love, then that is a still more perfect government."[48]

NOTES TO CHAPTER 3

[1] Georges Duby, *France in the Middle Ages 987–1460. From Hugh Capet to Joan of Arc*, trans. Juliet Vale (Cambridge, MA: Blackwell, 1991), pp. 268, 275.

[2] Jean Bodin, *The Six Books of a Commonwealth*, first published 1606 (Cambridge: Harvard University Press, 1962), especially Chapter IIII.

[3] A. M. C. Waterman, *Political Economy and Christian Theology Since the Enlightenment* (New York: Palgrave Macmillan, 2004), Chapter 2.

[4] Robin Briggs, *Early Modern France, 1560–1715* (New York: Oxford University Press, 1977); Perry Anderson, *Lineages of the Absolutist State* (London: New Left Books, 1974); Immanuel Wallerstein, *The Modern World System. Capitalist Agriculture and the Origins of the European World Economy in the Sixteenth Century* (New York: Academic Press, 1974); Philip T. Hoffman, *Growth in a Traditional Society. The French Countryside 1450–1815* (Princeton, NJ: Princeton University Press, 1996).

[5] Ralph Davis, *The Rise of the Atlantic Economies* (Ithaca, NY: Cornell University Press, 1973), p. 210.

[6] Steven L. Kaplan, *Bread, Politics and Political Economy in the Reign of Louis XV*, Volume 1 (The Hague: Martinus Nijhoff, 1976), p. 6.

[7] For an influential discussion of the English case, see E. P. Thompson, "The Moral Economy of the English Crowd in the Eighteenth Century," *Past and Present* 50 (1971), pp. 76–136.

[8] Kaplan, *Bread, Politics and Political Economy*.

[9] William Doyle, *Origins of the French Revolution*, 2nd edn (New York: Oxford University Press, 1988), p. 21.

[10] Lynn Hunt, *The Family Romance of the French Revolution* (Berkeley: University of California Press, 1992), p. 19.

[11] David Williams, "The Politics of Feminism in the French Enlightenment," in *The Varied Pattern: Studies in the 18th Century*, ed. Peter Hughes and David Williams (Toronto: A. M. Hakkert Ltd, 1971), p. 337.

[12] Olwen H. Hufton, *The Poor of Eighteenth-Century France 1750–1789* (Oxford: The Clarendon Press, 1974), p. 132.

[13] Bronislaw Geremek. *Poverty. A History.* (Cambridge, MA: Blackwell, 1994), p. 238.

[14] Alan Forrest, *The French Revolution and the Poor* (New York: St. Martin's Press, 1981), p. 15.

[15] Jean-Louis Flandrin, *Sex in the Western World. The Development of Attitudes and Behavior* (Paris: Harwood Academic Publishers, 1991); Angus McLaren, *Sexuality and Social Order. The Debate over the Fertility of Women and Workers in France, 1770–1920* (New York: Holmes and Meier, 1983), pp. 9–27.

[16] Hufton, *The Poor*; Alan Forrest, *The French Revolution and the Poor* (New York: St. Martin's Press, 1981), p. 119.

[17] Barbara Brookes, "The Feminism of Condorcet and Sophie de Grouchy," *Studies on Voltaire and the Eighteenth Century*" 189 (1980), p. 306.

[18] C. J. Betts, introduction to Montesquieu's *Persian Letters,* trans. C.J. Betts, first published 1721 (New York: Penguin, 1973) p. 17.

[19] Montesquieu, *Persian Letters*, p. 57.

[20] Ibid., p. 163.

[21] Ibid., p. 93.

[22] Ibid., p. 175.

[23] Ibid., p. 76.

[24] Ibid., p. 280.

[25] "Gentle methods of government have a wonderful effect on the propagation of the species. Evidence for this comes constantly from all the republics, especially Switzerland and Holland, which are the worst countries in Europe if the nature of their terrain is considered, and which are nonetheless the most populous. ... The species multiplies in a land where affluence provides enough for children to live on without reducing the quantity available for their parents." Ibid., p. 219.

[26] Baron de Montesquieu (Charles de Secondat), *The Spirit of Laws*, first published 1748 (Chicago: Encyclopedia Britannica Inc., 1952), p. 103.

[27] Ibid., p. 103.

[28] Ibid., pp. 118–119.

[29] Ibid., p. 117.

[30] Christine Fauré, *Democracy Without Women. Feminism and the Rise of Liberal Individualism in France*. Trans. Claudia Gorbman and John Berks (Bloomington: Indiana University Press, 1985) p. 76.

31 Montesquieu, *The Spirit of Laws*, p. 50.

32 Ibid., p. 21.

33 On slavery, see Montesquieu, *The Spirit of Laws*, p. 82; on progressive taxation, p. 21.

34 Ibid., p. 2.

35 "At our coming into the world, we contract an immense debt to our country, which we can never discharge". Ibid., p. 18.

36 A. J. Ayer, *Voltaire* (New York: Random House, 1986), p. 65. Voltaire described *bienveillance*, along with *l'amour propre* as a requirement of human society. See also Peter Gay, *The Enlightenment: An Interpretation. The Science of Freedom* (New York: W. W. Norton, 1969), p. 170.

37 See Voltaire's discussion on pp. 298–301 of his *Philosophical Dictionary* (New York: Penguin Books, 1971).

38 Ibid., p. 398.

39 Ayer, *Voltaire*, p. 3.

40 See Albert Hirschman, *The Passions and the Interests* (Princeton: Princeton University Press, 1977) and, for a different view, J. G. A. Pocock, *Virtue, Commerce, and History. Essays on Political Thought and History, Chiefly in the Eighteenth Century* (New York: Cambridge University Press, 1985).

41 Diderot, D'Alembert, and a Society of Men of Letters, *Encyclopedia. Selections,* trans. Nelly S. Hoyt and Thomas Cassirer (New York: The Bobbs-Merrill Company Inc., 1965), p. 230.

42 Forbonnais, "Commerce," in *Encylopedia*, p. 49.

43 Paul Hazard, *European Thought in the Eighteenth Century. From Montesquieu to Lessing* (Gloucester, MA: Peter Smith, 1973), p. 169.

44 Ibid., p. 165.

45 Jane Rendall, *The Origins of Modern Feminism: Women in Britain, France and the United States 1780–1860* (Chicago: Lyceum Books, 1985), p. 15.

46 Rendall, *Origins of Modern Feminism*, p. 15.

47 Diderot, "Sur les Femmes," in Diderot, *Oeuvres*, édition établie et annoté par André Billy (Paris: Gallimard, 1951), p. 957.

48 Voltaire, *Philosophical Dictionary*, p. 287.

CHAPTER 4

Free Trade but Not Free Love

You have heard it, my friend, as a common saying, that interest governs
the world. But, I believe, whoever looks narrowly into the affairs of it will
find that passion, humour, caprice, zeal, faction, and a thousand other
springs, which are counter to self-interest, have as considerable a part in
the movements of this machine.   The Earl of Shaftesbury

British advocates for the "interests" were even more eager than their French
counterparts to please themselves as well as God. With a more commercial
economy, and greater religious diversity, they cheerfully believed that God
himself, or at least a God-Given Nature, would sanctify the pursuit of self-
interest. One of the more naive efforts at such reconciliation came from the
Earl of Shaftesbury, who insisted that men were naturally benevolent. One of
the more cynical efforts came from Bernard Mandeville, who laid religious
concerns entirely aside to urge uninhibited self-indulgence. The clergyman
Joseph Butler and his chaplain Josiah Tucker outlined the most successful
formula: God himself ordained that self-interest and morality should coincide. A similar approach allowed both David Hume and Adam Smith to
insist that innate moral sentiments would temper the pursuit of self-interest.

These innate moral sentiments were presumably shared by men and
women. However, women were held to a higher standard of sexual responsibility than men on the grounds that their infidelities would have disastrous
results. Because they were under the sway of passions, rather than interests,

their choices could not be trusted. In this respect, Smith followed Locke's lead, prescribing individual freedom in the market, but male authority within the family.

Humanism

The early education of the third Earl of Shaftesbury was supervised by none other than John Locke. The young man's mind was no blank slate—he grew up to argue, contra Locke, that men must have innate moral sensibilities. He did not suggest that men *should* care for others, but insisted that they could never find satisfaction if they did not. Happiness could not be obtained without benevolence. The Earl's arguments influenced many of the most famous British Enlightenment philosophers:

> Thus the wisdom of what rules, and is first and chief in nature, has made it to be according to the private interest and good of everyone to work toward the general good, which, if a creature ceases to promote, he is actually so far wanting to himself, and ceases to promote his own happiness and welfare.[1]

Contrary to his emphasis on the complexity of the clock-like mechanism of human nature in the epigraph above, he seemed to believe that natural affections represented the true mainspring.[2] One could argue that it was easy in that day and age for an aristocrat to label pecuniary self-interest a vulgar, middle-class preoccupation.[3]

Shaftesbury's faith in natural benevolence was echoed by later writers, including Voltaire's favorite English poet, Alexander Pope, whose versified *Essay on Man* found a wide audience.[4] Pope initially echoes the Hobbesian argument that men imposed rules of government upon themselves in order to provide for their own defense.[5] But he quickly invokes natural benevolence: "Thus God and Nature link'd the gen'ral frame/ And bade Self-love and Social be the same."[6] The self feels so much affection for others that its own boundaries disappear. [7]

> God loves from Whole to Parts: but human soul
> Must rise from Individual to Whole.
> Self-love but serves the virtuous mind to wake,
> As the small pebble stirs the peaceful lake;
> The centre mov'd, a circle strait succeeds,

> Another still, and still another spreads,
> Friend, parent, neighbor, first it will embrace,
> His country next, and next all human race.[8]

Can such a boundless entity actually be called a self? Secular humanists like Shaftesbury and Pope praised Christian qualities but suggested that neither God nor the Church was necessary for their realization.[9] Most men of God found this argument rather aggravating, for the obvious reason that it rendered them unnecessary as well. Heretics who rejected Christian virtues altogether were easier to stigmatize.

Selfishness Celebrated

Such a heretic was Bernard Mandeville, who published a book in 1705 entitled *The Grumbling Hive*. Reissued in 1714 with additional prose commentary and a new title, *The Fable of the Bees,* it was widely interpreted as an inversion of Shaftesbury's argument, preaching that private vices led to private pleasure and to public benefits. Mandeville's view of human nature was modeled on earlier French writers such as Montaigne and La Rochefoucauld. But his lively style of presentation found a wider British audience and exercised a more tangible influence on its political economists.[10]

The *Fable* describes a prosperous bee hive whose members embrace true virtue and renounce their desire for gain. As a result, their productive efforts largely come to a halt. Religious doctrine is inverted: the apple of the Tree of Virtue leads to expulsion from economic paradise. Mandeville holds Avarice and love of Luxury forth as powerful engines of prosperity. Once tendered the respect they deserve, they bring redemption in the form of an improved standard of living:

> Thus Vice nurs'd Ingenuity
> Which join'd with Time and Industry,
> Had carry'd Life's Conveniences,
> It's real Pleasures, Comforts, Ease
> To such a Height, the very Poor
> Liv'd better than the Rich before
> And nothing could be added more.[11]

Mandeville believed that men pretended to altruism, but were actually motivated by a desire for praise or approval. Their opinions always reflect their own interests: "Self-Love pleads to all human Creatures for the different Views, still furnishing every individual with the Arguments to justify their Inclinations."[12] One could hardly ask for a better definition of ideology.

Greed could be conceptualized as a productive vice because it represented the expression of rational self-interest. The *Fable* imaginatively reiterated the various ways that petty intentions might lead to noble results. Love of luxury and vanity stimulated men's efforts and imaginations. The Hobbesian notion of short-run self-interest had a dark side—violence and anarchy. Mandeville, however, was unremittingly cheerful. None of the bee's vices were murderous or even illegal—the hive apparently enjoyed a social contract that prohibited violence, and there was no question of exploitation or injustice within it. Mandeville sweetened economic self-interest by associating it with benign expressions of rationality that allowed men choice, agency, creativity, and humor.

Economists often celebrate his wit while ignoring his less endearing qualities. Mandeville's views of women and the family were casually misogynist. In his tract *The Virgin Unmask'd,* a querulous spinster named Lucinda preaches the dangers of sex and marriage to her innocent niece, echoing Mary Astell: "Is not every Woman that is Married a Slave to her Husband?"[13] A caricature of nervous frigidity, Lucinda deplores the dangerous size and beauty of her niece's breasts. At times, she seems to speak for Mandeville himself, explaining that women have little capacity for reason.[14]

Like most of his contemporaries, Mandeville liked to visualize reproduction as a purely natural process. He compared the conception of a child with the brewing of beer, accomplished by the "senseless Engine, that raises Water into the Copper, and the passive Mash-tub".[15] One passage in the *Fable* referred approvingly to Jonathan Swift's imaginary land of Lilliputtia where children owed their parents nothing for their begetting, because conception was an unwitting by-product of concupiscence.[16] This makes perfect sense: no senseless engine could negotiate a social contract with a passive mash-tub.

Mandeville's appreciation of greed was complemented by his appreciation of male lust. He argued that men should be encouraged to satisfy their sexual needs outside the bounds of family life. Many European countries, including France, had developed municipal brothels as early as the fifteenth century.[17]

Mandeville praised the city fathers of Amsterdam for tolerating an "uncertain number of Houses in which Women are hired as publickly as Horses at a Livery Stable."[18] He went on to develop a detailed case for state-run brothels in a pamphlet entitled *A Modest Defense of Public Stews,* recommending three different price/quality levels for women's sexual services. The word "stew" derived from the use of warm and steamy public bathhouses for sensual venues.

Lust could not be checked, but it could, in Augustinian language, be channeled. A market for sex offered an efficient substitute for costly courtships and seductions. Prostitution could include regulations designed to reduce venereal disease. Only women who had already lost their virtue would be hired; in the event of shortage, more could be imported from abroad.[19] Having sown their wild oats, men would happily settle down to the cultivation of their wives.

Mandeville did not buy the argument that promiscuous women were unlikely to conceive. Rather, he claimed that prostitution could reduce infant mortality. Most children born out of wedlock were neglected or abandoned. Publicly supported and regulated brothels would require prostitutes to care for their bastard offspring. A legal market for sex would, he argued, encourage exchange, promoting population growth, and increasing national wealth. A twentieth-century advocate for legalizing prostitution, Milton Friedman, would later make a simpler case based on the principle that adults should be free to choose (See Chapter 19).

Mandeville also anticipated a claim that Malthus would later make in more detail: population growth would spur productive effort. Self-interest might not operate properly if life became too easy; the constant press of numbers provided a necessary stimulus. Perhaps he was poking fun at the existing class system as well as hypocritical reformers when he thanked God for the limitless children of the poor, "the willing hands for drudgery who make a civilized state possible."[20]

His warnings against public assistance did not include a hint of irony. In his *Essay on Charity and Charity Schools* he explained that the education of poor children would make them unfit for existing jobs and encourage them to aspire beyond their station. Shaftesbury's notion that the origins of society could be found in the family implied some collective responsibility for the care of the needy. Mandeville's story relieved affluent men of any such responsibility.

His confidence in both lust and greed was too exuberant for polite society. As one critic puts it, he "inherited the office of Lord High Bogy-Man, which Hobbes had held in the preceding century."[21] But even Mandeville stopped short of suggesting that women, as well as men, should relinquish virtue. And, in retrospect, the protagonists of his fable were poorly chosen. Bees of a hive, like many other social insects, are biologically related. One queen is mother to virtually all the worker drones. Not incidentally, they are altruistic creatures. Of the piquant fact that they are also matriarchal, Mandeville was comfortably unaware.

Sexual Regulation

Lust was generally viewed as a more dangerous force than greed, especially where homosexuality was concerned. French literature celebrated sexual pleasures: Voltaire warned against harsh repression of harmless practices, and Diderot challenged the very notion that some sexual practices were perverse.[22] Most countries of Northwest Europe, as well as the United States, had removed homosexuality from the list of capital offenses by the end of the eighteenth century.[23] In England, however, Puritan traditions reinforced a harsh legal climate that included ardent prosecution of sodomy.[24] Even those who privately disagreed, like Jeremy Bentham (discussed in Chapter 6), were reluctant to voice any public opposition.

The English were more relaxed about heterosexuality. Novels like Daniel Defoe's *Moll Flanders* and John Cleland's *Memoirs of a Woman of Pleasure* described sexual intercourse as an exchange from which both parties benefited. Prostitution was forgivable if a woman was forced into it by difficult circumstances. Promiscuity could be tolerated if accompanied by good will and good humor. James Boswell, who recorded the details of his numerous interactions with prostitutes as well as lovers, declaimed that there was no "higher felicity or Wealth enjoyed by man than the participation of genuine reciprocal amorous affection with an amiable woman."[25] He did not assess the felicity of sex that was not genuinely reciprocal, or define that term.

Philosophers were less forgiving than diarists, emphasizing that strict limits should be set on all women who were not prostitutes. Female infidelity would undermine men's confidence that their offspring were their own. David Hume patiently explained that women were so susceptible to the temptations of infidelity that civilized societies must impose shame, punishment, infamy, and dread upon the very idea of it. Relaxing the strictures on any group of women (such as those past the age of childbearing) would jeopardize this essential normative control.[26]

One might worry that relaxing the strictures on men (whose compliance is, after all, required) would also encourage promiscuity. Hume did not. He formalized his argument for a sexual double standard as follows:

> Tis contrary to the interest of civil society that men shou'd have an entire liberty of indulging their appetites in venereal enjoyment: But as this interest is weaker than in the case of the female sex, the moral obligation arising from it must be proportionably weaker. And to prove this we need only appeal to the practice and sentiments of all nations and all ages.[27]

This so-called proof was hardly worthy of an Enlightenment philosopher. As Poulain de la Barre would have pointed out, it could be reduced to "might makes right". At least one of Hume's contemporaries, Frances Hutcheson, argued that men should be bound to the same standards of sexual behavior as women.

The very notion that men could indulge their venereal appetites without corrupting virtuous women depended on the existence of those driven to sell their sexual services. Hume implicitly accepted Mandeville's argument that women who sold such services were engaging in socially beneficial commerce. He described male lust in relatively benign terms, detailing three different components of the amorous passions: the pleasure of beauty, the sexual drive itself, and generous kindness. These components were necessarily related: "One, who is inflam'd with lust, feels at least a momentary kindness towards the object of it, and at the same time fancies her more beautiful than ordinary."[28] Self-interest is benign and virtue tempers all. One finds a somewhat more realistic picture in Defoe's novels. Moll Flanders would have laughed herself to tears at the implication that all her customers were generous and kind.

Love Thyself

The philosophical apostasy of self-interest did not go unnoticed by the Church of England, but elicited more cooptation than confrontation.

In his Rolls Sermons, preached in the period immediately following publication of the *Fable of the Bees*, Bishop Joseph Butler reframed Mandeville's argument by arguing that self love, could, under some circumstances, represent a virtue rather than a vice: a man may be impulsively tempted to indulge an immoral desire, but if he reflects in a calm and considered way upon the likely outcome, he will realize that the virtuous decision serves his long run interests. To truly love one's self one must love virtue.[29]

Like Shaftesbury, Butler believed duty and self-interest would always coincide. Unlike Shaftesbury, he invoked both the prospect of salvation and the commandments of Christ. One must love oneself even as one loves one's neighbors. There is, in Butler's view, no trade-off between the two. Providence itself ensures that self-regarding actions lead to unintended social goods.[30]

Butler's brethren chimed in on the same note. Reverend Joseph Tucker anticipated Adam Smith even more directly: "The Self-Love and Self-Interest of each Individual will prompt him to seek such Ways of Gain, Trades and Occupations of Life, as by serving himself, will promote the public Welfare at the same Time."[31] The use of the masculine pronoun was hardly incidental. Neither Butler nor Tucker urged women to ways of gain, to trades or occupations. Most religious instruction for women urged them to love their families, not themselves. Women's primary virtue was "domestic love and Care, as the first Duty of her life, the very purpose of her being".[32] Only among evangelical groups such as the Methodists were women allowed to preach on the same terms as men—and to generalize the feminine rhetoric of love and care.

Anglican approval gave the discourse of male self-interest a powerful boost.[33] Still, disagreement with established religious views could hurt a man's career. Frances Hutcheson, who held the chair of Moral Philosophy at Glasgow University, was arraigned before the Presbyterian Church for promoting the dangerous doctrine that the standard of moral goodness was the "promotion of the happiness of others", which could be ascertained without God's explicit assistance.[34] Hutcheson succeeded professionally in part because he placed many of his ideas within a Christian context. David Hume was not so lucky. Though a great fan of Bishop Butler, his efforts to develop what he called "the moral sciences", along with his religious skepticism, contributed to his failure to secure the Chair of Moral Philosophy at Edinburgh in 1744.[35]

Hume developed Butler's arguments in more secular terms, reassuring his readers that self-interested men were not necessarily selfish and describing friendship and generosity as human passions. Criticizing Hobbes and Locke as advocates of the "selfish system of morals" he wrote, "I esteem the man whose self-love, by whatever means, is so directed as to give him a concern for others and render him serviceable to society, as I hate or despise him who has no regard to anything beyond his own gratifications and enjoyments."[36] In another famous quote, he referred to the "particle of the dove" that softened the elements of wolf and serpent in human nature.[37]

Another influential figure of the Scottish Enlightenment, Adam Ferguson, reiterated Shaftesbury's argument that benevolence gave pleasure to the giver, as well as the receiver.[38] The image suggests a pleasurable intercourse, an exchange in which the boundaries of the self become, at least temporarily, redefined. Adam Smith's first book, *The Theory of Moral Sentiments*, lay squarely within this optimistic tradition. Its title was based on a phrase Hume had made famous and the book itself reiterated many popular arguments concerning human nature.[39] Smith postulated, at the outset, that self-interest was subject to natural limits:

> How selfish soever man may be supposed, there are evidently some principles in his nature, which interest him in the fortune of others, and render their happiness necessary to him, though he derives nothing from it, except the pleasure of seeing it.[40]

Smith dismissed Mandeville as a scandalous thinker and adopted a far more refined approach. In the first chapter of the *Moral Sentiments* he announced that it was rude to eat voraciously, and that all strong expressions of sexual passion were indecent, even between married persons.[41] He praised sympathy, but argued that feelings alone mattered little: They should always be refracted through the eyes of an impartial spectator.[42] He explicitly contrasted the emotional (and feminine) trait of humanity with the moral (and masculine) trait of generosity, echoing the traditional distinction between the natural and the social.[43]

> Humanity is the virtue of a woman, generosity of a man. The fair sex, who have commonly much more tenderness than ours, have seldom so much generosity... Humanity consists merely in the exquisite fellow-feeling which the spectator entertains with the sentiments of the

persons principally concerned, so as to grieve for their sufferings, to resent their injuries, and to rejoice at their good fortune.[44]

On matters pertaining to women's rights, Smith was more conservative than his most famous Scottish predecessors. In his lectures on moral philosophy, later amplified and published in 1755, Francis Hutcheson had rebutted Locke's argument that men had a natural right to command within the family, and criticized civil laws that deprived women of property, as well as attacking the sexual double standard. Even David Hume had spoken out briefly but decisively against "male tyranny".[45] Smith never expressed opinions on such matters, and in one of his few references to sexual intercourse, described any breach of female chastity as an "irreversible disaster".[46]

Either because he was a bachelor or because he wanted to avoid mention of the bodily passions, Smith seldom alluded to the love of a husband for his wife, or vice versa. He did wax eloquent, in the *Moral Sentiments*, on the love of parents for children, brothers and sisters for one another, and the family in general for all its members. In an image that evokes Pope's metaphor of the circles of affection, he argued that men's sympathy for others diminished in proportion to his degree of relatedness and extent of social contact with them, and seldom extended beyond his country.[47] Of the possibility of universal benevolence, he promised that "The wise and virtuous man is at all times willing that his own private interest should be sacrificed to the public interest or his own particular order or society."[48] One wonders what proportion of the population he deemed wise and virtuous.

The Butcher, the Baker, and the Wife

In his more famous book, *The Wealth of Nations*, published in 1776, Smith forcefully prescribed the individual pursuit of self-interest. He has sometimes been accused of inconsistency on this score, but his earlier book had made the case that self-interest would generally take a benevolent form. *The Wealth of Nations* emphasized instead the important role that competitive markets could play in ensuring good social outcomes, consistent with the image of God as divine watchmaker.[49] Smith reiterated the Hobbesian notion that self-interest was a mainspring of a "well-contrived machine".[50] The gears of human nature would convert the energy of desire into the orderly and civilized progress of the clock's hands.

Smith also offered a spatial solution to the tension between virtue and self-interest, assigning one to the family (outside the economy) and the other to the market. In one of the most famous sentences in the history of economic thought, he wrote "It is not from the benevolence of the butcher, the brewer, or the baker that we expect our dinner but from regard to their self-interest."[51] Smith neglected to mention that none of these tradesmen actually puts dinner on the table, ignoring cooks, maids, wives, and mothers in one fell swoop.

Smith marveled at the efficiency of specialization in the factory but never in the household. Despite his great attention to the variety of occupations which men pursued in agriculture as well as in manufacturing, he seldom mentioned women's work either in the market or in the home.[52] Paid domestic service was widespread in his day, accounting for a significant share of all wage employment for women. Aristocratic families (such as the one in which he briefly served as a tutor) employed a panoply of servants. Smith gave them no attention.

His productive and unproductive labor ignored both paid and unpaid domestic work. Smith argued that only labor devoted to material production could create that all-important key to economic growth—a surplus. He insisted that labor devoted to what we now term "services" was essentially sterile.[53] If cooks and nannies and housekeepers were explicitly deemed unproductive despite their wages, the wives and mothers who often provided similar services to their own families were obviously also unproductive. As a modern feminist historian explains, domestic chores were "tainted by their association with perhaps the most unacknowledged form of women's work, that of simply attending to the needs of others."[54]

Smith judiciously noted that many occupations that failed to meet his standard of productivity (increasing the market value of a tangible commodity) were nonetheless necessary. Churchmen, lawyers, physicians, men of letters, the army, and the navy all graced the list of those who deserved the support of productive workers. Neither domestic servants nor wives nor mothers were included. This does not imply that Smith thought these women undeserving of support. It does suggest that he believed their efforts were irrelevant to economic growth. Such views were explicitly challenged by one of his female contemporaries, Priscilla Wakefield, as early as 1798.[55]

Smith did call attention to the importance of education and training of children.[56] He realized that some assumptions regarding population growth were necessary to a theory of wages: In the short run, subsistence could be defined as the wages necessary to enable the worker to return to work the next day; in the long run, subsistence required funds sufficient to compensate for the attrition of the adult work force by sickness, old age, and death. A predecessor, Richard Cantillon, had suggested that a man's wage must be sufficient to support two children, as well as the wage earner, assuming that a mother's productive activities were sufficient to provide for herself, but not for her children.[57]

Extending this reasoning, Smith added the astute qualification that more than two children must be borne, in order for two to survive to maturity. He went on to suggest that economic factors sometimes affected family size decisions. Where land was plentiful, as in England's colonies in the United States, families were large. Observing that children there were a "source of opulence and prosperity", Smith calculated their economic rate of return, noting that the "labour of each child, before it can leave their [parents'] home, is computed to be worth a hundred pounds clear gain to them."[58] Men, therefore, pursued their own self-interest when they married early and began to propagate. But despite his generalization that the "demand for men, like that for any other commodity, necessarily regulates the production of men," Smith offered an asymmetric explanation. Increased demand would bring forth more children, but reduced demand would not slow their production.[59] Infanticide and high infant mortality were the only factors Smith named as means of curtailing the size of families among the laboring poor.

Smith is often cited as a critic of state intervention in the economy. In the *Wealth of Nations*, he roundly criticized policies that interfered with free trade or the free mobility of labor. His discussion of the poor laws portrayed the state as a moral institution that could, like an overprotective mother, stifle male initiative. Yet he had few quarrels with the state's hold on women, including the denial of independent property rights to married women and children, or restrictions on access to education and apprenticeships.

In this respect, he resembled other men of his day and age and social class. The journalist and dictionary author, Samuel Johnson, with whom Smith dined at least once, was famous for his social repartee, much of it recorded by his faithful friend James Boswell. The conversation at a Mr. Dilly's home in the late 1770s turned to cookbooks, and Mr. Johnson opined that men could doubtless do a better job on these than women. His remark provoked a Quaker dinner guest:

> Mrs. Knowles affected to complain that men had much more liberty allowed them than women.
> Johnson: "Why Madam, women have all the liberty they should wish to have..."
> Mrs. Knowles: "Still, Doctor, I cannot help thinking it a hardship that more indulgence is allowed to men than to women. It gives a superiority to men, to which I do not see how they are entitled."
> Johnson: "It is plain, Madam, one or the other must have the superiority. As Shakespear says, 'If two men ride on a horse, one must ride behind.'"
> Dilly: "I suppose, Sir, Mrs. Knowles would have them to ride in panniers, one on each side."
> Johnson: "Then, Sir, the horse would throw them both."
> Mrs. Knowles: "Well, I hope that in another world the sexes will be equal."
> Boswell: "That is being too ambitious, Madam. We might as well desire to be equal with the angels."[60]

The tone, even more than the content of this exchange, shows how effortlessly women's protests could be dismissed. In his lively discussion of eighteenth-century confidence in the civilizing effects of commerce, Albert Hirschman repeats one of Samuel Johnson's most famous quotes: "There are few ways in which a man can be more innocently employed than in getting money."[61] Would Johnson have agreed that this was true for women as well? It is unfortunate that Mrs. Knowles did not ask him this more specific question.

The Balance

Like Shaftesbury, most British Enlightenment thinkers were heavily influenced by religious values. But like Mandeville, they also wanted to get on with their worldly affairs. In their efforts to reconcile spiritual with economic well-being, they struggled to encourage just enough self-interest, but not too much. Some influential spokesmen of the Church of England offered the comforting view that God-given self-love always takes a virtuous form. A healthy balance between concern for oneself and others was prescribed. Another, less explicit balance was based on gender. Men could pursue their self-interest because women would stay home to provide love and care. This was the natural order of things, but one that apparently required the exclusion of women from political participation and the restriction of their opportunities for economic independence.

Adam Smith is often described as the father of economics. Within the discourse of self-interest, however, he represented the end, not the beginning of an era. Smith's emphasis on moral sentiments and his confidence in masculine morality linked him strongly to his Enlightenment predecessors. Whether or not he actually changed his mind as he wrote the *Wealth of Nations*, his previous writings lent an air of genteel respectability to his endorsement of self-interest. The strict boundaries he drew around the market itself promised to protect society in general and the family in particular. Free trade, he seemed to promise, would never lead to free love, and self-interest would always stop well short of greed.

NOTES TO CHAPTER 4

[1] Anthony, Earl of Shaftesbury, *Characteristics of Men, Manners, Opinions, Times, etc.* Edited, with an introduction and notes by John M. Robertson, 2 volumes, first published 1711 (Gloucester, MA: Peter Smith, 1963), p. 338.

[2] Shaftesbury, *Characteristics*, Vol. 1, p. 77.

[3] See Thomas A. Horne, *The Social Thought of Bernard Mandeville. Virtue and Commerce in Early Eighteenth-Century England* (New York: Columbia University Press, 1978), p. 45.

[4] A.D. Nuttall, *Pope's Essay on Man* (London: George Allen and Unwin, 1984), p. 174.

[5] Alexander Pope, "Essay on Man," *The Poems of Alexander Pope* (Bungay, Suffolk: Methuen and Co. Ltd, 1865), p. 533, line 270.

[6] Ibid., "Essay on Man," p. 535, Epistle III, line 315.

[7] Nuttall, *Pope's 'Essay*, p. 111.

[8] Pope, "Essay on Man," p. 546, Epistle IV, line 361.

⁹ On responses to Shaftesbury, see John M. Robertson, Introduction to Anthony Earl of Shaftesbury, *Characteristics of Men, Manners, Opinions, Times* (Gloucester, MA: Peter Smith, 1963) p. xl. Robertson claims that Shaftesbury's ideas were quite similar to those of the Jewish philosopher Spinoza, another reason why the Church of England viewed them with great suspicion.

¹⁰ E. J. Hundert, "Bernard Mandeville and the Enlightenment's Maxims of Modernity," *Journal of the History of Ideas* 56:4 (1995), p. 580.

¹¹ Bernard Mandeville, *The Fable of the Bees; or Private Vices, Publick Benefits.* Vols. I and II. With a commentary by F. B. Kaye (Oxford: Clarendon Press, 1924), p. 26.

¹² Ibid., p. 333.

¹³ Bernard Mandeville, *The Virgin Unmask'd: or Female Dialogues betwixt an Elderly Maiden Lady and her Niece, on Several Diverting Discourses of the Times* (London: J. Morphero, 1709), p. 127.

¹⁴ Mandeville, *The Virgin Unmask'd*, p. 28.

¹⁵ Ibid., p. 228.

¹⁶ Ibid., p. 224. Mandeville also cited Solon of Athens as author of a law stipulating that fathers who failed to bring their sons up to any calling should not expect relief from them (p. 59).

¹⁷ Rossiaud, *Medieval Prostitution.*

18. Cited in Richard I. Cook, "The Great Leviathan of Lechery: Mandeville's Modest Defence of Publick Stews," pp. 23–33 in *Mandeville Studies. New Explorations in the Art and Thought of Dr. Bernard Mandeville*, ed. Irwin Primer (The Hague, Martinus Nijhoff, 1975), p. 22.

¹⁹ Bernard Mandeville, *A Modest Defense of Public Stews: or, an Essay Upon Whoring* (London: A. Bussy, 1924).

²⁰ Mandeville, *Fable*, p. 259.

²¹ Cited in Richard I. Cook, *Bernard Mandeville* (New York: Twayne Publishers Inc. 1974), p. 16.

²² Lester Crocker, *Nature and Culture. Ethical Thought in the French Enlightenment* (Baltimore: The Johns Hopkins Press, 1963), p. 362.

²³ Louis Crompton, *Byron and Greek Love. Homophobia in 19th-Century England* (Berkeley: University of California Press, 1985).

²⁴ Randolph Trumbach, "Sex, Gender, and Sexual Identity in Modern Culture: Male Sodomy and Female Prostitution in Enlightenment London," in *Forbidden History*, ed. John C. Fout (Chicago: University of Chicago Press, 1992), 89–106.

²⁵ Cited in Roy Porter, "Mixed Feelings: The Enlightenment and Sexuality in Eighteenth-Century Britain," in *Sexuality in Eighteenth-Century Britain*, ed. Paul-Gabriel Boucé (Manchester: Manchester University Press, 1982), p. 4.

²⁶ David Hume, *A Treatise on Human Nature and Dialogues Concerning Natural Religion* (London: Longmans, Green, and Co., 1882), Vol. II, p. 331.

[27] Ibid., p. 333.

[28] Ibid., p. 177.

[29] A.M.C. Waterman, "The Beginning of 'Boundaries': The Sudden Separation of Economics from Christian Theology," pp. 41–63 in *Economics and Interdisciplinary Research* edited by G. Erreygers (New York: Routledge, 2001), and "Recycling Old Ideas: Economics Among the Humanities," *Research in the History of Economic Thought and Methodology* 15: 237–49.

[30] Joseph Butler, Sermon 3.9, *The Works of Bishop Butler*, ed. S. Halifax, Vol. 1 (Oxford, 1874), p. 57; Waterman, "The Beginning of Boundaries," p. 3.

[31] Josiah Tucker, *Instructions for Travelers*, in *The Collected Works of Josiah Tucker*, with a new introduction by Jeffery Stern (6 vols.) (London: Routledge, 1993). First published in 1757, p. 48.

[32] John Brown, D.D. *On the Female Character and Education* (London: Printed for L. Davis and C. Reymers, 1765) pp. 13–14.

[33] Waterman states, "The Enlightenment in Britain was regarded as an opportunity rather than as a threat to established religion," ("The Beginning of Boundaries," unpublished manuscript), p. 1. Likewise, Gertrude Himmelfarb idealizes the British Enlightenment, stating, "Secular and religious institutions, civil society and the state, public relief and private charity complemented and cooperated with one another," ("The Idea of Compassion: The British vs. the French Enlightenment," *The Public Interest*, 2001, p. 9).

[34] Jane Rendall, *The Origins of the Scottish Enlightenment* (New York: St. Martin's Press, 1978), p. 74. See also A. W. Coats, *On the History of American Thought. British and American Economic Essays*, Vol.1, (New York: Routledge, 1992), p. 124.

[35] Gay, *The Enlightenment,* p. 8. See also Rendall, *Origins of the Scottish Enlightenment*, p. 32.

[36] David Hume, *An Enquiry Concerning the Principles of Morals*, reprinted from the edition of 1777 with an introductory note by John B. Stewart (La Salle, IL: Open Court, 1966), p. 139.

[37] Hume, *Enquiry*, p. 109.

[38] Gay, p. 341.

[39] On Smith's contributions relative to his predecessors, see A.W. Coats, "Adam Smith, The Modern Reappraisal".

[40] Adam Smith, *The Theory of Moral Sentiments*, with a biographical and critical memoir of the author by Dugald Stewart (London: G. Bell and Sons Ltd, 1911), p.3. See also, p. 27: "and hence it is, that to feel much for others, and little for ourselves, that to restrain our selfish, and to indulge our benevolent affections, constitutes the perfection of human nature"; and p. 214: "The man of the most perfect virtue, the man whom we love and revere the most, is he who joins, to the most perfect command of his own original and selfish feelings, the most exquisite sensibility both to the original and sympathetic feelings of others."

[41] Smith, *Moral Sentiments*, p. 33.

[42] Samuel Fleischacker, "Adam Smith," *Blackwell Companion to Early Modern Philosophy*, p. 4.

[43] Sumitra Shah, "Sexual Division of Labor in Adam Smith's Work," The *History of Economic Thought* 28:2 (2006), 221–41. See also Edith Kuiper, "The Construction of Masculine Identity in Adam Smith's Theory of Moral Sentiments," in D. Barker and E. Kuiper, eds., *Toward a Feminist Philosophy of Economics*, pp. 145–160 (New York: Routledge, 2003).

[44] See Jane Rendall, "Virtue and Commerce: Women in the Making of Adam Smith's Political Economy", in *Women in Western Political Philosophy*, ed. Ellen Kennedy and Susan Mendus, (New York: St. Martin's Press, 1987), p. 59.

[45] Gay, *The Enlightenment*, p. 34.

[46] Rendall, "Virtue and Commerce," p. 60; For a discussion of Smith's views on domestic law see Knut Haakonssen, *The Science of a Legislator. The Natural Jurisprudence of David Human and Adam Smith* (New York: Cambridge University Press, 1981), Chapter 5, section 5.

[47] Smith, *Moral Sentiments*, pp. 321–44.

[48] Ibid., p. 346.

[49] Anthony Waterman, *Revolution, Economics, and Religion: Christian Political Economy, 1798–1833* (Cambridge: Cambridge University Press, 1991).

[50] T. D. Campbell, *Adam Smith's Science of Morals* (London: George Allen & Unwin Ltd, 1971), p. 220.

[51] Smith, *Wealth of Nations*, I, p. 19.

[52] Robert W. Dimand, Evelyn Forget, and Chris Nyland, "Gender in Classical Economics," *Journal of Economic Perspectives* 18:1 (2004), 229–240; For a discussion of the few instances in which Smith does discuss women's work, see Michèle Pujol, *Feminism and Anti-Feminism in Early Economic Thought* (Aldershot: Edward Elgar, 1992) and Rendall, "Virtue and Commerce". For a more detailed critique of his masculinist assumptions, see Ulla Grapard, "Robinson Crusoe: The Quintessential Economic Man?" *Feminist Economics* I:1 (1995), 33–52 and "The Benevolence of the Butcher's Wife," manuscript, Department of Economics, Colgate University.

[53] Smith, *Wealth of Nations*, II, p. 84.

[54] Deborah Valenze, *The First Industrial Woman* (New York: Oxford University Press, 1995). Note, however, that Valenze offers a more generous interpretation of Smith than I do here.

[55] Robert Dimand, "An Eighteenth-Century English Feminist Response to Political Economy: Priscilla Wakefield's Reflections," 194–205 in *The Status of Women in Classical Political Economy*, ed. Robert Dimand and Chris Nyland (Cheltenham UK: Edward Elgar, 2003).

[56] Pujol, *Feminism and Anti-Feminism*, p. 19.

[57] Smith, *Wealth of Nations*, I, p. 91.

[58] Ibid., I, p. 95.

[59] Ibid., p. 108.

[60] James Boswell, *Boswell's Life of Johnson*, ed. George Birkbeck Hill, in six volumes (Oxford: The Clarendon Press, [MCMXXXIV], 1934), pp. 286–87.

[61] Albert Hirschman, *The Passions and the Interests: Political Arguments for Capitalism Before its Triumph*. (Princeton: Princeton University Press, 1977), p. 57.

CHAPTER 5

The Limits of Affection

There can never be any regular government of a nation without a marked
subordination of mother and children to the father.

John Adams, Letter to his Son

The American Declaration of Independence came to light the same year as
Smith's *Wealth of Nations*. It proclaimed men's right to happiness, as well as
life and liberty, describing the pursuit of self-interest as a natural virtue. The
colonists pronounced that they had come of age and outgrown the yoke of
royal authority. Their English supporters hailed the new revolution as
evidence that light and knowledge were gaining ground.[1] The task of
constitutional design would focus on the task outlined by Montesquieu—a
system of checks and balances that would prevent one group from imposing
its will upon another. A good society, like a good clock, would regulate itself.

The founding fathers of the new republic preached not just the ideals but
also the assumptions of the Enlightenment. Political victory and economic
progress would flow from the virtues of Christian love combined with individual initiative. John Adams located social affections in the human breast.[2]
Thomas Jefferson explained that the creator had planted them in the generous
soil of human nature.[3] Tom Paine, whose pamphlets rallied many behind the
revolutionary cause, credited Nature rather than God.[4] Whatever their location or origins, these affections would presumably civilize self-interest.

Their civilizing touch, however, remained light. The inhabitants of the colonies in 1776 were ethnically diverse—in 1776, the British colonial population numbered about 2.5 million; the enclaves of French, Spanish, Germans, and Dutch came to no more than 100,000. Native Americans were estimated at about 800,000, and enslaved Africans at least 500,000.[5] No English love was lost on the Native Americans or enslaved Africans who were excluded from the democratic brotherhood. Even the love of fellow white men extended only to establishment of political rights, stopping short of any economic obligations. The rights of women were circumscribed for reasons exactly opposite. They were presumably so loved that they required no independent representation.

Sweet Commerce

Adam Smith was a great fan of colonization. The opportunities available in the New World promised to increase the wealth of nations. Early immigrants struggled to gain a foothold; by the middle of the eighteenth century they could boast of considerable success. Many rural areas enjoyed a high level of self-sufficiency, and many individuals, including some outspoken residents of Amherst, Massachusetts expressed distaste for avarice.[6] Still, by 1776 evidence of the "market mentalité", that so-called capitalist state of mind, was widespread—and not just in New England and New York.[7]

The slave-based sugar and cotton plantations of the South were once described as the relics of a semi-feudal system antithetical to economic growth.[8] Adam Smith himself argued that slavery could never be an efficient system precisely because it was not in a slave's own interest to work hard.[9] But recent historiography offers considerable evidence that the planter aristocracy skillfully maximized its profits.[10] It was not necessarily doomed to economic extinction. Had such evidence been available in the eighteenth century, it might have weakened the confidence of those who believed that commerce would always lead toward higher virtue.

The struggle to end slavery represented a moral and political effort to restrict one particular type of market—a market for human beings themselves. It represented an effort to impose new limits on the pursuit of individual self-interest. The growth of markets, in the abstract, excited little opposition. Governance and regulation of the market were at issue, along with its cultural effects. How would markets and mobility affect the bonds of affection, the moral sentiments on which society relied?[11]

Then as now, that question was difficult to answer. But the centrifugal effect of new economic opportunities for men was particularly apparent. Most immigrants to the New World had departed from patriarchal tradition by leaving their own parents behind. They did not always have a choice: more than half of all English emigrants between 1718 and 1775 were felons, mostly young unmarried men with no property to their name. Women were more likely to accompany family members to New England than to other regions. Still, at mid-century 1.5 men lived there for every woman. In the Chesapeake the ratio was 4 to 1.[12]

When new families formed, they hoped their children would grow up happy to remain close at hand, contributing to a farm or family enterprise and providing mutual aid. Those hopes were often disappointed. The availability of land on the steadily expanding frontier, combined with the demand for hired workers in a labor-scarce environment, pulled many young men away from home. Fathers also became less dependent on their sons as a nascent labor market allowed them to hire substitutes. In New England in particular, men of the older generation complained bitterly of their reduced authority over the younger.[13] The growing sense that children had become less likely to defray their costs probably contributed to early fertility decline.[14]

Eighteenth-century women were seldom encouraged to develop any skills other than those that might complement their assigned roles as wives and mothers. The only occupation that invited their wage employment was domestic service, a luxury for most families in rural areas. Jobs as housekeepers and maidservants were more plentiful in more prosperous areas of early settlement. Daughters were more likely than sons to stay close to home, at least until they married. Sex ratios in New England were tilted due to the growing outmigration of young men from settled areas after 1800, making it harder for young women to find a husband.

At the same time, economic development reduced the relative importance of household production. The growth of factory-based cloth manufacture in Britain wrought a major transformation, rendering the traditional domestic responsibilities of spinsters largely obsolete. Patriotic commitment combined with the stringencies of war led to increased production of homespun cloth during the war itself. Afterwards, however, imports from abroad made such inroads that young women were in danger of becoming unproductive in the home—an argument in favor of developing local textile mills to provide them with employment. As Alexander Hamilton put it in his Report on Manufactures of 1791, "The husbandman himself experiences a new source of profit and support from the encreased (sic.) industry of his wife and daughters."[5] Hamilton's enthusiasm was borne out. After the War of 1812, protective tariffs promoted the development of the U.S. textile industry and brought the term "mill girl" into common parlance.

The American Revolution and what has been called a "market revolution" evolved hand in hand. Yet both revolutions affected women less powerfully than men because of explicit efforts to keep them in their place. Women's non-market work ensured their husbands and their children a generous supply of domestic service. It also offered a buffer of sorts against the anxieties of the market. Women would provide a haven in an increasingly impersonal if not completely heartless world.[16]

The Fraternal Compromise

Some opponents of British rule drew on the legacy of the Levellers. But the only published writer to directly challenge both slavery and patriarchy while demanding liberty for the colonies was James Otis, in his 1764 pamphlet, *The Rights of the British Colonies Asserted and Proved*. Whether white or black, he proclaimed, all colonists were by nature freeborn and women as free as men. The resulting firestorm of controversy caused him to back down.[17] Thomas Paine stepped forward to denounce slavery in 1775 and later wrote an eloquent defense of both the American and French Revolutions in *The Rights of Man*. In that book and his later *Agrarian Justice* Paine condemned the inequality of wealth, called for a progressive income tax, and outlined the principles of a welfare state.[18]

Paine also flirted with feminist ideas. His "Occasional Letter on the Female Sex" written in 1775, echoed Montesquieu, deploring the oppression of women in the despotic countries of Asia and calling for more appreciation of their contributions in Europe. His anonymously written *Common Sense* lashed out against the hereditary aristocracy. Like many of his more respectable counterparts, Paine chose to rally the troops around a youthful challenge to aging tyranny. That the colonies had prospered under British rule did not imply that they should remain under its thumb. As Paine put it, "We may as well assert that because a child has thrived upon milk, that it is never to have meat."[19] It was not in the interest of a man to be a boy all his life. But Paine never openly advocated democratic rights for women.

Like middle-aged men chafing at their fathers but mindful of the possible disobedience of their own sons, the founders of the Republic carefully delimited the bounds of legitimate authority. The King had overstepped the bounds of paternal authority even as his subjects had outgrown them.[20] Revolutionary rhetoric suggested that Britain was an uncaring father, an unnatural mother, or perhaps a horrid combination of the two, a feminized male, Queen Georgianna.[21] The British, for their part, reaffirmed parental authority. They were quick to ascribe disloyalty based on the fictive kinship of race: those favoring independence were drawing upon the assistance of "redskins and yellow-skins", "black-skins, blue skins"—savages rather than true men.[22] At best, American freedom fighters were rabble, men lacking distinction or property. Royalists pointed to gender inconsistencies as well: if men should be governed only by direct representation how then could women be excluded?[23]

The brothers united against their father, and fraternity helped forge a broad-based coalition of white men. Those with qualms regarding slavery set them aside in the interests of more unified resistance.[24] Once the war was joined the British promised manumission to any slaves who would abandon their rebel masters to support the loyalist cause. They made good on that promise even after they conceded to the revolution, and more than 3,000 African Americans emigrated to freedom in Nova Scotia.

The women who had helped keep farms and businesses running during the war were urged to devote themselves to "republican motherhood", raising a new generation of virtuous citizens.[25] Abigail Adams's injunction to her husband to "remember the ladies" while drafting the new constitution was fended off with the humorous objection that women would always be able to wield the "despotism of the petticoat". John Adams was opposed to any such leveling of distinctions, as indicated by the letter to his son in this chapter's epigraph.[26]

Thomas Jefferson feared that the expansion of trade and commerce would corrupt men, not to mention women. Federalists like Alexander

Hamilton, who believed that economic development would be a force for moral good, countered Jefferson's vision of an agrarian, family-based economy.[27] Hamilton insisted that factories could increase women's productivity. Neither he nor Jefferson foresaw the ways that productivity might further undermine the patriarchal order.

Montesquieu's metaphor of social engineering, the so-called "checks and balances" brought the framers to a compromise. Collective interests shaped these checks and balances. Although educated women played an important role in republican debates, they seldom challenged hierarchies of gender or race. Mercy Otis Warren, sister of James Otis and historian of the Revolution, criticized the Federalists for designing a constitution that gave the central government too much power. Judith Sargent Murray urged women to ambitiously pursue education and employment on the grounds that men themselves would benefit.[28]

The American Revolution has been described in terms of the "politics of liberty".[29] But its long run success hinged upon a new sense of national identity, nourished by the hope that citizenship might also confer some protection against ill health and bad luck. Wagering that the status quo could be shaken in Britain and France, as well as the United States, Thomas Paine outlined a remarkably detailed proposal: Taxes on low-income families should be replaced by a progressive tax on wealth, providing revenues sufficient to provide retirement benefits and payments for children under fourteen (provided they attended school). British authorities immediately condemned *The Rights of Man* and charged Paine with treason. His ideas, however, shaped British and American radicalism for years to come.[30]

Slavery and Evil

The ringing phrases of the Declaration of Independence would not be explicitly applied to women until 1848. Their relevance to slavery, however, was immediately apparent. Indeed, the original Declaration, authored by Thomas Jefferson, contained a distinctly anti-slavery sentence that was removed by Congress in 1776 to placate Southerners.[31] Patrick Henry, of "Give me liberty or give me death!" fame explained that while slavery was lamentable, its conveniences were great.[32] Observers in London made much of the contradiction. "How is it," asked a sarcastic Samuel Johnson, "that we hear the loudest yelps for liberty among the drivers of Negroes?"[33]

Political and economic expedience alone could not explain why the century of Enlightenment cast such a dark shadow on non-Europeans who lacked the power to defend themselves. An ideological rationale was required. The Church largely absolved Christians of responsibility for infidels. English political theorists relied more openly on the logic of national self-interest. Hobbes explained slavery as a result of war, and John Locke, who drafted a constitution for the Carolinas, described it as a state of war indefinitely continued. Likewise, Native Americans were described not as potential citizens, but as members of a foreign nation.

Neither social affections nor moral principles applied beyond the larger family of nations that conceived themselves as the civilized above the savage. The Bible described all humans as brothers and sisters descended from Eve and Adam. On the other hand, it named Cain and Abel as original sons, but no daughters, leaving the origins of the lineage unclear. Had there been, perhaps another race left out of the official story? Non-Europeans might have descended from the villainous Cain or Ham, inheriting some collective guilt. Among those who looked beyond the Bible, the notion that men were shaped by climate (as articulated, for instance, by Montesquieu) began to lose its force, replaced by notions of innate difference. Voltaire, for instance, believed that Negroes and Indians represented races separate from the white man.[34] The voice of the Scottish Enlightenment, David Hume, assumed Negroes were naturally inferior.

Racial difference was constructed in highly gendered terms. Negroes could be distinguished by their highly sexualized qualities. Their sexual organs, male and female, were described as larger and more exaggerated. The wanton lust of both Negro and Native American women was especially indicative. Their lack of shame brought their lineage into question, but it was also remarked that they experienced little pain in childbirth, unlike the true daughters of Eve who had been sentenced to such pain by God himself.[35] Negro women were often depicted with long breasts that could be flipped over to nurse a child upon their back. West Indian slave-holders, defensive about the low rate of natural increase of their human capital, explained that it was simply the result of polygamy and promiscuity, rather than maltreatment.[36]

Even abolitionists deplored the innate inferiority of the Negro, explaining why liberation would prove stressful to them, probably requiring deportation. Thomas Jefferson registered his disapproval of slavery in politically cautious ways even as he prospered from it.[37] In his view, Negroes lacked the ability to benefit from their exposure to Western civilization: "Nature has been less bountiful to them in the endowments of the head."[38] The best he could say of them was that they had fared better in the endowments of the heart. In this respect, descriptions of Negroes resembled descriptions of women. The Negro that Jefferson knew best was his slave Sally Hemings (his widowed wife's half-sister), who bore him at least one child. His paternity was dismissed as slanderous rumor until recently substantiated (if not completely proved) by the DNA testing of Sally's descendants. [39]

While theories of misplaced sexuality helped justify slavery, they also excited opposition to it. Abolitionists made much of the vulnerability of slave women, and the temptations it posed to even the most virtuous men. Few themes aroused more passionate condemnation than the lack of respect for marital ties and the separation of children from their parents. Such condemnations reached a crescendo when abolitionist Theodore Weld claimed that the high rate of slave population growth was attributable to raising children explicitly for sale.[40] When the British campaign to outlaw the slave trade won support from Parliament—and the Royal Navy—in 1808, the older, more established areas of the Southern U.S. began exporting slaves to the frontier areas. Lighter-skinned mulattoes generally yielded a higher price than their darker kin. In principle a man could buy a young female slave entirely for the purpose of profiting from the offspring he could sire upon her.

Opposition to slavery found especially fertile ground in parts of the country that enjoyed few economic benefits from it. In New England, New York, and Pennsylvania slavery was often described as the concatenation of both greed and lust. Denounced by most millenarian, perfectionist, and evangelical groups, its morality was most effectively challenged by the patient and persistent Quakers. Yet those who merely sought to establish their own virtues in opposition to it also favored the characterization of slavery as epitome of evil. An emerging class of industrial investors defended conditions in their factories by insisting that their employees were, after all, better off than slaves.[41]

Feminism and Abolition

Likewise, married white women were instructed to be grateful for their privileges. The comparison between their position and that of their Negro or Native American counterparts was particularly telling in the South, where women dissatisfied with their place in the patriarchal order tended more toward individual than public strategies of resistance.[42] The dissidents who spoke of women's rights almost always linked these with the rights of other unempowered groups. Frances Wright, a Scottish heiress influenced by the writings of Robert Owen, was scornful of inequalities based on class and race as well as gender. She established a utopian community in Nashoba, Tennessee in 1825, purchasing slaves in order to show that they could produce enough to buy themselves to freedom. The scandalized neighbors were less than cooperative. The utopians seemed to know more about social theory than growing food, and never became self-supporting. The emancipation of their slaves was not emulated.[43]

Sterner if hardly more effective emphasis on similarities between patriarchy and slavery came from the Quaker direction. Sarah Grimke, a Massachusetts member of the Society of Friends, was a fan of the French utopian socialist Henri de Saint-Simon.[44] In 1838 she published a set of letters on the equality of the sexes that described men as analogous to slave owners: "All history attests that man has subjected woman to his will, used her as a means to promote his selfish gratification, to minister to his sensual pleasures, to be instrumental in promoting his comfort; but never has he desired to elevate her to that rank she was created to fill."[45] She denounced male control over female sexuality, and argued that equal rights to person and property would release women from the "horrors of forced maternity".[46] She went on to complain that women's jobs were always paid less than men's.[47]

Slavery and patriarchal marriage did share some common features. Both slaves and wives were denied any legal rights over the products of their own labor. Until the latter part of the nineteenth century married women lacked legal rights over their own earnings or over their own children in the event of separation, abandonment or divorce. Runaway wives could be punished and forced to return home. The sexual double standard was advertised by the growing visibility of prostitution in urban areas. By law, slave owners and patriarchs were required only to meet the subsistence needs of their dependents, and could administer physical punishment without the close supervision of the law.

Within most white families it was likely that the force of patriarchal power was softened by personal affections. The same was said, of course, of slavery. Southerners insisted that plantation owners not only had a stake in the physical well-being of their chattel, but generally loved and cared for them. Altruistic behavior toward the powerless always has a contingent, variable quality. The slave owner, home from church, might offer his slaves an extra Sabbath ration. Faced with the prospect of a harvest shortfall, he might use a whip to stripe their backs. A suitor, overwhelmed with passion, might offer his heart. A husband, peeved with a disobedient wife, might slap her senseless. The mere threat of violence was often sufficient to enforce authority.

Altruistic behavior from the powerless, whether real or feigned, is a more predictable response. Affection is often coded as subservience, and pretending helplessness an effective way of blunting anger. The obligation to put others first requires either some repression of self-interest or a definition of the self that encompasses the well-being of the other.[48] Women were not— as Frederick Douglass pointed out—lynched on lampposts. What slaves and wives shared was the expectation of subservience—the repression of their own self-interest.

With a synergy that would be repeated more than a century later during the Civil Rights Movement, the movement to abolish slavery dislodged resistance to consideration of women's rights. Similarities in the lack of legal personhood and exclusion from the franchise were too obvious to ignore. Perhaps a willingness to offend public opinion on one count made it easier to be outspoken on another. Many other moral causes beckoned. In 1834 the New York Female Moral Reform society moved beyond parlor meetings to brothel visits, in efforts to embarrass patrons.[49] Most men were, however, reluctant to embrace the cause of sexual purity or of women's rights. Abolitionists feared distraction from their primary, overriding goal. The Conference on World Slavery held in London in 1840 voted to exclude women from official participation, despite the important role that they had played. Among the women who vowed redress was Elizabeth Cady Stanton, wife of a prominent anti-slavery activist. Eight years later she masterminded the convention in Seneca Falls, New York that inaugurated the campaign for women's suffrage.

Observers from Abroad

In the 1830s and 1840s, both the English and the French tended to regard the United States with the patronizing but affectionate curiosity of an elder sibling tending to a younger brother. The most famous English visitor of letters—a woman—urged the causes of feminism and abolition. The most famous French visitor of letters—a man—urged less and described more. Yet both Harriet Martineau and Alexis de Tocqueville were fascinated by inequalities based on gender and race, and both influenced America's understanding of its own discourse of self-interest.

Harriet Martineau, a Unitarian woman of educated background made her reputation—and her living—as a popularizer of the ideas of Thomas Robert Malthus (of whom, more in Chapter 8). She embraced the Malthusian argument that men as well as women should exert moral restraint—and that delayed (or even indefinitely postponed) marriage was no tragedy. Unlike Malthus, she hoped to reform, rather than abolish the Poor Laws. Also unlike Malthus, she was a staunch optimist and believer in the possibility of human progress.[50]

Once she found a publisher, her *Illustrations in Political Economy* became a best-seller, providing her with the means to plan a two-year tour of the United States—an adventurous plan not only due to the rigors of travel (especially compared with the more traditional European tour) but also to the contentious political environment. As the abolitionist movement gained visibility it also provoked a pro-slavery backlash. An installment of Martineau's *Illustrations*, "Demarara", had deplored the plight of West Indian slaves and invoked Smith's critique of the economic efficiency of slavery. The captain of Martineau's ship, knowing her reputation, feared that she could not safely disembark in New York.

Martineau's Unitarian friends, many of them active in the abolitionist movement, welcomed her with open arms, but pushed her to publicize her support for their cause. A turning point came when she witnessed William Lloyd Garrison dragged through the streets of Boston by a crowd threatening to tar and feather him. She found the Boston abolitionist's bravery infectious and risked her own physical safety at a meeting of the Female Anti-Slave Society in Boston in 1835 where she declared slavery "inconsistent with the law of God".[51] This declaration radicalized her reputation and circumscribed her welcome.

Two books written by Martineau in this period displayed a vehemence lacking in her other work.[52] Inconsistent individualism infuriated her. Her aptly titled chapter on "The Political Non-Existence of Women", in *Society in America* accuses Americans of hypocrisy because their Declaration of Independence holds that governments derive just powers only from the consent of the governed. It calls Thomas Jefferson to task for failing to carry democratic principles to their logical conclusion. It pooh-poohs James Mill's argument that women are effectively represented by their male relatives.[53] Beyond polemic, Martineau argues that extreme inequalities, whether based on race, gender, or class, create incentives for abuse. Inconsistent individualism, in other words, could undermine the moral sentiments and morph into pure, unadulterated greed.

Responses to Martineau, as to abolitionist feminists in general, were telling: The General Association of Massachusetts clergymen expressed alarm concerning possible "alterations in the female character" in the direction of political self-reliance. A consistent theme of condemnation was the departure of women from their proper sphere.[54] Martineau was personally ridiculed as an unattractive, masculine creature, and her popularization of Malthusian ideas increased her vulnerability to attack.[55] One critic described her as the "anti-Propagation lady a single sight of whom would repel all fears of surplus population as regards himself, her aspects being as repulsive as her doctrines."[56] Others described preoccupation with the sexual abuse of slaves as a form of hysteria endemic among old maids.[57]

Democracy in America

The abolitionist movement was not yet fully underway when Alexis de Tocqueville arrived in 1831, ostensibly to study prisons. While he came from an aristocratic French family, he was a less established writer than Martineau, less encumbered by the reputation of his earlier work. His impression on American culture, though less immediate, proved more enduring. Tocqueville's *Democracy in America* is widely considered a classic treatise on early nineteenth-century American morals and manners. It also offers a thoughtful, if pessimistic analysis of the political economy of individual and collective conflict.

De Tocqueville was an eloquent critic of slavery, and he went far beyond most of his contemporaries in his attention to the history of human exploitation.

> If we reason from what passes in the world, we should almost say that the European is to the other races of mankind what man himself is to the lower animals: he makes them subservient to his use, and when he cannot subdue he destroys them.[58]

While his explanation of the differences between African Americans and Native Americans relied on stereotypes, he correctly predicted that slavery would lead to armed conflict, and that Native American tribes were doomed to extinction.

Individualism was not, he observed, the same thing as selfishness, that "passionate and exaggerated love of self, which leads a man to connect everything with himself and to prefer himself to everything in the world".[59] He considered the Smithian claim that the social affections would temper self-interest, and wished that it were true. Yes, Americans often pursued self-interest in enlightened ways, recognizing the benefits of treating others in a kind and equitable manner. Yes, it was better to be self-interested in little ways than to engage in impractical hypocrisies. But in the long run, he insisted:

> No power on earth can prevent the increasing equality of conditions from inclining the human mind to seek out what is useful or from leading every member of the community to be wrapped up in himself. It must therefore be expected that personal interest will become more than ever the principal if not the sole spring of men's actions.[60]

At best, education might help combat destabilizing selfishness. But the sexual division of labor would also help. De Tocqueville praised Americans for adopting the principles of political economy and carefully distinguishing the duties of men from those of women. He castigated those Europeans who sought to confound the differences between the sexes. Equality, similarity, mixing of men and women in occupations or in business, would only degrade them both, making men "weak" and women "disorderly".[61] Like Rousseau, he found the very thought of female individualism almost too much to bear.

NOTES TO CHAPTER 5

[1] Richard Price, *Observations on the Importance of the American Revolution* (London, 1784).

[2] Gordon S. Wood, *The Radicalism of the American Revolution* (New York, Knopf, 1993), p. 220.

[3] Ibid., p. 239.

[4] Eric Foner, *Tom Paine and Revolutionary America* (New York: Oxford University Press, 1976), p. 219.

[5] Alan Taylor, *"The People of British America, 1700–1750,"* Foreign Policy Research Institute, available at www.fpri.org/orbis/ accessed January 10, 2006, p. 1 (based on chapters 8 and 14 in Alan Taylor, *American Colonies* (New York: Viking Penguin, 2001)).

[6] Christopher Clark, *The Roots of Rural Capitalism: Western Massachusetts, 1780–1860* (Ithaca: Cornell University Press, 1990).

[7] Winifred Barr Rothenberg, *From Market-Places to a Market Economy: The Transformation of Rural Massachusetts, 1750–1850* (Chicago: University of Chicago Press, 1992); Alan Kulikoff, "The Transition to Capitalism in Rural America," *William and Mary Quarterly*, 3rd Ser., 46 (1989), 120–44.

[8] Eugene D. Genovese, *The Political Economy of Slavery: Studies in the Economy and Society of the Slave South* (New York: Vintage, 1965).

[9] Adam Smith, *An Inquiry in the Nature and Causes of the Wealth of Nations* (Oxford: Clarendon Press, 1976), 411–2.

[10] Robert William Fogel and Stanley L. Engerman, *Time on the Cross: The Economics of American Negro Slavery* (New York: Little, Brown, 1974); Robert William Fogel, *Without Consent or Contract. The Rise and Fall of American Slavery* (New York: W.W. Norton and Company, 1989).

[11] Michael Merrill, "Putting 'Capitalism' in its Place: A Review of Recent Literature," *The William and Mary Quarterly*, 3rd Series, Vol. 52:2 (1995), 315–26.

[12] Taylor, *The People of British America*, p. 10.

[13] Phillip Greven, *Four Generations: Population, Land and Family in Colonial Andover, Massachusetts* (New York, 1970); Nancy R. Folbre, "The Wealth of Patriarchs: Deerfield, Massachusetts, 1760–1840," *Journal of Interdisciplinary History* 16:2 (1985), 199–220.

[14] Susan B. Carter, Roger L. Ransom, Richard Sutch, "Family Matters: The Life-Cycle Transition and the Unparalleled Antebellum American Fertility Decline," in Timothy W. Guinnane, William A. Sundstrom, and Warren Whatley, eds *History Matters: Essays on Economic Growth, Technology, and Demographic Change* (Stanford: Stanford University Press, 2002).

[15] Alexander Hamilton, *Papers* 10:252 (5 December 1791), available on line at http://press-pubs.uchicago.edu/founders/documents/v1ch4s31.html

[16] Charles Sellers, *The Market Revolution. Jacksonian America, 1815–1846* (New York: Oxford University Press, 1991), p. 226.

[17] Linda Kerber, *Women of the Republic: Intellect and Ideology in Revolutionary America* (New York: W.W. Norton, 1986), p. 30.

[18] Philip S. Foner, *The Complete Writings of Thomas Paine* (New York: Citadel Press, 1945), available online at http://www.thomaspaine.org

[19] *Common Sense*, in Foner, *Complete Writings*.

[20] Bernard Bailyn, *Ideological Origin of the American Revolution* (Cambridge, MA: Harvard University Press, 1967); Edwin G. Burrows and Michael Wallace, "The Ideology and Psychology of National Liberation," *Perspectives in American History* VI (1972), 167–306.

[21] Dror Wahrman, "The English Problem of Identity in the American Revolution," *The American Historical Review* 106: 4 (2001), p. 23.

[22] Wahrman, "The English Problem of Identity," p. 10.

[23] Wahrman, "The English Problem of Identity".

[24] Joseph J. Ellis, *Founding Brothers. The Revolutionary Generation* (New York: Vintage, 2002).

[25] Kerber, *Women of the Republic;* Mary Beth Norton, *Liberty's Daughters: The Revolutionary Experience of American Women, 1750–1800* (Boston: Little, Brown, 1980).

[26] Pauline Schloesser, *The Fair Sex. White Women and Racial Patriarchy in the Early American Republic* (New York: New York University Press, 2002), p. 18; cited in Gordon S. Wood, *The Radicalism of the American Revolution* (New York: Knopf, 1993), p. 147.

[27] Gertrude Himmelfarb, *The Roads to Modernity. The British French, and American Enlightenments* (New York: Knopf, 2004), p. 201.

[28] Schloesser, *The Fair Sex*.

[29] Himmelfarb, *The Roads to Modernity*.

[30] E. P. Thompson, *The Making of the English Working Class* (New York: Vintage Books, 1963), 93–4.

[31] David Brion Davis, *The Problem of Slavery in the Age of Revolution, 1770–1823* (Ithaca: Cornell University Press, 1975), p. 24.

[32] Bernard Bailyn, *The Ideological Origins of the American Revolution* (Cambridge: Harvard University Press, 1992), p. 236.

[33] Thomas F. Gossett, *Race. The History of an Idea in America* (Dallas: Southern Methodist University Press, 1963), p. 42.

[34] Gossett, *The History of an Idea*, p. 44.

[35] Kirsten Fischer, *Suspect Relations. Sex, Race, and Resistance in Colonial North Carolina* (Ithaca: Cornell University Press, 2002); Kathleen M. Brown, *Good Wives, Nasty Wenches, and Anxious Patriarchs. Gender, Race, and Power in Colonial Virginia* (Chapel Hill: University of North Carolina Press, 1996).

[36] Robert William Fogel, *Without Consent or Contract. The Rise and Fall of American Slavery* (New York: W.W. Norton and Company, 1989), p. 119.

[37] On Jefferson's ambivalence toward abolition, especially in his later years, see Davis, *The Problem of Slavery*, p 172–7.

[38] Gossett, *Race*, p. 43.

[39] Annette Gordon-Reed, *Thomas Jefferson and Sally Hemings: An American Controversy* (Charlottesville: University Press of Virginia, 1998).

[40] Robert William Fogel, *Without Consent or Contract. The Rise and Fall of American Slavery* (New York: W. W. Norton, 1989), p. 119.

[41] Davis, *The Problem of Slavery*.

[42] Rhys Isaac, *Landon Carter's Uneasy Kingdom: Revolution and Rebellion on a Virginia Plantation* (New York: Oxford, 2004).

[43] Carolyn Johnston, *Sexual Power. Feminism and the Family in America* (Tuscaloosa, AL University of Alabama Press, 1992), p. 75.

[44] Gerda Lerner, *The Feminist Thought of Sarah Grimke* (New York: Oxford University Press, 1998), p. 37.

[45] Sarah Grimke, *Letters on the Equality of the Sexes and Other Essays*, ed. Elizabeth Ann Bartless (New Haven: Yale University Press, 1988), p. 35. See also Gerda Lerner, *The Feminist Thought of Sarah Grimke* (New York: Oxford University Press, 1998).

[46] Grimke, *Letters*, p. 63.

[47] "In those employments which are peculiar to women, their time is estimated at only half of the value of that of men. A woman who goes out to wash, works as hard in proportion as a wood sawyer, or a coal heaver, but she is not generally able to make more than half as much by a day's work." Ibid., p. 59.

[48] Joan Tronto, "Beyond Gender Difference to a Theory of Care," *Signs: Journal of Women in Culture and Society* 12:4 (1987), 644–63 and *Moral Boundaries: A Political Argument for an Ethics of Care* (New York: Routledge, 1993).

[49] Charles Sellers, *The Market Revolution. Jacksonian America, 1815–1846* (New York: Oxford University Press, 1991), p. 244.

[50] James Huzel, *The Popularization of Malthus in Early 19th Century England* (Burlington, VT: Ashgate, 2006), 68–70.

[51] Deborah A. Logan, "The Redemption of a Heretic: Harriet Martineau and Anglo-American Abolitionism in Pre-Civil War America," 242–65 in Kathryn Kish Sklar and James Brewer, eds, *Women's Rights and Transatlantic Antislavery in the Era of Emancipation* (New Haven, CT: Yale University Press, 2007).

[52] Harriet Martineau, *Autobiography*, with Memorials by Maria Weston Chapman, 4th edn. (Boston: Houghton, Osgood and Co, 1879), vol. 2, pp. 562–74.

[53] Harriet Martineau, "The Political Non-Existence of Women," in Gayle Graham Yates, ed., *Harriet Martineau on Women* (New Brunswick: Rutgers University Press, 1985), p. 136.

[54] See Logan, "Redemption," and also Harriet Martineau, *The Martyr Age of the United States* (Boston: Weeks, Jordan and Company, 1839).

[55] See Note 12 in David M. Levy, "Taking Harriet Martineau's Economics Seriously," 262–84 in *The Status of Women in Classical Economic Thought*, eds Robert Dimand and Chris Nyland (Northampton, MA: Edward Elgar, 2003).

[56] Huzel, *The Popularization of Malthus*, p. 77.

[57] Levy, "Taking Harriet Martineau's Economics Seriously," p. 266.

[58] Alexis de Toqueville, *Democracy in America*, Vol. II (New York: Alfred A. Knopf, 1951) Book 1, Chapter XVIII.

[59] de Tocqueville, *Democracy in America*, Book 1, Ch. 2.

[60] de Tocqueville, *Democracy in America*, Book II, Chapter 8.

[61] Ibid., p. 211.

CHAPTER 6

The Perfectibility of Man

Never has a people perished from an excess of wine. All perish from the
disorder of women.   Jean-Jacques Rousseau

Revolutions spin on the conviction that men can perfect themselves as well
as their social institutions. The French expressed less confidence in the
social virtues than the British.[1] In the early eighteenth century they
seemed more open to women's rights than their British or American
counterparts. Perhaps the very strength of French patriarchy encouraged
sons and daughters to make a common cause. Once they had executed
their symbolic father, however, the sons found republican governance
more difficult than they had imagined and rejected political cooperation
with their sisters.

France's most celebrated eighteenth-century thinker, Jean-Jacques Rousseau, provided rhetorical support for this rejection. He described economic
development as a disruptive and corrupting force, particularly in its effects
on women, who could be tempted to pursue their own interests at the
expense of the common good. A less famous thinker, the Marquis de
Condorcet, developed a more optimistic and egalitarian view. At the opposite end of the individualist spectrum, rejecting the very concept of the
common good, were the writings of the Marquis de Sade, a believer in
immoral sentiments.

Progress?

In 1750, a group of eminent scholars known as the Academy of Dijon announced an essay competition on the following topic: "Has intellectual and economic progress contributed to the moral improvement of humanity?"[2] It is likely that Adam Smith would have answered "Yes." The Swiss-born Jean Jacques Rousseau won the prize for an essay explaining his resounding "No!" He developed his argument in a number of essays and books, including *The Discourse on Inequality* written in 1754 and in *The Social Contract* and *Emile*, both published in 1762 and banned by authorities in France and Switzerland.

Rousseau gained sufficient celebrity from his work to circulate with the best known philosophers of Paris, including Voltaire and Diderot. He was invited to write the essay on Political Economy for the first major compendium of French knowledge, the *Encyclopedia*. Lacking social skills, he broke off from most of his friends, spending the last years of his life in solitary obscurity. He never married, and although many of his later writings elaborated at length on the correct methods of raising children, he never welcomed parenthood. His lifetime companion, Therese Levasseur, bore him several children whom he deposited shortly after their births at a Paris orphanage.

Rousseau was no libertarian. He embraced ideals of benevolence.[3] He insisted, more vehemently than Montesquieu, Voltaire, or Diderot, that political and economic institutions should be designed to meet the basic needs of all citizens. When it came to political ideals, he, like other Enlightenment philosophers, wanted the law of nature on his side. His blazing rhetoric in the *Discourse on the Origin of Inequality* made him a favorite of revolutionaries for centuries to come: "It is manifestly contrary to the law of nature...that a handful of men should gorge themselves with superfluities while the starving multitude goes in want of necessities."[4]

But Rousseau was convinced that the growth of commerce, the development of so-called civilized society, would undermine natural benevolence. Perhaps he perceived his own internal conflicts in these terms: a natural desire to become a father undermined by fear it would threaten his social position. In any case, he dismissed the likelihood of any happy marriage of commerce and virtue. His imaginary state of nature was not unlike a

Garden of Eden inhabited by Robinson Crusoe: "I see him eating his fill under an oak tree, quenching his thirst at the first stream, making his bed at the base of the same tree that supplied his meal, and, behold, his needs are met."[5]

This was no Hobbesian warrior, wielding a broad axe. Rousseau envisaged natural man as a peaceable fellow who seldom came into prolonged contact with his fellows. Nature was bountiful, so he had little reason to fight. Natural man was not oblivious to his own self-interest, but had an inborn propensity for pity and sociability.[6] A nomenclatural distinction clarified his argument:

> One must not confuse vanity (*amour-propre*) and self-love (*amour de soi-meme*), two very different passions in their nature and in their effects. Self-love is a natural sentiment that prompts every animal to watch over its own preservation and that, guided in many by reason and modified by pity, produces humanity and virtue. Vanity is only a relative, artificial sentiment born in society, a sentiment that prompts each individual to set greater store by himself than by anyone else, that triggers all the evil they do to themselves and others.[7]

Other eighteenth-century Frenchmen used the term *amour-propre* to mean self-love. But the distinction Rousseau made echoed the English contrast between selfishness (what he termed vanity) and self-interest (*amour de soi-meme*). The State of Nature may be primitive and rude: but the State of Society feeds the vanities, making men "greedy, ambitious, and wicked".[8]

Other Enlightenment philosophers might sympathize with these arguments, to a point. But they were fairly confident that the state and the church, working in concert, could defend civic virtue. Rousseau believed in the existence of the Common Good and the General Will, to which all citizens of civic virtue should subordinate themselves. But he emphasized that individuals would not easily or automatically bow to such abstractions. In the process of pursuing their own self-interest, men might occasionally help others, but they would, more often, harm them.[9]

Hobbes had described the Leviathan as an aggregation; Rousseau offered the more organic picture of a body politic in which laws and custom were the brain, and economic wisdom fulfilled the functions of the heart.[10] Having established his metaphor, however, he went on to undermine it, observing that every political society is composed of smaller societies, each with its own interests. Feelings of humanity stretch only so far. Rousseau observed that Europeans did not feel as much pain at news of a disaster in Tartary or Japan as on their own continent.[11] As the body grew larger, and more complex, it began to lose its ability to function as a whole.

Rousseau's fear that individuals would not subordinate themselves to the General Will was expressed in elitist terms. Ordinary men might know how to define the Common Good but it would be difficult to persuade them to pursue it. Rousseau rejected the "social sentiments" solution. He summarized his argument in an early draft of Book I of *The Social Contract,* which included an appendix entitled "The General Society of the Human Race", asking whether a General Society is possible:

> It is false to say that, in a condition of independence, reason leads us to contribute to the common good through consideration for our own interests. Private interest and the general welfare, far from being combined, exclude each other in the natural order of things, and social laws are a tie which each man will gladly impose on others, but by which he will not be bound himself.[12]

The kind of religion that could solve this problem, he continued, was beyond the grasp of "the multitude". Men's interests may occasionally coincide with those of others, and justice may occasionally be expedient. But there is no reason to believe that these conditions will always hold.

Lacking confidence in both paternity and fraternity, Rousseau embraced maternity—on the condition that it remain firmly under male control. Mothers, sisters, and daughters could be held responsible for the future of civilization. In popular novels such as *Emile* and *La Nouvelle Héloïse* he shifted attention away from men to women's virtue, romanticizing the role of those who devoted themselves to the next generation. But because society remained so dependent on this virtue, the "disorder of women" posed a dire threat.[13] If only his lover Therese had not seized his affections and borne him children that he did not want—how much more orderly his life could have been.

Women had to be limited to the sphere of family life because this was the only uncorrupted, redemptive sphere of human experience, the only sphere that could be successfully defended from selfish preoccupations. Rousseau rejected the optimism of individualism.[14] Men might not be able to impose the Common Good directly upon themselves, but by imposing it upon women, they might protect future generations. One wonders what became of his own abandoned children.

Of Bread and Cake

While French philosophers debated the effects of commerce, French economists cheered it on. After 1700 both international and domestic trade picked up, and France's national income more than doubled, growing at about the same per capita rate as England's.[15] A new economic confidence found expression in demands for deregulation of the grain trade. François Quesnay argued that grain merchants should be left alone, and subsidies removed. An increase in the price of bread might cause some stress in the short run, he conceded, but in the long run, it would encourage farmers to plant more grain, averting future famines. What would happen to hungry peasants in the meantime? As Denis Diderot and other philosophers pointed out, bread was the most basic of necessities. It represented the very gluten of society, holding it together in ways that might be weakened by reliance on the market.[16]

Swayed by Quesnay, Louis XV chose the path of liberalization. Royal edicts of 1763 and 1764 rescinded most grain trade regulations, allowing both stockpiling and external export of grain and flour. By 1766, grain prices had risen dramatically and begun to excite unrest. Political pressure forced the King not only to reimpose rules on the Paris market, but also to spend royal funds increasing grain supplies there. Even when rules were extended to the country as a whole, shortages persisted. The injection of more money, or even more credit, into famine struck areas would have encouraged market networks and increased imports of the necessary food. But such policies would have made it more difficult to contain the costs of social obligation. The King managed to alienate both sides in the debate. Corruption and mismanagement of public subsidy programs generated anger at the grain control system. Market advocates argued that deregulation had been undermined by bad luck and inconsistent application. While grain regulation represented part of a moral economy, the emphasis on grain itself was overstated.[17]

Louis XV died in 1774, and his successor ascended the throne expressing his desire for the love of his people. He chose the economist Jacques Turgot as one of his ministers, and promptly agreed to another experiment with deregulation of the grain trade. The previous history repeated itself: bad weather, bad harvests, and poor market infrastructure. Grain prices went up and dissatisfaction mounted. The King had incurred debts that limited his financial flexibility. In 1789, the market women of Paris, angry at the high price of bread, marched for hours in the pouring rain to the palace at Versailles and demanded that the King force prices down. They also demanded that he return with them to Paris. Thus began women's active, organized participation in the Revolution.[18]

Initially, at least, Enlightenment optimism tempered political fury. The dissidents hoped to solve the country's bread problem, reform its family laws, and design a new democracy. Unified primarily by their dissatisfaction with the old regime, they complained that the King was no longer fulfilling his responsibility as a father to his people, and had therefore lost his right to rule.[19] But the revolution was not particularly successful at providing either bread or cake. Its leadership soon betrayed the very women who had marched upon the palace.

Interests and the Revolution

The initial unity of opposition was euphoric. The marvelously named Théroigne de Méricourt cut a particularly dramatic figure, dressed in a blood-red riding habit with two pistols at her waist. She described the atmosphere that year as follows:

> What struck me most was the air of general benevolence. Selfishness seemed banished from every heart. There was no longer a distinction between classes. People jostled together, talking to one another as though they were one family. The rich, at this moment of fermentation, mixed voluntarily with the poor and did not disdain to speak to them as equals. People's very expressions seemed changed.[20]

Women had their supporters among the highly educated theorists of change. Most prominent was the Marquis de Condorcet, student of Voltaire, mathematician, writer, and member of the political faction that hoped for a nonviolent transition to democracy, Condorcet had supported early efforts to deregulate the grain trade.[21] His most enduring passions, however, were democracy and the perfectibility of man, stepping-stones to equality of the sexes.

He outlined his views in an acceptance speech to the French Academy in the early 1780s. He was encouraged in them by the well-educated and highly opinionated Sophie de Grouchy, who soon became his wife. In 1787, he published a pamphlet reflecting on the American Revolution, arguing that it was unjust to exclude women from political representation. In 1789, he developed his ideas still further, contesting the claim that citizenship would take women away from their duties as wives and mothers, and therefore threaten the common good.[22] Many pamphlets, letters to editors, and delegations to the National Assembly convened in 1789 seconded his views.[23]

Still, the word "woman" was conspicuous by its absence from the famous rhetorical flourish known as the Declaration of the Rights of Man and Citizen, issued in 1789. Family law was transformed. New legislation weakened the power of fathers by stipulating that their property should, upon their death, be equally divided among their children. The age of majority was lowered to twenty-one. The infamous *lettres de cachet* were eliminated, and replaced by special family courts to provide arbitration for disputes.[24] Marriage became a civil contract, and both spouses gained the right to divorce. Homosexuality was decriminalized. As the Assembly debated a new Constitution, women's groups actively agitated for new rights, and Olympe des Gouges issued her *Declaration of the Rights of Woman and Citizen* in 1791, demanding that women be treated equally with men. She also insisted on the need for a new social contract that would include the right to sue fathers who failed to meet their paternal obligations.[25]

The role that women played in challenging the old regime, as well as the activism of groups such as the Society of Republican Revolutionary Women, seemed to create an opening for more radical reforms. After all, the Assembly had abolished feudal dues with the stroke of a pen. But reaction began to set in. Men complained that they wanted to come home from meetings to find their homes in order. As one anonymous male journalist put it, "We don't teach you how to love your children; kindly refrain from coming to our clubs to teach us the duties of a citizen."[26]

The King was beheaded in 1792, on the grounds that he was a traitor. The Queen, never particularly involved in politics, fell to accusations of sexual perversity. It was alleged, specifically, that she had fondled her son's genitals and taught him to masturbate.[27] Her execution the following year signaled a new willingness to take action against women, and scuffles between the Society of Republican Revolutionary Women and market women who had grown frustrated with price controls on bread created an excuse for new forms of repression.

Rather than merely taking action against one specific group, the Constitutional Convention outlawed all forms of female collective action, prohibiting all women's clubs and popular societies. The representative of the Committee on General Security explained that women could not exercise political rights because "they would be obliged to sacrifice the more important cares to which nature calls them".[28] Pierre-Gaspard Chaumette, a Commune official and disciple of Rousseau, rhetorically asked:

> Since when is it decent to see women abandoning the pious cares of their households, the cribs of their children, to come to public places, to harangues in the galleries, in the bars of the Senate? Is it to men that nature confided domestic cares? Has she given us breasts to feed our children?[29]

Up to 1793, the Girondin faction favoring a decentralized government that would not interfere in economic matters maintained control. Threats of invasion from abroad and a worsening economic situation intensified political tensions. Thomas Paine, believing that the French were fulfilling his vision of the rights of man, had triumphantly sailed to Paris to be elected as a deputy to the National Convention. He was almost immediately disillusioned, and said so publicly. The ascendant Jacobin faction packed him off to prison for eleven months. Their spokesman Robespierre took inspiration from a selective reading of Rousseau, proclaiming that morals should replace egoism, and that any man who wanted to pursue his own selfish interests should leave the country.[30] He went on to show just how profoundly the concept of The General Will could be corrupted by justifying the mass executions that he ordered:

> Terror without virtue is disastrous, virtue without terror is powerless. Terror is nothing but prompt, severe, and inflexible justice; it is thus an emanation of virtue; it is less a particular principle than a consequence of the general principle of democracy applied to the most urgent needs of the fatherland.[31]

Robespierre promised to restore the familial responsibility of the state and provide a state-funded welfare system. Those promises were never met.[32] At the public celebration of Unity and Indivisibility in August 1793, the Jacobin deputies ceremonially drank water spouting from the breast of a large maternal fountain in the form of an Egyptian goddess. Joan Scott explains the iconography as follows: "Woman as breast—nurturer but not creator. Man as citizen—the conqueror of nature. The differences between women and men were taken to be irreducible and fundamental; they existed in nature and therefore could not be corrected by law."[33]

Olympe des Gouges was sent to the guillotine. She had, according to a semiofficial paper, forgotten the virtues of her sex.[34] Méricourt was attacked on the street by a group of Jacobin women who stripped and beat her. She soon lost her mind and ended her days in an asylum. Perhaps any idealistic vision of human nature had begun to seem insane. Condorcet, an outspoken critic of Jacobin views, was forced into hiding. He distracted himself by writing a *Sketch for a Historical Picture of the Progress of the Human Mind,* a description of ten stages of social evolution that would culminate in the elimination of poverty, misery, and inequality.

He remained confident that the moral and political sciences would solve the problems that Rousseau had raised: "What are we to expect from the perfection of laws and public institutions, consequent upon the progress of those sciences, but the reconciliation, the identification of the interests of each with the interests of all?"[35] He was also confident that inequality between the sexes had no basis whatsoever in differences of intellect or moral sensibility. Men had simply failed to transcend the temptation to abuse their strength.[36]

Condorcet's formidable powers of imagination gave him some telling glimpses of the future. He correctly predicted that improved living conditions would lead to the use of contraception (an argument that Malthus would soon dismiss). But he never successfully explained why one group within society might exploit another. The possibility that such exploitation resulted from collective interests jarred with the assumption that men were naturally benevolent. If men had invented systematic means of oppression in the past, how could they be expected to behave any more virtuously in the present?

Condorcet left his refuge in Paris out of concern that he was endangering the friend harboring him there. Disguising himself as a woman, he managed to escape the city, but was soon captured, and died shortly after, possibly from self-inflicted poison.[37] His widow Sophie continued to promote their ideas, albeit in more cautious ways. After publishing her own French translation of Adam Smith's *Theory of Moral Sentiments*, she wrote of ways social institutions might be designed to strengthen the sentiment of sympathy.[38] In 1797 she happened to meet Napoleon at the house of a mutual friend, where he opined that women shouldn't meddle in politics. Her response: "In a country where their heads can be cut off, it's hardly surprising that they might want to ask why."[39]

Malevolence Theorized

The notion that it was always in men's interests to serve the common good had always invited cynicism. Still, many hoped that men were at least moving in a benevolent direction. As Republican France morphed into Terror and then into the military dictatorship of the Napoleonic Empire this hope faded. The Light of Reason began to seem just as faint as the Light of Faith. Perhaps historical events spotlighted problems easier to ignore in happier times. It was obviously difficult to balance the demand for individual liberty with the need to enforce social obligations.[40] It was also shockingly easy to reverse the assumption that men were naturally benevolent. The Marquis de Sade proclaimed that men could find pleasure only in other people's pain.

Though often dismissed as a mere pornographer, de Sade had a keen appreciation of the weaknesses of eighteenth-century moral philosophy. Some twentieth-century thinkers give him credit for the nihilist dissolution of the humanist ideals, because he showed how rational thought could be applied to what even secular thinkers would call evil ends.[41] That de Sade was so preoccupied with women and the family shows how well he understood their crucial place in moral discourse.

De Sade's first principle was radical individualism: Men were naturally egoistic and completely selfish. He went beyond Hobbesian assumptions to argue that interests of individuals are always and everywhere opposed to those of others: "The first and strongest inclination of man is incontestably to put his fellows in his power and to tyrannize them with all his might."[42] Unlike Rousseau, he considered this a law of nature, pointing to the child "who bites his nurse's nipple and breaks his rattle again and again."[43] He interpreted sexual intercourse (Boswell's favorite example of the benefits of reciprocal exchange) as another form of violence, arguing that pleasure was only diluted when it was shared.

Even the most skeptical philosophers had welcomed the possibility that virtue could bring pleasure. De Sade insisted that vicious behavior was much more fun, and that men who declared otherwise were hypocrites or weaklings. Nature had constructed men to derive pleasure from the domination of others, and Nature could not be contravened. Men should, therefore, pursue their selfish pleasures with abandon. De Sade put his principles into practice, abusing prostitutes and other women to such extremes that he spent much of his life in jail. His writings challenged presumptions of natural benevolence even more effectively than his actions.

De Sade argued that the concept of the common good was not only sentimental, but incoherent, because the competing demands of individuals could never be successfully arbitrated. Where could one draw the line between satisfaction of one's own desires, and those of others? Since the line could not be drawn, it should be abandoned. Any attention to the needs of others was, according to de Sade, unnatural. This conclusion reinforced some aspects of the individualist vision. Like Mandeville, for instance, de Sade argued that the rich had no responsibility for the poor. But the abrogation of all social obligations pushed individualism to extremes that few could tolerate. De Sade claimed that the sick should be left to die, friends should be betrayed, women should be raped, and family ties should be scorned.

Nature gave men the power, and therefore the right, to take women against their will. "All men are born free... no man may be excluded from possessing a woman. All men therefore have equal rights of enjoyment in all women."[44] In one of his most famous post-revolutionary pamphlets de Sade argued that the new regime should eliminate all rules against rape, incest, and sodomy, as well as any restriction on theft or murder. It should, in other words, remove any restraints on the war of all against all. Mandeville had argued for state support of prostitution; de Sade called for the organization of public establishments where human objects of all sexes and all ages should be freely available to the "caprices of libertines".[45] Weak men should be treated as women.

The meaninglessness of family is a consistent and recurrent theme in de Sade's work. In his ideal world the results of female promiscuity are irrelevant because men should not take responsibility for any children, not even their own. Parents owe nothing to children and children owe nothing to parents.[46] In many of his narratives, the protagonist derives ultimate pleasure from persuading a father to rape a daughter, or encouraging a young woman to rape her own mother with a dildo. It is impossible to outrage Nature itself, which tolerates, and therefore justifies all.

De Sade's work was never widely read, and remains difficult to find in English translation. Its relevance to political economy would be self-evident if it were retitled to emphasize its relationship to Adam Smith's early work. De Sade created a *Theory of Immoral Sentiments*. He asserted that human beings were naturally malevolent, not benevolent. It seems unlikely that they are naturally either one. But de Sade had a point: the wealth of nations was not created entirely by sweet commerce and voluntary trade.

Timid Egoism

Ideologies polarized in late eighteenth-century France, with Condorcet at one extreme and de Sade at the other. At every place on this spectrum, assumptions about gender shaped assumptions about self-interest, and vice versa. Rousseau, the man most worried that women might pursue interests separate from those of men, feared that self-interest would undermine social solidarity. Anticipating the later direction of the Revolution he proposed strict limits on women's rights. Condorcet, the idealist, shared Adam Smith's confidence in the moral sentiments. He expressed great faith in the rationality and morals of women, in particular. But he failed to explain what men had to gain by ganging up either on women or one another.

De Sade relieved himself of responsibility for either women or virtue by asserting that the strong had every right to dominate and exploit the weak. He rejected any double standard of morality because he had no standard of morality at all. He urged women to seize their birthright of sensuality, to pleasure themselves with one another as well as with men.[47] In his lexicon, greed and lust were simply the logical culmination of self-interest.

The dark side of self-interest cast an ominous shadow on the principles of individualist political theory. Why free men from their traditional chains if they would all follow de Sade's example, taking pleasure in other people's pain? It is easy to see why women, in particular, might develop some misgivings about the rational pursuit of self-interest as an organizing principle for society. As Simone de Beauvoir put it, most Enlightenment theorists were "timid egoists".[48] They could encourage men to be self-interested only because they believed men to be so good. Condorcet was, in this respect, no more naive than Adam Smith.

NOTES TO CHAPTER 6

[1] Gertrude Himmelfarb, *The Roads to Modernity: The British, French, and American Enlightenments* (New York: Knopf, 2004).

[2] "Introduction," by Patrick Coleman, to Jean-Jacques Rousseau, *Discourse on the Origin of Inequality* (New York: Oxford University Press, 1994), p. xi.

[3] Rousseau, *Discourse on the Origin of Inequality,* p. 47.

[4] Ibid., p. 85.

[5] Ibid., p. 26.

[6] Ibid., pp. 17, 47.

[7] Ibid., p. 115.

[8] Ibid., p. 67.

[9] Ibid., p. 95. "If I were told that society is so constituted that each man gains by serving others, I should reply that that would all be very well but for the fact that he gains even more by harming them. No profit is so legitimate that it cannot be surpassed by what can be done illegitimately, and a harm done to a neighbor is always more lucrative than any good turn."

[10] Jean-Jacques Rousseau, *Discourse on Political Economy and the Social Contract*, trans. Christopher Betts (New York: Oxford University Press, 1994), p. 6.

[11] Ibid., p. 17.

[12] Ibid., p. 172.

[13] Jean-Jacques Rousseau, *Politics and the Arts: A Letter to M. D'Alembert on the Theatre*, trans. A. Bloom (Ithaca, NY: Cornell University Press, 1968), p. 109; Carol Pateman, " 'The Disorder of Women': Women, Love, and the Sense of Justice," in *The Disorder of Women* (Stanford, CA: Stanford University Press, 1989), pp. 17–32.

[14] Lynda Lange, "Rousseau and Modern Feminism," *Social Theory and Practice* 7 (1981), 245–77.

[15] Ralph Davis, *The Rise of the Atlantic Economies* (Ithaca, NY: Cornell University Press, 1973), p. 288.

[16] Stephen L. Kaplan, *Bread, Politics, and Political Economy* (The Hague, Netherlands: Martinus Nijhoff, 1976) p. 601; Cyntha A. Bouton, *The Flour War: Gender, Class, and Community in Late Ancient Regime French Society* (State College PA: Pennsylvania State University Press, 1993).

[17] Thompson, "The Moral Economy"; Kaplan, *Bread, Politics, and Political Economy*; Elizabeth Fox-Genovese, *The Origins of Physiocracy. Economic Revolution and Social Order in Eighteenth-Century France* (Ithaca NY: Cornell University Press, 1976).

[18] Olwen H. Hufton, *Women and the Limits of Citizenship in the French Revolution* (Toronto: University of Toronto Press, 1992); Dominique Godineau, *The Women of Paris and Their French Revolution*, translated by Katherine Streip (Berkeley: University of California Press, 1998).

[19] Lynn Avery Hunt, *The Family Romance of the French Revolution* (Berkeley CA: University of California Press, 1993).

[20] Linda Kelly, *Women of the French Revolution* (London: Hamish Hamilton Ltd, 1987), p. 12.

[21] Barbara Brookes, "The Feminism of Condorcet and Sophie de Grouchy," *Studies on Voltaire and the Eighteenth Century* 189 (1980) p. 314.

[22] Ibid., p. 336.

[23] Jane Abray, "Feminism in the French Revolution," *American Historical Review* 80:1 (1975), p. 47.

[24] Hunt, *The Family Romance*, p. 41.

[25] Joan Wallach Scott, *Only Paradoxes to Offer. French Feminists and the Rights of Man* (Cambridge: Harvard University Press, 1997), 42–43; Abray, "Feminism," p. 49.

[26] Kelly, *Women of the French Revolution*, p. 50.

[27] Hunt, *The Family Romance*, p. 91.

[28] Scott, *Only Paradoxes*, p. 48.

[29] Ibid., p. 48; Williams, *Politics of Feminism*, p. 350.

[30] "The Unstable Boundaries of the French Revolution," in *A History of Private Life. From the Fires of Revolution to the Great War*, ed. Michelle Perrot (Cambridge: The Belknap Press of Harvard University Press, 1990) p. 15.

[31] Robespierre, "Republic of Virtue," in Richard W. Lyman and Lewis W. Spitz, eds, *Major Crises in Western Civilization*, vol. 2 (New York: Harcourt, Brace, and World, 1965), pp. 71–72.

[32] Forrest, *The French Revolution*, p. 172.

[33] Scott, *Only Paradoxes*, p. 50.

[34] Abray, "Feminism," p. 50.

[35] Antoine-Nicolas de Condorcet, *Sketch for a Historical Picture of the Progress of the Human Mind*, trans. June Barraclough (New York: The Noonday Press, 1955), p. 192.

[36] Condorcet, *Sketch*, p. 194.

[37] Brookes, "The Feminism of Condorcet," p. 352.

[38] Evelyn Forget, "Cultivating Sympathy: Sophie Condorcet's Letters on Sympathy," 142–164 in *The Status of Women in Classical Economic Thought*, eds Robert Dimand and Chris Nyland (Cheltenham: Edward Elgar, 2003).

[39] Ibid., p. 358.

[40] Some critics like Alasdair Macintyre argue that the Enlightenment project foundered on these difficulties. I consider this judgment premature. See his *After Virtue. A Study in Moral Theory* (Notre Dame, IN: University of Notre Dame Press, 1984).

[41] See Simone de Beauvoir, "Must We Burn Sade?" from *The Marquis de Sade. An Essay by Simone de Beauvoir,* with selections from his writings chosen by Paul Dinnage (New York: Grove Press, 1953). For a discussion of the views of other existentialist philosophers see Crocker, *Nature and Culture,* Ch. 6.

[42] Cited in Crocker, *Nature and Culture*, p. 409.

[43] Ibid.

[44] Hunt, *The Family Romance*, p. 138.

[45] Ibid., p. 136.

[46] Ibid., p. 143.

[47] Angela Carter, *The Sadeian Woman and the Ideology of Pornography* (New York: Pantheon Books, 1978).

[48] De Beauvoir, "Must We Burn Sade?" p. 57.

CHAPTER 7

The Greatest Happiness

It is the greatest happiness of the greatest number that is the measure of
right and wrong.   Jeremy Bentham

The pursuit of self-interest could lead to good results if selves were good.
How, then, to promote social virtues that rationality could rely upon? The
American Revolution showed that even a stable democracy could enforce
slavery. The French Revolution showed that social conflict could topple into
terror and imperial aggression. The British, looking first to their former
colony and then across the channel to their closest neighbor, had reason to
worry. Trade and commerce had expanded, putting the wealth of nations
easily within their reach. Yet the governance of nations—and of families—
began to seem more difficult. Confronting these problems, some urged the
benefits of tradition, a return to—or at least a more concerted defense of
what remained of—the patriarchal order. Religious doctrine and inherited
authority could help stabilize the market economy. The most energetic and
eloquent proponent of this conservative approach was Edmund Burke.
By contrast, radicals urged the need to end inherited privilege. William
Godwin took this stand, as did his wife Mary Wollstonecraft, who directly
challenged gender inequality. Jeremy Bentham planted the banner of liberal
individualism firmly in the imaginary towers of a welfare state, arguing that

individuals should subordinate themselves not to some mystical Common Good, but to the carefully calculated greater happiness of the greater number.

Chivalry versus Calculation

Early news of unrest in Paris did not initially disturb London. Few Britons were sympathetic to the traditional rulers of France, widely perceived as outmoded despots. Still, a prominent Irish-born Member of Parliament, Edmund Burke, felt certain that the revolutionaries would be even worse. His credibility in this matter was perhaps enhanced by his prior support (as a paid lobbyist) for the cause of American Independence. Democracy itself did not offend him. Burke moved in circles that included Adam Smith and Samuel Johnson. Paradoxically, he was both less conventional and more conservative than they.

In the years between the American and French Revolutions, Burke devoted much of his energy to criticism of the British East India Company, the chartered monopoly that had seized political control of much of India. Lucrative opportunities for trade emerged but the Company found it more profitable to use its military power to install local nabobs who paid them off with taxes extracted from the local population. Meanwhile, the company's managers enriched themselves far more successfully than their stockholders. To Burke, this seemed a scandalous example of runaway greed, and he urged Parliament to bring it under control.[1]

His efforts were largely unsuccessful, and shook his confidence in the virtues of self-interest. Few of his philosopher friends took so much interest in the ethics of empire. But rather than questioning British supremacy, Burke took refuge in the sanctity of tradition. He harkened back to an age in which a man's honor and manners counted for more than his economic interests. From this perspective the rhetoric of the French Revolution seemed even more alarming than the rape of India. Not surprisingly, he found a wider audience for his denunciations of the former. His *Reflections on the Revolution in France and on the Proceedings of Certain Societies in London Relative to That Event* won him great acclaim.

Burke's enthusiasm for the virtues of French royalty and the glittering beauty of Marie Antoinette was less winning than his larger critique of liberal individualism. He denounced both rational selfishness and the notion that laws should be designed anew by force of reason. He bemoaned the decline of traditional religious values, famously complaining that "the age of chivalry is gone and sophisters, economists, and calculators have taken over."[2] Wherever Burke himself belongs in the intellectual pantheon, his *Reflections* represented a bold attack of the very principles of the Enlightenment.[3]

The elevation of reason and depreciation of tradition would tear off "all the decent drapery of life" revealing an ugly, naked species. Women, in particular, would lie exposed and defenseless. They were after all, protected by the same drapery that protected royalty. "On this scheme of things," Burke wrote, describing the spirit of utilitarianism, "a king is but a man, a queen is but a woman, a woman is but an animal, and an animal not of the highest order. All homage paid to the sex in general as such, and without distinct views, is to be regarded as romance and folly."[4] While not an explicit commentary on de Sade, this analysis reflected some awareness of where male individualism could lead.

Burke often resorted to patriarchal precepts reminiscent of Sir Robert Filmer. Sons were bound by their fathers' promises of fealty.[5] Inheritance from forefathers was the source of everything of value.[6] In the most vivid passage of his *Reflections* he directly compared the state to an ailing father, and referred to the Greek myth of Peleas's daughters, tricked into killing their own father. (Medea, in a prequel to the murder of her own sons, had assured the girls that cutting their father to bits and cooking him in a special potion would allow him to be reconstituted with eternal youth).[7] The choice of myths seems to imply that French women were to blame.

The *Reflections* rallied conservative opposition and accurately foretold the chaos that would soon ensue in Paris. Published in 1790, when the French Revolution had gone no farther than establishment of a parliamentary democracy, it elicited no fewer than thirty-eight published replies, among them Thomas Paine's *Rights of Man* and Mary Wollstonecraft's *Vindication of the Rights of Women*.

The Vindication

Like most of her feminist predecessors Mary Wollstonecraft was a largely self-educated woman from a family of modest means. She penned a thoughtful tract on the education of girls in 1786 and befriended like-minded radicals among the Unitarians. Like other members of her circle, she was emboldened by events in France. Her *Vindication of the Rights of Man* contrasted Burke's affectionate praise of Marie Antoinette with his contempt for the poor. She gained more notoriety with her sequel, *Vindication of the Rights of Women*, which echoed and amplified the revolutionary fervor of Olympe des Gouges.

Wollstonecraft demanded that liberal democracy should be extended to women. She condemned all forms of authority modeled on that of royalty as "the pestiferous purple". Like her English predecessor Mary Astell, she pointed out that if kings required the consent of the governed, so too should husbands and fathers. Men, she argued, had monopolized not merely rights but rationality itself. They forced women into inferiority by encouraging "gentleness, docility, and spaniel-like affection" rather than rational self-assertion.[8] Education could solve this problem—but not the type of education that Rousseau had prescribed. Only complete freedom could foster the traits women needed to better fulfill their potential. Wollstonecraft openly appealed to male self-interest:

> Would men but generously snap our chains, and be content with rational fellowship instead of slavish obedience, they would find us more observant daughters, more affectionate sisters, more faithful wives, more reasonable mothers—in a word, better citizens.[9]

Despite her emphasis on the virtues of democratic citizenship Wollstonecraft was vilified, described as a "philosophizing serpent," "a hyena in petticoats," and an "usurping bitch."[10] Note the references to animals—as per Burke—and these "not of the highest order." Because she observed that poverty and misfortune sometimes forced women to sell sexual services, she was accused of encouraging prostitution. Her own extra-marital sex received far more attention than her work—particularly in the wake of a posthumous biography written by her husband, William Godwin.

Unlike many other radicals of her day (including Godwin), Wollstonecraft never condemned marriage. Yet her failure to conform to the sexual double standard condemned her work to illegitimacy. The reaction from male intellectuals on both sides of the Atlantic was overwhelmingly negative.[11] Still, the *Vindication of the Rights of Women* outlived her critics and came to be appreciated in later years. As one of Wollstonecraft's biographers waggishly put it, the book "worked a slow seminal effect."[12]

Godwin's Enquiry

More celebrated in its own day was the response her husband-to-be William Godwin aimed at Burke, a utopian manifesto brimming with confidence in men's natural virtues. William Godwin's *Enquiry Concerning Political Justice*, published in 1793 as France declared war on England, launched an attack on inequalities of wealth rather than of gender. Godwin shared Condorcet's optimism regarding perceptions of the common good, but was largely uninterested in women's rights. A radical individualist, he attacked the inheritance of both political and economic privilege: men should not be able to inherit offices from their fathers, nor should they be allowed to inherit wealth. Rather, they should be forced to rely on their own efforts and abilities.

At the same time Godwin attacked Smithian confidence in the pursuit of individual self-interest. Educated men should hue to civic virtue and recognize that equality would foster human development. It would, of course, be a slow process. Indeed, in his first edition, Godwin suggested that Negroes in the West Indies should continue in slavery until they could be gradually prepared for a state of liberty (his friends persuaded him to drop this comment from the second edition).[13]

Unlike Paine, Godwin wanted to eliminate private property itself. He was convinced that economic ambition was a dangerous force, "of all the passions of the human mind, the most extensive in its ravages".[14] Dismissive of merchants and money-grubbers, he felt that men should devote themselves to more noble causes. True, equal distribution of wealth would undermine the incentives that the poor currently had to work. But, in a chapter titled "Of the Objection to this System from the Allurements of Sloth", Godwin argued that the labor of one man in twenty would be sufficient to support the rest—or equally divided so that it occupied only the twentieth part of every man's time—if people were willing to resign themselves to a life of elegant simplicity.[15]

Godwin's description of subsistence requirements did not include any domestic labor.[16] Only a man who had never worked with his hands or prepared his own meals could so romanticize the concept of necessary labor. Mathematicians and poets would, he argued, derive a "new stock of cheerfulness and energy" from their small but regular assignments.[17] Godwin himself had a reputation for extensive begging and borrowing from his friends, suggesting he was not entirely fond of remunerative work himself.[18]

But Godwin's idealism cannot be reduced to its self-serving elements. It resided in an almost religious concept of benevolence closely related to Smith's concept of moral sentiments. What Smith had restricted to family and friends, Godwin extended to society as a whole. Central to his concept of political justice was the claim that men should treat their fellows as if they were kin. His chapter on justice asserted at the outset, "We are not connected with one or two percipient beings, but with a society, a nation, and in some sense with the whole family of mankind, of consequence that life ought to be preferred which will be most conducive to the general good."[19] Later, he suggested that the paternity of children was irrelevant, because all should be equally well cared for.[20]

Godwin, like Smith, placed women outside the realm of reason. As a result his egalitarian fantasy did not bode well for them. Conjuring the image of a palace in flames he asked his readers to imagine that, of two people in danger, only one can be saved—a famous French writer named Fenelon or an ordinary chambermaid. Fenelon's life, Godwin argued is the more valuable to society.[21] In later editions of the *Enquiry* he changed the example from chambermaid to valet. But one could argue that Burke's chivalry offered more advantages to women, especially in the event of fire.

Godwin is sometimes listed as a feminist because he criticized marriage, and, when he reluctantly capitulated to it, wedded the most notorious feminist of his day. But his opposition to marriage grew out of general opposition to any state regulation of personal life. Unlike Smith, he carried the principle of *laissez faire* to its logical conclusion, terming marriage the "most odious of all monopolies".[22] He ignored the possibility that men might abuse or exploit women even further without the restraints of marriage or the protection of the state. His hatred of greed freed him of any responsibility for lust. Indeed, he seemed to deny its very existence. In a well known passage of the *Enquiry*, famously ridiculed by Malthus, he prophesied that in the family of the future, "Reasonable men then will propagate their species, not because a certain sensible pleasure is annexed to this action, but because it is right the species should be propagated."[23]

Few men have suffered such unlucky confrontations with their own best principles. In 1796, when Godwin fell in love with Mary Wollstonecraft, she had been abandoned by her first lover, Gilbert Imlay, and was struggling to support herself and her daughter. Reason followed passion: when it became apparent that Wollstonecraft was bearing Godwin's child they married, though keeping separate residences. Wollstonecraft died in childbirth shortly after, leaving a new infant daughter, as well as three-year-old Fanny Imlay, in Godwin's care. While he garnered royalties from his biographical *Memoirs of Mary Wollstonecraft*, both his reputation and his earning power soon declined.

His daughter Mary, named after her mother, later eloped against her father's wishes with the poet Percy Shelley, who was married to another woman at the time. Experiments in family life as well as constitutional reform could easily go awry. Mary Shelley drove this point home when she later spun the tale of Frankenstein, a man-made monster who also rebelled against his own creator.

The Greatest Good

The traditional sin of selfishness played an important role in new efforts to reconcile individual desire with the common good. The utilitarian Jeremy Bentham built literally upon Montesquieu's notion that the state should promote civic virtue, drafting detailed blueprints for the architectural reform of prisons. But while he has often been portrayed as the very epitome of Big Brother, many of his arguments were aimed at subversion of the established sexual and economic order.[24] His commitment to state-sponsored reform of law, prisons, and education influenced a large group of political economists who came to be known as the Philosophic Radicals.

Bentham believed in both the force and the transcendence of self-interest. In his *Introduction to the Principles of Morals and Legislation* he described individuals as motivated by the desire to maximize pleasure and minimize pain.[25] Yet he also believed in the potential for a rational state that could, much like a rational deity, rule with complete benevolence. Bentham's implicit assumption, like Adam Smith's, seems to have been that well-educated men had the gentility required to represent the common interest. Certainly he never doubted his own gentility: "I am a selfish man," he wrote, "as selfish as any man can be. But in me, somehow or other, selfishness has taken the shape of benevolence."[26]

He was less impressed by the selfishness of his predecessors, and expressed disgust at the baroque inefficiencies and feudal remnants littering the British legal system. Rationality and common sense required legislative reform. In 1788, Bentham began a treatise on constitutional law urging the French government to remodel itself before it was forcibly overthrown, but history outran him.[27] He was an energetic critic of slavery and called for emancipation of all British colonies. He spoke out in favor of rights for women long before Mary Wollstonecraft's *Vindication* appeared.[28] He eventually became an outspoken advocate of extension of the franchise.

Bentham treated pleasure and pain as dimensions of "utility"—a term he appropriated from David Hume, but treated as a scientific concept analogous to Newton's concept of gravity.[29] Proponents of the neoclassical school of economics that emerged later in the nineteenth century carried the concept to higher levels of mathematical sophistication. In doing so, however, they relinquished a key aspect of Bentham's vision, the notion that the individual pursuit of utility should be subordinated to "the greatest happiness of the greatest number". Calculus tells us it is impossible to maximize two different magnitudes at once, and Bentham also ignored the difficulties of comparing the subjective feelings of two or more individuals.

Yet he correctly observed that, all else equal, poor people were likely to get more pleasure from an additional dollar of income than rich people ever would. Bentham never argued for complete equality, but praised the relatively egalitarian distribution of income in the non-slave regions of the United States.[30] Predisposed to an odd mixture of the paternalistic and the libertarian, he had little sympathy for public assistance to the poor, because he felt it would discourage work.

Bentham seemed to have more confidence than Smith in the state's ability to promote the common good. In matters relating to women and family life, however, he was a radical libertarian. He criticized all legal conventions governing marriage, divorce, and sexuality, on the grounds that these were private matters.[31] Contracts that could neither be broken nor renegotiated—like the traditional rules of marriage—were, in his opinion, inefficient.[32]

In his *Manual of Political Economy*, written between 1793 and 1795, Bentham listed arguments criticizing the prevailing mercantilist view that the state should promote population growth.[33] He called attention to the coercive pronatalism of laws that discouraged "marriages promising to be unprolific", "prolific venery out of marriage", and "venery necessarily unprolific" (venery is a now archaic term for sexual intercourse).[34] These arguments were followed by seven short paragraphs in Latin which defended the legitimacy of sexual pleasure, even when its intent was not procreative, and even when it was positively "unnatural".

Bentham reiterated these views in a series of unpublished manuscripts later deposited in the library of University College London, which apparently remained unpublished until C. K. Ogden included them in an appendix to a new edition of *The Theory of Legislation* in 1931.[35] Under the heading "All Comprehensive Liberty Proposed", he defended male homosexuality not only as an outlet for sexual desires thwarted by the need to avoid conception, but also as a perfectly reasonable activity in and of itself. By his account, it added to the mass of pleasure and prevented the injury "liable to be done to health by solitary gratification" (medical authority held that masturbation was dangerous). It could also diminish the amount of female prostitution.[36]

Bentham compared the legal prosecution of male homosexuality in England (which included the threat of capital punishment) with the repressive measures of the Spanish Inquisition. Not all his views were so enlightened. He was skeptical of the potential for self-control within heterosexual unions, particularly among the "savages of Asia, Africa, and America". His proposed solution to the problem of overpopulation was the legalization of infanticide. He was never fond of "rights"—in his view, the greatest happiness of the greatest number should take precedence over any such abstraction.

But unlike most of his contemporaries, Bentham was not afraid of what might happen if women were allowed to pursue pleasures of their own. His theory of utility assumed a fundamental similarity of psychological structure among all members of the species.[37] If the vote should be extended to a larger group of men, he argued, it should be extended to women as well. Bentham did not press hard for this demand because he perceived it as politically impractical. In his histories of legislation, however, he scoffed at the common argument that laws which discriminated against women were intended only to protect them.[38]

Many later feminists were influenced by Bentham's reasoning, including the writer Harriet Martineau and the economist John Stuart Mill. His contemporaries, however, did not share his libertarian views on sex. Like

Mandeville, Bentham believed that prostitution should be decriminalized. He stopped short of arguing for public support, and expressed confidence that few women would ever choose to sell their sexual services. Still, he raised the prospect of providing retirement annuities for prostitutes and homes for their children. His grand plans included details of architectural and interior design.[39]

Gendered Virtues

In Britain, as elsewhere, those who worried about virtue disagreed on how best to defend it—through tradition, revolution, or reform. Their disagreements were colored by different attitudes toward greed and lust, which began to play separate roles in the discourse of self-interest. Edmund Burke believed that religion could discourage both vices. William Godwin denounced greed, but declared that lust would never be a problem. His wife's life and his daughter's elopement seemed to undermine that declaration. Mary Wollstonecraft, less respected than her husband at the time, proved the more prophetic thinker. Her basic argument was bold in its simplicity: whatever rights men enjoyed, women should enjoy too. Jeremy Bentham also argued for a gender-neutral morality. He favored the indulgence of both economic and sexual self-interest, so long as they did no harm to others.

NOTES TO CHAPTER 7

[1] See Chapter 5 of Jerry Z. Muller, *The Mind and the Market. Capitalism in Western Thought* (New York: Anchor Books, 2002).

[2] Edmund Burke, *Reflections on the Revolution in France* (New York: Liberal Arts Press, 1955), p. 86.

[3] See Chapter 4 of Gertrude Himmelfarb, *The Roads to Modernity* (New York: Knopf, 2004).

[4] Ibid., *Reflections*, p. 86.

[5] Ibid., *Reflections*, p. 27

[6] Ibid., pp. 35–39.

[7] Burke wrote, on p. 109: "We have consecrated the state that no man should approach to look into its defects or corruptions but with due caution, that he should never dream of beginning its reformation by its subversion, that he should approach to the faults of the state as to the wounds of a father, with pious awe and trembling solicitude. By this wise prejudice we are taught to look with horror on those children of their country who are prompt rashly to hack that aged parent in pieces and put him into the kettle of magicians, in hopes that by their poisonous weeds and wild incantations they may regenerate the paternal constitution and renovate their father's life."

[8] Mary Wollstonecraft, *A Vindication of the Rights of Woman,* ed. Miriam Brody (New York: Penguin Books, 1992), p. 118.

[9] Ibid., p. 269.

[10] Claire Tomalin, *The Life and Death of Mary Wollstonecraft* (New York: Penguin, 1992), p. 142.

[11] Rendall, *The Origins of Modern Feminism,* p. 66.

[12] Eleanor Flexner, *Mary Wollstonecraft. A Biography* (New York: Coward, McCann and Geoghegan, 1972), p. 265.

[13] John P. Clark, *The Philosophical Anarchism of William Godwin* (Princeton: Princeton University Press, 1977), p. 284.

[14] Cited in Clark, *Philosophical Anarchism,* p. 263. Godwin, unlike Smith, had no respect for merchants and despised the way they resorted to "servile and contemptible arts".

[15] William Godwin, *An Enquiry Concerning Political Justice and Its Influence on General Virtue and Happiness,* ed. Raymond A. Preston (New York: Alfred A. Knopf, 1926).

[16] Though Godwin did not explicitly address this issue he seems to have assumed that women as well as children were economic dependents, burdens on men even among the working classes. In the same passage in which he deplores the increased inequality of wealth in Europe which threatens the viability of subsistence among the poor he writes "The women and children lean with an insupportable weight upon the efforts of the man, so that a large family has in the lower order of life become a proverbial expression for an uncommon degree of poverty and wretchedness". *Enquiry,* p. 17.

[17] Godwin, *Enquiry,* p. 249.

[18] Don Locke, *A Fantasy of Reason. The Life and Thought of William Godwin.* (Boston: Routledge and Kegan Paul, 1980).

[19] Godwin, *Enquiry,* p. 41.

[20] Ibid., p. 274. Fenelon, an advisor to French royalty, had written a famous allegory about the Greek character of Telemachus that illustrated the principle that a king could lose touch with those he ruled, and unwittingly oppress them. Earlier in the text Godwin also juxtaposes the value of the chambermaid's life with that of the archbishop of Cambrai.

[21] Ibid., p. 43.

[22] Ibid., p. 272.

[23] Ibid., p. 274.

[24] Michel Foucault, *Discipline and Punish. The Birth of the Prison* (New York: Vintage Books, 1979), Part 3, Ch. 3.

[25] Elsewhere he wrote, "In the general tenor of life, in every human breast, self-regarding interest is predominant over all other interests put together...Self-preference has place everywhere." See Jeremy Bentham, *Jeremy Bentham's Economic Writings,* ed. W. Stark (London: Allen and Unwin, 1954), vol. 3, p. 421.

[26] Brian Inglis, *Poverty and the Industrial Revolution* (London: Hodder and Stoughton, 1971), p. 206.

[27] Mary P. Mack, *Jeremy Bentham, 1748–1792* (New York: Columbia University Press, 1963), p. 415.

[28] Annie L. Cot, "'Let There be no Distinction Between the Sexes': Jeremy Bentham on the Status of Women," 165–193 in *The Status of Women in Classical Economic Thought*, eds Robert Dimand and Chris Nyland (Cheltenham UK: Edward Elgar, 2003).

[29] The gravity analogy seems to have originated with the French philosopher Helvetius. See the discussion in Joseph A. Schumpeter's *History of Economic Analysis* (New York: Oxford University Press, 1954), p. 130.

[30] E. K. Hunt, *History of Economic Thought. A Critical Perspective* (Belmont, CA: Wadsworth, 1979), p. 118.

[31] Mack, *Jeremy Bentham*, p. 212.

[32] Jeremy Bentham, *The Theory of Legislation*, ed. C. K. Ogden (New York: Harcourt, Brace, 1931), p. 224.

[33] The *Manual* was not actually published until 1811, and then in French translation. It first appeared in English in 1825.

[34] Bentham, *Jeremy Bentham's Economic Writings*, p. 272. W. Stark's editorial comments help explain the ways in which prevailing social norms discouraged consideration of the issue of gay rights. Of the cited passage, he writes on p. 57, "The economist need not give them more than a passing glance. Bentham speaks here, not as a social theorist, but as a teacher of morals (or, as some would say with equal justification, as a teacher of immorality)."

[35] Bentham, *The Theory of Legislation*.

[36] Ibid., p. 493.

[37] Lea Campos Boralevi, "Utilitarianism and Feminism," in *Women in Western Political Philosophy*, eds Ellen Kennedy and Susan Mendus (New York: St. Martin's Press, 1987), p. 163. As Boralevi explains, "Women could not only experience pains and pleasures, they also had interests which had to be taken into consideration. Whether women had souls or not, or whether they were less intelligent or less rational than men was not relevant, at least as far as the consideration of their interest was concerned."

[38] Ibid., p. 238.

[39] Cot, "Let There Be No Distinction," p. 174.

CHAPTER 8

Self-love, Triumphant

Benevolence yet lingering in a few bosoms, makes some faint expiring struggles, till at length self-love resumes his wonted empire, and lords it triumphant over the world.   Thomas Robert Malthus

Insistence that self-interest should be virtuous gradually began to dissipate, displaced by new interpretations of the tensions between moral and political economy. The English clergyman and writer Thomas Robert Malthus argued not only that the pursuit of self-interest would serve the common good, but that benevolence would undermine it. Malthus did not abandon the traditional religious emphasis on virtue. Rather, he recast virtue as control over lust rather than greed, describing poverty as punishment for the sexual self-indulgence of early marriage and rapid population growth. In his usage, the term "moral restraint" conveyed something quite specific: delayed marriage that could keep population growth in check.

Malthus's redefinition of vice represented an important conceptual innovation that has been described as part of a "demoralization of society".[1] It could better be described as a "remoralization", one sought a new compromise between religious values and political economy.[2] Malthus shifted concern away from greed (economic desire carried to harmful extremes) toward lust (sexual desire carried to harmful extremes). Indeed, the problem with the poor and working classes, he argued, was that they allowed their sexual interests to overwhelm their economic ones. Yet Malthus's arguments were also subversive of the established order, eliciting attacks from both right and left. He used economic reasoning to challenge the pronatalist notion that men and women had a God-given duty to replenish the earth by conceiving children regardless of the consequences.

Poor Relief

In late eighteenth-century Britain the expansion of commerce, combined with agricultural innovation, led to modest improvements in living standards and population growth. Yet the prospects for prosperity remained fragile. In the 1790s, the war with France created political turmoil, complicated by high unemployment in rural areas. The privatization of common lands through enclosure made it more difficult for families to gather food or fuel, making them more dependent on wages.[3] The system of poor relief came under increasing pressure. Localities could save money by enforcing the law of settlement that restricted their responsibility to those born in their own parish. But as Adam Smith had pointed out years before, such practices discouraged the mobility of labor.

Sympathy for the poor grew out of perceptions that they bore a large share of the high mortality and the high prices occasioned by the war. Evangelical revivalism applied the principles of Christian morality to social policy in the campaign against the slave trade.[4] The British poor, they pointed out, did not live much better than slaves abroad. A disappointing harvest in 1794 led to widespread protests, and occasional collective action against millers, middlemen, and bakers.[5] Those unable to feed their families despite long hours of drudging work could not be blamed but hostility was leveled at those suspected of laziness or malingering.[6]

The Poor Law of 1722 had authorized parishes to build workhouses and deny relief to anyone who refused to enter them—the equivalent of work requirements that are particularly strict in the U.S. today—but many parishes were inclined to provide more generous assistance. The magistrates of Berkshire County summoned a meeting in the parish of Speenhamland in 1795, where they calculated a minimum cost of living for a family based upon its number of members and the cost of bread. If the wages a man could earn fell below that level, the parish promised to make up the difference.

The so-called Speenhamland system was widely adopted in areas of the midlands and the south where factory jobs were scarce and economic conditions poor. It provided both a safety net for families and a public subsidy for employers, who could pay lower wages as a result.

Legislation setting minimum wages could have solved the problem, albeit on terms less favorable to employers. Such legislation was introduced into Parliament in 1795, but drew criticism from many quarters. In addition to interfering with the free operation of the labor market, the minimum wage violated mercantilist principles that valued population growth. Prime Minister William Pitt argued that it would give single men an unfair advantage over fathers, because each would earn the same no matter how many children they were supporting. He went on to defend the principles of the Speenhamland system:

> Let us make relief in cases where there are a number of children, a matter of right and an honour, instead of a ground for opprobrium and contempt. This will make a large family a blessing and not a curse; and this will draw a proper line of distinction between those who are able to provide for themselves by their labour and those who, after having enriched their country with a number of children, have a claim upon its assistance for their support.[7]

As Pitt put it, poor relief was actually a kind of family allowance system. The demands of war heightened awareness of the value of future manpower. But sheer manpower was becoming less relevant to military success than strategic development and deployment of technology, as exemplified by the force of British naval power. Few English politicians after Pitt spoke confidently of large families as a blessing to the nation. Indeed, they soon began to describe them as a curse.

The Essay on Population

In 1798, Thomas Robert Malthus published a superbly written polemic against the utopian visions of Condorcet and Godwin. He disliked their sentimental do-goodism and belief in the perfectibility of man. Any improvement in the conditions of the poor, he argued in his *Essay on Population*, would be canceled out by the resulting population growth. An increase in the supply of labor would drive wages down below subsistence level.

This view of future gloom and doom proved far less popular than Adam Smith's cheery confidence in the growing wealth of nations. Indeed, the intensity of critical responses to the *Essay* prompted later revisions with a more conciliatory, even hopeful tone.[8]

The long-lasting debate struck many dissonant chords, especially among members of the Anglican establishment. Religious doctrine offered a positive view of population growth: the Almighty would never bring more beings into the world than he prepares nourishment for.[9] The Malthusian emphasis on scarcity, diminishing returns, and the inevitable downward pressure of population growth on wages seemed heretical. In 1803, Malthus offered an amendment to his argument that would ultimately diminish—if not entirely resolve—conflict between the religious doctrine and the new discipline of political economy.

Rather than standing by and watching population growth overwhelm economic progress, men could practice moral restraint by delaying marriage.[10] No man should marry until he had gained sufficient means to support his family. The resulting decline in fertility would decrease the supply of labor and allow wages to gradually rise. Of even greater relevance to religious critics, the potential economic salvation offered by moral restraint evoked both the beneficence of God and the indispensable role of Christian virtue.[11] But wasn't moral restraint exactly what Godwin and Condorcet had earlier described as an aspect of the perfectibility of man?

Malthus took pains to distinguish his argument from theirs. The moral restraint he advocated relied less on benevolence than on self-interest.[12] By delaying marriage, men would make themselves and their children better off—but only if the institutions of private property and marriage remained firmly in place, and public relief for the poor was eliminated. Continued guarantees of a subsistence income would undermine economic welfare and moral virtue by tempting men to breed too much too soon.

In retrospect, this argument hardly seems persuasive. A delay in male marriage has little effect on fertility unless it is accompanied by a later age at marriage for women. Most British families, like most families in Northwestern Europe, already delayed marriage to a relatively late age.[13] But Malthus vividly emphasized the influence of the passions:

The cravings of hunger, the love of liquor, the desire of possessing a beautiful woman will urge men to actions, of the fatal consequences of which, to the general interests of society, they are perfectly well convinced, even at the very time they commit them. Remove their bodily cravings, and they would not hesitate a moment in determining against such actions.[14]

From this point on in the text, the first two forms of sensuality (desire for food and drink) play a distinctly subsidiary role to lust. Malthus never invoked the corrupting influence of passions in the form of violence, war, or fraud. Irrationality was concentrated, specifically, in the passion between the sexes—a powerful, God-given, and natural force.

In the new Malthusian cosmology, the desire for money required no restraints beyond the rule of law. Economic self-interest acted through cool considered calculation. Sexual self-interest, on the other hand, was hot and reckless, requiring social regulation. A man who married despite considerable risk of being unable to support the resulting offspring was a selfish fool. A man who declined to offer assistance to the poor, by contrast, was both virtuous and enlightened.

More than thirty years elapsed between Malthus's condemnation of the English Poor Laws and their legislative overhaul. But he influenced the debate from the very outset, advocating not merely for reform but for elimination of public assistance to the poor. His views were colored by a distinct sympathy for fathers, who, he believed, would never abandon their children were they not confident the public would assume responsibility for them.[15] He had less sympathy for dependents: "It may appear to be hard that a mother and her children, who had been guilty of no particular crime themselves, should suffer for the ill-conduct of the father; but this is one of the invariable laws of nature."[16] He went on to explain that it was evidently necessary for the sins of fathers to be visited upon their children.[17]

Malthus criticized the parish practice of pressuring men who had begotten children out of wedlock to marry, on two grounds. First, they would be likely to beget even more children within marriage, to unfortunate effect. Second, forced engagements profaned the true meaning of marriage. The best way to hold men accountable was not to impose rules upon them, but to deny their children any charity or assistance. Mothers who failed to marry before becoming pregnant were, in his view, heedless and immoral.[18]

Malthus conceded one reasonable objection to this argument that the poor were responsible for their own plight: poverty itself led to moral degradation. Reversing the traditional Catholic notion that poverty was ennobling, he described the miserable and disgusting habits of the poor. "When indigence does not produce overt acts of vice," he wrote, "it palsies every virtue."[19] But this was no reason, he added, to give up the good fight. The responsible classes should at least try to encourage moral restraint among the poor.

Against Benevolence

Whether one calls Malthus a "demoralizer" or a "moralizer" depends in large part on one's own moral standpoint.[20] Malthus challenged the traditional pronatalism of the established church as well as its reassurances that God would provide for his children. He also implicitly challenged some Christian ideals. According to his argument, charitable assistance to the poor could lead to the same population growth and immiseration as the official poor relief. Loving one's neighbor as thyself—in this way, at least—could do more harm than good.

Yet Malthus was a clergyman with strong moral principles who found ways to reconcile his arguments with established doctrine. He emphasized the religious doctrine of original sin, which urged all Christians to accept the imperfections of the status quo. The sufferings of the poor were transitory. The meek and virtuous among them would find reward in Heaven. An emerging Christian political economy insisted that poverty and inequality could be interpreted as a "deliberate contrivance by a benevolent God for bringing out the best in His children and so training them for the life to come."[21]

Smith had welcomed benevolence in its place; Malthus described it as a weak feminine sentiment. Describing the inevitable demise of Godwin's ideal state, he explained that self-love would "resume his wonted empire".[22] Men were not the masters of their own fate and should acknowledge forces beyond their control. Only the Deity could successfully practice benevolence.[23] Men should settle for less ambitious goals.

Smith had suggested that differences in social institutions were relatively unimportant, because of the natural benevolence of the wealthy. Malthus insisted that any society based on principles of equality or sharing was doomed to failure.[24] Any imaginable society would evolve into a system based on the distinction between rich and poor, a society, "divided into a class of proprietors, and a class of labourers, and with self-love for the main-spring of the great machine."[25] In a distinct break with Enlightenment principles, he argued that self-love did not need to be controlled, contained, domesticated, or tempered. He considered it a marker of civilization as well as an engine of progress:

> To the laws of property and marriage, and to the apparently narrow principle of self-love, which prompts each individual to exert himself in bettering his condition, we are indebted for all the noblest exertions of human genius, for everything that distinguishes the civilized from the savage state.[26]

Though Malthus never actually used the word "greed", he imposed few conceptual limits on self-love that might distinguish it from the vice still enshrined within the Christian lexicon. A footnote in an appendix to the 1806 edition distinguished between self-love and selfishness, describing the former as "that passion which under proper regulations is the source of all honourable industry, and of all the necessaries and conveniences of life," and the latter as "the same passion pushed to excess, when it becomes useless and disgusting, and consequently vicious."[27] Self-love equates with that which is good, selfishness with that which is bad. The operative distinction is virtually utilitarian: that which is good is that which has good consequences for society (though these are never specified), and vice versa. On closer consideration, the footnote is inconsistent with the larger thrust of the *Essay*. Malthus never described any necessary or proper regulations of self-love other than delayed marriage.

The Improper Arts

Moral considerations ruled other ways of reducing fertility out of order, such as a "promiscuous intercourse which prevents the birth of children".[28] Malthus tacitly conceded that delayed marriage might encourage prostitution.[29] But he held the "vicious practices" and "improper arts" of contraception to be economically undesirable as well as immoral, tantamount to prostitution.[30] Like Mandeville, Malthus asserted that God had imbued men with lust to protect them from sloth, and any human effort to subvert this causality was doomed to failure. Other political economists like McCulloch agreed; the law of population was part of a divine plan to encourage economic growth.[31] In an appendix to the 1817 edition of the *Essay*, Malthus re-stated his concerns:

> I should always particularly reprobate any artificial or unnatural modes of checking population, both on account of their immorality and their tendency to remove a necessary stimulus to industry. If it were possible for each married couple to limit by a wish the number of their children, there is certainly reason to fear that the indolence of the human race would be very greatly increased, and that neither the population of individual countries nor of the whole earth would ever reach its natural and full extent. But the restraints I have recommended are quite of a different character. They are not only pointed out by reason and sanctioned by religion, but tend in the most marked manner to stimulate industry.[32]

Greed alone was insufficient to keep workers motivated. Lust was another necessary evil.

J. R. McCulloch seconded this opinion.[33] But at least some of Malthus's contemporaries contested his reluctance to condone the improper arts. Bentham, who had long advocated contraception, became a fountainhead of support for it.[34] Bentham's good friend, James Mill, circumspectly endorsed it as well. In an article on "Colonies" which he wrote for the supplement to the eighth edition of the *Encyclopedia Brittanica,* he alluded to the problem of population growth and commented that "If the superstitions of the nursery were discarded, and the principles of utility kept steadily in view, a solution might not be very difficult to be found."[35] In *Elements of Political Economy*, published in 1821, Mill grew slightly bolder, describing the salutory effects of prudence, "by which either marriages are sparingly contracted or care is taken that children, beyond a certain number, shall not be the fruit."[36] Apparently, this was considered a racy turn of phrase; David Ricardo felt that the allusions to procreation in Mill's *Elements* made it unsuitable for the schoolroom.[37]

The most daring and, in retrospect, the most effective rebuttal to Malthus directly advocated contraception. In 1822, Frances Place, a successful tailor and autodidact committed to utilitarian principles, published *Illustrations and Proofs of the Principle of Population*. A passionate advocate of social reform, he also believed, like James Mill, that rapid population growth was problematic. In a section of the *Illustrations* entitled "Means of Preventing the Numbers of Mankind from Increasing" he advocated political and contraceptive reforms in virtually the same breath. He called for a repeal of all laws against combinations of working men, restraining emigration, or restricting trade, commerce, and manufactures. He also called on married couples to prevent unwanted conceptions, a process that would reduce the supply of labor and drive wages up.

> Those who really understand the cause of a redundant, unhappy, miserable, and considerably vicious population, and the means of preventing the redundancy, should clearly, freely, openly and fearlessly point out the means. It is "childish" to shrink from proposing or developing any means, however repugnant they may at first appear to be.[38]

Place conceded that such means might tempt a breach of chastity, but insisted that the problems arising from unwanted births would be worse. A year later he followed through on his own exhortations, boldly publishing three versions of a handbill entitled "To the Married of Both Sexes", describing the use of a vaginal sponge. These handbills were considered illegal as well as obscene. Among the men quietly arrested for distributing them was James Mill's son, the seventeen-year-old John Stuart Mill. The sins of youth were easily forgiven; Place himself suffered serious ostracism. Sadly, the advice he offered was neither effective nor safe. Natural sponge tends to fall apart, making it difficult to retrieve and conducive to infection. But the battle had been joined. Place became the mainspring of the contraceptive movement. Proponents of birth control came to be known as Neo-Malthusians.

In the early nineteenth century virtually anyone willing to allude to birth control celebrated its implications for women. Wives could not practice moral restraint alone, especially since they lacked a legal right to refuse their husbands. Prevailing medical theories held that abstinence for women was unhealthy—they needed periodic doses of male seminal fluid. Francis Place penned a letter to Harriet Martineau warning that delayed marriages would injure women's health.[39] Martineau herself, who never married and suffered long periods of invalidism, may have wondered at the possible connection.

The more radical enthusiasts of birth control proclaimed that it would end the sexual double standard, contributing to a paranoid fear that it would threaten chastity and motherhood itself. Even in France, a country tolerant of the improper arts, an early catechism for married people instructed husbands to ignore their wives' distaste for childbearing, condemning premature ejaculation, noncoital positions, and onanism as sins of lust.[40] In the 1840s, some doctors praised the rhythm method over coitus interruptus because husbands could employ it without revealing its secrets to their wives.[41]

More commonly, birth control was maligned as a selfish indulgence. Godwin himself dismissed it in his long-awaited reply to Malthus, published in 1820. With his knack for describing women as mere auxiliaries to men he wrote:

> It is one of the clearest duties of a citizen to give birth to his like, and bring offspring to the state. Without this he is hardly a citizen: his children and his wife are pledges he gives to the public for good behavior; they are his securities, that he will truly enter into the feeling of a common interest, and be desirous of perpetuating and increasing the immunities of his country from generation to generation.[42]

If men were always benevolent and dutiful, how could population growth ever be too fast or slow? Malthus was even more irritated than before, referring to Godwin's book as "the poorest and most old-womanish performance that has fallen from the pen of any writer of name."[43]

Malthus and Women

Despite that turn of phrase, Malthus viewed women of his own class in a favorable light, and many of them returned the favor. The concept of moral restraint appealed to women seeking to counter the sexual demands of their own suitors and sometimes even their own husbands. It elevated control over the sexual passions as a feminine virtue that men should emulate (at least where marriage was concerned). Malthus subtly challenged the traditional religious view that women were more susceptible to sensual temptation than men, describing virtue, like benevolence, as a feminine trait. Late marriage, he argued, "would be a most decided advantage to the more virtuous half of society."[44] The age at which an unmarried woman would be forced to consider herself an old maid would be pushed up.[45]

Two influential women writers helped popularize Malthus's theories, especially his views on the poor laws. Mrs. Jane Marcet's *Conversations on Political Economy*, published in 1816 and explicitly aimed at a female audience, was widely read.[46] In one of the dialogues a wise matron named Mrs. B. persuades the emotional young Caroline that assistance to the poor should be abolished because it does more harm than good. In 1834, Harriet Martineau, one of the most famous old maids of her day, chimed in with her enthusiastically Malthusian *Illustrations of Political Economy* (see discussion in Chapter 5).[47]

Eager to prove that Malthus had underestimated the power of moral restraint, William Hazlitt pointed to the example of calculating young Misses who dismissed suitors who did not command sufficient economic assets. Surely, if the "silliest women" would exercise such calculating restraint, men should be capable of it as well.[48] Hazlitt then alluded proudly to the many virtuous Englishwomen who had chosen never to marry at all.[49]

Enlightenment Redux

The most optimistic visions of the Enlightenment embodied a naïve faith in human progress that made them an easy target for Malthusian scorn. Malthus offered a compromise between the forces of tradition and modernity that was particularly appealing to those in the best position to gain from both. Men should restrain their desire for sex but not for wealth. If benevolence in the form of assistance to the poor could be checked, postponed marriage could bring prosperity in the form of economic growth. The poor in general, and unwed mothers in particular, were to blame for their own plight.

The rhetoric of self-interest continued to exercise almost hypnotic power. Malthus's *Essay* signaled a widening of its reach, bringing lust into social theory by calling attention to the impact of demographics on economics. Malthus warned that most individuals would not be rational enough to limit their fertility. It would soon became apparent that they were more rational than he thought they should be, becoming adept at the use of improper arts.

NOTES TO CHAPTER 8

[1] Gertrude Himmelfarb, *The Idea of Poverty. England in the Early Industrial Age* (New York: Alfred A. Knopf, 1984), and *The Demoralization of Society. From Victorian Virtues to Modern Values* (New York: Alfred A. Knopf, 1995).

[2] A. M. C. Waterman, *Revolution, Economics, and Religion. Christian Political Economy, 1798–1833* (New York: Cambridge University Press, 1991).

[3] Jane Humphries, "Enclosures, Common Rights, and Women: The Proletarianization of Families in the late Eighteenth and Early Nineteenth Centuries", *The Journal of Economic History* 50:1 (1990), 17–42.

[4] Raymond G. Cowherd, *Political Economists and the English Poor Laws. A Historical Study of the Influence of Classical Economics on the Formation of Social Welfare Policy* (Athens: Ohio University Press, 1977), p. 27.

[5] E. P. Thompson, "The Moral Economy of the English Crowd," *Past and Present* 50:1 (1971), 76–136.

[6] Brian Inglis, *Poverty and the Industrial Revolution* (London: Hodder and Stoughton, 1971), p. 50.

[7] Himmelfarb, *The Idea of Poverty*, p. 74.

[8] T. R. Malthus, *Essay on the Principle of Population,* The version published in 1803, with the variora of 1806, 1807, 1817, and 1826, ed. Patricia James (New York: Cambridge University Press, 1990), Vol. I, p. 325.

[9] A. M. C. Waterman, *Political Economy and Christian Theology Since the Enlightenment. Essays in Intellectual History* (New York: Palgrave Macmillan, 2004), Ch. 8, "The Sudden Separation of Political Economy," p. 119.

[10] Inglis, *Poverty and the Industrial Revolution*, p. 70.

[11] Waterman, *Revolution, Economics, and Religion*.

[12] Donald Winch. *Malthus* (New York: Oxford University Press, 1987), p. 40; Samuel Hollander, *Malthus* (London: University of Toronto Press, 1997), p. 939.

13   Mary S. Hartman, *The Household and the Making of History* (New York: Cambridge University Press, 2004).

[14] Thomas Robert Malthus, *An Essay on the Principle of Population as it Affects the Future Improvement of Society with Remarks on the Speculations of Mr. Godwin, Mr. Condorcet and Other Writers*. First published 1798 (London: Printed for J. Johnson in St. Paul's Churchyard. Reprints of Economic Classics, New York: Augustus M. Kelley, 1965), p. 255.

[15] Malthus, *On Population*, ed. James, Vol. II, p. 142.

[16] Ibid., p. 143.

[17] Ibid., p. 144.

[18] Ibid., Vol. I, p. 324.

[19] Ibid., Vol. II, p. 113.

[20] For an explicit critique of Himmelfarb's description of Malthus as demoralizer, see Donald Winch, "Robert Malthus: Christian Moral Scientist, Arch-Demoralizer or Implicit Secular Utilitarian," *Utilitas* 5:2 (1993): 239–53.

[21] Waterman, *Revolution, Economics, and Religion*, p. 258.

[22] Ibid., Vol. I, p. 321. In the following paragraph Malthus also describes benevolence in feminine terms.

[23] Ibid., p. 214.

[24] Interestingly, he claimed to disagree with Mandeville's version of this argument. Ibid., p. 214.

[25] Ibid., p. 326. Elsewhere Malthus refers to the desire to better one's condition as a "master-spring" (p. 145).

[26] Ibid., Vol. II, p. 202.

[27] Ibid., Vol. II, p. 214.

[28] Malthus, *Essay*, ed. James, Vol. II, p. 97.

[29] Samuel Hollander, *Malthus* (London: University of Toronto Press, 1997), 887–90.

[30] Donald Winch. *Malthus* (New York: Oxford University Press, 1987), p. 40.

[31] Angus McLaren, *Birth Control in Nineteenth-Century England* (London: Croom Helm, 1978), p. 50.

[32] Malthus, *Essay*, ed. James, Vol. II, p. 235.

[33] Angus McLaren, *Birth Control in Nineteenth-Century England* (London: Croom Helm, 1978), p. 50.

[34] Norman Himes, "Jeremy Bentham and the Genesis of English Neo-Malthusianism," *Economic History* 3:2 (1937), p. 267.

[35] Bruce Mazlish, *James and John Stuart Mill. Father and Son in the Nineteenth Century* (New York: Basic Books, 1975), p. 109.

[36] James Mill, *Elements of Political Economy*. 3rd edn, Revised and Corrected (New York: Augustus Kelley, 1963), p. 50.

[37] Patricia James, *Population Malthus* (New York: Routledge, 2006), p. 310.

[38] Francis Place, *Illustrations and Proofs of the Principle of Population*, with critical and textual notes by Norman Himes (New York: Augustus Kelley Publishers, 1967), p. 173.

[39] McLaren, *Birth Control in Nineteenth-Century England*, p. 96.

[40] McLaren, *Sexuality and Social Order*, p. 33.

[41] Ibid., p. 62.

[42] Cited in McClaren, *Sexuality and Social Order*, p. 71.

[43] James, *Population Malthus*, p. 381.

[44] Ibid., Vol. II, p. 99. See also p. 113, "virtue takes her flight away from the tainted spot".

[45] Ibid., p. 120.

[46] Jane Marcet, *Conversations on Political Economy* (London: Longman, 1817).

[47] Dorothy Lampen Thomson, *Adam Smith's Daughters* (New York: Exposition Press, 1973).

[48] William Hazlitt, "A Reply to the Essay on Population by the Rev. T. R. Malthus," *The Complete Works of William Hazlitt*, ed. P. P. Hower (London: J. M. Dent and Sons Ltd, 1930), p. 202.

[49] Ibid., p. 235.

CHAPTER 9

Production and Reproduction

Factory females have in general much lower wages than males, and they have been pitied on this account with perhaps an injudicious sympathy, since the low price of their labour here tends to make household duties their most profitable as well as agreeable occupation, and prevents them being tempted by the mill to abandon the care of their offspring at home.

Andrew Ure

Fear of contraception offered vivid illustration of the gendered double standard of self-interest. More profound evidence of the effect of patriarchal ideology on classical political economy lay in oversimplification of the relationship between production and reproduction. The two mechanisms emphasized by Malthus in his analysis of population growth—level of wages and age at marriage—represented a small subset of the factors affecting fertility decisions. Particularly significant were changes in the contribution of women and children to family income in the course of early capitalist development. None of the classical political economists recognized these changes, although they impinged directly on important policy issues, such as regulation of factory employment and reform of the poor laws.

The blind spot lay squarely in the core of David Ricardo's labor theory of value. Ricardo correctly viewed labor as a direct or indirect input into the production of commodities. But he never recognized that labor itself was the output of a production process that did not rely on commodities alone.

The wages that a worker earned never provided his or her subsistence, either in the long run or in the short. These wages were transformed into services—such as meals—and into replacement workers—namely children—by women's unpaid work, and were conditioned by children's own contributions to the family economy, which helped defray the costs of raising them.

The relationship among individuals, families, and the economy underwent especially rapid transformation in the early nineteenth century. Some of its changing dimensions can be traced through the development of regular national censuses, which documented the expansion of individual wage employment. Appreciation of the significance of this change, however, must be situated in a clear understanding of the structure of patriarchal capitalism. Contrary to the assumptions of historians like Alice Clark, R. H. Tawney, and Karl Polanyi (described in Chapter 1) capitalism did not represent a "disembedded" imposition of the pursuit of economic gain. The new institution of individual employment remained embedded in a distinctly patriarchal matrix.

Patriarchal Capitalism

Family-based farms and businesses were key to early capitalist development, active participants in trades that could make them better off. They were not, however, capitalist institutions. Operating under the strict authority of a male household head, their members could combine productive and reproductive efforts, alternating between market and non-market work and capturing some of the economic benefits of their childrearing efforts. Children began to do chores, run errands and look after one another at an early age. As teenagers they could provide substantial services. Their marriages often created new family alliances that generated new sources of capital. As working age adults they assumed responsibility for the support of their parents as well as that of sick or elderly family members.

The patriarchal family as a productive unit offered both advantages and disadvantages compared to a capitalist firm or corporation.[1] Family members often stood to gain from cooperation and mutual aid but enjoyed little flexibility. The head of the household could not hire or fire his basic labor force, and that labor force had even less scope for individual choice. Male household heads were obligated to provide for their dependents, and could not simply lay them off if they became sick or disabled. On the other hand, they were required to provide only subsistence, rather than a share of total family product. In terms of political economy, they maintained political and legal control over any surplus.[2]

Restricted economic opportunities outside the family put women and youth in a relatively weak bargaining position. Adult men could abandon their families more easily than their wives and children could abandon them. The subordination of men was typically a phase in their lifecycle, as sons short of the age of majority; the subordination of women changed only slightly when they left their fathers' households to become wives and mothers. Heads of family enterprises may have been averse to technological changes or alterations in the division of labor that might weaken their authority over women and younger household members.[3] Until they gained the opportunity to hire and fire a larger, non-kin labor force, family enterprises were limited in their ability to take advantage of new technologies that required a large capital investment or those that could pay off only if conducted on a large scale.

Family-based enterprises were typically integrated into a larger economic system shaped by inequalities based on class and race as well as gender. Feudal, slave, and tenant farming systems superimposed another layer of control over decentralized patriarchal authority. In France, feudal relations remained strong in the countryside until after the Revolution. In the Southern United States, slavery shaped the entire social order. In many areas of Britain and the northern United States, by contrast, family farms either paid rent or owned their own land, making their own decisions about what to produce and how. Even where property was unequally distributed, the opportunities for gain encouraged participation in the growing market economy.

Relations within both families and firms coevolved, and wage employment did not initially create a strong disjuncture between the two. Factory employment was often preceded by a period of proto-industrialization in which family members worked side by side producing such commodities as cloth or clothing for sale.[4] With the advent of factories, families sometimes continued to work as a group in new locations, with the father claiming the wages for his wife and children. Even when family members went to separate workplaces, men retained legal control over the earnings of their wife and minor children until the late nineteenth century in the United States and Britain, and until the early twentieth century in France.

With the expansion of wage employment to a larger percentage of individuals over a larger proportion of their lifecycle the implications of a new system of organizing labor were gradually realized. One of the earliest forms of wage employment was a paid version of the work that women and children typically performed—domestic service. By the early seventeenth century, a large percentage of English youth—about 60 percent of those between the ages of fifteen and twenty-four—worked as servants in other households.[5] Such opportunities offered the young a modicum of independence. But as long as they hoped to inherit assets, whether in the form of access to land, ownership of land, or a family enterprise, their economic futures were tethered to their parents. And as long as women were assigned primary responsibility for reproductive work, their productive contributions and their collective bargaining power would remain quite limited.

The Rise of Individual Occupations

The terminology of national censuses, as well as the numbers produced by them, reveals the gradual process of individuation. In 1801, the first census of the British population attempted to collect information on individual occupations of individuals. It failed, because ordinary people defined themselves in terms of the occupations of their families: The censuses of 1811, 1821, and 1831 returned to this traditional usage, tallying families rather than individuals. In 1821, for instance, overseers and schoolmasters were asked "What number of families in your parish, township, or place, are chiefly employed in, and maintained by agriculture, or by trade, manufacture or handicraft?"[6]

Not until 1851 was the concept of an individual worker engaged in the provision of goods or services for the market fully enshrined in the British census.[7] Discussion of the census results in that year noted that households were now no longer considered the same as families. "Formerly," explained an article in the *Westminster Review*, "the groups of inhabitants in separate houses were called families; but now, on account of the great number of single persons keeping house, the denomination is changed to households, under a *head* or occupier."[8] The Census enumerated 26 percent of those with paid occupations in agriculture. Persons engaged in "art and mechanic productions," represented 39 percent of all those tallied with paid occupations. The remainder was engaged in services of various kinds.[9]

The imprint of industrialization on the French labor force was less conspicuous. In 1851, the percentage of those with occupations who were engaged in agriculture was more than twice as high as in Britain, at 60 percent. Further, factories remained less prominent than small-scale enterprises. When the Paris Chamber of Commerce undertook a statistical analysis of local industries in 1851 it emphasized both the economic significance and the moral centrality of family-based enterprises, expressing discomfort with the concept of individual employment.[10] The French national censuses grouped entire households by occupation far longer than Britain or the U.S. Not until 1896 did the French census ask individuals to list their occupations, relegating housewives and children to the category of "inactive" (see further discussion in Chapter 17).[11]

At mid-century, the structure of employment in the U.S. resembled that of France, with 65 percent of the official labor force engaged in agriculture.[12] But farmers in the U.S. were far less dependent on inherited family property or use-rights than those in France—the relative abundance of land (among other factors) turned agriculture into a more entrepreneurial enterprise. It also increased the mobility of labor, literally stretching and thinning family ties. The Eastern seaboard in general and the New England states in particular traded extensively with Britain, and the relative scarcity of labor in those regions speeded adoption of new factory technologies. The 1850 census queried the "profession, occupation or trade of each male person over 15 years of age" and extended this query to women in 1860.[13]

As industrial employment shifted from cottage industry to factory work, mothers found it harder to combine productive employment with child care, and the growth of opportunities for women outside the home increased the amount of income foregone when they chose to stay at home. The payment of a wage based on the output of one worker meant that a man with five children would earn the same as a man with one. Furthermore, the economic insecurity and restless mobility fostered by factory employment may have discouraged family commitments among the least prosperous members of the working class.[14]

A majority of emigrants from Britain to the colonies were young men, a factor that both reduced parental control and tilted sex ratios.[15] The 1851

Census of Great Britain warned of a growing "spinster problem."[16] In the United States, internal migration to the West was predominantly male, leaving the more densely settled Eastern states with many young women relative to men. One result was lower marriage rates. In the 1830s the percentage of native-born adult women in Massachusetts who never married was far higher than the national average.[17] All these factors help to explain why an ethos of individual self-interest developed more rapidly in Britain and the U.S. than in France.[18]

The Labor Theory of Value

Malthus argued that wages largely determined men's decisions regarding when to marry. While he conceded that increases in the work effort of women and children could perhaps postpone the impact of lower male wages, he never explored the implications of changes in the relative economic contributions of family members.[19] David Ricardo also overlooked these factors as he sought to explain relative prices in terms of the relative amounts of labor devoted to production. His labor theory of value described wages as the cost of reproducing labor power. The origin and distribution of those wages within the family—as well as the role of non-wage labor—remained outside his field of vision. None of their contemporaries were any more perceptive. But Ricardo's assumptions proved particularly influential even among socialist critics like William Thompson and Karl Marx (see discussions in Chapters 11 and 15).

Ricardo followed the precedent set by Locke, treating labor as the most important factor of production, but one which was not itself produced (see discussion in Chapter 2). Quantification made this crystal clear: neither the hours devoted to rearing children nor those required to maintain adults entered into the equation. The value of a factory worker was determined only by the cost of the commodities that he purchased on the market, primarily the food that he needed to survive. This food requirement was often described, rather starkly, in terms of "corn"—the generic English term for grain. As with the rioting French women and the Speenhamland system of poor relief, wage determination came down to bread.

Ricardo believed that population growth would always drive wages to the subsistence level. He defined this level as one consistent with a stationary population, which would "enable the labourers, one with another, to subsist and to perpetuate their race, without either increase or diminution."[20] Like Malthus, he was nervous about the prospect of an actual decline in population, recognizing that it would put upward pressure on wages. Also like Malthus, he insisted that poor relief artificially increased the value of the subsistence package.

Neither economist speculated on how many children a subsistence wage would, ideally, support. The answer depended partly on the probability that a child would reach adulthood, a function of nutrition and living standards as well as health. Parish relief could have helped lower child mortality and therefore increased the efficiency of childrearing. Smith had referred in passing to such issues; Malthus and Ricardo never considered them.[21] The assumption that children were simply the fruit of sexual desire, rather than the product of parental time and effort, discouraged such considerations. Subsistence wage theory also sidestepped consideration of the productivity of families, ignoring the ways that higher wages and child labor regulation might contribute to improvements in the future quality of the labor force.

Children's contributions to the family income affected the net cost of rearing them. As a result, the effect of wages on population growth was mediated by the age at which children could begin to contribute to family income, helping support not only themselves but also their siblings. Families, not individuals, were the basic units of production in most agrarian settings; husbands and fathers wielded legal control over the earnings of their wives and minor children. Occupations were enumerated for all male children over the age of ten in the British Census of 1831, suggesting that those between the ages of eleven and eighteen were likely to contribute to family income.

Malthus and Ricardo, however, focused on adult male workers. When they claimed that a single man could subsist on less than a married man, they ignored both the market and non-market work of wives and children. A married man pooling income with a wife who provided him with household services that he would otherwise pay for was better off than a single man with a nominally higher market income. A man with several children over the age of ten working full-time for wages could easily enjoy a family income sufficiently high to compensate for additional expenses.

Children's contributions to family income posed a problem not only for the theory of subsistence wages, but also for the theory of population. It was

not rising wages or poor relief that fostered high fertility in late eighteenth-
and early nineteenth-century England, but rather increased economic
opportunities for young adults. The traditional controls that parents had
exercised over the age of marriage were weakened. The first stages of proto-
industrialization, based on a putting-out system in which capitalists provided semi-rural families with raw materials and purchased their final
products, made it easier for men and women to marry at a younger age
and utilize their own young children's labor.[22] The expansion of opportunities for factory employment reinforced this trend. As the British population
census of 1821 noted, "In many Manufactures, Children are able to maintain
themselves at an early age, and so to entail little expense of their Parents, to
the obvious encouragement of marriage."[23] British industrialization initially
increased the incentives to high fertility. Passion and reason worked in
concert.

Child Labor and the Poor Laws

Benefits for individual families did not however necessarily lead to benefits
for the working class as a whole. As Malthus correctly observed, an increase
in the supply of labor would, all else equal, lower wages. The supply of labor
was increased not only by higher fertility but also by declines in mortality.
Increased capacity to utilize the labor of young children also played a part.
More than two-thirds of the workers in the early factories of Northern
England were between the ages of seven and eighteen, working between
fourteen and sixteen hours a day.[24] Adults were, in a sense, in competition
with children. Yet they were increasingly dependent on their own children's
earnings.

The emerging textile industry was highly competitive, making it difficult
for employers unwilling to utilize child labor to stay in business. One notable
exception was Robert Owen, a benevolent yet upwardly mobile draper's
assistant who became a factory manager. The mills under his supervision in
New Lanark, Scotland employed no children under the age of ten, limited
working hours to ten and a half a day, and provided both schooling and
medical services for its employees. They became a model for reform, and
Owen became one of the influential spokesmen for the regulation of child
labor (and also, as Chapter 11 will elaborate, a socialist).

A bill introduced in 1815 proposed to extend the New Lanark model to the United Kingdom as a whole, prohibiting the employment of young children and setting limits on the work day. In factory towns children's earnings probably contributed as much to family income, overall, as any public assistance. Malthus quietly expressed support for some restrictions on child labor in the fifth edition of his *Essay*. Ricardo conspicuously failed to mention the issue, even in his published correspondence.[25]

The campaign to restrict child labor was couched in moral rather than economic terms. But the landed gentry had less to lose from restrictions on factory employment than the rising class of industrialists. Humanitarians such as the Seventh Earl of Shaftesbury threw their weight behind reform. Technological changes leading to increases in the intensity and skill required of factory work may have reduced the benefits of hiring children. A confluence of factors led to the passage of a Factory Act in 1833 that prohibited the employment of children under nine and limited children under twelve years to nine hours work per day.[26] In 1844, somewhat stricter regulations were imposed. While less common in French factories, child labor came under regulation there in 1841.[27]

The campaign to reform the Poor Laws, by contrast with the regulation of child labor, was framed in economic terms. Political economists, following Malthus's lead, rallied to the cause, as did an eager contingent of Benthamite lawyers. Abolition of relief outside the workhouse was described as the only possible means of discouraging excessive population growth. Malthus suggested that restrictions should be phased in gradually. Ricardo was the more draconian, approving the recommendations of a Poor Law Commission of 1817, which suggested taking the children of the poor away from their parents, the better to provide for them.[28] Elected to Parliament two years later, Ricardo used his inaugural speech to blast the existing system of poor relief.

Political economists took great pains to explain that their recommendations were motivated by their concern for the poor themselves. Theirs was not a callous view, they emphasized, but a scientific one. James Mill believed the causal effect of high fertility on low wages analogous to a proposition of Euclidean geometry.[29] Ricardo compared the inevitable effects of the Poor Laws to the principle of gravitation.[30] Malthus, as aforementioned, referred to the unfortunate vulnerability of mothers and young children as one of the invariable laws of nature. In 1834, the official report of the Poor Law Commission, influenced by the political economist Nassau Senior, recommended the abolition of all relief outside the workhouse. Parliament approved the recommendation. Many, though not all, parishes put new restrictive rules in place. Welfare had been reformed.

Fertility and Out-of-Wedlock Births

Did either of these two public policies, the regulation of child labor or the reform of the poor laws, have a discernable effect on British birth rates? The larger economic environment probably overshadowed both. It seems unlikely that parish allowances were ever high enough or reliable enough to induce more births.[31] In Ireland, a country that offered virtually no assistance to the poor, most families relied on an agricultural technology that allowed children to become productive at an early age. Fertility rates there far outstripped those in England in the early nineteenth century. Fear of the workhouse probably did more to discipline adult workers than to discourage births.

Accountability for out-of-wedlock births also became more openly contested. In the early eighteenth century, single men were held accountable for the support of children born out of wedlock. In the second half of the century, non-marital fertility increased in most of Northwestern Europe along with declines in age at marriage. The likelihood of premarital sex probably changed less than its consequences. Paternal desertion became easier in a world where men could find jobs outside their community of birth.[32] In France, before the revolution, an unmarried woman could sue the father of her child according to the doctrine of "creditur virgini" (literally, "give credence to the virgin").

New legislation passed in 1793 guaranteed an illegitimate child full rights if recognized by its father, but forbade any investigation into paternity and stipulated that no married man could acknowledge an illegitimate child. Similarly, the Napoleonic code forbade investigation of fatherhood unless the mother in question had been abducted. This restriction, which remained in force until 1912, left unmarried mothers—and their children—in a vulnerable position.[33] In the early nineteenth century, more than a third of all births in large cities such as Paris and Lyon took place outside of wedlock. Every year thousands of infants were deposited into foundling hospitals.[34]

A similar shift took place in England. Following the advice of Malthus, the authors of the Poor Law Report of 1834 (including Nassau Senior, Professor of Political Economy at Oxford) recommended elimination of legal responsibilities for fathers of bastard children. They quoted the observations of a vestry clerk in Cornwall to the effect that women were almost always responsible for seductions, often hoping to entrap the potential fathers.[35] The report explained that, "the virtue of female chastity does not exist among the lower orders."[36] Such women had been known to seduce even the most respectable of men. A Mr. Simeon explained:

> I rather believe we shall never be able to check the birth of bastard children by throwing the onus upon the man; and I feel strongly convinced, that until the law of this country is assimilated to the law of nature, and to the law of every other country, by throwing the onus more upon the females, the getting of bastard children will never be checked.[37]

The resulting legislation provoked such outrage that it was later revised to allow mothers to sue if they could meet stringent standards of proof.[38]

Reasoning about reproduction seldom took an explicit, calculating form. Still, the historical record shows that individuals responded to changes in the costs and benefits of family formation. Class interests were transparent. Factory owners had good reason to prefer the abolition of parish assistance to the regulation of child labor: the former policy would reduce their taxes, while the latter would decrease their profits. In the long run, regulation of child labor would benefit them as well, by improving the quality of the future labor force. Gender interests left a darker, more ambiguous mark. Men had a stake in future generations. But they could hedge their bets by avoiding responsibility for sexual mistakes. By and large, their calculations served them well.

The Wages of Virtue

If children complicated the issue of subsistence wages, so too did women, who were typically paid less than half what men earned. This discrepancy was explained in both natural and moral terms: women belonged in the home and should remain there. Even those enamored of the concept of wage labor worried about women's participation in it. Male trade unionists were acutely anxious, often exhorting women to stay home out of solidarity with the working class. The 1836 report of the National Trades Union meeting in the United States declared that the "physical organization, the natural responsibilities, and the moral sensibility of women prove conclusively that her labors should be only of a domestic nature."[39]

Women had long participated in the market as workers in a family enterprise. Guild restrictions that made it impossible for young women to acquire a trade on their own nonetheless gave them latitude, as wives or widows, to engage in business. In rural areas, access to common property resources allowed women access to fuel and fodder that made important contributions to their families' standard of living.[40] If enclosures of common land pushed women into factories, the pull of higher wages speeded them along. By the 1830s single women had begun to spill out of domestic service into forms of piecework and wage employment in which they competed more directly than ever before with men. By 1850 women accounted for about one third of the industrial labor force in both France and England.[41] Their level of participation was similarly high within the New England region of the U.S., though not in the South or the West.

Male wage earners in trades that did not require a great deal of physical strength, such as typesetting, were particularly vulnerable to competition, and made concerted efforts to limit women's participation.[42] Most trade unionists were more concerned with the wage effects of an increased supply of labor than with the potential to increase the earnings of their sisters, daughters, or wives. Even the reform-minded Francis Place argued that it was absolutely necessary to restrict women's employment. "It will be found universally," he testified before a government committee, "where men have opposed the employment of women . . . their own wages are kept up to a point equal to the maintenance of a family."[43] Ricardo had little if anything to say on the subject (there is, at least, no entry in the definitive edition of his collected works under "woman" or "workers, women").

Spokesmen for employers, such as Andrew Ure, defended the practice of hiring women, noting with satisfaction that the wages paid them were so low that they would not be able to neglect their family duties (see epigraph to this chapter).[44] Other discussions of women's work were infused with moral language. Lord Shaftesbury, serving as the first President of the Society for the Employment of Women, wrote that women's work could be defined as that which required "tact, sentiment, and delicacy."[45] He might well have added, that which "does not pay them enough to allow them to become assertive."

The French economist Jean-Baptiste Say, an admirer of Malthus's theory of population, made a more systematic effort to explain women's low wages. His *Treatise of Political Economy*, published in 1801, was widely cited in the English-speaking countries as well as his native France. While his views on women's pay were not particularly original, they were unusually explicit.[46] They received considerable elaboration at the end of the nineteenth century, in discussions of a male family wage (see Chapter 18).

Say argued that a man's wages should include the costs of supporting a wife and children, but a woman's wages should not.[47] He reasoned that the interplay between the family and the labor market would automatically lead to this result. Women wage earners seeking to support themselves on their own would always face competition from wives and daughters who were primarily supported by their husbands, and were therefore willing to work for a lower wage. This auxiliary supply of dependent labor would depress female wages.

Say's analysis, like that of his English contemporaries, ignored the unpaid domestic services that wives and daughters typically provided in return for their support, the limits that such unpaid work put on their supply of market labor, and their lack of property rights over their own earnings. It also ignored the logic of a perfectly competitive market that should, in principle penalize men as well as women for commitments to dependents. All else equal, men with children should earn the same wages as men without. An increase in the supply of men with no children should drive wages down. The only floor would be the costs of subsistence for a single worker. The resulting equilibrium wage would suffice only to support an adult without dependents.

In other words, "subsistence" means something different in the long run than the short run. Say seemed to recognize the problem more clearly than his peers. But he absentmindedly suggested that the market would anticipate the problem. Male wages would not decline, because this would drive the birth rate down only to drive wages up again. It was as though Say believed that Malthusian logic would work for women but not for men. The inconsistency in his reasoning can only be explained by his firm conviction that women were naturally designed to specialize in family work. He described women who try to "push ahead of men" as unnatural, representing a "third sex."[48] Those women who failed to find a husband could be allowed to seek employment in those occupations for which they were naturally suited—dressmaking, hairdressing, and cooking. So much for the virtues of competition.

Family Disruptions

Many contemporaries of Malthus and Ricardo revealed an intuitive understanding of the effect of capitalist development on the logic of the patriarchal family. As Peter Gaskell put it in 1833, the individual wage led to a "crying and grievous misfortune, namely that each child has ceased to view itself as a subordinate agent in the household; so far indeed loses the character and bearing of a child, that it pays over to its natural protector a stated sum for food and lodging, thus detaching itself from parental subjection and control."[49] The view that Andrew Ure expressed—that it was fortunate, in the long run, that women did not earn higher wages in the factories—would later be developed by the neoclassical economist Alfred Marshall in considerable detail.

Alice Clark feared that the capitalist wage employment would simply undo family ties, to ill effect. But capitalist institutions often reinforced gender inequalities that were already in place. The emergence of wage employment almost certainly gave women and young people more room to bargain over their family roles. Were women better or worse off as a result? The answer to this question depends on who they were and what they did. It also depends, obviously, on how individual welfare is defined. Most debates over trends in living standards focus on real wages. But changes in the value of non-market work are also relevant, as are changes in the distribution of family income over the lifecycle. Young women who managed to find good jobs almost certainly fared better than widows left upon the mercy of dispersed kin.

Those who had fared well in the old patriarchal order were frightened by its looming obsolescence, but even those who stood to gain were threatened by new forms of economic insecurity. The rise of factory technologies led to rapid shifts in relative prices, reducing the viability of cottage industries. The nineteenth-century economy grew in fits and starts with uneven and unpredictable effects. While a new class of investors grew rich, most workers did not, no matter when they married. Not surprisingly, the discourse of self-interest moved beyond issues of vice and virtue to more direct consideration of the interests that aligned individuals into groups.

NOTES TO CHAPTER 9

[1] For discussions of the institutional similarities and differences from a modern vantage point, see Robert A. Pollak, "A Transactions Cost Approach to Families and Households," *Journal of Economic Literature* 23:2 (1985), 581–608 and Paula England and George Farkas, *Households, Employment, and Gender. A Social, Economic, and Demographic View* (New York: Aldine Publishers, 1986).

[2] Elissa Braunstein and Nancy Folbre, "To Honor or Obey: The Patriarch as Residual Claimant," *Feminist Economics* 7:1 (2001), 25–54.

[3] Braunstein and Folbre, "To Honor or Obey."

[4] David Levine, *Family Formation in an Age of Nascent Capitalism* (New York: Academic Press, 1977).

[5] Ann Kussmaul, *Servants in Husbandry in Early Modern England* (New York: Cambridge University Press, 1981).

[6] "Proposals for an Improved Census of the Population," *The Edinburgh Review* (March 1829), p. 8, reprinted in *Population Problems in the Victorian Age*, vol. 1. (Westmead: Gregg International Publishers Limited, 1973).

[7] The 1841 census included some family workers and excluded others. See Catherine Hakim, "Census Reports as Documentary Evidence: The Census Commentaries, 1801–1951," *Sociological Review* 28:3 (1980), 551–80.

[8] "Occupations of the People," *Westminster Review* 48 (1854), reprinted in *Population Problems in the Victorian Age*.

[9] *1851 Census of Great Britain*, Occupations, Table XXIV.

[10] Joan Wallach Scott, "A Statistical Representation of Work. La Statistique de L'Industrie á Paris, 1847–1848," 113–38 in Joan Wallach Scott, *Gender and the Politics of History* (New York: Columbia University Press, 1988).

[11] Jacques Dupâquier, René le Mée, Joseph Goy, Maurice Garden, Hervé le Bras, Bernard Lepetit, Jean-Pierre Poussou, Daniel Courgeau, Jean-Pierre Bardet, Alain Bideau, Jean-Noël Biraben, Jacques Léonard, Bernard Lécuyer, Patrice Bourdelais, Agnès Fine, Martine Segalen, Yves Charbit, André Begin, *Histoire de la Population Française de 1789 á 1914* (Paris: Presses Universitaire de France, 1988); *Recensement de 1851, France*. Population Selon les Professions, Table 25; Christian Topalov, Une révolution dans les représentations du travail: L'émergence de la catégories statistique de 'population active' au XIXe siècle en France, en Grande-Bretagne et aux Etats-Unis," *Revue Française de Sociologie* 40:3 (1999), 445–73.

[12] *Historical Statistics of the U.S. Colonial Times to 1970*. Part I (Washington: Bureau of the Census), Series D 152–66, p. 138.

[13] Carroll Wright, *The History and Growth of the U.S. Census* (Washington, D.C.: Government Printing Office, 1900), pp. 135, 147.

[14] Wally Seccombe, *Weathering the Storm. Working-Class Families from the Industrial Revolution to the Fertility Decline* (London: Verso, 1993), p. 19.

[15] Bernard Bailyn, *Voyagers to the West* (New York: Random House, 1986).

[16] *1851 Census of Great Britain*, p. 86.

[17] L. V. Chambers-Schiller, *Liberty, A Better Husband. Single Women in America: The Generations of 1780–1840* (New Haven: Yale University Press, 1984), p. 5.

[18] Alan MacFarlane, *Marriage and Love in England 1300–1840* (New York: Basil Blackwell, 1986).

[19] Samuel Hollander, *Malthus* (London: University of Toronto Press, 1997), p. 778.

[20] David Ricardo, *On the Principles of Political Economy and Taxation. The Works and Correspondence of David Ricardo, Volume I*, ed. Piero Sraffa (Cambridge: The University Press, For the Royal Economic Society, 1966), p. 93.

[21] Michèle Pujol, *Feminism and Anti-Feminism in Early Economic Thought*, (Aldershot, Hants: Elgar, 1992) pp. 18–21; Mark Blaug, *Economic Theory in Retrospect*, 4th edn (New York: Cambridge University Press, 1985), 75–6.

[22] Wally Seccombe, *A Millenium of Family Change: Feudalism to Capitalism in Northwestern Europe* (New York: Verso, 1992);

[23] Census of Great Britain, Population: viz. Enumeration and Parish Registers; According to the Census of MD CCCXXI (1822), p. xxx.

[24] Brian Inglis, *Poverty and the Industrial Revolution* (London: Hodder and Stoughton, 1971) p.104.

[25] Gary Langer, *The Coming of Age of Political Economy, 1815–1825* (New York: Greenwood Press, 1987), p. 162.

[26] Clark Nardinelli, *Child Labor and the Industrial Revolution* (Bloomington: Indiana U. Press, 1990), p. 12; B. L. Hutchins and A. Harrison. *A History of Factory Legislation*, first published 1903 (New York: Augustus M, Kelley, 1966).

[27] Ibid., p. 137.

[28] Raymond Cowherd, *Political Economists and the English Poor Laws. An Historical Study of the Influence of Classical Economics on the Formation of Social Welfare Policy*, (Athens OH: Ohio University Press, 1977), p. 100.

[29] Raymond G. Cowherd, *The Humanitarians and the Ten Hour Movement in England* (Boston: Baker Library, Publication Number 10 of the Kress Library of Business and Economics, Harvard University, 1956), p. 5.

[30] Langer, *The Coming of Age*, p. 181.

[31] James Huzel, "Malthus, the Poor Law, and Population in Early Nineteenth-Century England," *Economic History Review* 22:3 (1969), 430–51; and "The Demographic Impact of the Old Poor Law: More Reflections on Malthus," *Economic History Review* 33:3 (1980), 367–81.

[32] Seccombe, *Weathering the Storm*, p. 50.

[33] Crane Brinton, *French Revolutionary Legislation on Illegitimacy, 1789–1804* (Cambridge: Harvard University Press, 1936), pp. 42, 50, 57.

[34] Susan K. Grogan, *French Socialism and Sexual Difference. Women and the New Society, 1803–44* (London: Macmillan, 1982), p. 7.

[35] Robert Dimand, "Women in Nassau Senior's Economic Thought," p. 224–40 in *The Status of Women in Classical Economic Thought*, ed. Robert Dimand and Chris Nyland (Northampton, MA: Edward Elgar, 2003).

[36] Cited in Cowherd, *Political Economists*, p. 276.

[37] *Report from his Majesty's Commissioners for Inquiring into the Administration and Practical Operation of the Poor Laws* (London: B. Fellowes, Ludgate St., 1834), p. 176.

[38] *Report from his Majesty's Commissioners*, p. 350; Cowherd, *Political Economists*, p. 269; Dimand, "Women in Nassau Senior," p. 233.

[39] Philip Foner, *Women and the American Labor Movement. From Colonial Times to the Eve of World War I* (New York: Free Press, 1979), p. 54.

[40] Ivy Pinchbeck, *Women Workers and the Industrial Revolution, 1750–1850* (London: Frank Cass), p. 22; Jane Humphries, "Enclosures, Common Rights, and Women: The Proletarianization of Families in the late Eighteenth and Early Nineteenth Centuries," *The Journal of Economic History* 50:1 (1990), 17–42.

[41] Seccombe, *Weathering the Storm*, p. 32.

[42] Felicity Hunt, "Opportunities Lost and Gained: Mechanization and Women's Work in the London Bookbinding and Printing Trades," *Unequal Opportunities. Women's Employment in England 1800–1918,* ed. Angela V. John (New York: Basil Blackwell, 1986): pp. 71–94.

[43] Pinchbeck, *Women Workers*, p. 179.

[44] Andrew Ure, *The Philosophy of Manufactures* (New York: Augustus M. Kelley, 1967), p. 475.

[45] Angela V. John, "Introduction," *Unequal Opportunities. Women's Employment in England 1800–1918*, ed. Angela John (New York: Basil Blackwell, 1986), p. 15.

[46] Evelyn L. Forget, "The Market for Virtue: Jean-Baptiste Say on Women in the Economy and Society," pp. 206–23 in *The Status of Women in Classical Economic Thought*, eds Robert Dimand and Chris Nyland (Cheltenham UK: Edward Elgar, 2003).

[47] Joan Wallach Scott, "L'ouvrière! Mot impie, sordide... Women Workers in the Discourse of French Political Economy, 1840–1860," in *Gender and the Politics of History* (New York: Columbia University Press, 1988), pp. 139–66.

[48] Forget, "The Market for Virtue," p. 211.

[49] Cited in Ivy Pinchbeck, *Women Workers and the Industrial Revolution, 1750–1850* (London: Frank Cass, 1969), p. 313.

CHAPTER 10

Whose Wealth?

...her floors and soil
Groan underneath a weight of slavish toil,
For the poor Many, measured out by rules
Fetched with cupidity from heartless schools,
That to an Idol, falsely called "the Wealth
Of Nations," sacrifice a People's health,
Body and mind and soul

William Wordsworth

Adam Smith always elicited more affection than his successors, and with good reason. In addition to his comforting confidence in the moral sentiments, he predicted that commerce would increase the wealth of nations, not merely of certain groups within them. Malthus and Ricardo were far less optimistic. Both believed that wages would never exceed subsistence in the long run, because population growth would only bring them down again. Ricardo warned that rents would likely rise and bring a halt to economic growth.

Small wonder, then, that the very phrase "the wealth of nations" began to elicit groans. It was ridiculed not merely by the great Romantic poets of early nineteenth century Britain but also by a popular novelist whose sensibilities had been shaped by his own childhood experience in the workhouse—Charles Dickens. Religious warnings that greedy merchants would land in hell were reborn as cultural critique—misers like Ebeneezer Scrooge would be condemned to nightmares.

Malthus and Ricardo were undeterred, or perhaps uninterested in this old debate. They shifted their attention from self-interest to collective interest, dividing Hobbes's Leviathan into three parts: landlords, capitalists of the new industrial order, and workers, defined as those who owned nothing but their own capacity to work. Men were assigned to classes by the great lottery of birth, mushrooms sorted into baskets by a divine hand. Malthus (a clergyman) was inclined to favor landlords, Ricardo (though in later life a landlord), capitalists. Their contending theories of rent and profit shaped debate over the abolition of tariffs on imported food, the Corn Laws that protected British agriculture from competition. They also informed the larger and even more contentious struggle over the meaning of free trade.

Wealth Demoralized

Smith had pronounced that the pursuit of self-interest would yield wealth and wealth in turn would strengthen the moral sentiments. A generation of English writers expressed fury at this claim. In 1813 the Romantic Percy Shelley made the title of Smith's master work the explicit focus of poetic scorn:

> The harmony and happiness of man
> Yields to the wealth of nations; that which lifts
> His nature to the heaven of its pride,
> Is bartered for the poison of his soul.[1]

The verse continued with a description of the "sordid lust of self", one of the few forms of lust of which Shelley did not approve.[2] In the more moderate and nostalgic language of the epigraph above, William Wordsworth described preoccupation with economic growth as a kind of perverse religion.[3]

Even more popular glosses on political economy were written by a man who avoided fancy language and initially published most of his novels in serial magazine installments. Most of Charles Dickens's novels portrayed the pursuit of economic self-interest as an excuse for hard-heartedness. *Oliver Twist*, published in 1837, parodied the reform of the poor laws. *A Christmas Carol*, published in 1843, pointedly contrasted the twisted priorities of the childless miser Ebeneezer Scrooge with those of his subordinate Bob Cratchit—a penniless but happy husband and father—and his dead partner Marley—who pronounced benevolence part of his business.

In *Hard Times*, Mr. Thomas Gradgrind personifies a kind of impersonal calculation that brings no one (including him) anything resembling happiness. Here too, the wealth of nations makes an appearance. A poor young girl insolently asks her teacher how she can know whether she lives in a prosperous nation or not, until she knows who actually has the wealth, and whether she is ever likely to enjoy any of it.[4] Mr. Gradgrind eventually needs help from a former student, but receives only a reminder of the catechism of self-interest which he had himself inculcated:

> It was a fundamental principle of the Gradgrind philosophy that everything was to be paid for. Nobody was ever on any account to give anybody anything, or render anybody help without purchase. Gratitude was to be abolished, and the virtues springing from it were not to be. Every inch of the existence of mankind, from birth to death, was to be a bargain across a counter. And if we didn't get to Heaven that way, it was not a politico-economical place, and we had no business there.[5]

As his contemporary Harriet Martineau complained, Dickens was more likely to find fault with the existing order than to offer remedies for it.[6] He never engaged with specific reformist efforts. But no one better satirized the underlying doctrine of political economy, or, in Dickens's own words, the doctrine of "everybody for himself and nobody for the rest."[7]

The Limits to Growth

The *Essay on Population* that made Malthus's reputation also gave him a strong voice in a new community of scholars. Joining a circle of men committed to the science of self-interest, he began to debate the nature of the business cycle, the implications of foreign trade and the future of economic growth. Despite his observation that moral restraint might slow the growth of population, he and virtually all his colleagues remained convinced that wages could not, in the long run, exceed subsistence.[8]

This skepticism was firmly rooted in assumptions regarding the limits of technological change. The quantity of land was fixed. Even if agricultural productivity grew, it could not, Malthus insisted, keep pace with population growth. In the words of one historian of economic thought, Malthusian arguments "cast a shadow over the optimism of early classicism."[9] Ricardian arguments cast an even darker shadow. Malthus emphasized the adverse effects of population growth on wages; Ricardo explained in more detail how population growth would increase the demand for food, which would require expansion of cultivation into less fertile and productive areas, increasing the price of food. Capitalists—whether in agriculture or in industry—would be forced to pay higher wages in order to feed their workers. This would necessarily lower their profits and bring a halt to economic growth. Ricardo was initially more optimistic about the potential for innovation in manufacturing. In the third edition of his *Principles of Political Economy*, however, he noted that labor-saving innovations could have the effect of throwing men out of work for more than a short while.

Such gloom and doom help explain why political economy was dubbed "the dismal science", though the author of that phrase, Thomas Carlyle, also registered distinctly racist, pro-slavery complaints.[10] What made the new pessimism both plausible and aggravating was the irregular rhythm of economic transformation. The growth of cottage industry contributed to a new prosperity, making it possible for men and women to marry at a younger age. But the handloom weavers soon became painfully vulnerable to relentless competition from new textile factories springing up in Manchester and other cities. In 1811, resentful saboteurs under the colorful banner of General Ned Ludd and his Army of Redressers began smashing machinery.

Trends in the standard of living of British workers in the era of industrialization have been hotly debated for many years. The emerging consensus suggests that the gains made before the 1840s were at best uneven.[11] The war with Napoleon, which lasted until 1815, consumed vast sums of money and manpower. Wealthy landowners who sought, above all, to keep taxes low dominated Parliament. Ordinary men and women had little voice. In 1819, workers gathered outside the city of Manchester to demand the right to vote. Among the many rabble rousers scheduled to speak was Mary Fildes, a leader of the Manchester Female Reform group (and known advocate of contraception). Fearing a riot, magistrates attempted to arrest the leadership. In the ensuing Peterloo Massacre, eleven people were killed, and many more wounded.[12]

A Reform Movement gradually gained momentum, leading to an expansion of the franchise in 1832 that was neatly calculated to allow working men with a modicum of property to vote.[13] The consequences of wealth inequality became apparent, and the Poor Law Reform of 1834 increased feelings of class antagonism. The cotton industry was particularly hard hit by economic contractions at the beginning and end of the 1840s.[14] Labor organizers began defying laws against trade unions. The Chartist Movement began demanding universal male suffrage.

Malthusian principles offered a shield of sorts, deflecting attention from specific policies toward putatively natural laws. They were invoked more officiously in Great Britain than in either France or the United States. Overpopulation was the least of French concerns, given the decimation of the French army by Napoleon's ill-fated visions of territorial conquest. And perhaps capitalists looked good compared to emperors. Jean-Baptiste Say, an industrialist himself, retained his Smithian optimism. In the second edition of his *Treatise,* published in 1814, he persuaded many of his countrymen of the productivity of capital and the self-regulating nature of the market.[15] His countryman Sismondi, less enthusiastic about market efficiency, faulted Malthus for not looking beyond England to the global economy as a whole, in which land was abundant.[16]

American economists were even more faithful to the ideal of progress. The white man's Enlightenment burned brightly on the western frontier, where civilization sought victory over something it called barbarism. Alexander Everett and Henry C. Carey, marveling at the abundance of land in the U.S., proclaimed that increased population was a boon, not a burden, because it promoted technical change and a more advanced division of labor.[17] Carey interpreted the Ricardian claim that population growth would limit the wealth of nations as a scandalous infidelity to Adam Smith.[18]

Collective Interests

Smithian alchemy had promised that economic growth would transform selfish lead into universal benefits. Ricardian chemistry suggested that the transformation might not last. The first sentence of the preface of his *Principles of Political Economy* called attention to distributional conflict: "The produce of the earth—all that is derived from its surface by the united application of labour, machinery, and capital, is divided among the three classes of the community, namely the proprietor of the land, the owner of the stock, or capital needed for its cultivation, and the laborers by whose industry is it to be cultivated."[19] He seemed to think that laborers themselves were a kind of natural crop, raised from the metaphorical seed corn in their wage bundle. Assuming they would always receive a subsistence wage, Ricardo turned his attention to the distribution of surplus between landlords and capitalists.

His story was simple and compelling. Landlords owned land, a fixed factor of production. Capitalist farmers paid rent for the use of the land, and the force of market competition tended to equalize their rate of profit. With population growth, the growing demand for food would lead to the expansion of agricultural production, leading to diminishing returns. Farmers would be forced to expand beyond the most easily cultivated areas to rocky hills and marshes where product per acre would be less. The price of food, and with it, the cost of subsistence wages would increase. Capitalist profits would thereby be lowered, but landlords would be able to charge much higher rents on productive land and grow rich at capitalist expense.

Ricardo has been described as the best economic spokesman of an emerging capitalist class that prided itself more on its skill than its genealogy. The description fit some aspects of his personal history. His parents were Sephardic Jews; he broke with his father at an early age; he made his fortune as a stockbroker, bought a landed estate and retired in his forties to devote himself to political economy. Most of his educated peers had simply inherited a stipend based on their parents' landed property. Without expressing any personal resentment, Ricardo observed they received a share of surplus without contributing to the common good. The interests of landlords were fundamentally at odds with those of other classes.[20]

His good friend Malthus disagreed. A class that devoted itself to luxurious expenditures, he pointed out, helped maintain demand for manufactured goods.[21] His *Principles of Political Economy Considered with a View to Their Practical Application*, published in 1820, warned that gluts and depression could result if luxury spending dropped too low. He went on to assert that what was good for the landlords was good for Britain as a whole: "It may be safely asserted that the interest of no other class in the state is so nearly and necessarily connected with its wealth, prosperity, and power as the interest of the landowner."[22]

The spotlight was now shining on a group rather unaccustomed to its glare. The Chartists hoping to expand the franchise used Ricardian reasoning to argue that landlord control over Parliament threatened the economic future of the country. Concepts like class and surplus raised uncomfortable questions. Why couldn't the working class claim a larger share? The French economist Simonde de Sismondi observed, in response to Malthus, that capitalists who were afraid of gluts could solve the problem by paying their employees more. Few landlords or factory owners liked that suggestion.

The Corn Laws

Bentham and his followers had long argued that Britain was politically monopolized by self-serving landlords. Many, though by no means all, political economists felt the franchise should be extended to a larger group of men. The most pressing issue concerned imports of grain. Government policy had traditionally sought to ensure that bread was neither too expensive (which would hurt the poor) nor too cheap (which would hurt farmers).[23] National security and self-sufficiency were also at stake.

During the Napoleonic wars, the costs of provisioning an army and the risk of ocean-going trade had combined to keep corn prices high. With the achievement of peace in 1815 came the prospect of renewed imports that would lower prices but also reduce landlords' incomes. Parliament immediately passed legislation prohibiting corn imports unless and until the price exceeded a very high level (about twice pre-war levels). These Corn Laws clearly violated the principles of *laissez faire*.

Class conflict met the principles of political economy head on. Landlords favored the restrictions in the name of rural tradition and national self-sufficiency. Malthus spoke eloquently on their behalf. In his defense of the Corn Laws, published in 1814, he conceded the abstract benefits of free trade but emphasized the adverse social effects of lowering the price of grain. As those familiar with his previous work might suspect, these included concerns about promoting population growth. But they also included apprehensions about excessively rapid growth of manufacturing, which would not be favorable to "national quiet and happiness." He went on to refer to fluctuations, which naturally tend to generate "discontent and tumult."[24]

Industrial capitalists opposed the restrictions in the name of economic efficiency. Most political economists weighed in on their side, including Robert Torrens, who explained quite clearly how the country could gain from reduced trade barriers. But no one systematized the argument better than Ricardo, in his *Principles of Political Economy*, published in 1817. As a Member of Parliament between 1819 and 1823, Ricardo had ample opportunity to expound his views and by most accounts, did so quite effectively.

The political influence of capitalists grew along with their pocketbooks, and on this issue their workers gained from coalition with them. With anti-Corn Law efforts centered in the factory city of Manchester, the political economists who favored their repeal were dubbed the Manchester School. Ricardo himself died prematurely in 1823. The continuing growth of the British population and swelling ranks of urban factory employment intensified the urgency of reform. Parliamentary debates focused not only on the detailed pros and cons, but also on the best method of relaxing tariffs. After several fits and starts and partial phase-outs, the Corn Laws were abolished in 1845.

Free Trade

A curious paradox lay at the heart of Ricardian theory. On the one hand, Ricardo emphasized distributional conflict, the factors affecting the division of the spoils. On the other hand, he insisted that free trade would benefit everyone. If his theory of rent led to unhappy conclusions, his theory of comparative advantage led to happy ones. The expansion of trade could help increase national income and mitigate diminishing returns to agricultural expansion. While it would not necessarily increase profits it would help to decrease rents.

Mercantilist theories had urged nations to export as much as possible, and import little, accumulating gold. Smith had persuaded most of his readers that the wealth of nations should be tallied by its overall consumption, not merely by its stores of gold. Smith's defense of free trade generalized his confidence in the division of labor. Let nations, like persons, specialize in what they could do best. Ricardo took Smith's reasoning one step further, building on earlier insights of Torrens and others to articulate the theory of comparative advantage. In a famous numerical example of the exchange of British cloth for Portuguese wine, Ricardo carefully specified the assumptions under which both countries could gain from trade, even if the absolute cost of producing both commodities were cheaper in Portugal.

If neither labor nor capital could cross national boundaries, and both countries were fully utilizing their factors of production (with no unemployment), differences in the relative efficiency of producing two goods had momentous implications. Modern economists often explain this argument in terms of opportunity cost and counterfactual comparisons. If Britain decided to make its own wine by reallocating labor from cloth production, it would give up a great deal because its cloth production was relatively more productive. Likewise, if Portugal decided to manufacture its own cloth by reallocating labor from wine production, it would give up a great deal because its wine production was relatively more productive.

The illustration that Ricardo chose was compelling partly because Portugal had an obvious absolute advantage in the production of wine, which was never very successfully produced in Britain. But his example also made it clear that the same results would follow even if it were cheaper to produce cloth as well as wine in Portugal. The reasoning behind comparative advantage only holds under strict assumptions. For instance, if capital could flow easily across national borders it might well be more efficient to produce both wine and cloth in Portugal.

Even in its modern formulation, the theory applies only when endowments are naturally given rather than socially created.[25] The declining importance of agriculture compared to high-tech services reduces the influence of natural endowments on comparative advantage. Some countries will always have the sunshine and rainfall better suited to grapes than others, but countries can invest in manufacturing, transportation, or the educational infrastructure that can develop a highly skilled labor force.

Ricardo's theory of comparative advantage pioneered the type of mathematical reasoning that would later come to dominate the discipline. Its analytical clarity was compelling; its assumptions, however limiting, were clearly stated. Furthermore, it resonated with utilitarian virtue. Elimination of tariffs would obviously threaten those who had taken advantage of their protection, leading not only to business failures but also to loss of jobs. But even if some were hurt, many more would benefit. The squawking protests might be more audible than more diffuse cheers, but by Ricardo's reasoning free trade would serve the greater good.

While his reasoning was correct, it was incomplete. All else equal, free trade could make everyone better off. But little else was equal. Countries could use their military power to force trade on their own terms, as the British did in India—where they virtually prohibited handloom weaving, and in China—where they sent their battleships to expand the opium trade. Imperial power often retarded technological development in the colonies and strengthened the political class that Ricardo himself believed was retrograde, namely landlords. Britain's head start in the development of new industrial technologies made it difficult for other countries to compete.[26] Most critics of the doctrine of free trade—and in the newly industrializing United States there were many—argued that it simply ratified British monopoly.

Protectionism

The principle of free trade was virtually inscribed on the Union Jack after 1845, but rhetoric waved far above reality. Britain not only maintained tariffs on a number of important goods until the last few years of the nineteenth century; its actual policies were, in some respects, more protectionist than those of France.[27] The United States, by contrast, both preached and practiced tariffs. Alexander Hamilton had, early on, advocated support for infant industries. With victory in the war of 1812 came a sharp increase in tariffs on cloth in particular, promoting transplantation of factory technologies from old England to new. Tariffs also became an important source of government revenue.

Like the German economist Friedrich List, eager to promote industrialization in his own country, American political economists defended the protectionist policies that their British mentors labeled heresy. The influential and prolific Henry Carey had few original ideas, and his reasoning was contradictory at times. Still, he outlined a passionate critique of both Malthus and Ricardo. If America needed anything, in his view, it was more children and more immigrants. Land was abundant, at least in the

West, and labor was scarce. In the absence of demographic pressures, there was no reason that wages could not rise along with labor productivity.

In England, landlords were, for the most part, men who inherited their wealth. In the United States, land was available to those with the energy, enterprise, and capital to claim it. Carey rejected the Ricardian theory of rent, the notion that landlords were simply claiming a portion of a surplus others had created. Land was not a completely non-produced good; investments in its clearing and improvement created a capital asset, which, like any other, offered a rate of return. Landlords, therefore, were no different than capitalists. Society was, Carey insisted, characterized by a harmony of interests, not a conflict.[28]

The only dissonance in Carey's intellectual world resulted from the dislocating effects of free trade. Carey went well beyond familiar arguments in favor of protection to argue that international trade could subvert the social order by separating producers from consumers, breaking the bonds of community and trust. Rhetorically, he sought to reconcile the competing doctrines of two Founding Fathers: Hamilton had argued that manufacturing would bring prosperity. Jefferson had insisted that family farms and small towns should be protected. Carey believed that protectionism could reconcile these goals. It was as though he hoped for capitalism only within countries, not among them.

Unable to challenge the logic of comparative advantage, Carey couched his argument in moral and cultural terms. He claimed that free trade would undermine what Smith had termed the moral sentiments. Malthus and Ricardo were urging the pursuit of self-interest at the expense of social responsibility. Carey warned that Britain had become a cold-hearted country dominated by the new religion of political economy which, thankfully, had not fully displaced Christian ideals: "That any feelings of kindness towards those who are so unfortunate as to be poor should still remain in England is due to the fact that those who teach it [political economy] have not in their doctrine sufficient faith to practice what they preach."[29]

Protection would indeed raise the prices of imports and perhaps inhibit demand for exports. But it would also raise wages, attract immigrants, and promote industrialization. Furthermore, he went on at length, it would benefit women in particular, by reducing the temptation to men to seek their fortunes on their own. It was policies of free trade, he argued, that had emptied men from the Highlands of Scotland and delivered them to the deserts of Australia, leaving women behind. Carey bewailed the tilted sex ratios of the Old World and bemoaned the deterioration of men's character when deprived of civilizing female influence. When "commerce is king," he wrote, describing the horrors of poverty and prostitution in London, his female subjects suffer.[30]

Like many others who rejected the march of liberal individualism, Carey emphasized the economic importance of families—the sites where labor power was produced and maintained. Influenced perhaps by Robert Owen (see Chapter 11) he pointed out that life expectancy itself had economic implications: "Of all machines, the most costly to produce is Man."[31] Machines could be programmed to pursue their own self-interest. If men ever programmed themselves that way, women and the family would be endangered. Carey concluded that the state should protect the natural harmony of interests from such unnatural disruption.

Selfish Classes

Mandeville's *Fable of the Bees* had described a hive that prospered by allowing its members to pursue their own self-interest. After Ricardo, however, the bee's honey became a metaphor for economic surplus. In response to the claim that economic growth meant that everyone was better off, Charles Hall observed that a great store of honey did not mean that the bees from which it had been taken were rich.[32] In his *Song to the Men of England*, Shelley asked why the Bees of England allowed "these stingless drones to spoil the forced produce of your toil."[33] Capitalists, of course, thought of themselves as bee-keepers, managers and protectors rather than as stingless drones.

Malthus and Ricardo made it clear that public policies could affect the distribution of surplus between landlords and capitalists. In the process, they called attention to larger forms of conflict. Capitalists were ascendant, as was free trade. Yet protectionists outside of Britain described her actions as those of a great monopoly, manipulating markets to her own advantage and draining honey from the nations, like India, in her thrall. Vice and virtue were less at issue now than the exploitation of one group by another. Some angry swarms or workers also wanted to reorganize the hive. Their efforts left political economists in both England and France abuzz.

NOTES TO CHAPTER 10

[1] Percy Shelley, "Queen Mab," V:79, *The Complete Poetical Works of Percy Bysshe Shelley*, ed. Thomas Hutchinson (London: Oxford University Press, 1947), p. 780.

[2] In the same poem he painted a glorious picture of dawning love "unchecked by dull and selfish chastity / That virtue of the cheaply virtuous / Who pride themselves in senselessness and frost." Shelley, "Queen Mab," IX:83, in *Complete Poetical Works*, p. 707.

[3] William Wordsworth, "Humanity," *Poetical Works*, ed. Thomas Hutchinson (New York: Oxford University Press, 1969), p. 393.

[4] Charles Dickens, *Hard Times* (New York: New American Library, 1961), p. 64.

[5] Ibid., p. 283.

[6] E. D. H. Johnson, *Charles Dickens: An Introduction to His Novels* (New York: Random House, 1969), p. 43.

[7] Johnson, *Charles Dickens,* p. 48.

[8] See the preceding chapter for a discussion of the imprecise meaning of the term "subsistence".

[9] William J. Barber, *A History of Economic Thought* (New York: Penguin, 1963), p. 68.

[10] David M. Levy, *How the Dismal Science Got Its Name: Classical Economics & the Ur-Text of Racial Politics* (Ann Arbor, MI: University of Michigan Press, 2001).

[11] Joel Mokyr, "The Factory System," pp. 120–61 in *Gifts of Athena. Historical Origins of the Knowledge Economy* (Princeton: Princeton University Press, 2002). For more background, see Peter Lindert, "Unequal Living Standards," in *The Economic History of Britain Since 1700*, 2nd edn, Vol. 1: 1700–1860, eds Roderick Floud and Donald McCloskey (Cambridge: Cambridge University Press, 1994), pp. 357–86; and Stanley Engerman, "Reflections on 'The Standard of Living Debate': New Arguments and New Evidence," in *Capitalism in Context: Essays on Economic Development and Cultural Change in Honor of R. M. Hartwell,* eds John A. James and Mark Thomas (Chicago: University of Chicago Press, 1994), pp. 50–79. On consequences for women, see Jane Humphries, "Enclosures, Common Rights, and Women: The Proletarianization of Families in the late Eighteenth and Early Nineteenth Centuries," *The Journal of Economic History* 50:1 (1990), 17–42.

[12] E. P. Thompson, *The Making of the English Working Class* (New York: Random House, 1966).

[13] Thompson, *Making of the English Working Class*, p. 821.

[14] George R. Boyer, "The Historical Background of the Communist Manifesto," *Journal of Economic Perspectives* 12:4 (1998), 151–74.

[15] Leonard P. Liggio, "Charles Dunoyer and French Classical Liberalism," *Journal of Libertarian Studies* I:3 (1977), 153–78.

[16] J. C. L. Simonde de Sismondi, *Political Economy* (1815), Ch. 7 available on line at <http://socserv2.socsci.mcmaster.ca/~econ/ugcm/3ll3/sismondi/poliec>.

[17] Alexander H. Everett, *New Ideas on Population, With Remarks on the Theories of Malthus and Godwin*, first published 1826 (New York: Augustus M. Kelley, 1970); Henry C. Carey, *Principles of Political Economy* (Philadelphia: Lea and Blanchard, 1840).

[18] Henry Charles Carey, *The Slave Trade. Domestic and Foreign, Why it Exists and How it May be Extinguished* (Philadelphia: Henry Cary Baird Industrial Publisher, 1853) available online at <http://yamaguchy.netfirms.com/carey/index.html> Chapter 5.

[19] David Ricardo, *The Principles of Political Economy and Taxation* (New York: E. P. Dutton, 1962), p. 1.

[20] Maurice Dobb, *Studies in the Development of Capitalism* (New York: International Publishers, 1963); Ricardo, *Principles*, p. 225.

[21] E. K. Hunt, *History of Economic Thought: A Critical Perspective* (Belmont, CA: Wadsworth, 1979); Fiona Maclachlan, "The Ricardo-Malthus Debate on Underconsumption: A Case Study in Economic Conversation," *History of Political Economy* 31:3 (1999), pp. 563–74.

[22] Thomas Robert Malthus, *Principles of Political Economy* (London: W. Pickering, 1836), Section VIII, "On the Strict and Necessary Connection of the Interests of the Landlord and of the State," paragraph 659, available on line at <http://oll.libertyfund.org/title/2188/202554/3333390>, accessed January 16, 2009.

[23] C.R. Fay, *The Corn Laws and Social England* (Cambridge: Cambridge University Press, 1932).

[24] T. R. Malthus, *Observations on the Effects of the Corn Laws, and of a Rise or Fall in the Price of Corn on the Agriculture and General Wealth of the Country* (St. Paul's Church-Yard: J. Johnson and Company, 1814), available on line at <http://socserv.mcmaster.ca/econ/ugcm/3113/malthus/cornlaws>, accessed February 17, 2006.

[25] The Heckscher-Ohlin theorem stipulates that a country has a comparative advantage in the production of a product if it is relatively well endowed with inputs that are used intensively in producing the product.

[26] For a modern version of this argument see Ha-Joon Chang, *Kicking Away the Ladder: Development Strategy in Historical Perspective* (London: Anthem Press, 2002).

[27] John Vincent Nye, "The Myth of Free Trade Britain and Fortress France: Tariffs and Trade in the Nineteenth Century," *Journal of Economic History* 51:1 (1991), 23–46.

[28] Henry Carey, *Harmony of Interests: Manufacturing and Commercial* (1851) available at <http://yamaguchy.netfirms.com/carey/harmony_20.html>

[29] Carey echoes Hamilton's arguments regarding the advantages of factory employment for women in Chapter 20, then invokes Jefferson in Chapter 21 of *Harmony of Interests*.

[30] Carey, *Harmony of Interests,* Ch. 20.

[31] Carey, *Harmony of Interests*, Ch. 22.

[32] Brian Inglis, *Poverty and the Industrial Revolution* (London: Hodder & Stoughton, 1971), p. 72.

[33] Shelley, *Collected Works*, p. 572.

CHAPTER II

The Social Family

If, then, due care as to the state of your inanimate machines can produce such beneficial results, what may not be expected if you devote equal attention to your vital machines, which are far more wonderfully constructed? When you shall acquire a right knowledge of these, or their curious mechanism, of their self-adjusting powers; when the proper mainspring shall be applied to their varied movements—you will become conscious of their real value.

Robert Owen

In the 1820s a small number of men and women who imagined a more cooperative and egalitarian world began to meet in London in Chancery Square. They challenged the notion that individual pursuit of self-interest would always benefit society as a whole. Reaching for an alternative to individualism they arrived at a new word: "socialism". The concept, if not the word, had religious antecedents. Both pagan worship of Mother Earth and Christian confidence in God the Father held the family up as a model for the organization of society as a whole. The early socialists departed from religious tradition by describing solidarity and concern for others as a feature of the natural rather than the spiritual order.

Socialism was typically described as kinship writ large, "as if one family had multiplied as to fill the earth" and was then "by the stipulations of kindred... pledged to co-operation in the full extent."[1] As Thomas Paine had explained in simple language, individuals had much to gain from commitments to mutual protection and support. Some socialists described a new society organized like a vast insurance company for the bearing of all losses from fire, shipwreck, old age, and widowhood.[2] Others developed a more ambitious vision of farms and factories as cooperative egalitarian enterprises.

Embracing the family as a model for society made it difficult to take the family for granted. Unlike their intellectual predecessors the early socialists defied complacency regarding traditional rules of marriage, the sexual double standard, and the gender division of labor. They hoped to banish both greed and lust. Most of their contemporaries felt that they hoped for way too much. But if their idealistic ardor diminished their political success, it also energized their vision.

The Social Father

As a leader of the early campaign to limit child labor, Robert Owen urged factory owners to practice the benevolence that the Third Earl of Shaftesbury had vaguely praised. Jeremy Bentham urged Owen on, investing in one of his humanitarian textile mills. Surely influenced by utilitarian reasoning, Owen often invoked a less hedonistic ideal: the development of human capabilities. In words that anticipated the winner of the 1998 Nobel Prize for Economics, Amartya Sen, he insisted on the following social goals: "to receive from birth the best cultivation of our natural powers—physical, mental, moral, and practical—and to know how to give this training and education to others," as well as to "have the inclination and means to increase continually our stock of knowledge."[3] Perhaps because he was a self-educated man, Owen prized education above all.

Members of the Parliamentary Committee considering restrictions on child labor expressed the fear that children under ten would be lazy and spoiled if not required to work. Owen insisted that his own experience at New Lanark showed that time spent in school made older children better workers. He also argued, with great prescience, that children could benefit enormously from education beginning at the age of three.[4]

Owen's followers sometimes referred to him as "The Social Father", and virtually everything he wrote was infused with parental solicitude. If the title evoked traditional reverence for the heavenly Father, it also called attention to Owen's disinterest in all forms of religion, which he considered little more than superstition.[5] Owen combined a humble sense of obligation toward the dispossessed with almost insolent disregard of cultural and religious precedent. Today he would probably be termed a secular humanist. The term secular paternalist would be more apt.

Owen's criticisms of the Church, like his advocacy of rights to divorce, invited derision from most supporters of the status quo. He was sometimes labeled an infidel. Yet his unwearying idealism neutralized at least some of the acid poured upon his reputation. He condemned all forms of violence. He denounced slavery. He campaigned tirelessly on behalf of reduced working hours for children and public education. Having made a fortune in manufacturing, he proceeded to invest his profits in efforts to develop a more egalitarian society. A good husband and committed father, he was by most accounts unfailingly courteous and kind.

He may have controlled his anger by channeling it into condescension. Owen viewed adults, like children, as innocent, unformed, blameless creatures. Conceding that men and women often behaved in selfish ways, he explained that they had been trained to do so. A social system based on cooperation would, he believed, foster greater concern for others. This argument was not far-fetched. Psychologists today (though not economists) treat the development of social affection and moral values as a stage of maturation.[6] Families and schools shape children's emotional, as well as cognitive intelligence.[7]

Owen's insistence that young children are malleable challenged the aristocratic conceit that heredity—or good breeding—determined character. But he carried his argument to metaphysical extremes reminiscent of theological doctrines that denied free will. On a more practical level, he aroused concerns regarding the extent to which men and women could be retrained—and by whom. Even his close supporters balked at the suggestion that men should not be held accountable for their own actions.[8] One of the subjects advertised for public discussion at a meeting of the London Co-operative and Economical Society in 1824 was the following question: "Is the position of Mr. Owen correct, that man is not properly the subject of praise or blame, reward or punishment?"[9] Given the framing, it is difficult to imagine anyone shouting "yes."

Like Che Guevara, who would issue an even more urgent call for a "new socialist man" in the twentieth century, Owen seemed to think the possibilities for heroic reconfiguration were within reach, but failed to explain exactly how it would take place. Perhaps educators could shape human character. But who would educate the educators? He found it difficult to say. As some put it, referring to the architectural plans associated with his communitarian experiments, Owen might "live in parallelograms but he argued in circles." Harriet Martineau observed rather tartly that he did not know how to argue at all.[10]

He was initially uninterested in expansion of the franchise, writing his manifestos for a political elite whose cultivated intelligence he always praised and whose motives he seldom questioned. It seemed self-evident to him that employers, even slave owners, would benefit from treating workers well.[11] He addressed his first public tract, *A New View of Society*, to His Royal Highness the Prince Regent, explaining the necessity not merely of educating, but of reforming the character of the poor and working classes.[12] *The Book of the New Moral World*, prefaced by a letter to His Majesty William IV, reiterated the vision of a rising generation that could be educated to superior social conduct.[13] In 1833, he published "An Appeal to the Rich", and in "Revolution by Reason" he proclaimed that "This great change ... must and will be accomplished by the rich and powerful." On his final trip to America, Owen appealed "To the Capitalists."[14]

This strategy often won him attention, if seldom agreement, from those in power. Not surprisingly, it also infuriated his natural constituency within the working class. "Why re-moralize the poor and not the rich?" asked Thomas Wooler in the radical magazine *Black Dwarf*, adding his own prescription: "Reduce the herd of locusts that prey upon the honey of the hive and think they do the bees an essential service!"[15]

The Great Dream

Owen's odd combination of traditional values and modern sensibilities shaped the experiments he financed. His success with the New Lanark mills as models of socially responsible capitalism led him to believe that the poor and unemployed could be put to work on cooperative enterprises that would eventually support themselves. His exhortations recalled the vision of the seventeenth century Levellers and Diggers. Other precedents were offered by religious orders whose members farmed in common and shared their bread. In the United States, the combination of religious freedom and inexpensive land encouraged the formation of so-called "backwoods utopias".[16]

Many small enterprises in both Britain and the United States embraced Owenite principles for at least brief periods of time. The most famous experiment, however, began to unfold in the United States in 1825, where Owen purchased a farm village in Harmony, Indiana, that had been established by German Protestants known as Rappites. He renamed it New Harmony and invited all who sympathized with his ideas of cooperation to join him. "I am come to this country," he announced, "to introduce an entire new state of society; to change it from an ignorant, selfish system to an enlightened social system which shall gradually unite all interests into one, and remove all causes for contest between individuals."[17]

Most communitarian enterprises established by religious groups had clear lines of authority, as well as strict rules of conduct that filtered out those undedicated to a larger cause. New Harmony lacked such features. Its vague rules of governance led to contention, and ultimately to litigation. Factionalism was rife—small interest groups formed and jostled for position. The open invitation to participants (without probation of any length) attracted opportunists. Yet the community held fast to the principles that everyone should be remunerated equally, regardless of effort or productivity. Three years later it fell apart, despite much enthusiasm for the quality of its schools.[18]

Many attributed the failure to excessive idealism. John Humphrey Noyes, himself the founder of the cooperative Oneida Community, published a classic account of American socialisms in which he seemed to echo the views of English political economy: "Mere benevolence, mere sentiments of universal philanthropy, are far too weak to bind the self-seeking affections of men."[19] He went on to describe "self-love" as though it were a demon, a "spirit which would not be exorcised."[20] Owen himself was less disappointed. Not surprisingly, given his views on the malleability of human character, he concluded that the attempt to persuade strangers to live together as a common family was simply premature.[21] Others like William Thompson and Charles Fourier (discussed later) believed that more specific managerial guidelines would solve the problem.

Owen left New Harmony for Mexico, where he requested a large portion of the Texas territory for further experimentation, to no avail. He returned to England in 1829, surprised and delighted to discover a frothing dissidence of factory workers and trades people eager to form local exchanges and currencies based on labor hours, to establish consumer cooperatives, to organize cultural and political events. Owen lent his voice, as well as much of his remaining fortune, to the Grand National Consolidated Trades Union and even more grandly named successor, the Association of all Classes of all Nations.

Class and Gender

Owen, however, remained a marginal figure, partly because he believed that women should work outside the home, and that domestic work should be socialized. Most Chartists and unionists were tradesmen who hoped to increase male wages. Many felt that women's proper place was in the home, where they could tend to family members rather than flooding the labor market and undercutting their own wages.[22] Marx and Engels urged their followers away from feminist socialism toward what they called scientific socialism. A hundred years later, trade union activists would continue to warn their members against the witcheries of utopian wish lists.[23]

Owen denounced the traditional patriarchal family ever more stridently after 1840. But his approach to gender inequality was, at best, incomplete. He believed that women should be educated to become "superior companions" rather than "family slaves".[24] He set up a patriarchal rather than democratic system of authority within his organizations, making it difficult for anyone to challenge him.[25] He seemed almost unconcerned about legal restrictions on women's property rights or their access to the vote. What bothered him most were the greedy allegiances of family life:

> The children within these dens of selfishness and hypocrisy are taught to consider their own individual family their own world, and that it is the duty and interest of all within this little orb to do whatever they can to promote the advantages of all the legitimate members of it. With these persons it is my house, my estate, my children, or my husband...No arrangement could be better calculated to produce division and disunion in society.[26]

Owen's critics were quick to warn of the risks that free love posed for mothers and children.[27] But Owen was convinced that male misbehavior, such as indulgence in prostitution, resulted only from the galling constraints of indissoluble marriage.[28] He never considered the possibility that other contractual obligations might be necessary for the support of dependents. He took both child care and child support as a given. Even in New Harmony, women's responsibilities for children extended above and beyond the "real work" they contributed to the collective.[29]

Like many of his left-leaning precursors Owen worried less about lust than greed. In his *Lectures on the Marriages of the Priesthood of the Old Immoral World*, published in 1841, he called celibacy a "great crime, necessarily leading to disease of body and mind."[30] "True chastity" he defined as "the intercourse of the sexes where there is a pure and genuine sympathy or sincere affection between the parties." The book was written after his wife had died; one wonders if a lover sweetened his old age.[31] Perhaps he was swayed in other ways by the younger generation.

Owen's Economics

Over the course of his long and committed career, Owen probably won more hearts than minds. Few took him seriously as a political economist, since his arguments on behalf of higher wages and cooperative self-management were drawn from the writings of others who had more directly studied Ricardo's *Principles*. Many of his ideas were inconsistent and far-fetched. Yet Owen effectively challenged Adam Smith's assumption that benevolent self-interest was a fact of Nature. He argued instead that self-interest was essentially shaped by social and family life. He initiated a furious debate over human malleability and the limits of socialization. He encouraged experimentation with egalitarian collectives whose failures, however painful, yielded important lessons for the future.

Owen's emphasis on the economic significance of developing children's capabilities was both practical and prophetic. None of his predecessors had paid much attention to the development of what we now term human capital. While Adam Smith had pointed to the advantages of public education he offered little by way of detail regarding regulations or provisions. Owen waxed eloquent on the subject of living machinery, applying the time-honored metaphor of mainspring to the clock.[32] He addressed factory managers directly when he insisted that the productivity of their vital machines—their workers—was as essential to their profits as their capital equipment.[33]

Society itself resembled a machine whose efficiency could be improved. The subsistence wages that most political economists accepted as a natural law led to the waste of children's capabilities. Prodded by democratic reforms, British employers began to recognize the economic logic behind the cooperative provision of at least some public goods. They accepted greater regulation of working hours and spending on common schools, along with public investments in transportation and utilities.[34]

Malthus had officially recognized his new challenger in 1817, when the revised fifth edition of his *Essay on Population* substituted criticisms of Owen's *New View of Society* for his original assault on Godwin. Malthus reiterated his view that movements toward equality would be undermined by population growth. Owen remained, as ever, optimistic. Reminiscing in extreme old age, he claimed that in his discussions with her husband, Mrs. Malthus always took his side.[35]

The Appeal of One-Half the Human Race

Most of the early socialists intuitively recognized that the extension of positive family values to society as a whole required a critique of gender inequality. The two thinkers who addressed this issue most directly were both members of the Irish landed gentry who had experienced both the chafe of English rule and the binding force of family law. William Thompson was initially angered by the plight of the Irish poor.[36] Anna Wheeler had more personal complaints. Married at the age of fifteen to an unregenerate drunkard, she bore six children within a space of twelve years. Only two survived, and when she finally managed to escape her husband's household she was forced to assume complete responsibility for their support.[37]

Once in London, both Thompson and Wheeler entered Bentham's circle, finding common cause in their criticisms of another Benthamite, James Mill. To the surprise of his friends and acquaintances (and later disapproval of his son John Stuart) Mill published an article in the 1819 *Encyclopedia Britannica* restating the familiar argument that women did not need political rights because they were well-represented by their fathers, husbands, and brothers.[38] The gist of Thompson and Wheeler's scathing retort was summarized in its title: *Appeal of One-Half the Human Race, Women, Against the Pretensions of the Other Half, Men, to Retain them in Political, and Thence in Civil and Domestic Slavery.*[39]

While the book appeared under Thompson's name, its long preface acknowledged Wheeler's contributions, and her voice rings in its most urgent passages.[40] The *Appeal* did more than assert women's right to vote. It systematically explored the contradictions of a theory of political economy that held men to be wholly self-interested in their dealings with each other, yet wholly altruistic in their dealings with women and children. This argument was put most concisely in the outline of topics covered in Part I, which directly addressed the issue of self-interest:

1. The general argument of the "Article" for Human Rights is founded on the universal love of power of all human beings over all their fellow-creatures for selfish purposes. This is stated to be the grand governing law of human nature...

2. But, if in the disposition of one half the human race, men, an exception from this grand governing law exists towards the other half, women, what becomes of the law itself and the arguments founded on it?[41]

The sections that followed made the case for a transition toward a more democratic and cooperative social system. In dialogue format, the authors rebutted every rationale they could imagine for denying women the same political and civil rights as men. They ridiculed the notion that marriage could be described as a contract between free and equal individuals, pointing to the asymmetrical property rights that gave husbands virtually absolute power over wives. Under English common law, they argued, the married woman could be treated as "an involuntary breeding machine and household slave."[42]

In a related article, published in *The Co-Operative Magazine*, Thompson laid out an argument that Owen later muddled. Patriarchal authority—not mere allegiance to kin—had distorted the natural instincts of cooperation.

> Every family is a centre of absolute despotism, where of course, intelligence and persuasion are quite superfluous to him who has only to command to be obeyed: from these centres, in the midst of which all mankind are now trained, spreads the contagion of selfishness and the love of domination through all human transactions.[43]

The family's ability to define its collective interests was pre-empted by its despot, the legal head of the household. Thompson and Wheeler seemed to blame patriarchal systems that antedated capitalism for resistance to cooperation. This interpretation, however undeveloped, made more sense than

Owen's vague complaints. It also helped explain why communitarian efforts that simply abjured class differences foundered on other types of inequality.

Feminist Socialism

If Thompson's socialism informed his feminism, the reverse was also true. It was as though he read Ricardo through Anna Wheeler's eyes. Many of his arguments paralleled those of other so-called Ricardian socialists who deployed the language of political economy. But Thompson offered a unique critique of the principle that individuals should be paid "according to their work," observing that individuals who cared for dependents would always be disadvantaged by it. Family care was based on obligation and commitment, tailored to the unpredictable needs of specific individuals. It was not a commodity to be bought and sold and could never be fully measured or rewarded by the metric of the market.

Thompson cared little for Ricardo's distinction between capitalists and landlords and, in asides clearly aimed at Owen, observed that appeals to the rich were unlikely to benefit the poor. The working class, he argued, must organize on its own behalf to lay claim to the products of its labor. Workers, like bees, were allowing their surplus honey to be stolen.[44] He called for the immediate abolition of slavery, insisting that the violation of human rights that it entailed was more damning than the violation of property rights that its abolition would require.[45] He opposed revolutionary redress only because he feared that violence would lead to brutalizing waste. Better for men and women to gradually lay claim to the surplus they produced, edging toward equality. The achievement of political democracy was necessary, though not sufficient to reach this goal.

Thompson condemned the inheritance of private property that distributed resources without respect to merit, effort, or ability. The unequal distribution of wealth led inevitably, in his view, to unequal exchange within the market.[46] He applied Benthamite logic to argue for a tax on wealth. A man with a thousand portions derived far less satisfaction from the last hundred than he did from the first, and egalitarian redistribution would contribute to the greatest happiness of the greatest number.[47]

Cooperative systems, Thompson insisted, could be efficient. Individuals might tend to shirk but a share of the surplus could potentially elicit more effort than a mere subsistence wage. How should that share be defined? Equal division was the simplest rule, but would put the hardest-working and most skilled workers at a disadvantage. Why not reward each according to his work, following the precepts of the labor theory of value? Many of Thompson's friends, as well as the French socialists discussed in the following chapter, urged this principle.

Thompson conceded that this would be a great improvement over the existing system of "constraint by mingled force and fraud."[48] But he pointed out that it was difficult to calculate each person's individual contribution, and that workers sometimes invested in skills that unexpectedly became obsolete. Like Owen, he feared that allowing workers to compete for higher individual rewards would foster selfishness and undermine the very basis of cooperation.[49]

Unlike Owen, Thompson pointed out that the labor theory of value ignored the labor devoted to the production and maintenance of laborers themselves. Competition would penalize people who devoted themselves to the care of those too young or old or sick to care for themselves.[50] Family responsibilities would always put women at a disadvantage. "In the race of individual competition for wealth," Thompson wrote, "men have such fearful advantages over women, from superiority of strength and exertion uninterrupted by gestation, that they must probably maintain the lead in acquisition by individual effort."[51]

Thompson insisted that women should never be forced into involuntary motherhood, and believed that prosperity would lead to fertility decline.[52] He was even more forthright than Owen in advocating contraception. He was likely referring to coitus interruptus when he wrote: "A mental effort on the side of refinement, not of grossness, is all the price necessary to be paid, and by only one party, for early marriages and mutual endearments, where the circumstances of society permit no increase of population."[53] Fertility decline could, in turn, reduce women's disadvantage.

Communities of cooperation could potentially benefit women more than men. Thompson offered detailed plans for redeploying domestic labor in his *Practical Directions for the Speedy and Economical Establishment of Communities on the Principles of Mutual Co-operation, United Possessions and Equality of Exertions and of the Means of Enjoyments*

(1830). Owen echoed many of its details in his *Book of the New Moral World* (1836), such as replacing the sexual division of labor with an age-based system (housework to be performed by children of eleven years or younger).

Before his untimely death in 1833 Thompson complained bitterly that the "leaders of the school of Competitive Political Economy" had simply ignored the "system of Cooperative political economy."[54] Though many of his arguments surfaced in the later work of Mill, Marx, and Engels, he received little credit for them. A portion of his estate was bequeathed to Anna Wheeler, the remainder left to trustees to advance the cause of socialism. Thompson's sisters immediately contested the terms of the will, keeping it in litigation for over twenty-five years. The value of the bequest was almost completely consumed by legal fees, poignant testimony to the costs of competition.[55]

Utopian and Scientific

The early English and Irish socialists have often been unfairly dismissed as emotional, unscientific thinkers.[56] Owen, Thompson, and Wheeler exposed important inconsistencies within classical political economy. Unlike Adam Smith, they refused to take the moral sentiments as a given, asking instead, how they were shaped by nature, culture, legal, and economic precedent.

Unlike Malthus and Ricardo, they challenged the claim that workers could never earn more than a subsistence wage. Workers could demand a larger share of the honey they produced, whether by threatening a collective sting or by changing the very structure of the hive. Early communitarian experiments seldom yielded sweet results, but they revealed obstacles to cooperation that later efforts would seek to overcome.

Thompson and Wheeler developed an explicitly feminist socialism. They argued that men and women represented groups whose interests were sometimes at odds and that gender roles themselves required reform. Efforts to understand both the ideals of family obligation and the concept of collective interests tangled socialists and feminists together from the start. The knots and tangles would vary from place to place, and the tapestry, unfolding over time, would tell a complicated tale.

NOTES TO CHAPTER II

[1] Barbara Taylor, *Eve and the New Jerusalem. Socialism and Feminism in the Nineteenth Century* (New York: Pantheon, 1983), p. 49.

[2] Ester Lowenthal, *The Ricardian Socialists* (New York: Longmans, Green, 1911), p. 98. See also Eileen Yeo, "Robert Owen and Radical Culture," in *Robert Owen, Prophet of the Poor*, eds Sidney Pollard and John Salt (Lewisburg, PA: Bucknell University Press, 1971), p. 87.

[3] Robert Owen, *The Revolution in the Mind and Practice of the Human Race*, in A. L. Morton, *The Life and Ideas*, p. 76; Amartya Sen, *Commodities and Capabilities* (London: Oxford University Press, 1999).

[4] For a modern version of this argument, see Jack P. Shonkoff and Deborah Phillips, *From Neurons to Neighborhoods: The Science of Early Child Development* (Washington, D.C.: National Academy Press, 2000).

[5] John Harrison, *Quest for the New Moral World. Robert Owen and the Owenites in Britain and America.* (New York: Charles Scribner's Sons, 1969), pp. 76, 157.

[6] P. L. Chase-Lansdale, L. S. Wakschlag, and J. Brooks-Gunn, "A Psychological Perspective on the Development of Caring in Children and Youth: The Role of the Family." *Journal of Adolescence* 18 (1995), 515–56.

[7] Daniel Goleman, *Emotional Intelligence* (New York: Bantam, 1997).

[8] Owen, *A New View of Society*, p. 108: "It becomes therefore the essence of irrationality to suppose that any human being, from the creation to this day, could deserve praise or blame, reward or punishment, for the prepossession of early education."

[9] Frank Podmore, *Robert Owen. A Biography* (New York: D. Appleton and Company, 1907), p. 375.

[10] Harriet Martineau, *Biographical Sketches, 1852–1868* (second edn) (London: Leypolt and Holt, 1869), p. 279.

[11] For Owen's views on slavery, see Cole's *Life of Robert Owen*, p. 249.

[12] Robert Owen, *A New View of Society: or, Essays on the Formation of the Human Character, Preparatory to the Development of a Plan for Gradually Ameliorating the Condition of Mankind,* third edn. (London: R. and A. Taylor, 1817), p. 15.

[13] Robert Owen, *The Book of the New Moral World, Containing the Rational System of Society* (London: Effingham Wilson, Royal Exchange, 1836).

[14] A. L. Morton, *The Life and Ideas of Robert Owen* (New York: Monthly Review Press, 1963), pp. 125, 149.

[15] See www.spartacus.schoolnet.co.uk?Rown. The reference is to *Black Dwarf*, August 20, 1817.

[16] Arthur Bestor, *Backwoods Utopias. The Sectarian Origins and the Owenite Phase of Communitarian Socialism in America: 1663–1829* (Philadelphia: University of Pennsylvania Press, 1950).

[17] Harry W. Laidler, *A History of Socialist Thought* (New York: Thomas Y. Crowell), p. 116.

[18] See Bestor, *Backwoods Utopias*; Mark Holloway, *Heavens on Earth. Utopian Communities in America 1680–1880* (London: Turnstile Press, 1951); John Humphrey Noyes, *History of American Socialisms*, first published 1870 (New York: Hillary House Publishers, 1961).

[19] Noyes, *History of American Socialisms*, p. 50.

[20] Noyes, *History of American Socialisms*, p. 64.

[21] Podmore, *Robert Owen,* p. 335.

[22] Taylor, *Eve and the New Jerusalem*, pp. 110, 268.

[23] John F. C. Harrison, *Quest for the New Moral World: Robert Owen and the Owenites in Britain and America* (New York: Charles Scribner's Sons, 1969), p. 3.

[24] Podmore, *Robert Owen*, p. 480.

[25] Taylor, *Eve and the New Jerusalem*, p. 88.

[26] Robert Owen, *Socialism or the Rational System of Society* (London, Effingham Wilson, 1840), p. 30.

[27] Taylor, *Eve and the New Jerusalem*, p. 187.

[28] He wrote, in his *Lectures on the Marriages of the Priesthood of the Old Immoral World*, "The pure and genuine chastity of nature is to have connection only with affection; and prostitution arises only when connection is induced or forced without affection; and it is always induced or forced by artificial causes, or forced by some necessity of law or custom, when it takes place without affection." See A. L. Morton, *The Life and Ideas of Robert Owen* (New York: International Publishers, 1969), p. 210.

[29] Carol A. Kolmerten, "Women's Experiences in the American Owenite Communities," pp. 38–51 in *Women in Spiritual and Communitarian Societies in the U.S.*, ed. Wendy E. Chmielewski, Louis J. Kern, and Marlyn Klee-Hartzell, (Syracuse NY: Syracuse University Press, 1993).

[30] Morton, *Life and Ideas*, p. 207.

[31] While he traveled a great deal, and lived apart from his wife much of the time, they seem to have had an amicable relationship. See Cole, *Life of Robert Owen*, p. 236.

[32] Robert Owen, *A New View of Society*, 3rd edn (London: Printed for Longman, Hurst, Rees, 1817), pp. 74–5.

[33] Alexander Gray, *The Socialist Tradition. Moses to Lenin* (New York: Longmans, Green and Co., 1947), p. 208.

[34] Wally Seccombe, *Weathering the Storm. Working-Class Families from the Industrial Revolution to the Fertility Decline* (London: Verso, 1993), p. 79.

[35] Patricia James, *Population Malthus* (New York: Routledge, 2006), p. 188.

[36] Chris Nyland and Tom Heenan, "William Thompson and Anna Doyle Wheeler: A Marriage of Minds on Jeremy Bentham's Doorstep," 241–61 in Robert Dimand and Chris Nyland, eds., *The Status of Women in Classical Economic Thought* (Cheltenham UK: Edward Elgar, 2003); Richard Pankhurst, *William Thompson, Pioneer Socialist* (London: Pluto Press, 1954), p. 18.

[37] Pankhurst, *William Thompson*, p. 52.

[38] James Mill, "Article on Government," reprinted in Susan Groag Bell and Karen M. Offen, editors, *Women, the Family and Freedom*: 1880–1950 (Stanford: Stanford University Press, 1983). Edmund Burke had made a similar argument years before, railing against expansion of the male franchise.

[39] William Thompson, *Appeal of One Half the Human Race, Women, Against the Pretensions of the Other Half, Men, to Retain Them in Political, and Thence in Civil and Domestic Slavery* (London: Printed for Longman, Hurst, Rees, Orme, Brown, and Green, 1825). For more discussion of the issue of authorship of the *Appeal*, see Taylor, *Eve and the New Jerusalem*, pp. 22–3.

[40] Abby L. Cory, "Wheeler and Thompson's Appeal: The Rhetorical Re-visioning of Gender," *New Hibernia Review*, 8:2 (2004), 106–20.

[41] Thompson, *Appeal of One-Half the Human Race*, p. B.

[42] Ibid., p. 63.

[43] Cited in Taylor, *Eve and the New Jerusalem*, p. 38.

[44] Thompson, *Labor Rewarded* (London: Hunt and Clarke, 1827).

[45] Pankhurst, *William Thompson*, p. 26.

[46] Thompson's approach foreshadows that of a contemporary economist, John Roemer, who rejects Marx's labor theory of value as a theory of relative prices but models the influence of unequal property allocations on the exploitation of labor. See his *Free to Lose. An Introduction to Marxist Economic Philosophy* (Cambridge: Harvard University Press, 1988).

[47] Thompson, *Inquiry*, p. 73.

[48] Ibid., p. 367.

[49] Ibid., p. 369.

[50] Ibid., p. 369.

[51] Ibid., p. 373.

[52] Ibid., pp. 544–5.

[53] Ibid., p. 549.

[54] William Thompson, *Labor Rewarded*, p. 46.

[55] Pankhurst, *William Thompson*, p. 134.

[56] Robert Heilbroner's classic *The Worldly Philosophers. The Lives, Times, and Ideas of the Great Economic Thinkers* warns that "There is no use trying to read the Utopians"

(New York: Simon and Schuster, 1986), p. 330. Mark Blaug ignores the early socialists altogether, attributing "the first appearance of the subject of socialism in a major treatise of economics" to John Stuart Mill's *Principles of Political Economy*. See his *Economic Theory in Retrospect*, 4th edn (New York: Cambridge University Press, 1985), p. 191. E. K. Hunt, a rare exception, gives William Thompson careful consideration. See his *History of Economic Thought: A Critical Perspective* (Belmont, CA: Wadsworth, 1979).

CHAPTER 12

Equal Opportunities

God has given me a mission to call the poor, and women, to a new destiny, to give admittance into the sacred Family of Man to all those who have hitherto been excluded from it, or treated only as minors therein.

Père Enfantin

The early French socialists, like their counterparts in Britain, clung to family values even as they rejected patriarchal norms. Prosper Enfantin—who called himself Father—published the announcement above in *Black's Morning Chronicle* in April 1832, hoping to recruit English-speakers to his cause.[1] Critiques of individualism flew back and forth across the channel. Anna Wheeler served as an important go-between and John Stuart Mill an occasional translator.[2] The French socialists put greater emphasis than their British counterparts on the simple principle of equal opportunity. They imagined grand communitarian schemes with an exuberance that Americans found particularly attractive.

France remained a relatively traditional, family-based economy, making uneven progress toward democratic governance. Critics of the existing order defined themselves more in opposition to patriarchal and feudal institutions than to capitalist ones. French feminists deployed the rhetoric of rights to challenge the sexual double standard, but they also invoked principles of social obligation, moving especially quickly to demand state support for motherhood.

Napoleonic Code

Revolutions tend to create opposite if not entirely equal forces of reaction. In France, such forces weakened progress toward democracy. Napoleon began installing himself in power in 1799, establishing a male meritocracy in which military and civil service promotions were based at least in part on actual performance rather than family origin. He also established a new legal code and a national educational system that featured secondary schooling for boys. These innovations helped provide a training ground for a new middle class. But Napoleon aspired to empire, and overreached on the battlefield. After his defeat at Waterloo the Bourbon monarchy returned to the throne. Despite small movements in a democratic direction in 1830, and later in 1848, France remained in the grip of a small, if somewhat factionalized political elite.

The French Civil Code of 1803 formalized many of the traditional prerogatives of patriarchal power. Men enjoyed the right to use physical force to compel the obedience of their wives and minor children and to control their earnings. Married women were allowed to retain some rights over property they brought into the marriage, but all income generated from such property belonged by law to their husbands. A man could force a woman who conceived his child out of wedlock to marry him if he chose, but an unmarried mother could make no claims upon the father of her child either for marriage or support. The right to divorce was heavily restricted and based on an explicit double standard (a wife's adultery, but not a husband's, provided grounds). Only single women retained any of the rights the Revolution had bestowed, remaining entitled, alongside their brothers, to an equal share of their parents' estates.[3]

Napoleon, famously outraged by his wife Josephine's infidelities, once referred to women as "mere machines for making children."[4] France's political economists were not quite so blunt, but Jean-Baptiste Say prescribed restrictions on women's opportunities (see Chapter 9). Catholics, invoking Pope XIII's Encyclical *Rerum Novarum*, declared that women were best suited to work as wives and mothers. Anti-clericalists often agreed with them on this point. Jules Michelet, the most famous historian of the period, reiterated Rousseau's fears that women would inevitably cause political disorder.[5] The artist and illustrator Honoré Daumier caricatured the "femmes nouvelles" who sought rights for themselves as neurotic hags.

Many French republicans, even the so-called anarchists, hoped to keep their women under control at home. Pierre-Joseph Proudhon, famous for his rejection of inherited privilege and his slogan that "property is theft" called for a decentralized economy based on agricultural production and handicrafts. He proclaimed that every man should be master of his own home, where women should serve their husbands and children and refrain from any contact with other men.[6] Separation of the male and female spheres seemed even more important to these French men than to prominent British thinkers.

Secular Humanism

Robert Owen had earned credentials as a capitalist; William Thompson inherited an estate. The best-known French socialists were, by contrast, men whose family fortunes had been dissipated or destroyed. It was as though they had little left to lose. Henri de Saint-Simon was an impoverished nobleman who had served with the revolutionary army in the United States. He sympathized with the French Revolution, and after surviving it, decided to conceptualize the next step forward for mankind. As he put it, he felt himself pregnant with the future of humanity.[7]

De Saint-Simon's basic views were less socialist than meritocratic. He argued that an economic system based on skill and effort would inevitably prevail over one based on privileges of birth. Men and women should be rewarded for virtue on earth, as well as in heaven.[8] France was already dependent on a new set of skills. What would happen if France lost fifty of her best physicists, chemists, mechanical engineers, businessmen, locksmiths, etc., comprising, in sum the top thousand scientists, artists, and artisans of the country? The effects would be far more ruinous, he predicted, than the loss of ten thousand members of the French nobility.[9]

But de Saint-Simon was not a simple individualist. He believed that a misplaced egoism was undermining French society.[10] His own studies of "universal interests" led him to divide men and women into three groups based on three different human capacities: feeling, thinking, and acting. Given the opportunity to harmoniously express these capacities, individuals would work happily in concert. The need to express one's own true nature trumped more abstract principles and pecuniary incentives.

The obstacles to the expression of de Saint-Simon's own true nature were formidable. He lived in penury, aided only by a few occasional collaborators. During one bout of depression he shot his own eye out in an unsuccessful suicide attempt. As he lay dying of natural causes in 1825 he reiterated the paternalistic convictions he shared with Owen. All members of society should be afforded the greatest possible opportunity to develop their capabilities.[11] Employers could increase efficiency by rewarding performance and fostering the loyalty and affection of their employees.[12]

The Sexual Radicals

De Saint-Simon's most passionate followers planned to redesign families rather than businesses. Under the leadership of Prosper Enfantin, they became known as sexual rather than economic radicals. Enfantin, literally "the childlike one", or, with his preferred title, Father Childlike, displayed theatrical flair. His followers dressed in blue waistcoats with red sashes, outfits that buttoned behind and therefore required mutual cooperation (you fasten me and I'll fasten you). Enfantin announced that the sentiment of love was superior to the faculty of reason and called for a new church with a Mother as well as a Father.[13] Like de Saint-Simon, he exhorted everyone to express his own true nature. Men and women alike should enjoy the freedom to change partners if they so desired.

Most appealing to Enfantin's female followers was his attack on the sexual double standard, accompanied by his denunciation of prostitution. Since about 1803, the French had sanctioned and regulated the sale of sexual services in two ways. Official tolerances were awarded to brothels that submitted their workers to periodic medical examination and observed certain rules, such as not locating near a school or a church. At the same time, the police could arrest virtually any woman they believed to be soliciting on the streets. With no right to trial or due process, women were legally subject to forced examination and possible incarceration.[14] Male clients enjoyed the benefits of medical supervision (a not inconsiderable benefit in the age of syphilis), while poor and working-class women were vulnerable to police harassment whether they sold their sexual services or not. Official policies were legitimated by an engineer named Alexandre Parent-Duchâtelet, whose quantitative analysis of prostitution in Paris proved enormously influential.[15] When asked why even the most debauched men were not subject to arrest for solicitation, he explained that they would never stand for such an obvious abrogation of "the sacred principle of individual liberty."[16]

Aquinas had likened prostitution to a sewer system (see Chapter 1). Parent-Duchâtelet's previous research (which he explained had mentally and physically prepared him for his new investigations) had focused on Parisian sewers. Still, he preferred a more modern, industrial metaphor for prostitution, likening it to the safety valve on a steam engine.[17] This particular safety valve let off impressive quantities of steam. By mid-century, the number of registered prostitutes in Paris, surely an underestimate of the total, numbered about 34,000, many of them lodged in official brothels.[18] This was almost three times the number of women the 1851 census enumerated as employees of textile mills; it amounted to one prostitute for about every sixteen married women.

De Saint-Simon's enthusiasts considered legalized prostitution the embodiment of bourgeois hypocrisy. Some women endorsed Enfantin's concept of free love as an alternative to the sexual double standard, wearing red ribbons to signal their own enthusiasm for what he called the "rehabilitation of the flesh." But free love was far riskier for women than for men. Out-of-wedlock births were on the increase, representing between 30 percent and 50 percent of all births in Paris and Lyon by mid-century.[19] Since the French Civil Code denied unmarried women legal recourse to paternity suits, abandonment was common. An illegitimate child himself, Enfantin had refused to marry the mother of his own son Arthur. Instead, he asked the men of the group to ceremonially accept joint responsibility for the boy as "social fathers". Arthur's specific fate remains unknown.[20]

Some of Enfantin's apostles traveled to England to woo influential thinkers like Thomas Carlyle and the young John Stuart Mill. Both Britons liked the emphasis on equal opportunity and the abolition of inherited privilege. Mill, at least, appreciated the criticisms of patriarchal power. But when French authorities arrested Enfantin and others on charges of public immorality in 1832, free love and prostitution trumped discussion of all other issues. Enfantin denounced French law for treating prostitutes as grapes harvested, fermented, and bottled for men's enjoyment, and announced that two of his women followers would present his case.[21]

The judge promptly ordered the women removed and sentenced the defendant to a year in jail.

Some of the apostles retreated to a rural estate where they vowed to live together chastely and share domestic tasks. Widely-circulated cartoons ridiculed men doing laundry and scraping carrots, and the group gradually disbanded.[22] Its more restless members traveled to Egypt in search of a new Messiah and more sunshine.

Le Tribune des Femmes

A small group of working-class women who had previously distanced themselves from Enfantin were more strongly drawn to the cause of economic rather than sexual reform. Suzanne Voilquin, Pauline Roland, and Jeanne Deroin, among others, founded a feminist newspaper written entirely by women.[23] Anna Wheeler, by then spending much of her time in France, urged them on. One of their proclamations, printed in Robert Owen's magazine *The Crisis*, called attention to the paradox of feminine altruism: "We are born as free as men— their infancy is as helpless as ours, and ours as theirs. Without our tenderness, our sympathy and our care, they could never grow up to be our oppressors."[24]

The founders of the *Tribune* called for a cross-class coalition of women bound by their common role as caregivers.[25] They criticized French family law and made a strong case for greater public spending on children. They explained why collective living would promote a more efficient organization of housework by taking advantage of economies of scale. In *The New Social Contract* Madame Casaubon argued that half of all communally held land should be vested in women to provide a "mother's tribute" that would repay women's reproductive services to society.[26] These maternalist values did not prevent them from reiterating principles of equal opportunity for women:

> If you preserve this old belief that women's sole purpose is to bear children, clean man's house, and give him pleasure; if you do not associate woman and the people, each according to their talents, in all branches of the social order; and if you do not give flight to genius in whatever sex or class it is found, you will not be following the path of god, who wants a place and happiness for everyone, and you will always fail.[27]

Other socialist feminists loosely associated with the de Saint-Simonians, such as Claire Démar, linked the exploitation of women to the exploitation of the proletariat. Flora Tristan gained a wide audience with an autobiography and a novel that publicized feminist ideas.[28] But success proved short-lived for *Le Tribune des Femmes*, which ceased publication in 1834. Two of its most important contributors later played a visible role in the French revolution of 1848, unsuccessfully demanding female suffrage.[29] Others were swept up in a new enthusiasm for yet another visionary scheme.

The Calculus of Harmony

Charles Fourier claimed to find inspiration in the exorbitant price of an apple in a Parisian restaurant. He became convinced that he could design a more efficient way to produce and deliver goods.[30] Many of his publications preceded those of de Saint-Simon, but his ideas seemed to find greater leverage when interpreted by others. Unlike other socialists of his day, Fourier believed that the pursuit of self-interest served as an effective incentive to productive work.[31] He simply did not believe that the market economy of his day successfully mobilized the pursuit of self-interest for the common good. Just the opposite, he argued—it was anarchic and inefficient. It allowed—it even encouraged—merchants to charge excessively high prices. A system of many small producers failed to take advantage of economies of scale. It condemned workers to repetitive and monotonous activities that inevitably sapped their energy and diminished their incentives to work. It confined women to repetitive and redundant domestic labor.

As a merchant and traveling salesman, Fourier came into contact with much suffering from poverty and unemployment. He was offended by the low productivity of labor. He argued that most people were employed in deadening jobs that failed to fully utilize their energies, and that nearly two-thirds of all workers were performing virtually useless tasks.[32] A more efficient economic organization promised enormous benefits to all—if only a benefactor-capitalist would advance the money necessary to set up the first community or "phalanstery".

These practical suggestions were packaged in strangely mystical terms. The proper combination of individuals within the phalanstery could create the necessary harmonic chords. The minimum number of individuals required was 814, a figure Fourier arrived at by calculating the probable permutations of the requisite passions (the details have been lost to history).

He christened the society that would emerge from these associations Harmony, and developed an elaborate conceptual framework based on the correspondence between the passions, the chromatic scale, and the colors of the spectrum. The mystical qualities of a plan influenced by the principles of both tarot and chess would align the forces of cooperation and create an army devoted to production rather than to warfare.

The phalansteries were not to be egalitarian communities. Members would be remunerated according to their individual contributions of capital, talent, and effort (the precise measurement of these contributions was not addressed). The dining rooms would offer meals at three different prices— luxurious, inexpensive, or takeaway to be consumed in one's own private room.[33] On the other hand, inherited privilege would be abolished.[34] A basic subsistence income or "social minimum" for those unwilling or unable to work would provide a safety net of sorts, as well as a guarantee that all individuals had the freedom to choose their employment. Variety was also assured, since Fourier believed that no one truly enjoyed performing the same activity for more than two hours at a time. Work tasks would, therefore, be organized in two-hour shifts. Any time lost in making the transition between different activities would be regained by the freshness and enthusiasm with which work would be performed. Some tasks might remain so onerous that no one truly enjoyed performing them: these could be performed by Drudges who would only be called upon to work occasionally.

Some unpleasant tasks could be assigned to those who would revel in them. Fourier believed that two-thirds of all boys and one-third of all girls between the ages of nine and fifteen loved getting dirty. This group, organized into a formal corps called the Little Hordes, would be assigned such tasks as cleaning the stables and maintaining the sewers. The children's enthusiasm and efficiency would provide a model for others and the community as a whole would honor and celebrate them. Every morning their charge would sound "in an uproar of bells, chimes, drums, and trumpets, a howling of dogs and a bellowing of bulls. Then the Hordes, led by their Khans and Druids, rush forward with a great shout, passing before the priests who sprinkle them with holy water."[35] Owen had suggested making children do the housework, but he had never made it sound like so much fun.

The greatest advantage of collective association would be the reorganization and centralization of domestic tasks, such as food preparation and childcare. Fourier announced that the constraints of domesticity had reduced women's productivity to one-fifteenth that of men, although they were potentially capable of producing, on average, three-quarters as much (the basis for his calculations remains unclear). Fertility decline would release women from maternal obligations and free them for more directly productive activities, in which they would be disadvantaged only by their lesser physical strength. These calculations help explain why Fourier believed that the status of women was an important indicator of the progress of civilization.

Recognizing the difficulties of a transition towards more equal opportunity, Fourier proposed a form of affirmative action that would reserve one-half of all jobs in the most lucrative fields for women, but explained that about one-eighth of all women had a natural inclination for performing childcare.[36] Fortunately, this number (plucked from his imagination, like all others) would be sufficient to meet collective needs, sparing men from responsibilities such as changing diapers. Fourier also believed that women were particularly skilled in the calculation of the erotic sympathies, the algebra of love. This gift would be put to good use in managing the sexual passions of the association, which were every bit as important to its harmony as total productive output.

The Sexual Welfare State

In the eighteenth century, interests had often been counterposed to the passions, as cooler, more rational, less violent motives.[37] But most nineteenth-century writers, including Fourier, considered the pursuit of profit a passion as well as an interest. Fourier outdistanced all his contemporaries in his eagerness to treat greed and lust in parallel terms:

> This theory of agricultural association, which is going to change the fortunes of the human race, appeals to the passions common to everybody, and seduces them with the allurements of profit and sensual pleasure; this guarantees its success among barbarians and savages as well as among civilized people, since the passions are the same everywhere.[38]

He also went further in challenging conventional sexual mores, although most of his specific proposals remained buried in manuscripts that might otherwise have landed him and his followers in jail. *The New Amorous*

World differed from Owen's *The New Moral World* exactly as its title suggested it would, celebrating sexual desire whether or not accompanied by sincere affections. He portrayed lust, like greed, as a human energy source that could be managed, channeled, and harnessed, but not repressed.

With characteristic attention to detail, he catalogued the *Gamut of the Misfortunes of the Conjugal State*, enumerating all imaginable forms and methods of cuckoldry, which he believed should simply be accepted. Monogamy was out of date. Like work, sex could be improved by variation. Such improvements should not be left to chance. Experienced experts, predominantly older women, would provide advice and guidance in determining and satisfying libidinal needs, according to Fourier's typology of passions and theory of omnigamy. Grandmotherly care and oversight would be combined with individual choice. The end result would be an increase in sexual satisfaction that a modern commentator has described as a "state of permanent orgasm."[39]

The parallels between the productive and the sensual dimensions of Fourier's utopia became explicit in the concept of the "sexual minimum", a safety net analogous to the minimum wage.[40] Individuals should not be denied satisfaction simply because they were unattractive, old, or cranky. Their needs would be met by altruists who, aspiring to sexual sainthood, were following a prescribed path that included seven stages or tests and payment of an amorous tribute to their elders. The ceremonial aspects of this process parodied Catholic ritual with serious intent. Just as no one would be forced to accept a job because it was his or her only alternative, no one would be forced to accept a partner because he or she was their only means of obtaining sexual services. Fourier's own disappointments in this arena were transparent.

Fourier's celebration of the passions has been compared to that of de Sade.[41] The comparison, however, is misplaced. Fourier condemned as a perversion any element of coercion or violence in sexual relationships. Sexual pleasure, in his view, was weakened rather than strengthened by possession and control. The phalanstery was designed not merely to pre-empt family responsibilities but also to extend them. Fourier described a "ralliement de famillisme" in which adult Harmonians would virtually adopt the children who worked alongside them on various tasks. The word passion, for

Fourier, encompassed parental and familial feelings, as well as sexual desire. Malthus embraced self-love as the mainspring of human society. Fourier embraced sexual love. No longer a "recreation which detracts from work," love was to be the "soul and vehicle, the mainspring of all works and of the whole of universal attraction."[42]

Such productive, optimistic hedonism violated Christian precepts. Dismissing the Malthusian assertion that contraception was immoral, Fourier veered to the opposite extreme, describing it as virtuous, obvious, and easy. He also expressed great interest in what he called a "third sex". He may himself have been bisexual, but he reserved his greatest enthusiasm for lesbianism, noting in his manuscripts that "sapphism = perfection." He believed that same-sex relationships would not only help women obtain their sexual minimum and free them to pursue other goals, but would also stimulate men to better behavior.[43] In order to compete with women for lovers men would be forced to adopt more gentle and attentive ways.

Such arguments were easily parodied at the time. Yet Fourier's basic economic vision of centralized, rationalized management was hardly radical. It did not depend on the reconfiguration of self-interest or the success of democratic governance. It did not demand perfect equality. Its exuberant promises of prosperity and plenty held more appeal than the vows of poverty associated with Christian communism. After his death in 1837 Fourier's fans winnowed the sexuality and fantasy from his approach, hoping to improve its harvest.

Brook Farm

Since few Americans could read French, selective translation could work wonders. The number of communitarian experiments explicitly based on Fourier's principles outnumbered those based on those of Owen or de Saint-Simon. A disciple named Albert Brisbane proved a most successful agent, compiling a collection entitled *The Social Destiny of Man*.[44] Horace Greeley, editor of the *New York Tribune*, was entranced. Some of America's most famous writers, including Nathaniel Hawthorne, Henry David Thoreau, and Ralph Waldo Emerson engaged one way or another with new communitarian schemes.

The Owenite experiment at New Harmony had failed in 1828, but other communities, founded by the religious groups such as the Rappites and the Shakers, remained afloat. Meanwhile, the ocean had become more turbulent. As factory employment grew, intense price competition and new waves of immigration combined to make prosperity seem precarious. Trade unions elbowed their way into existence. The young women mill workers of Lowell went out on strike in 1834. A major depression in 1837 was followed by several years of stagnation.[45]

These problems did not escape the attention of a New England intelligentsia whose disapproval of slavery sensitized them to the concept of economic immorality. Some, like Henry David Thoreau, expressed their distaste for the dictates of commercial capitalism by withdrawing from it. Others hoped to further the cause of cooperation. Experiments with names like "Hopedale" and "Fruitlands" began to multiply. In Northampton, Massachusetts, an abolitionist community invested in a new silk manufactory.[46] George Ripley, a Unitarian minister in Boston, bid farewell to his congregation in order to embark with friends on a collective enterprise known as Brook Farm.

Originally set up as a joint-stock company, Brook Farm officially converted to Fourierist principles (à la Brisbane) in 1845. Its avowed aim was to unify and more fairly distribute manual and mental labor. Ralph Waldo Emerson declined an invitation to join but expressed his sympathy for its basic principles, writing "In a day of small, sour, and fierce schemes, one is admonished and cheered by a project of such friendly aims."[47] Henry David Thoreau visited for at least a day, as did Margaret Fuller, author of *Women in the Nineteenth Century*. Nathaniel Hawthorne joined the farm for a while, cheerfully shoveling manure and later writing a fictionalized account of his experience that included a fearful caricature of Margaret.[48]

The farm became the symbolic center of the Fourierist movement in America, as Ripley took over editorship of its journal, *The Harbinger*. Still, the enterprise retained an Owenite emphasis on the fullest possible development of human capabilities, and Ripley himself echoed Owen when he described selfishness and cold-heartedness as "poisonous weeds that a false system of culture has produced."[49] Socialism would, he hoped, succeed by growing better fruit and producing more ample honey (the beehive was the official emblem of the farm). Sadly, a new phalanstery building caught fire the day after it had been finished, and two years of concerted collective effort went up in flames. The fragile finances of the farm collapsed.

In a way, Emerson had predicted its demise, arguing no system of social engineering could skip the "faculty of life, which spawns and scorns systems and system-makers, which eludes all conditions, which makes or supplants a thousand phalanxes and New Harmonies with each pulsation."[50] What Emerson did not explain was how this faculty of life might later modify the capitalist system, nudging it closer to a welfare state than its early advocates imagined possible. Both the concept of equal opportunity and the right to public education would later be inscribed in law.

Crazy Attempts

Apart from fans of the English school of political economy, like Jean-Baptiste Say, French political economists had little confidence in capitalism.[51] Yet moral condemnations of British and American greed were often grounded in patriarchal loyalties that limited room for socialist feminist maneuver. Those who raised issues of sexual as well as economic rights for women made themselves extremely vulnerable. In his *History of Political Economy in Europe*, first published in 1837, Jerome-Adolphe Blanqui remarked that de Saint-Simon's "crazy attempts at the emancipation of women" had discredited his larger arguments, a claim that Karl Marx and Friedrich Engels would reiterate.[52] August Comte, who served as de Saint-Simon's secretary for several years, later renounced his mentor's views, explaining that women's emotional and moral character suited them for family responsibilities alone.[53]

Still, de Saint-Simon and Fourier expanded the boundaries of economic vision, creating a cultural space for the more moderate ideas that John Stuart Mill and Harriet Taylor, among others, would soon articulate. Through modern eyes, their critiques of the sexual double standard look rather prescient. Individualist principles helped dislodge patriarchal ones. Socialist hopes for greater equality between the sexes, though not borne out for many years to come, would fare better than their hopes for more cooperation among men.

NOTES TO CHAPTER 12

[1] Richard K. P. Pankhurst, *The Saint Simonians Mill and Carlyle* (London: Lalibela Books, 1957), p. 84.

[2] H. Desroche, "Images and Echoes of Owenism in Nineteenth-Century France," in *Robert Owen. Prophèt of the Poor*, eds Sidney Pollard and John Salt (Lewisburg: Bucknell University Press, 1971), 239–84.

[3] James F. McMillan, *France and Women, 1789–1914* (New York: Routledge, 2000), p. 37.

[4] E. Bruce, *Napoleon and Josephine: An Improbable Marriage* (London: Weidenfeld and Nicholson, 1995), p. 155.

[5] McMillan, *France and Women*, p. 110.

[6] Claire Goldberg Moses, *French Feminism in the Nineteenth Century* (Binghamton, NY: State University of New York Press, 1985), p. 154.

[7] Susan K. Grogan, *French Socialism and Sexual Difference. Women and the New Society, 1803–44* (London: Macmillan, 1992), p. 149.

[8] Arthur John Booth, *Saint-Simon and Saint-Simonism. A Chapter in the History of Socialism in France*. (London: Longmans, Green, 1871), pp. 57, 88.

[9] Henri de Saint-Simon, "First Extract from the 'Organizer,'" in *Social Organization, The Science of Man and Other Writings*, ed. Felix Markham, first published 1819 (New York: Harper Torchbooks, 1964), pp. 72–3.

[10] Henri de Saint-Simon, "New Christianity," in *Social Organization*.

[11] Frank E. Manuel, *The Prophets of Paris* (Cambridge: Harvard University Press, 1962), p. 125.

[12] Ibid., p. 177; Alfred Cobban, *A History of Modern France* (New York: Braziller, 1965), 162–3.

[13] Claire Goldberg Moses, *French Feminism in the Nineteenth Century* (Albany, NY: State University of New York Press, 1984), p. 44.

[14] Jill Harsin, *Policing Prostitution in Nineteenth-Century Paris* (Princeton: Princeton University Press, 1985).

[15] Alexandre Parent-Duchâtelet, *La Prostitution á Paris au XIXieme Siecle,* First published 1836 (Paris: Editions de Seuil, 1981).

[16] Harsin, *Policing Prostitution*, p. 125.

[17] Ibid., p. 13.

[18] Grogan, *French Socialism*, p. 3.

[19] Claire Goldberg Moses, " 'Difference in Historical Perspective," pp. 17–84 in *Feminism, Socialism, and French Romanticism*, ed. Claire Goldberg Moses and Leslie Wahl Rabine (Bloomington: Indiana University Press, 1993), p. 57.

[20] Grogan, *French Socialism*, p. 151.

[21] Manuel, *Prophets of Paris*, p. 188.

[22] Moses, "Difference in Historical Perspective," p. 43.

[23] McMillan, *France and Women*, p. 82. See also Evelyn Forget, "Saint-Simonian Feminism," *Feminist Economics* 7:1 (2001), 79–96.

[24] Pankhurst, *The Saint-Simonians*, p. 109.

[25] Jeanne Deroin, "Call to Women," pp. 282–4 in Moses and Rabine, *Feminism, Socialism, and French Romanticism*.

[26] Grogan, *French Socialism*, p. 136.

[27] Jeanne-Désirée [Veret], "Improvement of the Destiny of Women and the People through a New Household Organization," p. 290 in Moses and Rabine, *Feminism, Socialism, and French Romanticism*.

[28] McMillan, *France and Women,* p 84.

[29] McMillan, *France and Women,* p. 82.

[30] Jonathan Beecher and Richard Bienvenu, Introduction to *The Utopian Vision of Charles Fourier. Selected Texts on Work, Love, and Passionate Attraction* (Columbia, Missouri: University of Missouri Press, 1983), p. 1.

[31] Charles Fourier, *The Theory of the Four Movements*, edited by Gareth Stedman Jones and Ian Patterson, first published 1808 (Cambridge: Cambridge University Press, 1996), p. 11.

[32] Jonathan Beecher, *Charles Fourier. The Visionary and His World* (Berkeley: University of California Press, 1986), p. 199.

[33] Alexander Gray, *The Socialist Tradition. Moses to Lenin* (New York: Longmans, 1947), p. 184.

[34] Harry Laidler, *A History of Socialist Thought* (New York: Thomas Y. Crowell, 1927).

[35] Charles Fourier, from *The Utopian Vision, Selected Texts*, p. 321.

[36] Grogan, *French Socialism*, p. 46.

[37] Albert Hirschman, *The Passions and the Interests: Political Arguments for Capitalism Before its Triumph* (Princeton: Princeton University Press, 1977).

[38] Fourier, *The Theory of the Four Movements*, p. 12.

[39] Manuel, *Prophets of Paris*, p. 228.

[40] Beecher, *Charles Fourier*, p. 305; Grogran, *French Socialism*, p. 63.

[41] Beecher, *Charles Fourier*, p. 222.

[42] Fourier, *The Utopian Vision*, p. 59.

[43] Grogan, *French Socialism*, p. 65.

[44] Albert Brisbane, *Social Destiny of Man, or Association and Reorganization of Industry* (Philadelphia: C.F. Stollmeyer, 1840).

[45] Samuel Resneck, "The Social History of an American Depression, 1837–1843," *American Historical Review* 40 (1935), 662–87.

[46] Christopher Clark, *The Communitarian Moment: The Radical Challenge of the Northampton Association* (Ithaca, NY: Cornell University Press, 1995).

[47] Ralph Waldo Emerson, "Fourierism and the Socialists," *The Dial* III (1842), 86–96.

[48] Sterling F. Delano, *Brook Farm: The Dark Side of Utopia* (Cambridge: Belknap Press, 2004).

[49] Cited in Lance Newman, "Thoreau's Natural Community and Utopian Socialism," *American Literature* 75:3 (2003), p. 530.

[50] Emerson, "Fourier and the Socialists," p. 88.

[51] Anthony Waterman, "The English School of Political Economy," in The *New Palgrave Dictionary of Economics,* 2nd edn (New York: Palgrave Macmillan, 2008).

[52] Jerome-Adolphe Blanqui, *History of Political Economy in Europe* (New York: G.P. Putnam's Sons, 1880), p. 502.

[53] Oscar Haac, ed., *The Correspondence of John Stuart Mill and Auguste Comte* (New York: Transaction Press, 1995).

CHAPTER 13

The Subjection of Women

All the selfish propensities, the self-worship, the unjust self-preference, which exist among mankind, have their source and root in, and derive their principal nourishment from, the present constitution of the relation between men and women.
John Stuart Mill

The early socialist feminists celebrated female altruism and regarded it as a model for society as a whole. In this sense they emphasized the importance of differences between men and women. The early liberal feminists chose a simpler, and in the short run, more successful strategy, celebrating the masculine pursuit of self-interest as a strategy that women could and should adopt for themselves. Demanding equality, they de-emphasized gender differences. It is, however, difficult to find perfect examples of either extreme, and both feminisms were united by their discomfort with the traditional dualism that encouraged self-interest in men but demanded altruism from women.

Liberal feminism emerged most vigorously in countries with a strong tradition of individualism and adherence to *laissez faire*. Still, the French utopian socialists influenced even writers as confident of individualism as John Stuart Mill, who recognized the need to redefine and, in a sense, redistribute the pursuit of individual self-interest. The sexual double standard also came under scrutiny. Those who professed horror at the very mention of free love could not ignore the moral inconsistencies and economic realities of state-regulated prostitution. The line separating desire from lust, like that separating self-interest from greed, was drawn differently for women than for men. Efforts to redraw these lines in less gendered terms provoked magnificent contention.

The Census of England and Wales began enumerating individual occupations in 1851, often assigning married women the same occupation as their husband on the presumption that the couple worked side by side. In 1871, women accounted for 31 percent of those defined as "economically active," significantly more than in the United States at the same time (but probably reflecting an upward bias). Domestic service was similarly predominant, accounting for 46 percent of the total. Agricultural employment was much lower and manufacturing employment concomitantly greater than among women in the United States or France.[1] Women in manufacturing (a term defined more broadly in the English than in the U.S. census) accounted for 40 percent of all women with gainful occupations.[2] English economists were forced to take heed of an increasingly visible transformation of women's work.

The Partnership

John Stuart Mill was the heir apparent of the British tradition of classical political economy. His father, the eminent James Mill, instructed him in Latin and Greek before the age of six, and helped him complete his first survey of political economy at age thirteen. Jeremy Bentham became his friend and tutor in utilitarian principles. As a young adult, John Stuart worked under his father's supervision for the British East India Company. Perhaps because he was too carefully groomed, his grooming went awry.

A certain nonconformity became apparent with his arrest in 1823 at the tender age of seventeen for distributing Francis Place's handbills of contraceptive advice. The young Mill was also drawn to arguments on behalf of female emancipation. Rather than courting a suitable merchant's daughter who would devote herself to his creature comforts (and provide him with income from her property), Mill fell in love with a married woman who loved political debate. He met Harriet Taylor in 1830, and devoted himself to a circumspect friendship and correspondence with her until her husband's death in 1849. After a decent mourning period, they married. Over the long course of their relationship, Taylor deepened Mill's sympathy for both socialist and feminist views.[3]

Mill made his formal intellectual debut in 1848 with the publication of his *Principles of Political Economy, with Some of their Applications to Social Philosophy*. The book restated many of the principles of Ricardian and Malthusian theories of production but emphasized the need for more attention to the distribution of income. He clung to the basic utilitarian creed—promoting the greatest good of the greatest number. He noted that while laws of nature could not be changed, social institutions such as marriage and inheritance could be redesigned. He favored competition but criticized the accumulation of unearned property and privilege. He disliked the prospect of a potentially intrusive central government and feared the abrogation of individual rights.

Historical context often determined whether Mill was called a socialist, a liberal, or an authoritarian, an issue on which eminent scholars have often disagreed.[4] His socialist tendencies would have seemed more radical had publication of his *Principles* not coincided with the French Revolution of 1848. In the context of policies already being put into place in Paris, Mill's tone seemed cautionary.[5] Left-leaning economists who characterized Mill as a timid wishful thinker ignored his radical arguments on behalf of contraception and women's rights writ large.[6] Insistence that such issues lay outside the provenance of political economy made it easier to deprecate Mill's contributions.[7]

Mill's interest in gender equality led him to develop a more sophisticated analysis of self-interest than his predecessors. He and Taylor (with whom he discussed the writing of the *Principles* in some detail) agreed that classical political economists offered a simplistic view of human motivation. In a chapter devoted to a discussion of communism, Mill emphasized that individual values were culturally constructed and susceptible to change: "Mankind are capable of a far greater amount of public spirit than the present age is accustomed to suppose possible. History bears witness to the success with which large bodies of human beings may be trained to feel the public interest their own."[8]

This idealistic pronouncement was reinforced by the shrewd observation that the existing capitalist system did not actually make very good use of self-interest, because it offered workers a wage determined by a prevailing market wage, rather than a share of the total product. An entirely rational worker would minimize his effort on the job, knowing that only his employer would benefit from it. A socialist system that adhered to the de Saint-Simonian principle "from each according to their ability, to each according to their work" might actually elicit higher productivity. If individuals could learn to compete with each other over whom could best contribute to the public good, so much the better.

In Mill's view the very ubiquity of self-interest decreed the need for democratic guarantees of individual rights. He invoked Ricardo's analysis of landlords, capitalists, and workers in terms that paralleled his analysis of relations between men and women:

> All privileged and powerful classes, as such, have used their power in the interest of their own selfishness, and have indulged their self-importance in despising, and not in lovingly caring for, those who were, in their estimation, degraded, by being under the necessity of working for their benefit. I do not affirm that what has always been must always be, or that human improvement has no tendency to correct the intensely selfish feelings engendered by power, but though the evil may be lessened, it cannot be eradicated, until the power itself is withdrawn.[9]

Mill's comments on gender inequalities in the *Principles* converged with his larger economic analysis. The traditional patriarchal family, he observed, was outmoded because it was inconsistent with large-scale production and more complex forms of economic organization.[10] Owen was right—despotism within the family would invariably lead to despotism without. Self-interest could be a positive force, Mill implied, only in a world of equal rights for all.

The most striking chapter of the *Principles* called for a transition to more cooperative modes of production that could preserve the benefits of competition. It also predicted that the future well-being of the working class would depend on improvements in women's position. Mill described the sexual division of labor in paid employment, which crowded women into a small number of occupations, as inefficient and unfair. He argued that many women were forced prematurely into marriage and motherhood.[11] He predicted that greater economic independence for women would lead to fertility decline.

This prediction was hardly noticed by Mill's readers. It enjoyed far less attention from economists than Malthus's prediction that population growth would keep wages at subsistence level, or Ricardo's prediction that economic growth would inevitably level off. Yet fertility decline, already underway in many areas, would accelerate in Britain, France, and the U.S. in the late nineteenth century, long before the advent of modern contraceptives. Combined with technological change, the expansion of education and increases in women's labor force participation, fertility decline helped bring significant improvements in working class standards of living (though not, it should be emphasized, without a fight).

Mill's awareness of the force of economic self-interest always tempered his utopian impulse. In one of the very few disagreements with Harriet documented in their correspondence, he wrote:

> I cannot persuade myself that you do not greatly overrate the ease of making people unselfish. Granting that in "ten years" the children of a community might by teaching be made "perfect" it seems to me that to do so there must be perfect people to teach them. You say "if there were a desire on the part of the cleverer people to make them perfect it would be easy"—but how to produce that desire in the cleverer people?[12]

Mill made it clear in his *Autobiography* that he looked forward to a time when people would be more willing to work for the common good. But he did not believe that time was imminent.

He had more confidence in the project of freeing women to pursue their own interests, and he and Harriet concentrated much of their joint intellectual energy on this task. Excited by reports of conferences on equal rights held in America in 1850, they began work on an essay entitled "The Enfranchisement of Women", which appeared in the *Westminster Review* in July 1851. The particularly bold tone of this article suggests that Harriet may actually deserve more credit for it than her husband, and Mill himself explained later that he had done little more than edit the piece (for this reason it is sometimes attributed to Taylor even though it did not appear under her name).[13] The substance of the argument reveals more confidence in the principles of liberal individualism than had been apparent in the *Principles*.

The motive may have been strategic. The intellectual influence of political economy was expanding and individualism becoming more acceptable. Mill and Taylor appealed to the predominant theory of *laissez faire* when they wrote "[S]o long as competition is the general law of human life, it is tyranny to shut out one-half of the competitors."[4] They applied the now-familiar rhetoric of "no taxation without representation," as well. Mill and Taylor pushed the limits of respectability by suggesting that the rules of reason should be applied to family-size decisions.

They also insisted that married women could attain full equality only if they earned an income outside the home. Otherwise, their bargaining power within marriage would be limited: As they put it, "Even under the present laws respecting the property of women, a woman who contributes materially to the support of the family, cannot be treated in the same contemptuously tyrannical manner as one who, however she may toil as a domestic drudge, is a dependent on the man for subsistence."[5] Mill inserted a similar phrase in the 1852 edition of his *Principles of Political Economy,* though he backed off somewhat in a later revision.[16] Women's bargaining power within marriage received virtually no more attention from economists until the 1980s (see discussion in Chapter 20).

"The Enfranchisement of Women", published in the year of the author's marriage, was the finest product of their direct collaboration. Taylor, plagued by poor health probably related to tuberculosis, died seven years later. Mill was devastated. "The spring of my life is broken," he wrote, announcing he had no further interest in life but to fulfill her wishes.[17] Having retired from his post at the India House, he began work on an essay he and Harriet had planned to write together.

The Subjection of Women

Its title boldly announced its theme. In *The Subjection of Women* Mill explored the links between greed, lust and gender, developing a theory of male domination and male/female differences that drew heavily from his socialist feminist predecessors. He also drew heavily from classical political economy. In a logical extension of Ricardian class analysis, Mill explained both patriarchy and slavery as expressions of the collective self-interest of a powerful group. The motive in these cases was the "love of gain, unmixed and undisguised" combined with physical and military superiority.[18] The most insidious aspect of this strategic collective action, he observed, was that oppressors used the state to institutionalize inequality, then exercised their cultural influence to justify it. "Was there ever any domination," he asked, "that did not appear natural to those who possessed it?"[19]

His theory of patriarchy as a system analogous to slavery gave substance to his claim that social institutions could pervert the natural pursuit of self-interest into repugnant selfishness: He elaborated further on the arguments outlined earlier in the *Principles*:

> Such being the common tendency of human nature; the almost unlimited power which present social institutions give to the man over at least one human being—the one with whom he resides, and whom he has always present—this power seeks out and evokes the latent germs of selfishness in the remotest corners of his nature—fans its faintest sparks and smouldering embers—offers to him a licence for the indulgence of those points of his original character which in all other relations he would have found it necessary to repress and conceal, and the repression of which would in time have become a second nature.[20]

The fanning of the flames, turning selfishness into greed and lust, evokes the image of hell. The word "repression" (and the notion that it could become a second nature) reappears prominently in the later writings of Sigmund Freud, who not only admired Mill, but also translated many of his essays into German. Mill appealed to his Christian audience by describing selfishness as a form of idolatry: self-worship. This term, which also appears in the epigraph to this chapter, has a more negative inflection than the term that Malthus had made famous, self-love.

Mill's account suggested that the oppression of women was in some historical sense the original sin, the form of inequality that enabled and promoted others. It followed that gender equality was an absolute prerequisite for progress on other fronts, including socialism. Owen's emphasis on socialization echoes through Mill's arguments. "All the moralities," he wrote, "tell them [women] that it is the duty of women, and all the current sentimentalities that it is their nature, to live for others; to make complete abnegation of themselves, and to have no life but in their affections."[21] The tendency to describe femininity as essentially submissive was, he argued, a form of enslavement.[22]

Mill's approach allowed him to explain the moral double standard of his day without agreeing that it was either inevitable or desirable. He went so far as to argue that the ideals of human character should be degendered; women should become more self-interested and men less so:

> If women are better than men in anything, it surely is in individual self-sacrifice for those of their own family. But I lay little stress on this, so long as they are universally taught that they are born and created for self-sacrifice. I believe that equality of rights would abate the exaggerated self-abnegation which is the present artificial ideal of feminine character, and that a good woman would not be more self-sacrificing than the best man: but on the other hand, men would be much more unselfish and self-sacrificing than at present, because they would no longer be taught to worship their own will as such a grand thing that it is actually the law for another rational being.[23]

In short, women should become more masculine, men more feminine. Some of Mill's literary contemporaries leaned in a similar direction. Charles Dickens's heroes were often nurturing, mother-like men; Alfred Tennyson romanticized androgyny.[24] But Mill put the argument in explicit terms that elicited enormous opposition. An article in the highly respected *Edinburgh Review* accused him of hypothesizing that women were simply men in petticoats.[25]

This was a simplistic criticism. Mill's argument built carefully on the previous discourse of self-interest. Many of the thinkers described in preceding chapters worried about the balance between individual rights and social obligation: Smith had optimistically argued that innate moral sentiments, combined with competitive markets, would solve the problem. Mill, like his socialist feminist predecessors, insisted that the issue was more complicated and more directly linked to gender roles. But he never argued that women and men were identical or that economic reform could or should eradicate all differences between them.

His conviction that women would naturally choose to specialize in family labor was expressed both in the *Subjection of Women* and in 1865 revisions to the *Principles*.[26] In each case he explained that it was not actually desirable that a wife contribute to family income. The impersonal processes of competition would likely sort men and women into different types of jobs. In fact, Mill chided those who assumed that women would not choose to become mothers unless forced to do so.[27] He was not terribly worried that the emancipation of women might, as one twentieth-century commentator put it, "simply universalize the competitive and acquisitive ethos, the unbridled envy and egoism, of bourgeois civil society."[28]

Mill was, however, concerned that freedom to divorce would encourage selfish calculation at the expense of family obligation. He cautiously detailed the terms under which marriages might be gracefully terminated.[29] He believed that parents should set a good example for their children and discourage selfishness. This paternalism infused his vision of social reform. The state, like parents, should establish clear rules and implement them with tough love.

In the end, Mill remained remarkably confident of women's moral sentiments. On the one hand, he argued that women who commit themselves to family care would sacrifice their economic independence and along with it their potential for equality. On the other hand, he argued that even once they gained equality they would freely make this sacrifice.[30] Mill could have returned to the proposals offered by Owen, Thompson, and others regarding the collectivization of housework. He could have proposed ways of increasing paternal responsibility for the support and care of children. But such changes would have required rather forceful social policies. It was easier to hope that women would naturally choose to devote themselves to family care.

Political Activism

Harriet Taylor's daughter Helen had enjoyed a brief period of independence from her family, pursuing a career as an actress. After her mother's death, however, she devoted herself to her stepfather, who depended on her for both personal assistance and political advice. In conjunction with other prominent figures like Harriet Martineau and Barbara Bodichon in England, and in close communication with feminists in both the United States and France, they campaigned for new political rights and expanded economic opportunities for women.

Mill had never been fond of Harriet Martineau and had little regard for her grasp of political economy. Martineau was, however, a shrewd ally in the effort to budge public opinion. A famously self-supporting spinster herself, she emphasized that "the footing of women" was changing as a result of declining marriage rates. She published an article in the *Edinburgh Review* using data from the British census of 1851 to call attention to the impact of male outmigration on the English sex ratio.[31] The article helped jolt the middle class into greater awareness of the problem of "redundant" women. Those unable to find respectable work outside the home were likely to become a burden on their fathers and brothers.[32]

The more radical Barbara Bodichon questioned the assumption that married women should ideally devote themselves exclusively to family life. "There are thousands of married women," she wrote, "who are in want of a pursuit—a profession. It is a mistake to suppose marriage gives occupation enough to employ all the faculties of all women."[33] Her arguments eerily anticipated those the U.S. feminist Betty Friedan would make a hundred years later in *The Feminine Mystique* (see discussion in Chapter 20).

Political progress was slow and uneven, but discernible. In 1857, Parliament approved a bill making it possible (though not easy) to sue for official separation or divorce in a secular, rather than an ecclesiastical court. It also gave married women some control over their property in the event of desertion or divorce. In the same year, the first Married Women's Property Bill was introduced into Parliament, and roundly defeated.[34] In 1865, Mill agreed to run for election to Parliament—on the condition that he would not canvass, spend any money, or compromise his political views. He gained support from those hoping to extend the male franchise as well as from women's groups and was, somewhat to his surprise, elected.

Strategic considerations dictated a proposal to extend the suffrage only to women of property. Barbara Bodichon spearheaded an effort to gather the signatures of nearly 1,500 women (including Martineau's) on a formal petition. On the appointed day, June 7 1866, the women came to Westminster carrying a large scroll. Hoping to keep it a surprise, they asked a woman selling apples near the entrance to conceal it under her cart. She kindly agreed, and upon learning of its intent, pulled it out and added her own name. It seemed an auspicious omen and Mill collected the scroll, exclaiming "This I can brandish to good effect."[35] The effect, if good, was small. Still, it laid the groundwork for Mill's most famous speech in Parliament proposing an amendment to the Reform Bill of 1867. He asked that the word "person" be substituted for the word "man" at every place in the bill.

In making his case, Mill reiterated the criticisms William Thompson and Anna Wheeler had leveled against his father James Mill over thirty years before, directing them with blistering irony at those who claimed support for the interests of the working class:

> The interests of all women are safe in the hands of their fathers, husbands, and brothers, who have the same interest with them, and not only know, far better than they do, what is good for them, but care much more for them than they care for themselves. Sir, this is exactly what is said of all unrepresented classes. The operatives, for instance; are they not virtually represented by the representation of their employers? Are not the interests of the employers and that of the employed, when properly understood, the same? ... And, generally speaking, have not employers and employed a common interest against all outside the family? And what is more, are not all employers good, kind, benevolent men, who love their workpeople, and always desire to do what is most for their good? All these assertions are as true, and as much to the purpose, as the corresponding assertions respecting men and women.[36]

In order to make his meaning absolutely clear, Mill went on to describe the horrors of domestic violence against women. He did not win the franchise battle, but his arguments built support for the married women's property acts, approved in 1870 and considerably extended in 1882. By that time, Mill had lost his seat in Parliament, not only because his views on women's rights were controversial, but also because he had contributed to the campaign of another politician who was a public atheist and advocate of birth control.

Mill also risked his political reputation to publicly oppose a new initiative to regulate prostitution. In 1869, the English government, increasingly concerned about the spread of venereal disease, passed legislation modeled on that in effect in France. The Contagious Diseases Acts empowered local authorities to force any women suspected of prostitution to submit to periodic medical examination. The authorities underestimated the opposition that such explicit, yet one-sided regulation would elicit. Many women were outraged by their own vulnerability to accusation and medical examination without due process. That men remained utterly exempt from public scrutiny made it difficult to justify the policy as one intended only to preserve public health. Mill denounced the sexual double standard, arguing that men should also be examined for venereal disease and held legally responsible if they infected an innocent woman.

Other critics emphasized that state regulation of prostitution implied social approval of it. Harriet Martineau welled with moral fury. When one supporter of the Acts opined that prostitution was a necessity, she asked him if he was unaware that fornication was denounced in the Holy Scriptures.[37] No one dared bring forward Bernard Mandeville's ancient brief. Invoking the value of the home as the "nursery of all virtue", a stalwart middle-class woman named Josephine Butler provided formidable leadership for an international movement against state regulation of the health of prostitutes.[38] In 1883, English advocates for such regulation backed off.

A Fundamental Question

Economists have typically regarded Mill's feminist concerns as social rather than economic, peripheral to his grand systematization of classical political economy. Yet Mill always described the "woman question" as an economic issue. His most influential writings explained how women's rights influenced population growth, the labor market, the distribution of income, and the social definition of self-interest. In 1871, he argued that the woman question was more fundamental than the nationalization of land or the relationship between labor and capital. The Married Women's Property Acts, which he championed, represented "one of the greatest expropriations and reallocations of property" in English history.[39] John Stuart Mill died in 1873. He bequeathed almost half of his estate to the cause of women's education.

NOTES TO CHAPTER 13

[1] In France, by contrast, agriculture occupied not only half the total number of "economically active" (engaged in market work) individuals but also almost half the "economically active" women. The predominance of agricultural employment signaled the predominance of a more family-based economic system. The nineteenth-century French censuses are neither detailed nor consistent, and do not break out "domestic service" as a specific occupation. However, the fact that only 20 percent of French women with occupations in 1866 were in the larger category of Services suggests that paid domestic service was less widespread than in

England and the United States. Kin-based forms of domestic service, in which female relatives worked in return for their room and board, were probably more significant. B. R. Mitchell, *International Historical Statistics*, Europe, 1750–1993, 4th edn (1998), Table B1, p. 149. See also Jacques et Michel Dupâquier, *Histoire de la Démographie. La statistique de la population des origines a 1914* (Paris: Librarie Académique Perrin, 1985).

[2] Edward Higgs, "Women, Occupations, and Work in the Nineteenth Century Censuses," *History Workshop* 23 (1987), 59–80; See also B. R. Mitchell, *British Historical Statistics* (New York: Cambridge University Press, 1988).

[3] John Stuart Mill, *Autobiography* (New York: Oxford University Press, 1952), p. 195.

[4] Joseph Schumpeter explained that, "J. S. Mill was exactly what is meant by an evolutionary socialist." See his *Principles of Economic Analysis* (New York: Oxford, 1954), p. 531. Mark Blaug, on the other hand, insisted that, "Despite his sympathetic treatment of socialist arguments, however, he [Mill] was not socialist. Indeed, he is a perfect example of what we mean when we call someone a 'classical liberal'." See his *Economic Theory in Retrospect*, 4th edn, (New York: Cambridge University Press, 1985), p. 220. On Mill as authoritarian, see Maurice Cowling, *Mill and Liberalism* (New York: Cambridge University Press, 1963); Joseph Hamburger, *John Stuart Mill on Liberty and Control* (Princeton, N.J.: Princeton University Press, 1999); Linda C. Raeder, *John Stuart Mill and the Religion of Humanity* (Columbia, MO: University of Missouri Press, 2002).

[5] Neil de Marchi, "The Success of Mill's Principles," *History of Political Economy* 6:2 (1974), 119–57.

[6] Robert L. Heilbroner, for instance, describes Mill's doctrine as "English to the core: gradualist, optimistic, realistic, and devoid of radical overtones." See his *The Worldly Philosophers* (New York: Simon and Schuster, 1961), p. 110. E. K. Hunt writes that Mill looked forward to the day that the rich would simply become less greedy, and give the poor their due. See his *History of Economic Thought. A Critical Perspective* (Belmont: Wadsworth, 1979), p. 179.

[7] Joseph Schumpeter, though clearly sympathetic to Mill's socialism, could not bring himself to mention his feminism, and describes him in effeminate terms, e.g. "that impression of stunted growth and lack of vital strength that comes to us from many passages in the imposing work of his life," and "the note of hysteria in the Preface to the essay *On Liberty*." See his *History of Economic Analysis*, p. 528.

[8] John Stuart Mill, *Principles of Political Economy with Some of Their Applications to Social Philosophy*, Books I and II, based on the seventh edition (London: Routledge and Kegan Paul, 1965), p. 205.

[9] Mill, *Principles*, IV, p. 759.

[10] Ibid., p. 769.

[11] As he put it, "The ideas and institutions by which the accident of sex is made the groundwork of an inequality of legal rights, and a forced dissimilarity of social functions, must ere long be recognized as the greatest hindrance to moral, social, and even intellectual improvement." Ibid., p. 765.

[12] Mill, *Principles*, Appendix G, p. 1030. For the remainder of their correspondence, see F. A. Hayek, *John Stuart Mill and Harriet Taylor. Their Correspondence and Subsequent Marriage* (Chicago: University of Chicago Press, 1951).

[13] John Stuart Mill, *Dissertations and Discussions* (London: John D. Parker, 1859), vol. II, p. 411. On Harriet Taylor's distinctive contributions, see Michèle Pujol, "The Feminist Thought of Harriet Taylor," 82–102 in R. W. Dimand and E. L. Forget, eds, *Women of Value. Feminist Essays on the History of Women in Economics* (Aldershot, UK: Edward Elgar, 1995).

[14] Harriet Taylor, "The Enfranchisement of Women," in John Stuart Mill and Harriet Taylor, *Essays on Sex Equality*, ed. Alice Rossi (Chicago: University of Chicago, 1970), p. 105.

[15] Ibid.

[16] Richard W. Krouse, "Patriarchal Liberalism and Beyond: From John Stuart Mill to Harriet Taylor," pp. 145–72 in Jean Bethke Elshtain, ed., *The Family in Political Thought* (Chicago: University of Chicago Press, 1982); Gertrude Himmelfarb, *On Liberty and Liberalism: The Case of John Stuart Mill* (New York: Alfred A. Knopf, 1974).

[17] Josephine Kamm, *John Stuart Mill in Love* (London: Gordon and Cremonesi, 1977), p. 129.

[18] John Stuart Mill, *The Subjection of Women*, with an introduction by Wendell Carr (Cambridge: M.I.T. Press, 1970), p. 11.

[19] Ibid., p. 13.

[20] Ibid., p. 37. See also p. 80, where Mill writes, "All the selfish propensies, the self-worship, the unjust self-preference, which exist among mankind, have their source and root in, and derive their principal nourishment from, the present constitution of the relation between men and women."

[21] Ibid., p. 16.

[22] Mill writes, "All men, except the most brutish, desire to have, in the woman most nearly connected with them, not a forced slave, but a willing one, not a slave merely, but a favourite. They have therefore put everything in practice to enslave their minds." Ibid., p. 16.

[23] Ibid., p. 43.

[24] Carol Christ, "Victorian Masculinity and the Angel in the House," pp. 146–62 in Martha Vicinus, ed., *A Widening Sphere. Changing Roles of Victorian Women* (Bloomington: Indiana University Press, 1977).

[25] Wendell Carr, from his introduction to Mill, *Subjection of Women*, pp. xx.

[26] In the *Principles*, he wrote "It cannot, however, be considered desirable as a permanent element in the condition of a laboring class, that the mother of the family (the case of single women is totally different) should be under the necessity of working for a living, at least elsewhere than in their place of abode" (II, p. 394). In *The Subjection of Women* he wrote, "In an otherwise just state of things, it is not, therefore, I think, a desirable custom, that the wife should contribute by her labour to the income of the family" (p. 48).

[27] Mill, *Subjection of Women*, p. 28.

[28] Krause, "Patriarchal Liberalism," p. 168.

[29] For a discussion of Mill's "fence-sitting" with respect to divorce see Kamm, *John Stuart Mill*, p. 200.

[30] See Michèle Pujol, *Feminism and Anti-Feminism in Early Economic Thought* (Aldershot: Edward Elgar, 1992).

[31] Martineau, "Female Industry," *Edinburgh Review* 222 (1859), p. 300. See also her "Independent Industry of Women," in Yates, ed., *Harriet Martineau*, pp. 224–9.

[32] Lee Holcombe, *Victorian Ladies at Work* (Newton Abbot, Devon: David and Charles, 1973), p. 10; "Household Education," in Yates, ed., *Harriet Martineau*, pp. 95–6.

[33] Barbara Bodichon, *Women and Work* (New York: C.S. Francis, 1859) p. 29. See also the discussion of Bodichon in Pujol, *Feminism and Anti-Feminism*.

[34] Lee Holcombe, "Victorian Wives and Property," pp. 3–28 in Martha Vicinus, ed., *A Widening Sphere. Changing Roles of Victorian Women* (Bloomington: Indiana University Press, 1977), p. 11.

[35] Kamm, *John Stuart Mill in Love*, p. 151.

[36] Mill, "Speech Before the House of Commons," May 20 1867, reprinted in Susan Groag Bell and Karen M. Offen, eds, *Women, the Family and Freedom* (Stanford: Stanford University Press), p. 486.

[37] Kamm, *John Stuart Mill in Love*, p. 183; Martineau, "On the Contagious Diseases Acts," in Yates, ed. *Harriet Martineau*, pp. 247, 259.

[38] Jane Lewis, *Women in England 1870–1950: Sexual Divisions and Social Change* (Sussex: Wheatsheaf, 1984), p. 89.

[39] Holcombe, "Victorian Wives and Property," p. 27.

CHAPTER 14

Declaring Independence

The history of mankind is a history of repeated injuries and usurpations on the part of man toward woman, having in direct object the establishment of an absolute tyranny over her.

Declaration of Sentiments, Seneca Falls Convention

The famous woman's rights activists of the nineteenth-century United States, such as Elizabeth Cady Stanton and Susan B. Anthony, have seldom been considered contributors to economic theory. The issues they pursued, including gender inequality and family law, were not of interest to most economists. Their ideas were presented, for the most part, in speeches and newspaper articles, rather than in weighty tomes. Their style was often narrative and discursive rather than analytical. Within the realm of political economy, their formidable English allies Harriet Martineau, John Stuart Mill, and Harriet Taylor upstaged them.[1]

Yet Stanton and her sister activists were fascinated by a central theme of political economy—the tension between individual self-interest and collective welfare—and, like Mill and Taylor, interpreted this tension in highly gendered terms. While U.S. feminists drew inspiration from the abolitionist movement, they also influenced it, emphasizing the corrupting effect that slavery had on family life. They also advanced discussion of three specific economic issues: collective interests based on gender, the economic significance of family work, and the importance of family law and reproductive rights.

Peculiar Institutions

The home-grown political economy of mid-nineteenth-century U.S. had a conservative slant. Most recognized authorities dismissed the notion that women or slaves had distinct collective interests or were vulnerable, as groups, to economic exploitation. In addition to defending the institution of slavery, the southerner Thomas Dew pronounced that women's qualities of mind fitted them for subservient roles.[2] The influential Amasa Walker explained that women's wages were low because "the prevailing ideas of the community restrict them to easily dispensable occupations."[3] Those who longed for some explanation of how such ideas came to prevail found precious little explanation.

Early advocates of women's rights drew from a dissident anti-slavery Quaker tradition. With a synergy that would be repeated more than a century later during the Civil Rights Movement, efforts to redress racial exploitation were both inspired and strengthened by consideration of women's rights. Similarities in the lack of legal personhood and exclusion from the franchise were too obvious to ignore. A willingness to offend public opinion on one count sometimes made it easier to be outspoken on another. Utopian and communitarian ideals tinged both movements. Frances Wright, an Owenite, founded a community in Tennessee based on the principle of emancipation for women and for slaves.[4] Sarah Grimke, an abolitionist activist and stalwart of the Massachusetts Society of Friends was a fan of Henri de Saint-Simon.[5]

As the abolitionist cause gained momentum, its supporters feared distraction from their primary, overriding goal. The Conference on World Slavery held in London in 1840 voted to exclude women from official participation, despite the important role that they had played. Among the women who vowed redress was Elizabeth Cady Stanton, wife of a prominent anti-slavery activist. Eight years later she masterminded the convention in Seneca Falls, New York that inaugurated a campaign for women's suffrage.

The convention's manifesto begin with a paraphrase of the Declaration of Independence that added two small words—"and women."

> We hold these truths to be self-evident: that all men and women are
> created equal; that they are endowed by their Creator with certain
> inalienable rights; that among these are life, liberty, and the pursuit of

happiness; that to secure these rights governments are instituted, deriving their just powers from the consent of the governed.[6]

The document drew a clear analogy between the Revolutionary War slogan "no taxation without representation" and demands for the political representation of women. Public response to the Seneca Falls convention was hardly enthusiastic. One newspaper described the women as "erratic, addle-pated comeouters."[7] But emphasis on the goal of woman's suffrage—not achieved until 1920—understates their success. Concerted efforts to publicize the cause of women's rights contributed to major improvements in married women's property rights over the course of the nineteenth century, which in turn strengthened the suffrage effort.[8] The connections were personal as well as political. Elizabeth Cady Stanton's inheritance from her father increased her bargaining power within marriage and enabled her to advance the cause of women's rights while also tending to responsibilities as a wife and mother.[9]

In the wake of the Civil War, women's rights advocates suffered serious setbacks. Progressive political energies focused on the fifteenth Amendment to the Constitution giving black men the right to vote. Horace Greeley, prominent newspaper editor and Fourierist sympathizer opposed woman suffrage as an innovation "openly at war with a distribution of duties and functions between the sexes as venerable and pervading as government itself."[10] When Elizabeth Cady Stanton and Susan B. Anthony successfully solicited his wife's signature on a petition for women's suffrage he retaliated with the news that they would never be published in his newspaper again.[11]

Angered by public willingness to give black men, but not women, the vote, Stanton and Anthony became more willing to emphasize gender interests. In the process they resorted to racist rhetoric, complaining that men of the "lower orders" should not take precedence over native-born white women.[12] With the financial assistance of a notorious opponent of black male suffrage, they inaugurated a new women's rights journal called *The Revolution* in 1868. It became the voice of militant feminism, publishing the writings of Mary Wollstonecraft, Harriet Taylor, and John Stuart Mill and entertaining its readers with articles about bread and babies and the ballot. It lionized women who took on non-traditional jobs, including female farmers, inventors, sailors, and thieves.

True to its name, *The Revolution* quickly generated a backlash, and not just among opponents of women's rights. Many reform-minded activists felt that Stanton and Anthony were going too far too fast, alienating potential supporters. Disagreements over votes for black men (and over policies towards Reconstruction in the South) were exacerbated by debates over the issue of divorce. The movement split. In 1869, the National Woman Suffrage Association, formed under the leadership of Stanton and Anthony, remained open to all women believers in woman suffrage. The more cautious American Woman Suffrage Association led by Henry Ward Beecher and Lucy Stone was organized on a delegate basis, inviting only representatives from recognized organizations.[13] Not until 1890 did the two organizations reconcile and rejoin.

The split reflected temperamental differences—the contentious versus the compromising. But theoretical tensions were also evident. Stanton and Anthony leaned more toward the discourse of political economy than the discourse of morality. Stanton, frustrated by the continual invocation of scripture against the cause of women's rights, publicly campaigned against literal adherence to the Bible. Henry Ward Beecher, by contrast, was a man of the cloth.[14]

A quasi-religious approach to women's rights found vivid expression in the temperance movement, which included ax-wielding attacks against saloons selling demon rum. Temperance leader Frances Willard called on women to listen to their "mother-hearts" and serve as a conscience for the world. In her view, gaining the franchise was less a political right than a moral duty for women who wanted to better fulfill their responsibilities for the care of others.[15] By the 1890s, the organization she commanded, the Women's Christian Temperance Union, enjoyed a membership one hundred times larger than the National Woman Suffrage Association.[16] But the smaller group under the leadership of Stanton and Anthony ultimately proved more influential, perhaps because its embrace of political economy contributed to the development of new ideas.

Equality and Difference

Nineteenth-century feminists often alternated between efforts to improve gender equality and efforts to improve men's appreciation of women's distinctive contributions. Historians like Nancy Cott emphasize that the dialectic between "equality" and "difference" contributed to feminism's intellectual and political vitality.[17] The same dialectic linked feminism to the tensions among concepts of selfishness, altruism, and moral obligation in political economy. As earlier chapters have pointed out, early socialists, such as Robert Owen, William Thompson, Henri de Saint-Simon, and Charles Fourier, criticized individualism more than capitalism *per se.*

Feminists like Stanton shared John Stuart Mill's conviction that institutional change could establish a better balance between individual and collective interests. This did not always bring them into direct opposition to those who believed in women's moral superiority. For instance, Harriet Beecher Stowe's popular novel, *Uncle Tom's Cabin,* explained most social ills as the result of inadequate maternal love. The generic slave trader was a man who would "sell his own mother at a good percentage—not wishing the old woman any harm, either."[18] If slaves behaved badly, it was because they had been torn from their mothers—or had their children torn from them. Still, Stowe's morality tale led many of its readers to agree that slavery itself was the source of the problem. Abraham Lincoln referred to her as the little lady who helped start the Civil War.[19]

On the other hand, the moralists feared that women might be tainted by too much participation in a men's world. Catherine Beecher's *Treatise on Domestic Economy,* published in 1841, foreshadowed arguments that were laid out in the even more successful *The American Woman's Home,* coauthored with her sister Harriet and published in 1869. In addition to providing a great deal of practical advice, it described women's great mission as self-denial and self-sacrifice, necessary to counterbalance the growing selfishness encouraged by the market economy.[20] As one of Beecher's biographers put it, "She led her readers to conclude that by removing half the population from the arena of competition and making it subservient to the other half, the amount of antagonism the society had to bear would be reduced to a tolerable limit."[21]

Stanton and other woman's rights advocates countered with the argument that such self-sacrifice made women vulnerable and tempted men to misbehavior. But they never went to the opposite extreme of arguing that women should imitate men.[22] Even Lois Banner, who describes Stanton as a staunch individualist, immediately notes her great appreciation of maternal virtues.[23]

More recent scholarship challenges the notion that Stanton can simply be characterized as an individualist.[24]

Stanton's engagement with political economy reveals similar complexities. Sometimes she adopted a liberal tone, emphasizing the merits of competition relative to the dangers of monopoly. In 1902 Theodore Roosevelt campaigned for president on a platform denouncing evil giants such as Standard Oil and preaching the virtues of a marketplace that allowed small farmers and small businesses to thrive. Stanton praised his efforts, but went on to plead, "Surely there is no greater monopoly than that of all men in denying to all women a voice in the laws they are compelled to obey."[25]

Sometimes Stanton adopted socialist rhetoric, arguing that capitalism was exploitative: men were to women as capitalists were to workers, extractors of labor.[26] Her essays in *The Revolution* advocated fair wages and an eight-hour workday. In her view, political power would allow women to use their maternal gifts to guarantee "equal distribution among all."[27] When she identified women with the "unselfish, the moral, the diffusive" she was paraphrasing the French sociologist August Comte who had served as secretary to de Saint-Simon.[28]

The Revolution sometimes looked down on women who were only housewives. Nonetheless, its editors often invoked the virtues of motherhood as evidence of women's moral superiority. They called for more equality in the workplace even as they encouraged more freedom of choice in the home. Conflicts between rights and duties shaped feminist discourse. Susan B. Anthony offered a concise critique of the way that norms and obligations of care for others had been gendered in a speech delivered in 1889:

> We women have been taught that the object of a woman's life is to help a man. No one seems to have suspected that any man was ever born for any purpose except his own happiness and self-development. Now, after forty years of agitation, the idea is beginning to prevail that women were created for themselves, for their own happiness, and for the welfare of the world.[29]

The argument inverts a proverb: what's sauce for the gander is sauce for the goose. If men should be self-interested, women should be too. Ironically, Anthony herself could not resist adding "the welfare of the world" to women's burdens.

Collective Interests

Unlike the Beecher sisters Stanton and Anthony did not want such burdens to be assigned to women alone. Rather, they envisioned a world in which both men and women would share responsibility for others, a new "equilibrium of the masculine and feminine elements."[30] Unfortunately, they pointed, out, men would not relinquish their privilege without a fight. Early feminists articulated an analysis of collective economic interests based on gender that paralleled the concept of class interests articulated by David Ricardo and the early socialists. In 1838 Sarah Grimke published a set of letters on the quality of the sexes that described men as analogous to slave owners: "All history attests that man has subjected woman to his will, used her as a means to promote his selfish gratification, to minister to his sensual pleasures, to be instrumental in promoting his comfort; but never has he desired to elevate her to that rank she was created to fill."[31] She denounced male control over female sexuality, and argued that equal rights to person and property would release women from the "horrors of forced maternity."[32] She went on complain that women's jobs were always paid less than men's.[33]

The Declaration of Sentiments at Seneca Falls began with an emphasis on individual rights, but moved rather quickly to a militant emphasis on collective action, as indicated in the epigraph of this chapter. The list of more specific observations that followed protested women's subordination in the family, in the church, and in the economy. Occupational segregation, as well as lack of property rights, was deplored: "He has monopolized nearly all the profitable employments... He closes against her all the avenues to wealth and distinction which he considers most honorable to himself."[34]

This rhetoric drew heavily on the tropes of classical political economy as well as liberal political theory. Male power was often described as analogous to that of feudal lords, slaveholders, or capitalists. Like the landlords that fascinated Ricardo, men inherited their access to wealth and power, rather than earning it. Stanton's term "aristocracy of sex" treated women as an unrepresented class or caste, an approach later fleshed out in some detail by the twentieth-century feminist economist, Barbara Bergmann.[35]

Yet Stanton also situated her analysis of male collective power in a larger context: "As I read history old and new the subjection of women may be clearly traced to the same cause that subjugated different races and nations to one another, the law of force, that made might right, and the weak the slaves of the strong."[36] Like John Stuart Mill, she believed that the purpose of the democratic state was to curb such subjugation, to impose limits on efforts at collective aggrandizement. In her essay on "The Subjection of Women", adopting the title of Mill's famous tract, she argued that all those who struggled for equality would advance the cause of woman's rights.

Like Friedrich Engels, whose *Origins of the Family, Private Property and the State* was first published in 1884, Stanton drew on the work of early anthropologists like Johann Bachofen and Henry Louis Morgan, who provided some evidence that early human civilizations venerated women and mothers, and were possibly even ruled by them. She believed that anthropology and history provided a powerful alternative to the religious account of Eve's original Garden of Eden transgression. In her "Matriarchate or Mother-Age," published in 1891, she emphasized that men had used physical force and military power to wrest control of society away from women. These arguments foreshadowed those of twentieth-century feminist historian Gerda Lerner and others seeking to understand the emergence of patriarchal systems.[37]

An odd grammatical detail of nineteenth century feminism was its use of the singular "woman's rights" rather than the plural "women's rights". At first glance, this might seem to represent its individualism. In practice, however, the singular invoked a symbolic unity. Emphasis on men's collective action obviously helped justify the need for collective action on women's part. If women wanted individual rights, they would need to work in concert. Even in its most liberal form, feminism appealed to female solidarity. The most serious weakness of this argument, then as now, was its failure to articulate a vision of competing collective interests, or any clear model of systemic inequality—other than slavery itself.

The Economic Significance of Family Work

Living standards varied enormously among women, determined not only by family background but by marital status. On a day-to-day basis, most women tended to family and home—as managers of domestic servants, if not as workers. Beecher and Stowe offered detailed, practical advice to support their claim that household management was a demanding craft rather than a menial task.[38] In their view, the housewife's successful performance of her God-given role was crucial to the welfare of society as a whole. Stanton and Anthony went beyond both practical advice and moral praise to ask why women who worked without a wage lacked rights over the products of their labor.

The Married Women's Property Acts passed in many states after 1848 represented a straightforward extension of liberal political theory, gradually giving women control over inherited wealth and their own market earnings.[39] Members of the National Woman Suffrage Association offered a more radical critique, raising concerns about lack of economic remuneration for housework and childrearing.[40] In an article in *The Revolution*, Elizabeth Cady Stanton argued that women who surrendered themselves to their family's needs deserved decent egalitarian compensation and that the work of wives and mothers was unique only because it was "unpaid, unsocialized, and unrelenting."[41] Elizabeth Blackwell, the first woman doctor in the United States, contested the vocabulary of dependence, asserting that, "The theory that a wife who...bears her fair share of the joint burdens, is yet 'supported' by her husband has been the bane of all society."[42]

Nineteenth-century common law required that a husband support his wife, but the meaning of support was nowhere clearly defined, and many women were forced to beg their husbands for money.[43] In 1873, an article in *The Woman's Journal* explicitly demanded wages for housework. In 1878, the National Woman Suffrage Convention passed a resolution calling for legal recognition of women's rights to "the proceeds of her labor in the family."[44] Elizabeth Cady Stanton, Susan B. Anthony, and Mathilda Gage called more explicitly for a law guaranteeing the wife the absolute right to one half the joint earnings of her and her husband.[45]

Another writer pointed that if housewives were to adopt the eight-hour-day that trade unions were demanding for their members, many workers would be forced to go to bed without their supper.[46] Feminist proposals for a shorter working day anticipated late twentieth-century debates over family policy.[47] Yet few of today's activists realize that their late nineteenth-century counterparts argued that men and women alike would welcome paid employment that required only a few hours per day, and such an arrangement would also allow men to assume more responsibilities for family care.[48] Coops and cohousing also came under discussion, under the rubric of "cooperative housekeeping".[49]

Divorce and Reproductive Rights

Stanton and Anthony argued that existing family laws—even beyond property rights over labor—had harmful economic consequences for women. Restrictions on divorce left women vulnerable to physical abuse. Husbands' unlimited rights to their wives' sexual services violated women's "self-sovereignty". However, Stanton and Anthony never argued that complete freedom of choice should rule family life. Sex outside of marriage remained outside the pale, as did any *de facto* legalization of prostitution through regulation.

The incidence of marital separation (including desertion) increased over the course of the nineteenth century and Western states, magnets for many men who had left families behind, liberalized their divorce laws. While the overall divorce rate remained low, it increased dramatically after the Civil War, prompting many Eastern states to impose more restrictive rules. But as divorce became more common it also became less stigmatizing. Many pundits linked the rising divorce rate to the emancipation of women and some, at least, argued that the association between the two was a healthy one.[50]

Divorce was a divisive issue for nineteenth-century feminists, however, because it hinted at female pursuit of selfish pleasure. The distinctive threat of female lust lay in the prospect of indulging romantic love. A woman who could not restrain her passionate impulses until they were sanctified by legal and religious approval could not be trusted to subordinate her own interests to those of others. Hence, a woman who would abandon her legal husband and his offspring to attach herself to another man was considered the bane of polite society. The slogan "free love" has been described as the "single most odious epithet that one could attach to a respectable citizen of the post-Civil War era."[51] Even by the end of the twentieth century, it retained vulgar connotations, which may help explain why many historians have insisted that the free love melodrama remained peripheral to the larger women's movement.[52]

In the eyes of moderates like Lucy Stone, advocating freedom to divorce was like calling turnabout fair play. She conceded that the sexual double standard bound women far more tightly than men. But why not then bind men more tightly rather than loosening women? In a sense, she echoed Harriet Beecher Stowe's hero, Uncle Tom: better to endure wrong than to perpetrate it. Not incidentally, Stowe and her sister Catherine Beecher aligned themselves with Stone. They embraced a concept of femininity imbued with the virtue of self-sacrifice.

Victoria Woodhull, spiritualist, faith-healer, con-artist, and stockbroker represented the opposite extreme. With help from the wealthy Commodore Vanderbilt, also a spiritualist, Victoria and her sister Tennessee Claflin struck it rich on the stock market. They used the pages of their newspaper, *Woodhull and Claflin's Weekly*, to endorse the cause of women, workers, and free love. Victoria famously declared, "Free love will be the religion of the future. Yes! I am a free lover. I have an inalienable constitutional right to love whom I may, to love as long or as short a period as I can, to change that love everyday if I please!"[53] Karl Marx, reading press accounts in London, was sufficiently horrified to insist on Victoria's expulsion from the First International Workingman's Association.[54]

Elizabeth Cady Stanton was, to all outward appearances, the embodiment of middle-class respectability. But she had a profound appreciation of the problem of domestic violence and a keen eye for the asymmetries of the marriage contract, which she interpreted in economic terms as a set of property rights and contractual restrictions. As early as 1860, she wrote powerfully and persuasively on behalf of divorce law reform.[55] She observed that the liberalization of divorce laws had something in common with the liberalization of trade. "Laissez-faire with all my heart", she wrote, explaining that unhappy marriages should be ended.[56]

Stanton's advocacy of birth control within marriage—primarily in the form of abstinence, was also couched in political and economic language. Herself the mother of seven children, Stanton invoked the concept of self-ownership that John Locke had claimed for men: A woman's body should be her private property. This particular sexual property right had momentous demographic implications. Anglo-American common law gave husbands unlimited sexual access to their wives. When Stanton and others demanded "voluntary motherhood" what they meant was that wives should have the right to kick their husbands out of bed.

Marital abstinence, along with use of folk methods of contraception such as withdrawal and douching, contributed to a dramatic decline in completed fertility rates in the United States over the course of the nineteenth century, from eight to about three children per woman.[57] Many forces favored sexual self-control. The growth of public education, the declining value of young children's labor, and the increasing independence of elder children—combined with a desire to ensure the prosperity of the next generation—increased awareness of the costs of large families. Late nineteenth-century medical literature compared the virtues of saving sperm to saving money—investments that would pay off at a future date.[58]

Evangelical Protestantism found a ready audience among those shaken by the new economic order. Religious virtue was becoming harder to sell, in part because men were under less obligation to buy. Those marketing a new religious persuasion reached out to women. Evangelical preachers, uncomfortable with doctrines emphasizing Eve's original sin and women's susceptibility to lust, began to suggest that women were actually more predisposed to virtue than men. The price of virtue for most women, however, was a kind of passionlessness that could explain their relative immunity from temptation.[59]

Men, on the other hand, enjoyed new sexual freedoms. All the forces that drew youth away from home—urban migration, Westernization, and military conscription—expanded the market for paid sexual services. In 1858, the physician William Sanger published his *History of Prostitution: Its Extent, Causes and Effects Throughout the World*, with tantalizing descriptions of Greek and Roman practices. Sanger's accounts of sexual relations in what he called "barbarous" and "semi-civilized" nations suggested that the Western practice of marriage represented a magnificent accomplishment simply because it protected many, if not all women, from "common use".

The book also included the results of a survey of several thousand prostitutes in New York City, reporting that nearly half claimed to have been infected with syphilis.[60] Like most physicians, Sanger strongly favored French-style regulation. In the United States, however, regulatory efforts met especially concerted opposition. Women's rights advocates linked arms both with religious groups who feared that Parisian values would undermine American morals and with civil libertarians who opposed unwarranted search and seizure. This rather unexpected alliance effectively blocked most efforts to regulate and medicalize prostitution (including campaigns in New York in 1867 and Chicago in 1871).[61] The resulting uncertainties reduced customer demand.

A true libertarian would argue that women should have the right to freely sell their sexual services. Of course, he would also suggest that men and women should have the individual right to sell themselves into slavery. Stanton seized on the parallel, and used her opposition to prostitution to illustrate her larger concerns about gendered self-interest: "Just as slavery in the South, with its lessons of obedience, degraded every black man in the Northern States, so does an accepted system of prostitution, with its lessons of subjection and self-sacrifice, degrade the ideal of womanhood everywhere."[62]

Balancing Acts

Elizabeth Cady Stanton and Susan B. Anthony questioned the traditional assumption that only men had rights and only women had responsibilities by calling for a better balance between the two. They sought to balance selfishness and altruism along with equality and difference. They developed a theory of collective interests, an emphasis on the economic value of non-market work, and an analysis of sexual property rights.

In her autobiography, *Eighty Years and More*, Stanton conceded that there was truth to the observation that she had forged the thunderbolts, while Susan Anthony had fired them.[63] Whatever their division of labor, their collaboration proved heroic. True, it avoided serious consideration of the persistent racial, ethnic, and class inequalities that divided women.[64] Still, Stanton and Anthony made enduring contributions that reached well beyond the liberal discourse of individual rights. They argued that political reform could change human behavior.

The notion that women had been—to modernize Mill's claim—brainwashed to put others' interests before their own suggested not only that that process could be reversed, but that it could be imposed on men. In modern parlance, women could take assertiveness training, while men could practice sensitivity. Then, as now, the big unanswered question was just how far and fast such regendering could go, and at what balance of assertiveness and sensitivity it should come to rest.

NOTES TO CHAPTER 14

[1] Mary Ann Dimand, Robert W. Dimand, Evelyn L. Forget, *Women of Value: Feminist Essays on the History of Women in Economics* (Aldershot: Elgar, 1995); Janet A. Seiz, Michele A. Pujol, "Harriet Taylor Mill," *American Economic Review* 90:2 (2000), 476–9; Stanton and Anthony are not included in Robert W. Dimand, Mary Ann Dimand, and Evelyn L. Forget (eds), *The Biographical Dictionary of Women Economists* (Cheltenham: Elgar, 2000).

[2] Joseph Dorfman, *The Economic Mind in American Civilization* (New York: Augustus Kelley, 1969), p. 908.

[3] Ibid., p. 750.

[4] Carolyn Johnston, *Sexual Power. Feminism and the Family in America*. (Tuscaloosa, AL: University of Alabama Press, 1992)

[5] Gerda Lerner, *The Feminist Thought of Sarah Grimke* (New York: Oxford University Press, 1998), p. 37.

[6] Aileen Kraditor, *Up from the Pedestal. Selected Writings in the History of American Feminism* (Chicago: Quadrangle Books, 1968), p. 184.

[7] Judith Wellman, *The Road to Seneca Falls. Elizabeth Cady Stanton and the First Woman's Rights Convention* (Chicago: University of Illinois Press, 2004), p. 209.

[8] Carole Shammas, "Re-Assessing the Married Women's Property Acts," *Journal of Women's History* 6:1 (1994), 9–29.

[9] Wellman, *The Road to Seneca Falls; Lois W. Banner, Elizabeth Cady Stanton, A Radical for Women's Rights* (Boston: Little, Brown, 1980).

[10] Ellen Carol Dubois, *Feminism and Suffrage. The Emergence of an Independent Women's Movement in America, 1849–1869* (New York: Cornell University Press, 1978), p. 87.

[11] Barbara Goldsmith, *Other Powers. The Age of Suffrage, Spiritualism, and the Scandalous Victoria Woodhull*. (New York: Alfred A. Knopf, 1998), p. 133.

[12] Stanton wrote, "If you do not wish the lower orders of Chinese, Africans, Germans, and Irish, with their low ideas of womanhood to make laws for you and your daughters... demand that women, too, shall be represented in the government," cited in Dubois, *Feminism and Suffrage*, p. 174. Another indicative quote: "If you will not give the whole loaf of suffrage to the entire people, give it to the most intelligent first." Elizabeth Cady Stanton, Susan B. Anthony, and Matilda Jocelyn Gage, *History of Woman Suffrage*. Volumes 1–3 (New York: Fowler and Wells, 1882), p. 379.

[13] Eleanor Flexner, *Century of Struggle. The Woman's Rights Movement in the United States* (New York: Atheneum, 1971), p. 152.

[14] Aileen S. Kraditor, *The Ideas of the Woman Suffrage Movement, 1890–1920*. (New York: Anchor Books, 1971), p. 65.

[15] Suzanne M. Marilley, *Woman Suffrage and the Origins of Liberal Feminism in the U.S., 1820–1920* (Cambridge, MA: Harvard University Press, 1996), p. 108.

[16] Ibid., p. 101.

[17] Nancy F. Cott, *The Grounding of Modern Feminism* (New Haven: Yale University Press, 1987), p. 20.

[18] Harriet Beecher Stowe, *Uncle Tom's Cabin; or Life Among the Lowly* (Boston: John P. Jewett, 1852), Vol. 1, p. 59.

[19] Josephine Donovan, *Uncle Tom's Cabin. Evil, Affliction, and Redemptive Love* (Boston: Twayne Publishers, 1991).

[20] Catherine Beecher and Harriet Beecher Stowe, *The American Woman's Home* (New York: J.B. Ford and Company, 1869), p. 19.

[21] Katherine Kish Sklar, *Catherine Beecher. A Study in American Domesticity* (New Haven: Yale University Press, 1973), p. 156.

[22] Linda Kerber, "Women and Individualism in American History," *Massachusetts Review* (1989), 589–609. See also William Leach, *True Love and Perfect Union. The Feminist Reform of Sex and Society* (New York: Basic Books Inc., 1980), p. 97.

[23] Lois Banner, *Elizabeth Cady Stanton, A Radical for Woman's Rights* (Boston: Little Brown, 1980) p. 76.

[24] Richard Cándida Smith, "Stanton on Self and Community," 66–81 in *Elizabeth Cady Stanton. Feminist as Thinker. A Reader in Documents and Essays,* Ellen Carol DuBois and Richard Cándida Smith, eds (New York: New York University Press, 2007).

[25] *Elizabeth Cady Stanton, Eighty Years and More. Reminiscences 1815–1897* (Boston: Northeastern University Press, 1993), p. 369.

[26] Leach, *True Love,* p. 172.

[27] Leach, *True Love,* p. xv.

[28] Ibid., p. 148.

[29] Lynn Sherr, ed., *Failure is Impossible. Susan B. Anthony in Her Own Words* (New York: Random House, 1995), p. 58.

[30] Elizabeth Cady Stanton, "The Equilibrium of Sex," *Commonwealth* 6 (June 24, 1899), 12–13.

[31] Sarah Grimke, *Letters on the Equality of the Sexes and Other Essays*, ed. Elizabeth Ann Bartless (New Haven: Yale University Press, 1988), p. 35. See also Gerda Lerner, *The Feminist Thought of Sarah Grimke* (New York: Oxford University Press, 1998).

[32] Ibid., p. 63.

[33] "In those employments which are peculiar to women, their time is estimated at only half of the value of that of men. A woman who goes out to wash, works as hard in proportion as a wood sawyer, or a coal heaver, but she is not generally able to make more than half as much by a day's work." Ibid., p. 59.

[34] Ibid., p. 185.

[35] Barbara Bergmann, *The Economic Emergence of Women* (New York: Basic Books, 1986).

[36] Elizabeth Cady Stanton, "The Subjection of Women," in Gordon, ed., *The Selected Papers*, p. 626.

[37] Gerda Lerner, *The Creation of Patriarchy* (New York: Oxford University Press, 1986).

[38] Catherine Beecher and Harriet Beecher Stowe, *The American Woman's Home* (New York: J.B. Ford and Company, 1869), p. xiii.

[39] Shammas, "Reassessing the Married Women's Property Right Acts."

[40] Reva B. Siegel, "Home as Work: The First Woman's Rights Claims concerning Wives' Household Labor, 1850–1880," *Yale Law Journal* 103 (1994), 1073–217.

[41] Elizabeth Cady Stanton, *The Revolution*, December 24, 1868.

[42] Ibid, August 27, 1868.

[43] Siegel, "Home as Work."

[44] Leach, *True Love*, p. 194.

[45] Siegel, "Home as Work."

[46] Leach, *True Love,* p. 193.

[47] Janet Gornick and Marcia Meyers, *Families that Work* (New York: Russell Sage, 2005).

[48] "Let no women give all their time to household duties, but require nearly all women, and all men also, since they belong to the household, to bear some share of the common household burdens. Many hands make light work, and hearts would be lightened in proportion ... I should rejoice to see springing up in every city, distinct classes of three to five hour industries, with a fresh relay of workers at stated intervals, arranged for the express benefit of men and women, who desire to give but a small portion of their time to outside pursuits." Antoinette Brown Blackwell in Aileen Kraditor, *Up from the Pedestal. Selected Writings in the History of American Feminism* (Chicago: Quadrangle Books, 1968) p. 155.

[49] Dolores Hayden, *The Grand Domestic Revolution. A History of Feminist Designs for American Homes, Neighborhoods, and Cities* (Cambridge: M.I.T. Press, 1981), p. 80.

[50] Elaine Tyler May, *Great Expectations. Marriage and Divorce in Post-Victorian America* (Chicago: University of Chicago Press, 1980).

[51] Mary Gabriel, *Notorious Victoria. The Life of Victoria Woodhull, Uncensored* (Chapel Hill, NC: Algonquin Books, 1998), p. 96.

[52] Eleanor Flexner, in *Century of Struggle*, refers to Stanton's alignment with Woodhull as brief and unfortunate (p. 153). Aileen Kraditor, in *The Ideas of the Woman Suffrage Movement*, (New York: Doubleday, 1971) writes that Stanton and Anthony supported Woodhull "only out of a sense of sex solidarity, but neither they nor any other suffragists ever espoused her views" (p. 93). Stanton never espoused all her views. But she did espouse some of them, particularly her advocacy of divorce.

[53] Cited in Johnston, *Sexual Power*, p. 77.

[54] Goldsmith, *Other Powers*.

[55] See "Address to the Tenth National Women's Rights Convention on Marriage and Divorce, New York City, May 11, 1860," and "Divorce versus Domestic Warfare," in *Elizabeth Cady Stanton, Feminist as Thinker. A Reader in Documents and Essays*, Ellen Carol DuBois and Richard Candida Smith, eds (New York: New York University Press, 2007).

[56] Elizabeth Cady Stanton, "Reasons Why Some Marriages are Unhappy," *The Revolution*, October 15, 1868.

[57] Daniel S. Smith, "Family Limitation, Sexual Control and Domestic Feminism in Victorian America," *Feminist Studies* 1:3–4 (1973), 40–57; Paul A. David and Warren C. Sanderson, "Rudimentary Contraceptive Methods and the American Transition to Marital Fertility Control," 307–90 in *Long-Term Factors in American Economic Growth* (Chicago: University of Chicago Press, 1986).

[58] G. J. Barker-Benfield, *The Horrors of the Half-Known Life: Male Attitudes Toward Women and Sexuality in Nineteenth-Century America* (New York: Harper and Row, 1976).

[59] Nancy Cott, "Passionlessness: An Interpretation of Victorian Sexual Ideology, 1790–1850," pp. 162–81 in Nancy F. Cott and Elizabeth H. Pleck, eds, *A Heritage of Her Own: Toward a New Social History of American Women* (New York: Simon and Schuster, 1979).

[60] William Sanger, *The History of Prostitution. Its Extent, Causes and Effects Throughout the World* (New York: Eugenics Publishing Company, 1939), p. 676.

[61] Ruth Rosen, *The Lost Sisterhood. Prostitution in America, 1900–1918* (Baltimore: Johns Hopkins, 1982), pp. 3, 10.

[62] Elizabeth Cady Stanton, "Has Christianity Benefited Woman," in Dubois and Smith, *Elizabeth Cady Stanton*, p. 249.

[63] Elizabeth Cady Stanton, *Eighty Years and More. Reminiscences, 1815–1897* (Amherst, New York: Humanity Books, 2002), p. 165.

[64] Robert W. Dimand, "Nineteenth-Century American Feminist Economics: From Caroline Dall to Charlotte Perkins Gilman," *American Economic Review* 90:2 (2000), 480–4.

CHAPTER 15

The Icy Waters

The wife is the breadwinner while her husband stays at home to look after the children and to do the cooking and cleaning....In Manchester alone there are many hundreds of men who are condemned to perform household duties. One may well imagine the righteous indignation of the workers at being virtually turned into eunuchs.   Friedrich Engels

By most Eurocentric accounts, the nineteenth was the most capitalist of centuries. The expansion of trade and technological change in the now affluent countries of Britain, France, and the U.S. gained visible momentum. The factory became the iconic site of production, and the corporation its iconic legal form. Karl Marx, largely responsible for the term "capitalism", became its most iconic critic. The German political economist spent most of his life in London, the epicenter of the new and apparently dominant mode of production, trying to understand its laws of motion. He enjoyed the friendship, support, and collaboration of his countryman, Friedrich Engels, whose father was a financially successful factory owner.

Capitalism was not a sufficiently specific word to characterize nineteenth-century economic systems shaped by patriarchy, slavery, and imperialism as well as the expansion of wage employment. The effort to attribute most social ills to the exploitation of wage earners by capitalists called attention to the dynamics of collective conflict, but oversimplified these dynamics in dangerously misleading ways. By distancing themselves from their socialist feminist antecedents, Marx and Engels gained support from a growing male trade union movement. But their single-minded emphasis on the internal contradictions of capitalism generated a simplistic theory of socialism that proved vulnerable to patriarchal and authoritarian appropriation.[1]

In their passion to understand—and hopefully eliminate—class interests, Marx and Engels understated the importance of collective interests based on nation, race, and gender. While they acknowledged differences within the global working class, they viewed these as political and cultural, rather than economic in character. The oppression of the working class, unlike that of other groups, was based in the appropriation of surplus value, the linchpin of capitalist accumulation. Their embrace of a labor theory of value that disregarded family labor deflected their attention from gender inequality in particular. Yet many of their fellow travelers avoided this mistake. August Bebel, among others, developed an analysis of patriarchal capitalism that highlighted the parallels between collective interests based on class and gender.

Despite their departures from the earlier socialist feminist tradition, Marx and Engels always insisted that a better world was possible. Their conviction that members of the working class could successfully exert collective power countered individualist views of the war-of-all-against-all variety. At first glance, Charles Darwin's theory of evolution seemed to strengthen the case for emphasis on individual competition. Proponents of social evolution, like Herbert Spencer, seemed to argue that poverty and inequality were the outcome of necessary, natural processes. Yet Darwin himself tried to reconcile relentless individual competition with evidence of cooperation based on both real and fictive kinship. In the twentieth century, debates over the role of collective interests would often be framed in the Darwinian language of individual versus group selection.

Revolutions

Marx and Engels issued the *Communist Manifesto* in 1848, just as John Stuart Mill published his *Principles of Political Economy* and women's rights advocates in Seneca Falls, New York issued their own manifesto. In that same year a revolution in the streets of Paris extended the right to vote to all French men and also proclaimed their right to work, establishing workshops for the unemployed. Though short-lived, these gains became a model for collective protest elsewhere. "There is a spectre haunting Europe," Karl Marx and Friedrich Engels had proclaimed, with perfect timing. Though they called for proletarian ownership of the means of production, their demands were mild by current standards, featuring a progressive income tax and free education for all children in public schools.[2]

The aura of de Saint-Simon colored their confidence in science and industry, the development of the "forces of production". A hint of Fourier appeared in their vision of a future in which men would be able to hunt in the morning, fish in the afternoon, herd cattle in the evening, and criticize philosophy after dinner.[3] But the early writings of Marx and Engels distanced them from the "critical-utopian" socialism that they believed was premature, lacking the support and guidance of a proletariat. The *Communist Manifesto* did not endorse cooperative experiments. It called for revolutionary change.

The first volume of *Capital*, published in 1867, provided a compelling account of the role of force and violence in the early stage of primitive accumulation in Britain. It went on to develop a critique of capitalism that drew heavily from the doctrines of classical political economy even as it emphasized their ideological character. Locke had originally offered the labor theory of value as a justification for private property. Ricardo had applied it to a very different end, the demonstration of a difference between the costs of production and a surplus that was appropriated by landowners who provided absolutely no labor or services in return. Extending Ricardo's analysis to argue that capitalists extracted a different kind of surplus from workers, Marx turned the labor theory of value into a theory of capitalist exploitation. One need not accept his specific formulation to support the claim that the relative bargaining power of capitalists and workers affects the distribution of income. In the late twentieth century, a new generation of Marxist economists would develop more analytical versions of a general theory of exploitation.[4]

Marx's analysis of class conflict was joined to a prophecy of a future in which the vicious conflicts of capitalism would be transcended. The falling rate of profit would force an economic crisis and a transition, first, to a socialist system based on de Saint-Simonian principles—from each according to their ability, to each according to their work. The next stage would be communism—from each according to his ability, to each according to his need. The teleology drew heavily from the German philosopher Georg Wilhelm Friedrich Hegel's abstract formulation of the laws of history. The stage theory neatly transcended earlier debates about equality of opportunity versus equality of outcomes by suggesting that they should come in sequence.

Scientific Self-Interest

Embedded in this theory was a radical, though indirect departure from previous theories of self-interest. First, Marx and Engels aspired to treat self-interest in scientific rather than moral terms. They rejected all preaching as ineffectual, laughing at Owen's "appeal to the capitalists" and de Saint-Simon's Christian exhortations. What they meant by "scientific socialism" was an approach that did not depend upon the success of philosophical assumptions about justice, equality, or the transcendent importance of developing human capabilities. Would-be revolutionaries could stop wagging their fingers and shaking their fists at the ruling class, and prepare for a wave of historical transformation that would render their enemy obsolete.

Marx and Engels sharply rejected Fourier's notion that individual self-interest was a natural or inherent passion. They argued instead that men were largely the product of their own environment. Obviously, men had to meet their basic economic needs (Marx admired Darwin's theory of the survival of the fittest). But economic self-interest was grotesquely amplified by capitalist development. Greed, in other words, was capitalism's unholy offspring. Marx and Engels decried bourgeois culture, which "drowned the most heavenly ecstasies of religious fervor, of chivalrous enthusiasm, of philistine sentimentalism, in the icy water of egotistical calculation."[5]

They were joined in this view by many of the English romantics of their century, fascinated by what Marxist historian Eric Hobsbawm describes as "the demonic element in capitalist accumulation, the limitless and uninterrupted pursuit of *more,* beyond the calculation of rationality or purpose, need or the extremes of luxury."[6] Owen and Mill had both observed that human character was molded by economic circumstance, pointing to the unfortunate legacies of patriarchal, as well as capitalist power. Marx and Engels focused more narrowly on the ideology of accumulation, the claim that capitalist greed would benefit everyone.

The Marxian theory of ideology challenged the basic premise of the liberal theory of the social contract. Individuals did not only form societies they were also formed by them; and once formed, they might find it difficult to reform. The theory of ideology also rejected a traditional elitism of the educated that reflexively treated great thinkers as arbiters of the public good. Marx and Engels showed in scornful detail how prevailing economic theories served the interests of the rich and powerful.

To condemn the ideology of greed was to raise the issue of how it might be transcended in the next stage of human progress. The explanation that Marx and Engels offered here was far less compelling than their emphasis on ideology writ large. They claimed that in a society governed by a proletarian majority, *self-interest* would become *universal interest* and thus—poof!—disappear. This rabbit, pulled from the magic hat of Hegelian theory, proved difficult to pin down. It depended entirely on the assumption that individuals had no interests apart from those of their economic class. All would be one, and one would be all. A classless society would be without conflict, and therefore would require little attention to democratic governance or efficient management. Ricardo believed that classes as a whole had economic interests; Marx and Engels assumed, in effect, that individuals could have no interests *other* than those based on class. This assumption, perhaps more than any other, undermined the twentieth-century Marxist regimes that collapsed under the weight of authoritarian bureaucracy.[7]

The Holy Family

Apart from a few tantalizing comments in the *German Ideology* and his nominal condemnation of the sexual double standard, Marx endorsed a traditional vision of family life. The German philosopher he loved, Georg Wilhelm Friedrich Hegel, probably bore responsibility for this. He articulated many of the arguments that English speaking intellectuals typically refer to as Victorian, based on the prescription of entirely separate spheres for men and women. Hegel argued, for instance, that the family was a wholly ethical realm that would counter the selfishness of market society and provide a stable foundation for civil society. He described men as the active force of reason, women as the passive expression of love.[8]

Marx's own personal life conformed neatly to this picture. By most accounts, he adored his wife Jenny, who hand-copied most of his manuscripts before they were sent to a publisher and cared for a family living hand-to-mouth. Constantly in debt, and occasionally even forced by economic circumstance to withdraw their daughters from school, the Marx family became dependent on financial assistance from Engels, who also accepted paternity of a child born to the family's loyal unmarried housekeeper, Helene Dumuth. Evidence from his daughter Eleanor's papers strongly suggests that Marx was the biological father.[9]

Marx and Engels did not dismiss their feminist predecessors. Both agreed with Fourier that woman's position was a measure of the general level of social development and her wretched condition under capitalism one more indicator of the need to supersede that system. In their early writings, they often used the adjective "patriarchal" to modify the word "family". Yet they located patriarchy in the past, describing it as an outmoded, anachronistic inequality. Where it did exist under capitalism, it lacked significant economic implications, because the working-class family unit was unified by mutual benevolence. As Marx explained, "Individual labour powers, by their very nature, act only as instruments of the joint labour power of the family."[10]

Engels, far more interested than Marx in the internal dynamics of family life, blamed capitalism for its malfunctions. *The Condition of the Working Class in England*, a detailed descriptive study he published in 1845, dwelt at length on the perversities that resulted when high male unemployment made husbands dependent on their wives' earnings (see the epigraph to this chapter).[11] Forced to adopt feminine responsibilities, he implied, they were in effect demasculinized. While Engels condemned the pre-existing domination of husbands over wives that had simply been reversed by the new factory system, he steered clear of any discussion of contemporary women's rights.[12] The weight of his argument supported the popular view that men and women should be segregated in the workplace, and that men—but not women—should earn a wage sufficient to support a family.

The Response to Bebel

In the 1880s, both the "woman question" and the "population question" were hotly debated by German Social Democrats. August Bebel's *Women and Socialism* (1879) enjoyed international acclaim, but was greeted unenthusiastically by Marx and Engels. Shortly after Marx died, Engels took time off from the task of editing the final volumes of *Capital* to write a response to Bebel. His manuscript was based on the findings of the American anthropologist Lewis Morgan and on Marx's notes on the subject. *The Origin of the Family, Private Property, and the State* applied the theory of historical materialism to explain the coevolution of class relations and family types. Engels described the overthrow of an original matriarchy, based on "mother right" as the result of the emergence of forms of property that men wanted to control and pass on to their heirs in the male line. Men's desire to ensure paternity led them to establish control over women's sexuality in the form of strict female monogamy; their monopoly over economic activities outside the home enhanced their power over the emergent state.

The *Origin* persuasively argued that gender inequality was rooted in the process of social evolution, not in biological differences between men and women. But the argument lacked much contemporary relevance. Engels carefully absolved the proletarian family of any potential for internal conflict. Both husband and wife were propertyless, dependent on wage employment, and therefore equals. The transition to socialism, and the concomitant increase in women's participation in social labor, would guarantee their complete liberation, because domestic labor and child rearing could easily be industrialized. Whatever domestic cares remained, women would naturally and lovingly assume.

Consolidating the reputation of a tradition unsympathetic, though not overtly hostile, to feminist concerns, *The Origin* became known as the classic Marxian account of women's oppression. Only a few Marxists dissented from the view that gender inequality could not affect capitalism's laws of motion. The Hegelian assumption of family unity, echoing James Mill's famous explanation of why women had the need to vote, helped make Marxism more politically palatable to working-class men than earlier feminist socialisms had been. As one of his contemporaries put it, Marx "represented the manhood of socialist thought."[13]

Some historians argue that he remained largely unaware of issues that were only later labeled feminist.[14] But as noted in the previous chapter, Marx recommended expulsion of a faction of the International Working

Men's Association in the United States, headed by Victoria Woodhull, on the grounds that they put the rights of women above those of workers. In a letter to a friend in the late 1860s, Marx spoke derisively of female suffrage, explaining that "German women should have begun by driving their men to self-emancipation" rather than "seeking emancipation for themselves directly."[15] Marxist theory rode a wave of larger efforts to define the interests of the proletariat as the interests of proletarian men.[16]

Bebel and Social Democracy

Still, many socialists—especially those outside France—embraced the cause of women's rights. The German social democrats considered hopelessly reformist by orthodox Marxists were a case in point. August Bebel's *Woman and Socialism,* first published in 1879 and widely translated, became an international bestseller. By 1910 it had gone through fifty editions and far outsold the critique that Engels had penned.[17] Bebel strongly supported feminist efforts. Within the Second International Workingmen's Association, left-wing militant Vladimir Lenin argued that issues such as sexuality, marriage, and divorce were diversionary, because they were not class-based.[18] Still, Bebel's views influenced some of the policies implemented by the Bolshevik regime in Russia in 1917, and exerted an even stronger influence on the platforms of social democratic political parties all over Western Europe.

The first sentence of *Woman and Socialism* boldly asserted the parallels between class and gender: "Woman and the workingman have, since old, had this in common—oppression."[19] Bebel went on to argue that all social dependence and oppression were rooted in economic dependence, or lack of independent property rights. He recited a catechism of arguments in defense of women's capabilities, rebutting misogyny from Plato to Schopenhauer. His sweeping history of the emergence of patriarchal and capitalist hierarchy dwelt on the role of force and violence and the establishment of arbitrary laws and social norms. It asserted the need for sweeping democratic reform.

Bebel addressed issues that political economists had typically ignored, ranging from general themes such as asymmetric property rights to colorful specifics, such as the Prussian law giving the husband the right to dictate how long his wife should be required to suckle his child.[20] The increased costs of raising children, Bebel argued, were forcing women to resort to illegal abortions that threatened their health.[21] He documented new laws in France and Germany making it difficult for unwed mothers to gain any support from the fathers of their children. He deplored the increasing use of contraception not because it was immoral, but because under a socialist regime all children would be considered economic assets. Like John Stuart Mill, he predicted that improvements in women's position would result in fertility decline:

> Leaving exceptions aside, intelligent and energetic women are not as a rule inclined to give life to a large number of children as "the gift of God" and to spend the best years of their own lives in pregnancy, or with a child at their breasts. This disinclination for numerous children, which even now is entertained by most women, may—all the solicitude notwithstanding that a Socialist society will bestow on pregnant women and mothers—be rather strengthened than weakened. In our opinion, there lies in this the great probability that the increase of population will proceed slower than in bourgeois society.[22]

Like Engels, Bebel saw children as essentially women's responsibilities, cheerfully predicting that under socialism "nurses, teachers, female friends, and the rising female generation" would be on hand to help individual mothers.[23] Also like Engels, he believed that housework would soon be obsolete. His evidence on this count included a glowing description of the centralized modern kitchen exhibited at the Chicago Exposition of 1893 and details of a recently invented shoe-polishing machine.[24] But unlike Engels and other orthodox Marxists, Bebel refused to blame women's oppression simply on the interests of the ruling class. He emphasized, instead, men's collective interest in protecting their own privilege.[25] "The icy waters of egotistical calculation," it seems, could lap at many different shores.

The Survival of the Altruistic

Marxists had a point when they observed that capitalist culture seemed to reward both individual and collective greed. The new science of evolution, as well as political economy, harped upon this point. Reading Malthus's

Essay on Population in 1838, Charles Darwin experienced an epiphany—the relentless pressure of population growth could help explain why and how natural selection took place.[26] Also inspiring, perhaps, had been the example of a parson who rejected the notion that God must be benevolent. Both men challenged the vision of a heavenly Father looking after his children, or a shepherd taking care of his flock. Their God seem more detached, sadly observing the cycles of demographic boom and boost and watching a gladiatorial contest for the prize of "most fit".

Advocates of *laissez faire*, like the English philosopher/sociologist Herbert Spencer, had long argued that fierce competition would bring out the best in individuals and society. Charles Darwin appropriated Spencer's phrase, the "survival of the fittest" in his *Origin of the Species*. Spencer, in turn, developed the theory of Social Darwinism, which gradually replaced Malthusianism as a bludgeon against public assistance to the poor. Spencer was a militant individualist, insisting on the "permanent supremacy of egoism over altruism."[27] Evolution, after all, appeared to be a winner-take-all game.

In his later volume *The Descent of Man*, however, Darwin shifted tone, hypothesizing that some degree of altruism would give the tribe, or group, an evolutionary advantage. In a page that could have been lifted from Montesquieu's parable of the Troglodytes he wrote:

> Selfish and contentious people will not cohere, and without coherence nothing can be effected. A tribe rich in the above qualities would spread and be victorious over other tribes: but in the course of time it would, judging by all past history, be in its turn overcome by some other tribe still more highly endowed. Thus the social and moral qualities would tend slowly to advance and be diffused throughout the world.[28]

Darwin did not fully explain his version of group selection, which remains a controversial issue within evolutionary theory today. But his confidence in "coherence" weirdly echoed Marx's confidence in class solidarity. The argument Darwin saved for last in *The Descent of Man* betrayed surprisingly sentimental views. There can hardly be a doubt, he explained, that we are descended from barbarian tribes. Was it necessarily worse to be descended from an ape? Recalling men who had enslaved women and butchered children, he declared that he would rather be descended from a heroic monkey who had saved its keeper's life, or an old baboon who saved a younger from a pack of dogs. It was a surprising turn of argument for a scientist, to claim that an altruistic ape was at least as good a forebear as a selfish man.

Herbert Spencer also took pains to distinguish selfishness from self-interest. He worried what might happen if women became selfish. Their individual interests were at odds with those of their children. The ultimate rationale for altruism was the survival of the family, and this, he noted rather presciently, implied an intergenerational contract: "a society, like a species, survives only on condition that each generation of its members shall yield to the next, benefits equivalent to those it has received from the last. And this implies that care for the family must be supplemented by care for the society."[29] In Darwinian terms, kin-based altruism would be rewarded, and members of a society were often either actual or potential kin.

The Free Development of All

The problem was not just to understand morality, but to improve it. Maybe socialism would never create a new socialist man. But institutional design could make a difference. Democratic rights, social solidarity, and economic safety nets could discourage, if not eliminate the worst forms of exploitation. They could narrow the avenues of greed. Marx and Engels helped illuminate the role of ideology in historical change, ironically providing tools by which to critique their own capitulations to the status quo. In retrospect, it may be too easy to admire their predecessors and successors more than they.

If there was one aspect of the family that all socialists embraced, it was parental concern for the self-realization of the next generation, extended to society as a whole. Marx and Engels stated the ideal with characteristic boldness in the *Communist Manifesto*: "The old bourgeois society with its classes and its conflicts of classes gives way to an association where the free development of each individual is the condition of the free development of all."[30] At this, Owen, Thompson, Wheeler, de Saint-Simon, and Fourier would all have cheered. Mill and Stanton would have murmured at least some assent. Each would have gone on to explain, in their own distinctive voice, why the unregulated pursuit of individual self-interest could never achieve this nurturant ideal.

NOTES TO CHAPTER 15

[1] Lydia Sargent, ed., *Women and Revolution* (Boston: South End Press, 1981); Alex Nove, *The Economics of Feasible Socialism* (Boston: Allen and Unwin, 1983).

[2] Karl Marx and Frederick Engels, "Manifesto of the Communist Party," in Robert Tucker, ed., *The Marx-Engels Reader* (New York: W. W. Norton and Company Inc., 1972), p. 352.

[3] Marx and Engels, "The German Ideology," in Tucker, *Marx-Engels Reader*, p. 124.

[4] John Roemer, *Free to Lose. An Introduction to Marxist Economic Philosophy* (Cambridge, MA: Harvard University Press, 1988).

[5] Karl Marx and Friedrich Engels, "The Communist Manifesto," in Robert Tucker, ed., *The Marx-Engels Reader* (New York: W. W. Norton, 1972), p.337.

[6] E. J. Hobsbawm, *The Age of Revolution, 1789–1848* (New York: The World Publishing Company, 1962) p. 259.

[7] See Alec Nove, *The Economics of Feasible Socialism* (Boston: Allen and Unwin, 1983).

[8] Joan Landes, "Hegel's Conception of the Family," pp. 125–44 in Jean Bethke Elshtain, ed., *The Family in Political Thought* (Amherst: The University of Massachusetts Press, 1982), pp. 131, 137.

[9] For more on this point, see Frank E. Manuel and Fritzie P. Manuel, *Utopian Thought in the Western World* (Cambridge: Harvard University Press, 1979), 708–109.

[10] Karl Marx, *Capital*, Vol. 1. Trans. Ben Fowkes (New York: Vintage Books, 1977), p. 171. Joint labor power, in this context, is directly analogous to the neoclassical economic concept of joint utility.

[11] Frederick Engels, *The Condition of the Working Class in England*. Translated and edited by W. O. Henderson and W. H. Chaloner (Stanford: Stanford University Press, 1958), p. 162.

[12] Ibid., p. 164.

[13] David McLellan, *Karl Marx. His Life and Thought* (New York: Harper and Row, 1973), p. 177.

[14] Lise Vogel *(Marxism and the Oppression of Women*, 1983) is entirely unconvincing when she claims that, "his sources were poor." (p. 59).

[15] Mary Jo Buhle, *Women and American Socialism, 1870–1920* (Urbana: University of Illinois Press, 1981), p. 11.

[16] Harold Benenson, "Victorian Sexual Ideology and Marx's Theory of the Working Class," *International Labor and Working Class History* 25 (1984), 1–23.

[17] The greatly expanded ninth edition of 1891, which incorporated some of Frederick Engels's arguments in its historical section, became the best-known and most widely cited

version. Lise Vogel, *Marxism and the Oppression of Women* (New Brunswick: Rutgers University Press, 1983), 97–98.

[18] For an articulate modern version of this argument, see Vogel, *Marxism.*

[19] August Bebel, *Woman Under Socialism*. Translated from the original German of the thirty-third edition by Daniel De Leon (New York: Schocken Books, 1971), p. 9.

[20] Ibid., p. 216.

[21] Ibid., p. 109.

[22] Ibid., p. 370.

[23] Ibid., p. 347.

[24] Ibid., pp. 338–41.

[25] Ibid., p. 187.

[26] Frances Darwin, *The Life and Letters of Charles Darwin* (New York: D. Appleton and Co., 1888), Vol. I, p. 68.

[27] Herbert Spencer, *The Principles of Ethics* (New York: D. Appleton, 1910), p. 187.

[28] Charles Darwin, *The Descent of Man* (New York: Encyclopedia Britannica, Inc., 1952), p. 321.

[29] Herbert Spencer, *The Principles of Ethics* (New York: D. Appleton, 1910), p. 216.

[30] Marx and Engels, *Communist Manifesto*, p. 353.

CHAPTER 16

The Sacred Sphere

The most valuable of all capital is that invested in human beings; and of that capital, the most precious part is the results of the care and influence of the mother, so long as she retains her tender and unselfish instincts, and has not been hardened by the strain and stress of unfeminine work.

Alfred Marshall

Socialism and feminism were creative responses to destabilization of the traditional patriarchal order, but they were not particularly popular ones. Most people found it easier to reiterate the traditional moral division of labor and to condemn the indulgence of greed and lust everywhere except the masculine marketplace. Queen Victoria, who ruled the British Empire from 1837 to 1901, assumed a traditionally male prerogative but also encouraged the notion that women and men were essentially different. Victorian values encouraged separate spheres for men and women that reflected contrasts between selfishness and altruism, the market and the family. This social cosmology offered men the possibility of inhabiting both worlds, buying their cake and having it homemade for them, too. It created a sacred space in which traditional moral values remained exempt from the demands of economic rationality.

The concept of a sacred feminine sphere found expression in manuals of household advice and conservative denunciations of market society. Its legacy was stamped on the writings of Stanley Jevons and Alfred Marshall, the best known of the English neoclassical economists. Their world view presumed God-given differences between men and women that closely corresponded to the distinction between rational self-interest and moral obligation. Jevons and Marshall may have shared many of Adam Smith's basic views, but they lived in an era in which the boundary between the work of men and women was shifting rapidly. Perhaps as a result, they devoted more energy to boundary defense.

Domestic Advice

Economic development pulled men out of the home more quickly than women, intensifying the gender division of labor. Within the prosperous classes, wives and mothers were seldom required to contribute income to the household. They were, however, required to devote substantial time and effort to domestic work, supervising and often working side by side with their cooks, maids, and nannies. Many of these relatively well-educated women developed a hunger for both technical and moral advice. In both Britain and the United States, a burgeoning literature of domesticity explained how women could become queens and angels of the home.

Even the liberal Harriet Taylor had acknowledged the power of the so-called "civilizing influence" argument: Women should defend their own sacred sphere in order to counterbalance the violence and corruption that men were inflicting on the profane world. The concept of virtuous womanhood had contradictory implications. On the one hand, it could be deployed against any threat that women might withdraw their services in the home, helping to keep them in their place. On the other, it carried anti-capitalist connotations, identifying masculinity and the market as dangerously kindred forces that could only be controlled and civilized by women.

In the mid-nineteenth century women, once considered temptresses, were increasingly depicted with a glow of selfless virtue. The moralization of femininity was particularly prominent in the United States and England, where it percolated through the culture, from manuals of domestic advice to philosophical treatises, from poetry to political economy. Traditional ideals of domesticity offered a buffer against rapid social and economic change. Queen Victoria became the emblem of moral fortitude as well as prudish etiquette.[1]

The Victorian frame of mind was characterized by considerable anxiety about religious values. In 1865, the prominent Irishman William Lecky reiterated the traditional Christian vision: A man with foreknowledge of heaven and hell should recognize that he would be punished for selfishness. Fear of punishment, however, seemed to be declining. If the progress of civilization could be expected to encourage virtue, its effects would come primarily through women, whose moral superiority over men was, Lecky, believed, unquestionable: "Self-sacrifice is the most conspicuous element of a virtuous and religious character and it is certainly far less common among men than among women, whose lives are usually spent in yielding to the will and consulting the pleasures of another."[2] Not incidentally, Lecky referred to Mandeville's economic defense of greed and lust as "grotesque" and "repulsive".[3]

Economic development seemed to increase the temptations toward selfish behavior even as it weakened religious self-confidence.[4] If men could not love one another, it seems, they could at least love their wives. How could they not? The very purpose of women was to bring out the best in men. As Coventry Patmore explained in his versified paean to domesticity, *The Angel in the House,* "Man must be pleased; but him to please is women's pleasure."[5] The two-volume work blending exhortations to virtue with romantic passion was received with great enthusiasm and widely quoted throughout the second half of the nineteenth century.

Moral inspiration was easily added to lists of women's household duties. In her famous book of advice to the mothers of England, Mrs. Sarah Ellis described mother love as far too powerful a force to be "trifled with in the nursery or expended in infantine indulgence." It should be extended to the "great family of earth."[6] A later instruction book, *Female Piety: The Young Woman's Friend and Guide*, made women's responsibilities absolutely clear: "It is essential to your making home happy that there should be much self-denial, a spirit of forbearance, an occasional surrender, for the sake of peace, of supposed rights, a willingness to forego what you could rightfully claim as your own."[7] Not all domestic advice books struck such a submissive tone. Mrs. Beeton, author of *Household Management*, a classic cookbook and instruction manual published in 1861, emphasized simpler virtues such as frugality, charity, and rising at an early hour.[8]

Ironically, the most Victorian manual of household advice was published not in England but in the United States. The Beecher sisters' *American Woman's Home*, published in 1869 (discussed briefly in Chapter 14) praised women's self-abnegating virtues. Catherine Beecher has been described as a domestic feminist because she so enthusiastically celebrated women's contributions to society. The term seems a misnomer for someone who disapproved of female participation in public life.[9] Beecher later became more tolerant of feminist impatience. Women could and should leave the home, she argued, but not to become factory workers. They should work as teachers, as reformers, as moral guardians to benefit the nation as a whole rather than a "self-interested class of businessmen".[10] Women, in other words, should become the mothers of civilization.[11]

The Meaning of Motherhood

Not all men were convinced that the angel of the house could redeem the sins of capitalist individualism. After all, brotherhood itself, metaphor for male solidarity, was under attack. The English essayist Thomas Carlyle condemned the disruption of traditional feudal—and patriarchal—order: To live in the business world, he wrote, was like "living without father, without child, without brother."[12] An equally passionate, but more systematic critique of the new economic world was presented in John Ruskin's *Unto This Last*, subtitled *Four Essays on First Principles of Political Economy* and published in 1862. The tract took its name and its moral from the New Testament parable, "Christ and the Vineyard", in which all workers were paid the same even though some had worked longer than others. Men's wages, Ruskin argued, should be determined by their level of need—and their need for dignity—rather than by the dictates of the labor market.

Ruskin was a Tory conservative, uninterested in the principles of economic justice or equality, but committed to the concept of social obligation, which was, in his view, being undermined by the new emphasis on self-interest. Classical political economy, he argued, was at odds with England's religious principles.[13] He lambasted John Stuart Mill, among others, for his preoccupation with individual rights rather than moral virtue. A "strange political economy," he wrote, "being but the fulfillment of that which once brought schism into the Polity of Angels and ruin into the Economy of Heaven."[14]

Rather than exhorting the wives of England to solve this problem, Ruskin used examples of maternal altruism to counter the conventional presumptions of individualism. He described a mother and child with only a crust of bread between them. An obvious conflict of interest there, he observed, since if one ate the other would go hungry. Yet the antagonism between them was limited by mutual affection. So should it be between employers and workers.[15] The true measure of economic success, he wrote, echoing Robert Owen, was not accumulated treasure, but the creation of human capabilities: "like a Mother, leading forth her sons, saying 'these are my jewels'."[16] Ruskin was a great fan of Patmore's *Angel in the House*. Beyond poetry, however, he longed for an economic system, which, like a family, would train its youth, provide them with employment, and take care of the old, the sick, and the destitute.

He painted an oddly maternalist vision of a patriarchal past. Fathers, after all, had retained legal and economic control over both mothers and their jewels. Like many critics of emergent capitalism, Ruskin romanticized his country's history. Unlike many others, he also romanticized slavery and expressed distinctly racist and ethnocentric views.[17] Still, Ruskin's imagery helps explain why socialists and conservatives were sometimes allied against new economic policies. It also helps explain why defenders of the new economic order strained to explain why it should not cross the threshold of the home.

Neoclassical Altruism

When utilitarians like Jeremy Bentham first articulated their guiding principle—to seek the greatest happiness of the greatest number—it seemed to contravene religious values. It presumed that men could exercise virtually divine judgment, and elided concerns for salvation or eternal life. By the 1870s, however, utilitarianism had begun to seem too moralistic, its redistributive implications tilting men like John Stuart Mill in the socialist feminist direction. A new generation of neoclassical economists, departing from classical concerns with capital accumulation and growth, attacked utilitarianism as imprecise, even incoherent. They properly noted that it is impossible to maximize two things at once: which should take precedence, the greatest happiness or the greatest number? The question played well in a period of conscious efforts to limit family size, particularly among the middle and upper classes. Limiting the numbers of the family—or nation—could enhance per capita income.

Could happiness itself be meaningfully measured? One man (especially a man of wealth, education, and refinement) might have a great deal more capacity for happiness than another (especially one raised in poverty, ignorance, and squalor). In this case, taking a dollar from a rich man redistributed to a poor one might lower the sum total of human happiness. This was a fascinating possibility. Francis Edgeworth (later the editor of the prestigious *Economic Journal*) spelled out its implications for gender inequality when he observed in 1881 that women have less capacity for happiness than men.[18]

Continental scholars such as Leon Walras and Wilfredo Pareto made important contributions to the emerging theory, but within Anglo-American circles, William Stanley Jevons gained attention as an innovator. His *Theory of Political Economy*, published in 1871, stripped Bentham's utilitarianism of its subversive emphasis on redistribution, arguing that the true essence of political economy lay in the study of individual choice.[19] What some have called a scientific revolution initiated a new era of mathematization.[20] The notion that individuals were pleasure-seeking machines suggested the kind of predictability that engineers aspired to: "In its action on the body," explained Jevons, "the mind must follow a simple and universal law of seeking the most pleasure, and follow it as implicitly as the railway train follows the curves and turns of the line upon which it is running."[21]

Jevons's early life was not pleasurable. As the eldest son of a family that suffered a major financial setback, he was forced to interrupt his education in England to accept a job in Australia. He remitted a considerable share of his paycheck to help support his two unmarried sisters and his younger brother. His letters from Australia reveal a restless frustration only partly assuaged by a growing fascination with political economy. As soon as his father died, he politely apologized to his siblings for withdrawal of his support and returned home to university.

His letters to his sister Henrietta describe the personal conflict he experienced: "I have often entered into sorts of long mental discussions as to what the word (of all the most disagreeable) 'selfish' means."[22] Jevons was attracted to the accommodation that the Smithian view offered: Self-interest was not necessarily selfish, because individuals could derive pleasure from the happiness of others, through sympathy. He took great pleasure from Richard Whateley's lectures on Political Economy, reassured by the notion that God as well as Nature might sanction the pursuit of self-interest.[23]

These letters urged his sister to begin supporting herself as a teacher. She should make the best of things, he explained, despite the obstacles she faced. Nor should she make excuses: "A woman's field of action and her available means are considerably less than those of a man, but she has no reason to complain and remain idle, so long as the field is really so little occupied and still so wide, and while all her disadvantages are fully recognized and allowed for."[24] Jevons himself reached for success. After completing his studies in Political Economy, he published a well-received essay on the economics of coal mining and won a professorship at Owens College of Manchester. Favorable reception of his *Theory of Political Economy* won him an appointment to University College, London. His younger brother also achieved prosperity. His sister Henrietta, however, suffered a breakdown and spent much of her adult life in an asylum.[25]

Jevons's own theory offered something of an explanation: "Every mind is thus inscrutable to every other mind, and no common denominator of feeling seems to be possible."[26] Adam Smith had emphasized the powers of sympathy; Jevons seemed to deny these. There is no way, he emphasized, to compare the quantity or intensity of feelings between two individuals. It follows that no man could be expected to think about what was best for anyone but himself. Of course, the basis for ascertaining the greatest good for the greatest number had always been vague. But as a principle, it had, at the very least, required its proponents to consider the impact of their actions upon others. The more formal aspects of Jevons's theory implied that such considerations were futile.

Jevons's individualism was tempered by his willingness to invoke moral principles and common sense in support of some specific social reforms. He was sympathetic to the advantages of industrial cooperation, and suggested that profit-sharing might have a salutary effect on the productivity of labor.[27] Where mothers and children were concerned, he was explicitly opposed to *laissez faire*. Expressing horror at the high levels of infant mortality and child neglect in factory towns, he recommended that mothers of children under the age of three be excluded from factories and work-shops, with the possible exception of establishments that provided nurseries with medical supervision.[28] His statistical analysis of the causes of infant mortality was cursory, but his philosophy was clear: Maternal responsibil-ities for children were sacred, and therefore lay within the purview of state regulation and control.[29] He anticipated and dismissed the individualistic rebuttal to this argument:

> The objection may no doubt be made, that the exclusion of child-bearing women from works in public factories would be a new and extreme case of interference with the natural liberty of the individual. Philosophers will urge that we are invading abstract rights, and break-ing through the teachings of theory. Political economists might, no doubt, be found to protest likewise that the principles of political economy are dead against such interference with the freedom of contract. But I venture to maintain that all these supposed natural entities, principles, rules, theories, axioms, and the like, are at the best but presumptions or probabilities of good ... If we find that freedom to work in factories means the destruction of a comfortable home, and the death of ten out of twelve of the offspring, here is palpable evil which no theory can mitigate.[30]

Morality itself dictated restrictions on mothers.[31] Yet Jevons expressed little concern regarding the enforcement of fathers' responsibilities toward young children. Several women interlocutors challenged him on this point, forcing him into a revealing dialogue. Most systematic in her criticisms was a Mrs. Bright, who noted that the problem might be ameliorated by granting women the right to vote. Jevons agreed, but insisted this was a separate issue. Mrs. Bright then protested that wives lacked any legal claim on their husbands' earnings unless they enrolled themselves as paupers, and were therefore often forced to work for wages. Jevons agreed this legal defect required some remedy.

Several correspondents objected that the problem lay with drunken fathers rather than wage-earning mothers. In response, Jevons explained that women were at fault for that as well. "I answer that nothing can possibly tend more to drive a husband to the public-house than to have a wife coming home tired from the factory, and beginning perhaps to do the housework and prepare the meal, when she ought to have all things comfortable and cheerful for him."[32] Apparently, she *ought* to have all things comfortable and cheerful for him, whether this was in her self-interest or not.

Jevons's allegiance to appropriate gender roles softened his otherwise pro-market views. Yet his focus on individual decisions had profoundly conservative implications, deflecting attention from the distribution of wealth and the formation of individual preferences. Jevons believed human nature to be variable but largely fixed, a view consistent with and perhaps influenced by scientific racism.[33] Men, like trains, could only start and stop on tracks that they could never change.

Women's Duties

Alfred Marshall expounded a gentler version of individualist reasoning from his Cambridge University chair.[34] The title of Marshall's famous textbook, *The Principles of Economics*, signaled the replacement of "political economy" by a less contentious term. The book was ecumenical in tone and rich in institutional detail. Unlike Jevons, Marshall did not unequivocally reject the possibility of interpersonal utility comparisons. But then, he was reluctant to unequivocally reject anything. He liked to clinch his opponents so closely that they could land no hard blows. On the one hand, he praised the ethical neutrality of the mathematical approach. On the other, he appealed to the "higher values".[35]

Many found his tone of reasoned compromise appealing. He was more optimistic and idealistic than most of his neoclassical counterparts. His watchword was "duty", a kind of amalgam of social responsibility and Christian obligation reminiscent of Smith's moral sentiments:

> Political economy will help us rightly to apply the motive force of duty, but the will to do one's duty must come from some other source. Still political economy will doubtless show, in many cases, that selfish action is also foolish and suicidal. And on the whole it does show, in almost every case, that when a man adopts action which injures others, he injures himself more than he thinks he does.[36]

At some points, Marshall went so far as to suggest that economic man could not be considered selfish because he was making provision for his family.[37] His most systematic treatment of the issue came in an article entitled

"The Social Possibilities of Economic Chivalry", in which he described himself as a socialist in the sense of being one who wants to promote the "social amelioration of the people." But he reproved social critics for exaggerating the evils of present economic conditions. Businessmen, like knights of old, were capable of chivalry, though not enough to sustain the collectivist programs that socialists liked to advocate.[38] Marshall seemed to offer chivalry, or gallantry toward women, as a substitute for solidarity.[39] Those whose definition of socialism involved actual redistribution of wealth rather than simple kind-heartedness were not won over.

Marshall's concept of chivalry was embedded in Victorian views of appropriate gender roles. Like Jevons, he fretted that women might behave in selfish ways and favored strict limits on their choices. One reviewer welcomed his *Principles of Economics* as an excellent source of arguments for excluding women from wage employment.[40] Not all his colleagues agreed with such arguments. Marshall's immediate predecessor at Cambridge, Henry Fawcett, had spoken out in favor of women's rights. Fawcett's wife Millicent, an activist in the campaign for women's property rights, published popular books on economics similar to those of Harriet Martineau.

Marshall himself fell in love with an economist. At a time when women were allowed to take courses at Cambridge but not to matriculate for degrees, his brilliant student Mary Paley became the first woman lecturer in political economy. Marriage represented a violation of the terms of Marshall's employment, but he took the chivalrous plunge and moved to University College, Bristol (he would later return to Cambridge). Mary Paley had begun work on an elementary text entitled *The Economics of Industry*; the newlyweds collaborated on completion of the book, which bore both their names. The coauthored volume introduced many of the arguments later spelled out in *The Principles of Economics* but, unlike its successor, addressed the issue of gender differences in wages.[41]

With that publication, Paley's career came to an end. She did not publish again until after her husband's death. Marshall's students recall a devoted wife who never participated in intellectual discussion. John Maynard Keynes described her as a woman who neither asked nor expected anything for herself.[42] The well-known sociologist David Reisman wrote, "If Alfred Marshall's mission was economics, then Mary Paley Marshall's mission was Alfred."[43] Both testimonies suggest that she found fulfillment in her self-abnegation. A more disturbing interpretation emerges from consideration of Alfred's views concerning women and marriage. The prominent reformer Beatrice Webb described a conversation with Marshall as follows:

> He holding that woman was a subordinate being, and that, if she ceased to be subordinate, there would be no object for a man to marry, that marriage was a sacrifice of the masculine freedom and would only be tolerated by male creatures so long as it meant the devotion, body and mind, of the female and no longer. Hence the woman must develop in no way unpleasant to the man: that strength, courage, independence were not attractive in women, that rivalry in men's pursuits was positively unpleasant. Therefore masculine strength and masculine ability in women must be firmly trampled on and "boycotted" by men. Contrast was the essence of the matrimonial relation: feminine weakness contrasted with masculine strength, masculine egotism with feminine self-devotion.[44]

Marshall said as much outright in his *Principles of Economics*, explaining that the employment of women was a "great gain in so far as it tends to develop their faculties; but an injury in so far as it tempts them to neglect their duty of building up a true home, and of investing their efforts in the personal capital of their children's character and abilities."[45] Constant revision of the book was Marshall's main preoccupation in life; virtually all of its many editions contain this or similar warnings.

Marshall rejected feminism because it questioned women's assignment to sacred moral duties. He described the demand for women's suffrage as an example of "a selfish desire among women to resemble men."[46] The only constructive role he could foresee for women in the academy lay in pursuing "certain delicate inquiries related to women and children in which a man would be out of his element (such was the advice he offered Beatrice Webb).[47]

In 1896, Marshall actively campaigned against the granting of Cambridge degrees to women. At this time, every university in Britain, with the exception of Cambridge and Oxford, admitted women to degree study; even Cambridge had allowed women unofficially to take the degree examination. Marshall had no objection to some sort of lesser associate status, but he was appalled by the prospect of full equality. In an eight-page flysheet that he circulated to members of the Cambridge University Senate, he warned that women, better at taking exams than men, were far less capable of creative research. Further, he emphasized, the pursuit of a competitive degree would conflict with women's duties:

> However severe the illness of those dear to her, however urgent the need for her presence at home, she must keep her terms under penalty of losing recognition for her work. If she decides to go her own way, and let her family shift for themselves, she gets her honours; but her true life is impoverished and not enriched by them.[48]

Most male students cheered Marshall's views. In 1897, over two thousand of them signed a petition to the chancellor asking that women be excluded from the university. Not until 1948 were full privileges accorded to women students at Cambridge (and then, under conditions that limited their numbers).[49]

Marshall's economic theory provided a theoretical basis for such restrictions. He argued that child rearing and education fulfilled national needs that could not be satisfied by the mere operation of individual self-interest. By interpreting these domestic activities in terms of human capital Marshall emphasized their essential complementarity with the larger process of capital accumulation.[50] Though never entirely comfortable with the analogy between self-interested investments in physical capital and altruistic investments in children, he praised middle-class fathers for investing in their children's education.[51]

He exhorted fathers, as well as mothers, against selfishness. But he viewed familial altruism as a moral dictum rather than an empirical issue. As a result, he seldom considered the possibility that parents might abuse their children, even at a time when social reformers were calling for policies that would limit patriarchal power, including restrictions on child labor and the expansion of mandatory education. As the epigraph to this chapter indicates, Marshall idolized motherhood without expressing much concern for mothers themselves.[52] Many of Marshall's contemporaries worried that men's wages were insufficient to support a full-time homemaker (see discussion in Chapter 18). Marshall worried that women's work outside the home would both diminish virtue and reduce economic growth by lowering the quality of the nation's work force.[53] Those worries probably refracted personal disappointment: the Marshalls never became parents.

Virtue and Consequences

The views of Jevons and Marshall exemplify a moral double standard: men should pursue their own self-interest whatever it might be, but women should subordinate themselves to the needs of others. Marshall reframed the classical exclusion of reproductive labor, mapping it onto a new distinction between market and non-market work. The putative motive behind work became the arbiter of its productivity: in the new Marshallian framework a woman who provided domestic services in order to earn money was considered productive while a woman who provided them out of a sense of moral duty was not (even though she received a share of her husband's income in return).[54] The market/non-market distinction solidified the Victorian concept of separate spheres, soon deeply embedded in the conceptual infrastructure of economic classification: censuses and national income accounts.

NOTES TO CHAPTER 16

[1] Walter E. Houghton, *The Victorian Frame of Mind, 1830–1870* (New Haven: Yale University Press, 1957).

[2] William Edward Hartpole Lecky, *History of European Morals from Augustus to Charlemagne* (New York: D. Appleton and Company, 1869), p. 380.

[3] Lecky, p. 6.

[4] Houghton, p. 348.

[5] Coventry Patmore, *The Angel in the House,* Vol. 1, *The Betrothal* (Boston: Tickner and Fields, 1937), p. 135.

[6] Mrs. Sarah Ellis, *The Mothers of England; Their Influence and Responsibility* (New York: D. Appleton and Co., 1844), pp. 5, 149.

[7] Jenni Calder, *The Victorian Home* (London: B. T. Batsford, 1977), p. 145.

[8] Graham Nown, *Mrs. Beeton. 150 Years of Cookery and Household Management* (London: Ward Lock Limited, 1986).

⁹ Kathryn Kish Sklar, *Catherine Beecher: A Study in American Domesticity* (New Haven: Yale University Press, 1973).

¹⁰ Sklar, p. 174.

¹¹ Mary P. Ryan. *Womanhood in America. From Colonial Times to the Present* (New York: New Viewpoints, 1975), p. 150.

¹² Thomas Carlyle, *Past and Present*, (London: Vision, 1976) Book IV, Ch. 4, p. 274.

¹³ John Ruskin, *Unto This Last and Other Writings* (New York: Penguin, 1985), p. 203.

¹⁴ Ruskin, *Unto this Last*, p. 222.

¹⁵ Ruskin, p. 168.

¹⁶ Ruskin, p. 189.

¹⁷ David M. Levy, *How the Dismal Science Got Its Name: Classical Economics & the Ur-Text of Racial Politics* (Ann Arbor, MI: University of Michigan Press, 2001).

¹⁸ Francis Isidro Edgeworth, *Mathematical Psychics. An Essay on the Application of Mathematics to the Moral Sciences* (New York: Augustus M. Kelley, 1967), p. 78.

¹⁹ William Stanley Jevons, *The Theory of Political Economy* (New York: Augustus M. Kelley, 1965), p. 23.

²⁰ Margaret Schabas, *A World Ruled by Number. William Stanley Jevons and the Rise of Mathematical Economics* (Princeton: Princeton University Press, 1990).

²¹ William Stanley Jevons, in R. D. Collison Black and Rosamand Könekamp, eds, *Papers and Correspondence of William Stanley Jevons*, Vol. I. (London: Macmillan, 1972), p. 133.

²² Jevons, *Papers and Correspondence*, Vol. II, p. 240.

²³ Jevons, *Papers*, pp. 158, 288, 326.

²⁴ Ibid., pp. 360–61.

²⁵ Schabas, *A World Ruled by Number*, p. 13.

²⁶ Jevons, *Theory of Political Economy*, p. 14.

²⁷ Ibid., pp. 108, 123.

²⁸ Ibid., p. 172.

²⁹ Michael V. White, "Following Strange Gods: Women in Jevon's Political Economy," 46–78 in *Feminism and Political Economy in Victorian England*, Peter Groenewegen, ed. (Aldershot: Edward Elgar, 1994).

³⁰ Ibid., p. 177.

³¹ In an earlier speech to the trades society in 1868, Jevons invoked the notion of parental duty against efforts to reduce the work day: "But what I wish especially to point out to you is that a man's duty to himself after all should give place to his duty to his children and his wife. It is right for a man or for anyone who works to desire to reduce his working hours from ten to eight, but I think he should abstain from doing so until his children are put to

school, and kept there till they are well educated and likely to do better than their parents,"
Ibid., p. 109.

[32] Jevons, *Papers and Correspondence*, Volume V, Letter 710.

[33] Schabas, *A World Ruled by Number*, p. 38, p. 150, note 25.

[34] Mark Blaug, *Economic Theory in Retrospect*, 4th edn (New York: Cambridge University Press, 1985), p. 296.

[35] David Reisman, *Alfred Marshall's Mission* (New York: St. Martins Press, 1990), p. 98.

[36] Ibid., p. 33.

[37] Alfred Marshall, *Memorials of Alfred Marshall* (New York: Augustus M. Kelley, 1966), p. 160.

[38] Ibid., p. 25.

[39] Alfred Marshall, "The Social Possibilities of Economic Chivalry," *The Economic Journal* 17 (1907), pp. 7, 17.

[40] Peter Groenewegen, "Alfred Marshall—Women and Economic Development: Labor, Family, and Race," 79–109 in Peter Groenewegen, ed., *Feminism and Political Economy in Victorian England* (Aldershot: Edward Elgar, 1994).

[41] Reisman, *Alfred Marshall's Mission*, p. 22; Pujol, *Feminism and Anti-Feminism in Early Economic Thought*, p. 129.

[42] Keynes, *Essays in Biography,* p. 242.

[43] David A. Reisman, *Alfred Marshall's Mission* (Palgrave Macmillan, 1990) p. 28. This interpretation was based partly on John Maynard Keynes's reflections in his *Essays on Biography*.

[44] Beatrice Webb, *The Diary of Beatrice Webb, Vol. 1, 1873–1892. Glitter Around and Darkness Within*, Norman and Jeanne McKenzie, eds (Cambridge: Harvard University Press, 1982), p. 273.

[45] Alfred Marshall, *Principles of Economics,* first published 1890, 8th edn, (London: Macmillan, 1962) p. 570.

[46] Marshall, letter to Louis Dumur, July 2, 1909, in *Memorials*, pp. 459–61.

[47] Marshall, manuscript note, May 28, 1894, Marshall Archive, cited in Groenewegen and King, p. 1.

[48] Cited in Reisman, *Alfred Marshall's Mission*, p. 210.

[49] Rita McWilliams-Tullberg, "Women and Degrees at Cambridge University, 1862–1897," p. 117–45 in Martha Vicinus, ed., *A Widening Sphere. Changing Roles of Victorian Women* (Bloomington: Indiana University Press, 1977).

[50] Michèle Pujol, "Gender and Class in Marshall's Principles of Economics," *Cambridge Journal of Economics*, 8 (1984), 217–34; *Feminism and Anti-Feminism in Early Economic Thought* (Aldershot: Edward Elgar, 1992).

[51] Pujol, *Feminism and Anti-Feminism*, p. 136.

[52] Marshall, *Principles of Economics*, 8th edn, p. 564.

[53] Groenewegen, "Alfred Marshall," p. 102.

[54] Marshall did acknowledge, in passing, the problematic character of his definition "There is however some inconsistency in omitting the heavy domestic work which is done by women and other members of the household, where no servants are kept," *Principles of Economics*, p. 80.

CHAPTER 17

The Unproductive Housewife

The more we have concentrated on money values the more we have overlooked that part of our economic system which is not organized on a profit basis.   Margaret Reid

Numbers often seem less easily twisted than mere words. Census reports and national income accounts lend an aura of objectivity to economic history, generating numbers that trace consistent narratives of increased female labor force participation along with economic growth. But the categories behind the numbers tell their own story, reflecting philosophical assumptions, economic theories, and collective interests.[1] Ironically, economic growth itself seems to unleash forces that can retrospectively affect its measurement and interpretation.

At the outset of the nineteenth century Britain, the U.S., and France began to invest considerable time and money in regular censuses to enumerate their citizens and workers through regular censuses. As noted earlier, Britain and the U.S. moved more rapidly than France to ask individuals rather than households to designate an occupation. Small differences also categorized the treatment of the family work that remained, for the most part, the mainstay of wives and mothers. Beneath these differences, however, a fundamental similarity emerged: family work would not be categorized as work at all, because it took place in the sacred, rather than the selfish sphere.

This categorization did not go uncontested. Early advocates for women's rights recognized its perverse implications. But once established in the national censuses, the concept of the "unproductive housewife" carried over into the national income accounts, and even into calculations of the value of a human life. Some feminist thinkers, conceding that non-market work within the family was unproductive—or, at the very least disempowering—urged women to move as quickly as possible into wage employment. Others insisted on the need to revalue family work as a step toward demanding more generous public support for it.

Counting Workers

The 1851 Census of England and Wales offered a poignant tribute to the work of wives and mothers. Under the direction of the physician William Farr, who likely had some direct experience of women "in labor" as well as laboring, it reasserted the mercantilist principle that a country's most important product was its population.[2] The census officially acknowledged the occupation of housewife, placing "wives, mothers and mistresses" who did not work for pay in a category by themselves, the "Fifth Class". Another class (the "Seventeenth" to be precise) was reserved for "dependents" or those supported by the community—"children, the sick and infirm, gypsies and vagrants, and certain ladies and gentlemen of independent means."[3]

After Farr retired the census moved toward greater conformity with the double standard of liberal political theory. In 1881 wives and other women engaged in domestic duties were explicitly placed in the "Unoccupied Class" which replaced the earlier "Indefinite and Non-productive" category. The discussion noted that many of the "unoccupied" were women, "who can only be called unoccupied, when that term is used in the limited sense that it bears in the Census Returns. Many more of these women, though unmarried, were also engaged in domestic duties, or were assisting their fathers or other near relatives in the details of business."[4] The comment seemingly apologizes for demoting housewives to the unoccupied category.

In 1890, a Parliamentary committee was convened to consider improvements to the census, and Alfred Marshall was called to testify. Among his many reservations, he expressed dissatisfaction with the large numbers in the "Unoccupied" column and urged the committee to reduce them by adopting the German practice of describing married women as "dependents".[5] Following his advice, the 1891 Census of England and Wales restricted the Domestic Class to those employed in paid domestic service. The Unoccupied Class was simply struck from the list of categories. The text explained that most important of female occupations was omitted from the reckoning; otherwise the proportion of occupied women would resemble that of men.[6]

In 1890, the British colony of New South Wales (soon to become part of the Commonwealth of Australia) shifted its terminology in the same direction. Advocates of a clear emphasis on men as breadwinners won a decisive victory when it was agreed that wives would be classified as dependents unless they stipulated that they worked for pay. The chief census director believed that women's participation in productive labor could only lower men's wages and the community's standard of living.[7] National statistics showing a low rate of female labor force participation would, he hoped, enhance the colony's ability to attract British investment.

French census-takers postponed these problems by continuing to record occupations only on the household level. When they finally switched, in 1896, to individual enumeration, they fell into line with the new international standard. Domestic servants, once simply lumped along with family members under the occupation of the household head, were categorized with separate occupations. Family members providing services without pay, however, were designated "inactive".[8] This term sounds even more irrelevant than "unproductive", though perhaps less burdensome than "dependent".

The U.S. and Massachusetts Censuses

The federal census of the U.S. never conceded the economic significance of family work. Although the forms filled out in longhand by census-takers often listed "housewife" as married women's occupation, these results were never tabulated. In 1870, the census came under the direction of Francis Amasa Walker, son of the well-known political economist Amasa Walker,

President of the Massachusetts Institute of Technology and, later, the American Economics Association.[9] Walker supported women's right to vote, and argued that they should have greater access to jobs outside the home. But he endorsed the standard economic assumption that household work was...not really work.

This assumption was directly challenged by the officers of the Association for the Advancement of Women (AAW), an eminent group of women scholars sometimes dubbed the "Ladies Social Science Association."[10] In a letter sent to Congress in 1878 they insisted on the need to "make provision for the more careful and just enumeration of women as laborers and producers." They complained that women's domestic efforts were "not even incidentally named as in any wise affecting the causes of increase or decrease of population or wealth."[11] In other words, they quarreled with the official assumption that housewives and mothers were unproductive workers. But the federal census never budged from its assumptions. In 1900 it deployed a new term, "breadwinners," to describe persons who earned market income. As in England and Australia, wives and daughters without paying jobs officially became "dependents".

The consensus of the U.S. Census was briefly challenged by the state of Massachusetts, which conducted its own surveys using categories influenced by the British example. In 1875, housewives and unmarried women who performed housework without remuneration were included in the larger category of Domestic and Personal Office, along with subcategories for paid employment such as housekeepers, servants, nurses, and washerwomen. The introduction to the first volume clearly departed from economic orthodoxy, "The terms non-productive and unemployed are applied to all who take no part in the work of life."[12] Idle gentlemen were more likely to land in this category than energetic housewives: the "propertied" were lumped in with the "non-productive".

Rather than simply assuming that all married women were housewives the enumerators inquired into the actual nature of their daily activities. Some were described as "having nothing to do but superintend the households," and some as doing even less than that. The census enumerated "4,786 wives of heads simply ornamental."[13] One wonders if they all wore feathers. In any case, they amounted to less than 2 percent of all wives. In 1885, the state modified its terminology, redefining housewives as "the female heads of household, that is, the wife or some person in the family who has general charge of the domestic affairs."[4] This definition seemed to exclude the possibility of a purely ornamental wife. Still, the term "housework," used to describe the work of unmarried persons who performed unpaid domestic labor, retained a specific meaning at least somewhat independent of gender. Of 89,062 people so engaged, 77 were males.

The 1889 report of the Massachusetts Bureau of Statistics of Labor emphasized the economic value of this unpaid domestic labor.[5] But in 1905, the Massachusetts Census surrendered its distinctive approach, placing housewives and housework in the "not gainful" class, along with scholars, students, retirees, those unemployed for twelve months, and dependents. The Domestic and Personal Service category was limited to those who received a wage or salary. In 1900, a woman named Flora Thompson won first prize in a contest for best essay on "the servant" question in *Cosmopolitan*. As she put it, "Women have forced economic recognition of their labor in men's spheres, but especial woman's work remains the economic cipher. Domestic labor is accorded no rational recognition in the mind of political economy or in the heart of labor reform."[6]

The mind of political economy remained divided, but most dissenters offered, at best, glancing remarks. Richard Ely, founder of the American Economics Association, noted that failure to take the decline of women's non-market work into account overstated the rate of economic growth.[7] Carroll Wright, director of the Massachusetts Bureau of Labor and later, of the U.S. Bureau of Labor Statistics, almost certainly sympathized with this point, but did not explore it in any of his published work.

The little-known Scottish economist William Smart deserves credit for the most forthright analysis. Like the nameless authors of the Massachusetts Bureau of Statistics Report, he insisted that non-market work generated implicit income:

> the value of which might be guessed if we imagine what we should have to pay to servants for doing work now done by wives, sisters, and daughters, and how entirely impossible it would be to get similar work done for money. If such women went to the factory or into professional life, we should have to withdraw probably a much greater number from the factory or professions to take their place, and should lose something with it all.[8]

Smart went on to dispute the claim that men should be paid more than women because they had more dependents to support. If men's pay was to be determined by the value of what they produced, women's pay should be determined by the same principle. He chided his colleagues in terms that made it quite clear that he understood the larger implications of their conceptual double standard: "We cannot hunt with the individualist hounds and run with the socialist hare."[19] He was, perhaps, hinting at the possibility that men were dogs.

A Double Bind

Women's rights advocates were by no means unified in opposition to the concept of the "unproductive housewife". They recognized, even emphasized, a double bind. Too much emphasis on the importance of women's work in the home could strengthen the case that women should be confined there. Burgeoning opportunities in wage employment seemed both more exciting and more empowering.

No one captured the implications better than a remarkable independent intellectual named Charlotte Perkins Gilman, a distant relative of the Beecher sisters who lacked their enthusiasm for domesticity. Gilman's ideas were less embedded in political economy than in the emerging theories of social evolution that were shaping the new field of sociology. Yet she managed to engage a broad audience in a broadside against the Marshallian argument that women should specialize in motherhood.[20]

Gilman's *Women and Economics*, published in 1898, made her name. *The Nation* magazine pronounced it "the most significant utterance on the subject of women since Mill's Subjection of Woman."[21] Its enthusiastic reception enabled her to make a living as a journalist and lecturer, traveling widely in Europe as well as the U.S. In addition to writing more books on the same subject, she pioneered the genre of feminist science fiction, and published, edited, and wrote most of the content of a regular magazine, *The Forerunner*. A self-described socialist feminist, Gilman was never partisan or doctrinaire. Her naïve but charming confidence in economic progress led her to believe that the inevitable dissolution of the patriarchal household would lead to increased social cooperation.

Taking her cue from earlier feminists, Gilman carefully acknowledged the value of domestic labor:

> For a certain percentage of persons to serve other persons, in order that the ones so served may produce more, is a contribution not to be overlooked. The labor of women in the house, certainly, enables men to produce more wealth than they otherwise could; and in this way women are economic factors in society.[22]

"But," she immediately added, "so are horses." She gently suggested that both housewives and horses would soon become obsolete. *Women and Economics* included a chapter entitled "Socializing the Household Industries" that advocated innovations such as apartment living and collective meal provision.

Deftly invoking economic principles, Gilman pointed out that households were small-scale, inefficient enterprises, resistant to technological change. Incentives within them were misaligned: However hard wives and mothers worked, they could never capture the benefits of their efforts.[23] In response to the argument that women earned their livelihood as mothers, rather than merely domestic workers, Gilman pointed out that there was no relationship between the quantity or quality of motherhood and the quantity and quality of pay.[24] Although she never used Marxian terminology, it would have served her here. Essentially, she argued that capitalism had left women behind within a semi-feudal system.[25]

Gilman observed that wives and mothers remained dependent on men for financial support. In a public debate sponsored by the Women's Trade Union League in 1909 on the question "is the wife supported by her husband?" Gilman, arguing "yes", lost the audience vote.[26] Yet many of her readers and listeners sympathized with her argument that women's complete specialization in motherhood was no longer necessary or desirable. Gilman noted that many families were seeking to limit their number of children, partly in order to devote more resources to the care and education of a smaller number.[27] Even if domestic labor and childrearing were productive activities, she emphasized, they could never fully utilize women's productive capabilities.

Some critics labeled her "antimaternalist". She was, certainly, less enthusiastic about maternity than European counterparts such as Ellen Key, the Swedish activist who had already begun to call for state support of both married and unmarried mothers.[28] Unlike Key, Gilman was not particularly interested in sexual liberation. Indeed, she voiced prudish concern that competition among women for male support encouraged them to flaunt their sexuality.[29] But Gilman's conviction that family work was fundamentally different from market work was widely shared by a new generation of professional women learning how to make a life and a living for themselves outside the home.

Home Economics and Household Production

As women in the U.S. gained greater access to higher education, they also began to seek employment as teachers. Few were able to penetrate the sanctum of political economy, but they flocked in increasing numbers to the new discipline of home economics that elevated ideals of domesticity through application of the scientific method. Long emphasized in women's colleges, home economics promised both practical gains and respectable segregation from men. By the 1920s, more women held academic positions in this discipline in the United States than in any other of the social sciences.[30]

The divide between home economics and economics reflected the legacy of separate spheres. Even within the masculine discipline, Alfred Marshall's notion that women could best make their contribution by studying other women was apparently widely shared. Between 1886 and 1924, women represented less than 10 percent of all those indexed as authors of articles appearing in economic journals, but 63 percent of all those who published on the topic of "women and children."[31]

This niche strategy reinforced sex segregation, but enabled a few talented and hard-working individuals to gain professional cachet. Most successful scholars avoided the issue of women's non-market work to focus on their contributions to family income through informal market work—their contributions to family farms and businesses. The argument that women "had always worked" (for pay) lent support to the argument that they should now be allowed to seek wage employment. The first Englishwoman to publish in the eminent *Economic Journal* emphasized this point, explicitly chiding men for their fear that married women with independent access to income would abandon their families (which she termed "the veriest scooped-out, sheet-draped turnip that ever made a village dolt take to his heels and run").[32] The English economist Clara Collett pursued similar themes, as did historians Alice Clark and Ivy Pinchbeck.[33]

In the U.S. Edith Abbott, who completed a Ph.D. in economics at the University of Chicago in 1905, published seven articles in the *Journal of Political Economy* (two of them coauthored with Sophonisba Breckinridge), and wrote a classic history entitled *Women in Industry*.[34] Neither Abbott nor Breckinridge were offered jobs in economics, but they created a beachhead in the new School of Social Work at the University of Chicago. They threw their institutional weight behind a demand for a joint appointment for Hazel Kyrk in the departments of Home Economics and Economics in 1929.[35]

Kyrk had just completed a book entitled *Economic Problems of the Family* that directly addressed the issue of non-market work.[36] She estimated the number of women engaged in full-time homemaking between 1890 and 1920 and cited early time use studies administered by home economists to illustrate the extent and variety of homemakers' productive contributions. "Care of members of the family" was included along with meal preparation, laundering, and other more tangible activities. Kyrk used the data to measure the impact of additional children on the total amount of time that Oregon farm homemakers spent in homemaking.[37] She pointed out that women working in the home had every interest in performing their work efficiently. Posing the question "Is home-keeping a full-time job?" she sidestepped polemical debate to observe dispassionately that men and women could choose to share household responsibilities.[38]

Kyrk's student Margaret Reid developed a more systematic theoretical perspective, couched more explicitly in the terminology of the discipline. Her *Economics of Household Production* argued that both non-market and market work were governed by the principle of seeking maximum returns at minimum costs.[39] Like Gilman, Reid observed that the increasing costs of raising children were prompting many women to plan and reduce births, and predicted that women's participation in wage employment would increase.[40] In response to criticisms that the home was a site of consumption, rather than production, she patiently explained that no one person could consume on behalf of another and that many homemakers engaged in activities that directly benefited their husbands and their children.[41]

Like Kyrk, Reid focused primarily on full-time homemakers, but her definition of work as something that could, in principle, be performed by someone else (the "third party" criterion) provided a basis for classification and measurement of household members' activities that is widely utilized today.[42] Her book elicited negative reviews from two other women economists, both rather hostile to emphasis on home production, but it helped win her a position in the University of Chicago economics department.[43] She was personally appreciated there, and Milton Friedman gratefully acknowledged her contributions to his theory of consumption.[44] Widespread appreciation of Reid's *Economics of Household Production*, however, would not be expressed for more than fifty years.

National Income and the Value of Labor Services

In the first half of the twentieth century, interest in counting non-market work occasionally cropped up only to wilt beneath the disapproving eye of economic orthodoxy. National income accounting and efforts to assign an economic value to human lives built upon the restrictive and gender-biased assumptions of prior census and labor force studies.

One of the first efforts to develop a national accounting system for the U.S., sponsored by the National Bureau of Economic Research in 1921, essentially followed William Smart's recommendation, estimating the number of women primarily engaged in housework without monetary remuneration in 1910 and multiplying that by the average income of persons engaged in the paid occupational category of Domestic and Personal Services. The study concluded that the value of housewives' services had declined from 31 percent of market national income in 1909 to 25 percent in 1918.[45] A similar imputation exercise can easily be applied to a much longer historical period.[46]

Subsequent efforts to construct national accounts ignored the issue, perhaps because they were driven by concerns regarding market income and expenditures. The Great Depression created concerns about disequilibria in the labor and credit markets. In his famous efforts to explain these,

John Maynard Keynes completely ignored non-monetary assets and non-market work, despite their potential contribution to the living standards of families struck by unemployment. With the outbreak of World War II, governments needed a clear picture of their tax base in order to estimate the tax revenues that would constrain their military expenditures. Modern national income accounting grew out of efforts to finance war.[47]

Simon Kuznets took the lead in efforts to develop accounts that could shed some light on patterns of international economic development.[48] He warned repeatedly that his measures of Gross National Product omitted the value of non-market work, and were therefore incomplete. In this respect he was more enlightened than many of his contemporaries. Yet Kuznets never called for major efforts to address this problem or tried to estimate the extent of bias that it might introduce. Nor did he ever cite the research of Hazel Kyrk or Margaret Reid. Most subsequent national income accountants cited his authority and followed his precedent.[49]

A similar trajectory is evident in efforts to assign a value to humans themselves. William Farr, the early director of the British census, had argued that the capital value of the population could be represented by the discounted value of future earnings "less the value of the subsistence of the labourer as child and man." Since relatively few married women worked for wages at this time, their valuations would necessarily be lower than those of married men. Farr sidestepped this issue by averaging total earnings across the population to arrive at a per person measure of about 110 pounds sterling.[50] Later efforts to capitalize the value of human life assigned the value of future earnings to the individuals receiving them, resulting in a much higher average valuation for men.

In both the U.S. and Britain, the growth of the life insurance industry and law suits seeking to recover damages for wrongful injury or death was shaped by English common law, allowing damages to family members for the probable value of the services of the deceased from the time of his death (net of maintenance costs), but no compensation for emotional losses. By the end of the nineteenth century even young children in the U.S. could be insured for a sum equivalent to their prospective net earnings.[51] By this measure, young boys were considerably more valuable than young girls.

Louis Dublin and Alfred Lotka's *The Money Value of a Man,* first published in 1930, offered a detailed justification and extension of calculations based on earnings net of maintenance costs. In the same year, Irving Fisher, writing in a more theoretical vein, argued that the costs of actually producing human capital needed to be taken into account.[52] Dublin and Lotka, more attentive than Fisher to the empirical problem, confessed the limitations of their methodology, especially where the valuation of adolescent lives was concerned. Noting that the value of a mothers' time should be included in estimates of expenditures on children, they expressed regret that they lacked a pecuniary measure of that value.[53]

Yet they could have provided a lower-bound estimate by adopting the replacement cost approach suggested by the earlier National Bureau of Economic Research study, as well as by Margaret Reid. A better explanation for Dublin and Lotka's decision emerges from their reluctance to view childrearing as an economic activity: "The bringing up of children is not altogether a voluntary enterprise, entered upon with deliberate forethought and casting of a balance sheet of the profit and loss to be expected. It is a situation forced upon men and woman by innate instincts."[54] Lust, in other words, should take the blame.

Ironically, the costs of raising children could also be crossed out for the exactly opposite reason. Perhaps parents had already taken the costs into account, balanced against and entirely repaid by the subjective benefits— love and adoration of the little darlings. In a classic treatise of public finance published in 1938 Henry Simons wrote, "it would be hard to maintain that the raising of children is not a form of consumption on the part of parents, whether one believes in the subsidizing of such consumption or not."[55]

The notion that children could be treated like luxury goods was challenged eloquently by economist William Vickrey in 1947, in an explicit rebuttal of Henry Simons:

> This reduction of children to a status comparable to that of a household pet is hardly acceptable. Almost everyone will concede that the community has a greater interest in the welfare of children than in the welfare of pets, even though there may be widespread disagreement as the nature of that interest. A more satisfactory approach, on the whole, is to regard minors and other dependents as citizens in their own right.[56]

Vickrey had a point. But he missed the opportunity to point out that the community's interest in the welfare of children derives not just from their citizenship, but also from their future productivity as workers and taxpayers. Resources devoted to children represent an investment in everybody's future, not just their own.

The Meaning of the Adjectives

Dependent, unoccupied, inactive, non-gainful—to the casual reader the words may seem like routine jargon harmlessly applied. But these adjectives reinforced the assumption that men contributed more than women to economic growth. They promoted the claim that husbands supported wives without receiving any significant services in return and justified lower wages for women than for men on the grounds that they could live on less. These adjectives also literally devalued women's lives, promoting estimates of the value of a human life based primarily on the value of a future earning stream.[57] Such estimates remain in effect today: when the U.S. awarded compensation to families for the victims of 9/11, average compensation for male deaths far exceeded that for female deaths.[58]

Much also rides on the seemingly abstract debate over economic metaphors for children. Are they like pets, consumer durables, citizens, or investment goods? If investment goods, do they yield benefits only to themselves or also to their parents or to society as a whole? Many public policies reflect the assumption that children, like pets, are primarily consumption goods. In 1939 the U.S. Board of Tax Appeals held that childcare expenses should not be deductible as a work-related expense because they simply reflect a preference for a particular form of consumption.[59] Changes in U.S. tax law since then have allowed only a small proportion of actual childcare expenses to be deducted. The U.S. subsidizes childrearing—especially by single mothers—less generously than Britain or France.[60]

The notion that family work is sacred provides a kind of buffer against the sharp edge of selfish calculation. One could argue that the work of wives and mothers is so infinitely valuable that it would only be demeaned by estimation of a market price. But the exclusion of non-market work from the definition of "the economy" had distributional consequences that marked the influence of collective interests: it weakened women's claims on the income of other family members and the larger income of the polity. It also diverted economists' attention from an important determinant of living standards.

NOTES TO CHAPTER 17

[1] Joan Scott, *Gender and History* (New York: Columbia University Press, 1988), pp. 113–38.

[2] *Census of Great Britain, 1851, vol. 1. Population,* British Parliamentary Papers (Dublin: Irish University Press, 1970) p. lxxxviii.

[3] Celia Davies, "Making Sense of the Census in Britain and the U.S.A.: The Changing Occupational Classification and the Position of Nurses," *Sociological Review* 28:3 (1980), pp. 581–609.

[4] *1881 Census of England and Wales,* 1881, British Parliamentary Papers (Dublin: Irish University Press, 1970), p. 63.

[5] Ibid., p. 66.

[6] *1891 Census of England and Wales*, 1891, British Parliamentary Papers (Dublin: Irish University Press, 1970), p. 58.

[7] Desley Deacon, "Political Arithmetic: The Nineteenth Century Australian Census and the Construction of the Dependent Woman," *Signs: Journal of Women in Culture and Society* 11:1 (1985), p. 35.

[8] Christian Topalov, "Une révolution dans les representations du travail: L'émergence de la catégories statistique de 'population active' au XIXe siecle en France, en Grande-Bretagne et aux Etats-Unis," *Revue Francaise de Sociologie* 40:3 (1999), p. 469.

[9] James Phinney Munroe, *A Life of Francis Amasa Walker* (New York: Henry Holt and Company, 1923), p. 328; Robert Solow, "What Do We Know that Francis Amasa Walker Didn't?" *History of Political Economy* 19:2 (1987), pp. 183–90.

[10] William Leach, *True Love and Perfect Union*, (New York: Basic Books, 1980), pp. 292–322.

[11] Memorial of Mary F. Eastman, Henrietta L. T. Woolcott, and others, officers of the Association for the Advancement of Women, praying that the tenth census may contain a just enumeration of women as laborers and producers, *Senate Miscellaneous Documents*, 45th Congress, 2nd Session, Vol. 2, No. 84 (Serial Set, 1786).

[12] *The Census of Massachusetts: 1875* (Boston: Albert J. Wright, 1876), p. xlix.

[13] Ibid., p. l.

[14] Ibid., p. xxv.

[15] Massachusetts Bureau of Labor Statistics, *Twentieth Annual Report of the Bureau of the Statistics of Labor* (Boston: Wright and Potter Printing Company, December 1889), p. 579: "To be sure, they (housewives) receive no stated salary or wage, but their work is surely worth what it would cost to have it done, supposing that the housewife, as such, did no work at all. There were 372,612 housewives in Massachusetts in 1885, and only 300,999 women engaged in all other branches of industry. If a housewife were not expected nor required to

work, then for the labor of 372,612 women paid service would have to be substituted. Such a demand for labor could not be supplied by the inhabitants of the State itself. Consequently, as the labor of the housewives was absolutely necessary to allow society to exist in its present form, the housewife is certainly 'in industry.' As has been stated, she is excluded from the previous tables in this Part for conventional and arbitrary reasons alone. The housewife is as much a member of the army of workers as the clerk or cotton weaver, and too often supplements the toil of the day, 'in industry' with household duties performed at home, but outside of the 'in industry' classification."

[16] Flora McDonald Thompson, "The Servant Question," *Cosmopolitan* XXVIII (March 1900), pp. 521–8.

[17] Richard T. Ely and George Ray Wicker, *Elementary Principles of Economics: Together With A Short Sketch of Economic History* (New York, Macmillan Co., 1904), p. 117.

[18] William Smart, *The Distribution of Income* (New York: The Macmillan Company, 1899), p. 69.

[19] William Smart, *Studies in Economics* (London: Macmillan and Co., 1895).

[20] Irene van Staveren, "Feminist Fiction and Feminist Economics," 56–69 in *Toward a Feminist Philosophy of Economics*, Drucilla K. Barker and Edith Kuiper, eds (New York: Routledge, 2003); Ulla Grapard, "The Trouble with Women and Economics: A Postmodern Perspective on Charlotte Perkins Gilman," in Stephen Cullenberg, Jack Amariglio, and David Ruccio, eds., *Postmodernism, Economics, and Knowledge* (New York: Routledge, 2001); Mary Ann Dimand, "The Economics of Charlotte Perkins Gilman," in Mary-Ann Dimand, Robert Dimand, and Evelyn Forget, eds, *Women of Value: Feminist Essays on the History of Women in Economics* (Aldershot: Edward Elgar, 1995).

[21] *The Nation* 68 (June 8, 1899), p. 443.

[22] Charlotte Perkins Gilman, *Women and Economics*, first published 1898, Carl N. Degler, ed. (New York: Harper and Row, 1966), p. 13.

[23] Gilman, *Women and Economics*, p. 14. See also Charlotte Perkins Gilman, *The Home: Its Work and Influence* (Chicago: University of Illinois Press, 1972).

[24] Gilman, *Women and Economics*, p. 16.

[25] Some modern Marxist theorists describe patriarchal systems as examples of a feudal mode of production. See Harriet Fraad, Steven Resnick and Richard Wolff, *Bringing It all Back Home* (London: Pluto, 1999).

[26] Nancy Cott, *The Grounding of Modern Feminism* (New Haven: Yale University Press, 1997), p. 189.

[27] Gilman, *Women and Economics*, p. 169.

[28] Cott, *Grounding of Modern Feminism*, p. 47.

[29] Gilman, *Women and Economics*, p. 96.

[30] Margaret W. Rossiter, *Women Scientists in America. Struggles and Strategies to 1940* (Baltimore: Johns Hopkins, 1982), p. 172.

[31] Nancy Folbre, "The 'Sphere of Women in Early-Twentieth-Century Economics," pp. 35–60 in Helene Silverberg, ed., *Gender and American Social Science* (Princeton: Princeton University Press, 1998), p. 49.

[32] Ada Heather-Bigg, "The Wife's Contribution to Family Income," *The Economic Journal* IV (1894), p. 55.

[33] Peter Groenewegen, "A Neglected Daughter of Adam Smith: Clara Elizabeth Collet (1860–1948)," 147–72 in Peter Groenewegen, ed., *Feminism and Political Economy in Victorian England* (Aldershot: Edward Elgar, 1994); Clara Collet, "Female Labour," *Palgrave Dictionary of Political Economy*, vol. 2, pp. 49–50 (London: Macmillan, 1896); Alice Clark, *Working Life of Women in the Seventeenth Century* (New York: Augustus Kelley, 1967); Ivy Pinchbeck, *Women Workers and the Industrial Revolution, 1750–1850* (New York: Augustus M. Kelley, 1969).

[34] Folbre, "The 'Sphere of Women' "

[35] Folbre, "The 'Sphere of Women' " p. 50.

[36] For more biographical background as well as a broader discussion of her ideas, see Susan van Velzen, "Hazel Kyrk and the Ethics of Consumption," 38–55 in *Toward a Feminist Philosophy of Economics*, Drucilla K. Barker and Edith Kuiper, eds (New York: Routledge, 2003).

[37] Hazel Kyrk, *Economic Problems of the Family* (New York: Harper and Brothers Publishers, 1929), p. 42.

[38] Kyrk, *Economic Problems*, p. 106.

[39] Margaret Reid, *Economics of Household Production* (New York: John Wiley and Sons, 1934), p. 255.

[40] Reid, *Economics of Household Production*, p. 348.

[41] Reid, *Economics of Household Production*, p. 8.

[42] Katherine Abraham and Christopher Mackie, *Beyond the Market. Designing Nonmarket Accounts for the United States*. (Washington, D.C.: The National Academies Press, 2004).

[43] Ruth Allen, "Review of Economics of Household Production," *American Economic Review* 24 (1934), 761–62; Hildegarde Kneeland, "Review of Economic of Household Production," *Journal of Home Economics* 26 (1934), p. 525.

[44] Theodore Schultz, personal communication.

[45] Willford I. King, Wesley G. Mitchell, Frederick Macaulay, and Oswald W. Knauth, *Income in the United States, Its Amount and Distribution* (New York: Harcourt, Brace, and Co., 1921).

[46] For examples of such imputations see Nancy Folbre and Barnet Wagman, "Counting Housework: New Estimates of Real Product in the U.S., 1800–1860" *The Journal of Economic History* 53:2 (1993): 275–88, and Barnet Wagman and Nancy Folbre, "Household Services and Economic Growth in the U.S., 1870–1930," *Feminist Economics* 2:1 (1996), pp. 43–66.

[47] E. A. G. Robinson, "John Maynard Keynes 1883–1946," in *Keynes' General Theory. Reports of Three Decades*, ed. Robert Lekachman (New York: St. Martin's 1964).

[48] Simon Kuznets, *National Income and Its Composition, 1919–1938*. Assisted by Lillian Epstein and Elizabeth Jencks (New York: National Bureau of Economics Research, 1941).

[49] Marilyn Waring, *If Women Counted. A New Feminist Economics* (New York: Harper and Row, 1988).

[50] William Farr, "On the Economic Value of Population" reprinted in *Population and Development Review* 27 (2001) p. 567.

[51] Viviana A. Zelizer, *Pricing the Priceless Child. The Changing Social Value of Children* (New York: Basic Books, 1985), p. 123.

[52] Irving Fisher, *The Nature of Capital and Income* (New York: Macmillan, 1906).

[53] Louis I. Dublin and Alfred J. Lotka, *The Money Value of a Man* (New York: Ronald, 1930) p. 40.

[54] Dublin and Lotka, *The Money Value*, p. 48.

[55] Henry Simons, *Personal Income Taxation. The Definition of Income as a Problem of Fiscal Policy* (Chicago: University of Chicago Press, 1938), p. 140.

[56] William Vickrey, *Agenda for Progressive Taxation* (New York: The Ronald Press Company, 1947), p. 292.

[57] Thomas R. Ireland, "Compensable Nonmarket Services in Wrongful Death Litigation: Legal Definitions and Measurement Standards," *Journal of Legal Economics* 7:2 (1998), pp. 15–34.

[58] Kenneth Feinberg, *What Is Life Worth? The Inside Story of the 9/11 Fund and Its Effort to Compensate the Victims of September 11th* (New York: Public Affairs, 2006).

[59] Edward J. McCaffery, *Taxing Women* (Chicago: University of Chicago Press, 1997), p. 111.

[60] Nancy Folbre, *Valuing Children: Rethinking the Economics of the Family* (Cambridge MA: Harvard University Press, 2008).

CHAPTER 18

The Nanny State

> People rear children for the State and the future and if they do that well,
> they do the whole world a service, and deserve payment just as much as if
> they built a bridge or raised a crop of wheat.　　　　H. G. Wells

The term "nanny state" is often used to deprecate public policies that seem
fussy, intrusive, and expensive, policies that would perhaps be unnecessary if
individual women were more virtuous. But the term can also convey the
ways that early welfare state policies encouraged motherhood and limited
women's reproductive choices. Apprehensions about the quantity and quality of the nation's population helped motivate the development of social
safety nets, family allowances, and tax subsidies for rearing children.
Women's groups played an important role in the fight for maternalist
programs, which, nonetheless often had the effect of reinforcing women's
traditional nanny role.[1]

Neither public opinion nor public policy in France, Britain or the U.S.
condemned men's efforts to postpone or avoid fatherhood, whether through
abstinence, delayed marriages, purchase of sexual services from prostitutes,
or the use of condoms. Yet women's efforts to postpone or avoid motherhood
were often interpreted as selfish efforts to escape female obligation. A small
but vocal minority, including many well-known feminists, challenged the

inconsistencies of the sexual double standard.[2] In doing so, they often invoked the glories of sexual self-interest.

Fear of Fertility Decline

By the close of the nineteenth century observers in both Britain and the United States recognized that birth rates were dropping, particularly within the upper class. Efforts to discourage female selfishness began to take the form of exhortations to bear more children. Particularly influential in Britain were the writings of the eugenicist Karl Pearson, who believed that the imperial race (guess which one that was) needed to expand demographically.[3] It followed that the state should make every effort to increase the birth rate among families with the best genetic endowments.

That the education of women seemed to lower their desired number of children seemed, well, unfortunate. "If child-bearing women must be intellectually handicapped," wrote Pearson, in a rather ominous hypothetical, "then the penalty to be paid for race-predominance is the subjection of women."[4] In 1908, the Secretary of the British National Birth Rate Commission proclaimed that the difference between the number of cradles and the number of coffins would determine "the existence and persistence of our Empire."[5] Alfred Marshall explained that fertility decline was attributable partly to a "selfish desire among women to resemble men," and suggested that a "national protest against the restriction of births from selfish motives" might help.[6] Petitions were circulated stipulating that only women who had borne at least four children should be allowed the vote.[7]

Fertility decline had begun even earlier and spread more rapidly in France. Prominent conservatives there joined with politicians to counter the effects of liberal individualistic policies and encourage population growth, a prescription in keeping with Catholic dictates from the Pope. Feminist activists blamed male egoism—their reluctance to support children—for the problem, and suggested mothers should go on strike to demand more public support for their efforts. By most accounts, the conservative efforts proved more influential, motivating many large employers to include family allowances as part of their compensation packages.[8]

In the United States, the reproductive reluctance of white American-born women took center stage. The eminent political economist Francis Walker argued that economic competition from immigrants was undermining the desire and ability of true Americans to reproduce themselves.[9] Eugenic analysis quickly penetrated mainstream economics journals. An article published in the *Journal of Political Economy* in 1900 ridiculed those who believed that inherited racial differences were unimportant, and concluded that the ambitious classes should be encouraged to reproduce.[10]

President Theodore Roosevelt publicized his fears regarding "race suicide" in the *Ladies Home Journal* in 1906. Explaining that married women needed to bear at least four children a piece to maintain the population he attributed the waning performance of "old New England stock" partly to the "highly welcome emancipation of woman" but went on to explain that "this new freedom has been twisted into wrong where it has been taken to mean a relief from all those duties and obligations which, though burdensome in the extreme, women cannot expect to escape."[11] Roosevelt was wrong. Many women ardently hoped and expected to escape the burdens or rearing four or more children. Some began to support policies that would help them do just that.

The Family Wage

The concept of a family wage, a wage sufficient to allow a man to "support a wife and children", was rooted in the tension between an economy based on family production and one based on individual wage employment. If workers were to be paid only on the basis of what they produced for their employers, and children were to be sent to school instead of to work, who would pay for the increased costs of raising the next generation? The male trade union movement, eager to assert its economic rights, offered an unambiguous answer. Employers should pay for their future labor force, paying higher wages to men so that they could better support their wives and children.

Most conservatives and most economists invoked the forces of supply and demand to reject the notion of a family wage or, as it came to be more broadly defined, a living wage.[12] The very idea that workers' needs should be taken into account, rather than the "market rate of wages as determined by the laws of the universe" was sometimes labeled "pure and simple communism."[13] Male trade union activists seized an opportunity to make common cause with social conservatives who worried that the new economic order was disrupting family life. Pope Leo XIII's Encyclical on Capital and Labor had pronounced women, by nature, "fitted for home-work".[14]

The concept of a family wage was often deployed in efforts to exclude married women from paid employment and to justify lower earnings for single women than for men. Spokesmen for the American Federation of Labor, such as Samuel Gompers, were particularly vociferous in their denunciation of married women's labor force participation. Father John Ryan, of the Catholic University of America, wrote that, "the welfare of the whole family, and that of society likewise, renders it imperative that the wife and mother should not engage in any labor except that of the household."[15] A more empirically oriented defense of the family wage was mounted in England by Seebohm Rowntree and Frank Stuart, who provided detailed estimates of the distribution of responsibilities for supporting dependents among men and women workers. Counting housewives, like children, as dependents, they argued that male wage earners, on average, bore a higher burden.[16] F. Y. Edgeworth, editor of the *Economic Journal*, echoed these arguments, observing that "If the bulk of working men support families, and the bulk of working women do not, it seems not unreasonable that the men should have some advantage in the labour market" (he seldom if ever invoked need-based arguments in other discussions of wages).[17]

Despite protests from the many women workers who supported families on wages that averaged less than half of men's, the concept of a male family wage remained influential, with discernable implications for public policy. During World War I, the National War Labor board in the U.S. used family-wage based budget studies in its wage adjustment determinations. In England, the Departmental Committees on Teachers and the Majority of the War Cabinet Committee on Women in Industry did the same.[18] Gradually, however, the notion that employers should pay men directly for the childrearing services of their wives was displaced by a new emphasis on public support.

The Fabians

No group did more to enliven debates over state support of parenthood than the Fabian Society, a loose-knit group of British intellectuals that assembled in 1893 to pursue democratic socialist ideals. They took their name from the story of a Roman general named Fabius who had patiently waited for his enemies to overreach themselves. They sought reform, not revolution and most of them showed more wit than patience. Among the best known were H. G. Wells and George Bernard Shaw, both brilliant writers and popularizers of political economy.

The Fabians as a group were initially reluctant feminists, but added a clause to their creed in 1907 insisting on equal citizenship of men and women.[19] They typically described unregulated capitalism as selfishness run amuck, a problem that could be solved by intelligent state regulation by experts like themselves. Their distinctly technocratic point of view betrayed more confidence in bureaucratic process than democratic participation. A remarkably unselfconscious confidence in the superiority of the white race—and unapologetic nationalism—animated their fears of fertility decline.

H. G. Wells, famous for his science fiction novella, *The War of the Worlds*, devoted volumes of fiction and non-fiction to the need to reconcile women's need for independence with their traditional mothering role by offering them a childcare stipend.[20] He was convinced that childrearing created a public good: "People rear children for the State and the future," he thundered, and "if they do that well, they do the whole world a service, and deserve payment just as much as if they built a bridge or raised a crop of wheat."[21] Some feminists objected on the grounds that public stipends would encourage women simply to stay home and breed, rather than develop their capabilities through paid employment.[22]

The Fabian Women's Group, however, felt that public support would allow women to reconcile personal independence with a commitment to a form of work that was unremunerated. It was not marriage, after all, but mothering that was to be rewarded. As Mrs. Pember Reeves put it, "the woman who shrinks from the feeling that her wifehood is a means of livelihood will proudly acknowledge that her motherhood is a service to the state."[23] The broader demand for state services, such as meals for schoolchildren, represented a compromise that reflected concerns about the health and quality of the nation's future work force.

A similar convergence of feminist and socialist concerns was personified in Beatrice Webb. An elegant patrician who married the self-made civil

servant Sidney Webb, Beatrice's early political views were distinctly conservative.[24] She initially regarded the feminist demand for suffrage as selfish,
and went on record against it until 1903. Her change of heart was closely
related to her emerging vision of women's activism as a force for social
amelioration. In a letter to the suffragist Millicent Fawcett, she explained
that "The raising of children, the advancement of learning and the promotion of the spiritual—which I regard as the particular obligations of
women—are, it is clear, more and more becoming the main preoccupations
of the community as a whole."[25]

The notion that the state should guarantee a decent standard of living for
every child fit perfectly with Fabian emphasis on the efficiency of public
provision. It also provided a way of reconciling the ideals of Victorian
femininity with the reform of the state. As Beatrice put it in one of her
autobiographical tomes, "We saw that to the Government alone could be
entrusted the provision for future generations, to which neither producers
nor consumers would attend as such. In short, we were led to the recognition
of a new form of state, and one which may be called the 'house-keeping
state,' as distinguished from the 'police state'."[26]

The future generations that concerned the Webbs were those to whom
they were linked by ties of citizenship and race. Citing Pearson, Sidney
Webb warned in 1907 that, in the absence of public support for childrearing,
the country would fall to the Irish and the Jews.[27] Later, in 1919, Beatrice
reframed the argument, suggesting that the nation might be forced to resort
to alien immigration on a large scale.[28] One could argue that such rhetoric
simply represented political expedience. But the concept of the nation (and
the predominant racial-ethnic group within it) as a family relied on strict
boundaries between those who were and were not kin.

Many of George Bernard Shaw's plays, including the famous *Pygmalion*
which became the basis for the Broadway musical cum Hollywood hit, *My
Fair Lady*, explored the intersections between class and gender. Near the end
of his life Shaw offered a charming, if somewhat pedantic, reprise of Fabian
views in a book he described as his "last will and testament to humanity",
the *Intelligent Woman's Guide to Socialism and Capitalism*.[29] The book
patiently explained that both British and U.S. society as a whole would
benefit from the reduction of monstrous inequality within their own borders. It also pointed out that markets could never reward individuals who

produced goods that would not be bought and sold, such as children. Like his fellow-Fabians, Shaw endorsed state endowment of parentage. He also prescribed two additional public policies: limits on the number of children a family could raise, and public instruction in methods of contraception.

The Endowment of Motherhood

The Fabian proposal for endowment of motherhood gradually gained credibility in Britain, partly due to the relentless efforts of a middle-class feminist named Eleanor Rathbone. In an article published in the *Economic Journal* in 1917 and, later a book entitled *The Disinherited Family*, Rathbone reviewed English and European precedents for public support.[30] She also summarized British experience during World War I, when the government had paid soldiers' wives separation allowances that were explicitly based on family size rather than merely on rank. Children's welfare had improved discernibly as a result.

Unlike many political advocates, Rathbone framed her practical arguments in theoretical terms, castigating the entire economics profession for its lack of attention to childrearing:

> I do not think it would be an exaggeration to say that if the population of Great Britain consisted entirely of adult, self-propagating bachelors and spinsters, nearly the whole output of writers on economic theory during the last fifty years might remain as it was written, except for a paragraph or phrase here and there, and those unessential to the main argument.[31]

For empirical support, she drew on a genre of working class budget studies that had been widely cited by advocates of a male family wage, noting wide variation in family size. Since not all workers had four dependents, the demand that a man should receive a wage sufficient to support that number, she editorialized, implied "phantom wives and children." If trade unions were successful in garnering a family wage for all male workers, she calculated, the nation's wage bill would provide for about 16 million phantom children, while many real children in families larger than this supposed norm would go wanting.

Further, Rathbone argued, the counter-claim that all men without dependents were saving up to support them later was suspect. Bachelors were likely to spend their surplus on football, cigarettes, and other luxury items. Unlike Rowntree and others who consistently described wives as dependents, Rathbone emphasized the importance of women's domestic labor. With some irony, she noted that the provision of "phantom wives" was not completely farfetched, because a man who lacked a wife had to pay someone to do his cooking, washing, and housekeeping for him—a landlady, a mother, or some other female relative.[32] Women's domestic labor on behalf of a husband concerned her less than the labor of mothering, which was essentially unremunerated.

The economics establishment remained unmoved. Francis Edgeworth expressed his disapproval of family allowances in *The Economic Journal* on the grounds that they would sap male incentives to work and would encourage a growth in the "least desirable classes."[33] Alexander Gray of the University of Aberdeen leveled even more scornful criticisms.[34] Still, Rathbone cleverly deployed economic reasoning to argue that the organization of childrearing was inefficient as well as unfair. She also developed a strategic analysis of political divisions among women, who could, she argued be sorted into two major groups, those who worked for wages (primarily younger unmarried women) and those who provided non-market services such as childrearing in the home. Female wage earners were competing with the men who provided the market income that many wives, mothers, and children relied on, generating conflict. A family allowance system could unify women around the principle of equal pay for equal work without penalizing mothers, who could receive the additional support needed to raise children from the state instead of hoping for higher wages for their husbands.

Rathbone argued that men would instinctively resist any effort to provide public rather than spousal support for childrearing. She explained this resistance in polemical terms, describing male desire for domination over women as "the Turk complex"—an irrational, uncivilized selfishness embedded in human nature but particularly rife in Islamic culture.[35] Her wording reflected the strategic racism that she shared with many of her contemporaries, as well as frustration with those unwilling to engage her arguments: "When a proposal presents itself which is obnoxious to the hidden Turk in man, he stretches up his hand from his dwelling in the unconscious mind and the proposal disappears from the upper regions of consciousness."[36]

While this theory of masculine ideology won few adherents, Rathbone's case for family allowances gradually gained traction. The Family Endowment Society that she founded wrested endorsements from major women's groups and helped her gain a seat in Parliament. Though her efforts were initially unsuccessful, the devastation of World War II gave her countrymen a more profound appreciation of the work of creating and maintaining soldiers and citizens. Like other participants in that War—the United States notably excepted—Great Britain put modest publicly-financed family allowances into place in 1945.

Minimum Wages for Women in the U.S.

In the U.S., the stubborn consensus that men needed higher wages in order to support their families was tempered somewhat by widespread agreement that the labor market did not function effectively where women and the family were concerned. Proposals for the establishment of a national minimum wage for women were among the many examples of protective legislation designed to address this problem. The American Federation of Labor (AFL) opposed minimum wage legislation for men, but not for women and children. Twelve states passed mandatory minimum wage laws for women and children between 1912 and 1920.[37] Before these were declared unconstitutional in 1923, they provoked considerable debate. Critics of wage earning women insisted that no minimum was necessary because most worked only for "pin money", an extra but unnecessary bit of income. At the other end of the political spectrum, the boldest feminists argued that women should earn enough to support dependents of their own.

Virtually all participants in the debate cited a growing number of budget studies conducted by the U.S. Bureau of Labor Statistics (BLS). A vast collection of survey data supported the claim that women's earnings were a necessary component of working class family incomes. Women work for wages, the reports emphasized, because they must. The tone implied that no motive beyond sheer necessity could justify female wage employment.[38] The survey data was also used to support the claim that men needed higher wages. Conforming to the precept that non-market work was unproductive, the BLS surveys focused on market income alone. Several independent researchers, however, including those associated with Jane

Addams's Hull House in Chicago, sought to establish that households with no full-time homemaker required more market income to purchase substitutes for home-provided services.[39]

Another, more subtle issue concerned the costs of what economist Frank Taussig called "expense-reducing cooperation". Objecting to the claim that a minimum wage for women should be based on their cost of living independently, he pointed out that most wage-earners lived with family members, and were able to take advantage of economies of scale.[40] Dorothy Wolff Douglas, also publishing in the *Economics Journal*, pointed out that wage earners typically contributed to the support of a "housekeeping mother" whose:

> services are just as real a part of the necessary cost of living in a family as are the food she markets and cooks and the clothes she launders. If the working daughter, therefore, is to share evenly in the necessary household expenses, she must bear her share of the mother's costs just as much as her share of the rent or of the fuel bill.[41]

Douglas was reluctant to suggest that women should earn enough to help support other dependents, but others advanced the argument that women as well as men deserved a family wage. Mary Van Kleeck, head of a government agency that would shortly become the Women's Bureau, argued that men and women worked together to support dependent children, and older daughters were just as responsible as older sons for contributions to this end. A fierce advocate of equal pay for equal work, Van Kleeck opposed efforts to set a female minimum wage at a level lower than the minimum wage for men. Sophonisba Breckinridge of the University of Chicago School of Social Work also called attention to women's need for higher earnings. Marshalling data from the decennial censuses as well as the Bureau of Labor Statistics budget surveys, she documented the number of married women contributing income to their families, concluding that, "no safe line can be drawn between the sexes on the basis of the support of dependents."[42]

Economist Paul Douglas, best known to economists for his contribution to the eponymous Cobb-Douglas production function, argued that wage earners should be paid on the basis of work performed, not family size, noting that it was impossible to determine whether they actually contributed their wages to family support. Douglas and his wife, Dorothy Wolff Douglas (referred to above) were both impressed by Eleanor Rathbone's arguments. A family allowance system would make it reasonable to stipulate an equal minimum wage for men and women without penalizing those with large numbers of children to support. Douglas published a book on the subject, entitled *Wages and the Family*, but was soon distracted by a distinguished career as a U.S. Senator.[43] Few other academic economists favored family allowances, even as they were widely adopted in many European countries.[44]

Birth Control

The decline in fertility that animated these policy debates was enlivened by melodramas of repression and dissent in which risk-takers and trouble-makers played an important role. Middle-class advocates of birth control within marriage like Margaret Sanger and Marie Stopes demanded permission for women to pursue their own self-interest in bed. In doing so, they carried the banner of liberal individualism much further than their male predecessors had ever dared.[45]

Scholars differ on the extent to which feminists advanced the cause of birth control in Britain and elsewhere.[46] But it seems indisputable that new information about contraception offered greater gains to women than to men, by offering them techniques that did not require the successful cooperation and self-control of their male partner. French advocates of contraception were particularly eloquent on the redemptive possibilities for enhancing women's sexual pleasure. Social critics like the anarchist Paul Robin were thrilled by the possibility that women could go "on strike" against the state and refuse to bear children until social conditions had improved.[47]

These attitudes help explain the repression of both contraceptive information and technology that intensified in Britain and the United States in the late nineteenth century. Most of this repression came from the top down, enforced by male elites anxious to defend female morality. In Britain the popular demand for contraceptive information was so great that efforts to legally suppress it simply publicized it further. The London obscenity trial of Annie Besant and Charles Bradlaugh became the talk of the town in 1877. They escaped conviction on a legal technicality (other free-thinkers were not so lucky) but sales of their publication skyrocketed.[48] Most liberal feminists were horrified and many socialists were dismissive. But Annie Besant soon became a spokesperson for socialist feminism, denouncing retrograde comrades who believed that the birth control problem would go away after the revolution. As women became more educated and more economically independent, she argued (contra Marshall), they would refuse to serve as "mere nurses of children throughout the whole of their active life."[49]

In the United States, the so-called Comstock Law passed in 1873 made it illegal to ship any information or devices that could be used for preventing conception, which were defined as obscene, on either public or private freight carriers. The first application of the law came with the incarceration of the feminist activist Victoria Woodhull. After she published an article denouncing the sexual hypocrisy of a famous preacher, other material in the same issue of her weekly magazine was deemed obscene, and all copies were seized. The prosecution effectively ended her political career in the United States.[50] The Comstock law was later used against the anarchist Emma Goldman as well.

Sleeping Beauty Awakes

Margaret Sanger is best known to demographers as an early advocate of birth control; indeed she is said to have invented the term. But she was also a utopian feminist who believed that sexually liberated women could lead mankind to a happier world. Her optimism blossomed most luxuriantly in her 1922 book, *The Pivot of Civilization*.

> Through sex, mankind may attain the great spiritual illumination which will transform the world, which will light up the only path to an early paradise.... If I am criticized for the seeming 'selfishness' of this conception it will be through a misunderstanding. The individual is fulfilling his duty to society not by self-sacrifice but by self-development.... This is fundamentally the greatest truth to be discovered by womankind at large. And until women are awakened to their pivotal function in the creation of a new civilization, that new era will remain an impossible and fantastic dream.[51]

Until women are awakened... Sleeping Beauty needed more than just a kiss. She needed a diaphragm.

Sanger was arrested in 1914 for violations of the Comstock Act, but the charges were soon dropped, and she boldly published a pamphlet entitled

Family Limitation that represented the first widely-distributed update on contraceptive methods since the Comstock Act had gone into effect. In 1917, she spent thirty days in jail after being convicted of actually dispensing contraceptive devices. As soon as she was released she resumed her activities, hampered more by social disapproval than by legal persecution.[52]

Sanger was not particularly successful in her efforts to garner support from either socialist feminists or more liberal mainstream groups such as the League of Women Voters. The reasons were profoundly ideological. Despite her awareness of the strategic risks, she was irrepressible in her emphasis on individual sexual pleasure as well as the "good of the race". Sanger believed that female desire was a radiant force, and hoped to reduce the fears of pregnancy that inhibited it. Even free-thinking feminists like Charlotte Perkins Gilman were taken aback by what they regarded as her "over-sexualization".[53]

Sanger was heavily influenced by proponents of a new sexual psychology, such as Edward Carpenter and Havelock Ellis, reframing their arguments to develop a philosophy of feminine self-interest. In *Woman and the New Race*, she pronounced that women were inexorably driven to greater self-development. If given free play, they would assert themselves in beneficent ways; if repressed, they could become destructive.[54] In *Pivot of Civilization*, published in 1922 and graced with an introduction by H. G. Wells, she explained that birth control was key to reconciling the conflict between altruistic commitment and individual autonomy.[55] Women would freely choose motherhood, but if they were coerced by lack of reproductive choice, the consequences would be dire not only for themselves but also for their children. Forced maternity was, for Sanger, a metaphor for forced submission to the welfare of others.

Sanger initially denounced eugenic prescriptions, pointing out that their discussion of who was "fit" and who was not betrayed a distinctly middle-class bias. She lampooned talk of a "cradle competition" in which educated women should sacrifice their own interests in order to advance the race. If contraception was a selfish act, she asked, why wasn't the state more unselfish in offering to help unwed mothers to support their children? Sanger seemed to believe that feminine self-interest held redemptive potential because women's natural bond with children would ensure their devotion to the future of the race. In the 1920s, she became far more conservative, responding to and aligning herself with growing backlash against immigrant families in the U.S.

As the leader of an increasingly respectable movement to advance reproductive rights, she found it necessary or at least expedient to relinquish other progressive ideals. At the Sixth International Birth Control conference in New York in 1925, she criticized the French system of awarding allowances to families for raising children and proposed that the United States do just the opposite: award bonuses to undesirable families who limited fertility.[56] No longer concerned about middle-class bias, she was apparently confident that she could determine which families were undesirable and which were not.

The Glorious Unfolding

The birth control movement also gained momentum in Great Britain, dramatized by another woman eager to assert sexual self-interest, the paleobotanist Marie Stopes. Her initial involvement in the birth control movement grew out of her own sexual frustration in her first marriage, as well as her friendship with Sanger. In 1918 she published a book entitled *Married Love,* marketed as a marriage manual. While it did not include details about how to avert births, it provided an exceptionally clear explanation of how conception took place, using words such as penis, erection, semen, clitoris, and vagina. Since these words were considered obscene, readers were warned that the book was "unexpurgated" and Stopes was labeled a pornographer.[57] The book soon found its way to the bestseller list.

Married Love urged married couples to limit births in order to improve the quality of their personal relationships. Its style was florid. The first sentence declared, "Every heart desires a mate." The chapter titles included "The Fundamental Pulse" and "The Glorious Unfolding." Stopes offered a scientifically accurate explanation of why many married women fail to reach orgasm and announced that it was healthy, not sinful, for women to enjoy sexual intercourse. Better sex would lead to better marriages, she argued, and better marriages would benefit society as a whole.

Stopes brilliantly reversed the traditional religious notion that sensual and spiritual love were at odds, hinting that sexual intercourse allowed men and women to transcend selfish individuality. Each partner's hormones affected the other, she argued, creating a conjugal unit far greater than the mere sum of its parts: "In union with the beloved there will be added powers of every sort which have no measure in terms of the ordinary unmated life."[58] Stopes never openly advocated extramarital sex (though she apparently indulged in it), and insisted on sexual self-control.[59] She declared that husbands as well as wives should be freed of the fear of unwanted pregnancy.

By 1927, *Married Love* had gone through eighteen editions and been translated into twelve languages.[60] A sequel, *Wise Parenthood*, offered a more explicit guide to contraceptive methods, so that couples could practice what had been preached. Stopes became a famously egocentric partisan, who alienated many if not all of her colleagues. Nonetheless she poured much of her money and energy into the establishment of birth control clinics, and remained a relentless advocate of sex education and promoter of birth control technology. A cervical cap she designed was registered with the trademark "Pro-Race".[61]

That trademark was emblematic of the point that both she and Sanger constantly reiterated. Karl Pearson and Teddy Roosevelt were wrong. Women's pursuit of their own self-interest would strengthen the human race, not weaken it. Both women believed that birth control would reduce poverty, the primary cause of social degeneracy. Both women rejected eugenic claims that bad behavior was inherited, but tried to harness eugenic concerns about the well-being of the future labor force.[62] Good motherhood, by which they meant intelligent, reasoned, planned motherhood, would lead to redemption. In the words of the socialist hymn, "Bread and Roses", the "rising of the women is the rising of the race."

Later advocates of birth control adopted a similar response to the eugenic challenge. It was, after all, politically easier as well as less expensive to increase the choices available to the poor than to restrict the choices of affluent women. Sanger and Stopes argued that if parents could exercise better birth control they would have fewer children. If they had fewer children, the public would be more willing to help provide education and social services for them. Both hypotheses were borne out in succeeding years.

Public Support *and* Reproductive Rights

Few, if any, feminists today would argue that the English family allowance represents a good model of public support for childrearing. Indeed, the

United Kingdom stands out as one of the least generous countries of North-western Europe where support for parenting is concerned.[63] The task of designing and implementing an equitable and efficient family policy remains a daunting one. Still the arguments articulated by early advocates of social motherhood raise a pointed question: If the seemingly private work of raising children creates benefits for society as a whole, how should that work be supported?

Early twentieth-century feminists sought to expand state policies in some arenas, but to limit them in others. They insisted on women's individual rights to reproductive choice, rights that the early nanny state explicitly denied. Sanger and Stopes took Adam Smith in the direction he had started, promising that women's pursuit of self-interest—even in bed—would serve the social good. Women wanted more of everything—more public support for parenting along with greater scope for individual choice. Over the next fifty years they would attain both, though not in the generous measure that they hoped for.

NOTES TO CHAPTER 18

[1] Susan Pedersen, *Family, Dependence, and the Origins of the Welfare State. Britain and France 1914–1945* (New York: Cambridge University Press, 1993); Seth Koven and Sonya Michel, *Mothers of a New World. Maternalist Politics and the Origins of Welfare States* (New York: Routledge, 1993); Theda Skocpol, *Protecting Soldiers and Mothers. The Politics of Social Provision in the United States, 1870s–1920* (Cambridge: Harvard University Press, 1993).

[2] For an interesting take on the sexual double standard in twenty-first century U.S. where sexually active women are often termed "sluts" while their male counterparts are termed "players", see Paula England, Emily Fitzgibbons Shafer, and Alison C. K. Fogarty, "Hooking Up and Forming Romantic Relationships on Today's College Campuses," in *The Gendered Society Reader*, ed. Michael Kimmel. (New York: Oxford University Press, 2007).

[3] Theodore M. Porter. *Karl Pearson. The Scientific Life in a Statistical Age*. (Princeton NJ: Princeton University Press, 2004), p. 283.

[4] Karl Pearson, *The Ethic of Free Thought* (London: Adam and Charles Black, 1901), p. 373.

[5] Jane Lewis, *The Politics of Motherhood. Child and Maternal Welfare in England, 1900–1939* (London: Croom Helm, 1980), p. 201.

[6] Alfred Marshall, Letter to Louis Dumor, in *Memorials of Alfred Marshall*, A. C. Pigou, ed. (New York: Augustus Kelley, 1966).

[7] Lewis, *Politics of Motherhood*, p. 143.

[8] Pedersen, *Family, Dependence, and the Origins of the Welfare State*, pp. 25–78.

[9] Frances Walker, "Restriction of Immigration," *Atlantic Monthly* 25 (June 1896): 822–9.

[10] Carlos C. Closson, "The Real Opportunity of the So-Called Anglo-Saxon Race", *Journal of Political Economy* 9 (1900), p. 96.

[11] "Mr. Roosevelt's Views on Race Suicide", *Ladies Home Journal*, February 1906, p. 21. Roosevelt reiterated these views in his book *The Foes of Our Own Household* (New York: George Doran, 1917).

[12] Lawrence B. Glickman, *A Living Wage. American Workers and the Making of Consumer Society* (Ithaca: Cornell University Press, 1997); Alice Kessler-Harris, *A Woman's Wage. Historical Meanings and Social Consequences* (Lexington: University of Kentucky, 1990).

[13] Martha May, "Bread Before Roses: American Workingmen, Labor Unions and the Family Wage," in Ruth Milkman, ed., *Women, Work and Protest. A Century of U.S. Women's Labor History* (Boston: Routledge and Kegan Paul, 1985), p. 2.

[14] See section 42; available online at http://www.vatican.va/holy_father/leo_xiii/encyclicals/ accessed January 11, 2009.

[15] John Ryan, *A Living Wage*, (first published 1906) (New York: The Macmillan Company, 1920), p. 101.

[16] B. Seebohm Rowntree and Frank D. Stuart, *The Responsibility of Women Workers for Dependents* (Oxford: Clarendon Press, 1921).

[17] F. Y. Edgeworth, "Equal Pay to Men and Women for Equal Work," *Economic Journal* XXXII:128 (1922), p. 449. See also his "Women's Wages in Relation to Economic Welfare", *Economic Journal* XXXIII:132 (1923), 487–95.

[18] Sophonisba Breckenridge, "The Home Responsibilities of Women", *The Journal of Political Economy* 31:4 (1923), p. 538.

[19] Margaret Cole, *The Story of Fabian Socialism* (Stanford: Stanford University Press, 1961).

[20] H. G. Wells, *Socialism and the Family* (London: A. C. Fifield, 1906); *New Worlds for Old* (New York: MacMillan, 1919); *The Work, Wealth, and Happiness of Mankind* (New York: Doubleday, Doran, 1931).

[21] *Independent Review*, November 1906, cited in G. R. Searle, *A New England. Peace and War 1886–1918* (New York: Oxford University Press, 2005) p. 380.

[22] Pedersen, *Family, Dependence, and the Origins of the Welfare State*.

[23] Jane Lewis, *Women in England 1870–1950: Sexual Divisions and Social Change* (Sussex: Wheatsheaf, 1984), p. 51.

[24] Carole Seymour-Jones, *Beatrice Webb* (Chicago: Ivan Dee, 1992).

[25] Lewis, *Women in England*, p. 97.

[26] Beatrice Webb, *Our Partnership* (London: Longmans, Green, 1948), p. 149.

[27] Sidney Webb, *The Decline in the Birth Rate* (London: The Fabian Society, 1907), pp. 16–17.

[28] Beatrice Webb, *The Wages of Men and Women: Should They be Equal?* (London: The Fabian Society, 1919), p. 68.

[29] George Bernard Shaw, *The Intelligent Woman's Guide to Socialism and Capitalism* (New York: Brentano's, 1928). The "last will and testament to humanity" quote appears on the cover of this edition.

[30] Eleanor Rathbone, "The Remuneration of Women's Services", *The Economic Journal*, XXVII (1917): 54–68; *The Disinherited Family* (London: Edward Arnold and Company, 1924).

[31] Rathbone, *The Disinherited Family*, p. 10.

[32] Rathbone, *The Disinherited Family*, p. 16.

[33] F. Y. Edgeworth, "Equal Pay to Men and Women for Equal Work", *The Economic Journal*, XXXIII:131 (1922), p. 445.

[34] Pedersen, *Family, Dependence and the Origins of the Welfare State*, p. 181.

[35] Rathbone's use of the word "Turk" may reflect Prayer Book usage. Anglican Good Friday prayers used to intercede for "all Jews, Turks, heretics and infidels" where the word "Turk" was synonymous with Muslim (A. M. C. Waterman, personal communication),

[36] Rathbone, *The Disinherited Family*, p. 217.

[37] U.S. Women's Bureau, *State Laws Affecting Working Women*, Bulletin No. 16. Washington: Government Printing Office, 1921.

[38] Nancy F. Cott, *The Grounding of Modern Feminism* (New Haven: Yale University Press, 1987), p. 205.

[39] Residents of Hull House, *Hull House Maps and Papers*, first published 1895 (New York: Arno Press, 1970).

[40] Frank W. Taussig, "Minimum Wages for Women", *Quarterly Journal of Economics* XXX:3 (1916), 411–42.

[41] Dorothy Douglas, "The Cost of Living for Working Women: A Criticism of Current Theories", *Quarterly Journal of Economics* XXXIV:2 (1920), 209–59.

[42] Sophonisba B. Breckinridge, "The Home Responsibilities of Women", *Journal of Political Economy* 31:4 (1923), p. 535.

[43] Paul H. Douglas, *Wages and the Family* (Chicago: University of Chicago Press, 1925).

[44] Edward Heiman, "The Family Wage Controversy in Germany", *Economic Journal* XXXIII (1923): 509–15; J. H. Richardson, "The Family Allowance System", *Economic Journal* XXXV (1924), 373–86.

[45] Nancy Folbre, "Sleeping Beauty Awakes: Self-Interest, Feminism, and Fertility in the Early Twentieth Century", *Social Research* 71:2 (2004), 343–56.

[46] J. A. and Olive Banks argue that it played virtually no role. See their *Feminism and Family Planning in Victorian England* (New York: Schocken Books, 1964). Angus McLaren

persuasively argues just the opposite in *Birth Control in Nineteenth-Century England* (London: Croom Helm, 1978).

[47] Alain Corbin, *Women for Hire. Prostitution and Sexuality in France after 1850,* translated by Alan Sheridan (Cambridge: Harvard University Press, 1990); Francis Ronsin, *La grève des ventres. Propagande néo-malthusienne et baisse de la natalité en France 19e-20e siècles* (Paris: Éditions Aubier Montaigne, 1980).

[48] Richard Allen Soloway, *Birth Control and the Population Question in England, 1877–1930* (Chapel Hill: University of North Carolina Press, 1982), p. 54.

[49] McLaren, *Birth Control*, p. 179.

[50] Barbara Goldsmith, *Other Powers. The Age of Suffrage, Spiritualism, and the Scandalous Victoria Woodhull* (New York: Alfred A. Knopf, 1998).

[51] Margaret Sanger, *The Pivot of Civilization* (New York: Brentano's, 1922), pp. 271–2.

[52] On Sanger's life, see Ellen Chesler, *Woman of Valor. Margaret Sanger and the Birth Control Movement in America* (New York: Simon and Schuster, 1992) and David M. Kennedy, *Birth Control in America. The Career of Margaret Sanger* (New Haven: Yale University Press, 1970).

[53] Carole R. McCann, *Birth Control Politics in the United States, 1916–1945* (Ithaca: Cornell University Press, 1994), p. 48.

[54] Margaret Sanger, *Woman and the New Race* (New York: Brentano's, 1920).

[55] Margaret Sanger, *Pivot of Civilization* (New York: Brentano's, 1922).

[56] Margaret Sanger, *My Fight for Birth Control* (Elmsford, New York: Maxwell Reprint Company, 1931), p. 290. See also the discussion in David Kennedy, *Birth Control in America. The Career of Margaret Sanger* (New Haven: Yale University Press, 1973).

[57] Marie Stopes, *Married Love. A New Contribution to the Solution of Sex Difficulties* (New York: Eugenics Publishing Co., 1932).

[58] Ibid., p. 162.

[59] "The fullest delight, even in a purely physical sense, can be attained only by those who curb and direct their natural appetites." Ibid., p. 76.

[60] June Rose, *Marie Stopes and the Sexual Revolution* (Boston: Faber and Faber, 1992), p. 186.

[61] Ibid., p. 198.

[62] On Stopes, see Lewis, *Politics of Motherhood*, p. 205; on Sanger, see McCann, *Birth Control Politics*.

[63] Gosta Esping Anderson, *Three Worlds of Welfare Capitalism* (Princeton: Princeton University Press, 1990).

CHAPTER 19

Human Capitalism

The world is *not* so governed from above that private and social interest always coincide. It is not so managed here below that in practice they coincide. It is not a correct deduction from the principles of economics that enlightened self-interest always operates in the public interest. Nor is it true that self-interest generally is enlightened; more often individuals acting separately to promote their own ends are too ignorant or too weak to attain even these. John Maynard Keynes

The addition of a final "e" to the adjective "human" shifts its meaning in the direction of benevolence, as in "humane capitalism". During the twentieth century, the role of state spending and social insurance in Great Britain, the U.S., and France expanded along with increased female labor force participation.[1] Debates over the appropriate roles of public programs and private enterprises cycled along with the rise and fall of state socialism, periods of economic stress, and military conflict. Those who believed that public action could help solve coordination problems, like John Maynard Keynes, demanded a larger role for government. Those with greater confidence in self-interest, like Milton Friedman generally cheered for market forces. True believers in both camps were sure that they could achieve the greater good of the greater number.

Economists in both camps were impressed by the contribution of increased education to technological change and improvements in living standards.

Since education has typically been both mandated and subsidized by governments, one might assume that enthusiasm for it would lend support to advocates of the public sector. But economists Theodore Schultz and Gary Becker developed a compelling model of education as the outcome of individuals' decisions to invest in their own and their children's human capital. Employers would gain from rewarding such investments unless they fell prey to an economically irrational, discriminatory preference to choose workers based on superficial traits such as sex or race.

Originally built on individualist foundations, the neoclassical theory of human capital led almost inevitably to an emphasis on family decisions and an appreciation of family work. In this respect, Gary Becker's *Treatise on the Family* transcended the most conspicuous inconsistency of the Marshallian legacy. Yet Becker's allegiance to the virtues of self-interest made him reluctant to concede its implications for conflict within the family. Despite brilliant insights into the causes of gender inequality, the role of the state and the formation of preferences, Becker relied heavily on the assumption that altruism would pervade—but seldom reach beyond—family life.

Social Welfare

Economic growth in the late nineteenth and early twentieth centuries lifted many boats but sank others. Its stormy wake contributed to the success of socialist and reform movements that challenged the primacy of *laissez-faire*. The Russian Revolution of 1917, as well as the gradual consolidation of Communist Party rule in China seemed to offer a distinct alternative to a capitalist economic system. Even economists suspicious of the very concept of social welfare were forced to grapple with public perceptions of its relevance.

Alfred Marshall had carefully noted that individual transactions often had positive or negative effects, "external economies" that spilled over onto others.[2] His prize student Arthur Pigou further developed the concept of "externalities", explaining how taxes and subsidies could be used to bring private and social costs closer together and advocating, among other policies, family allowances.[3] Many of Pigou's contemporaries warned that government policymakers might lack both the motivation and the information necessary to maximize social welfare. But as previous chapters have shown, many were persuaded that individual decisions would not necessarily yield the optimal rate of population growth. The concept of externalities would later come to play a titanic role in debates over environmental degradation and global warning.

In the early twentieth century, however, issues of instability trumped issues of sustainability. After the stock market crash of 1929, the U.S. economy spiraled into a downturn characterized by persistently high unemployment rates. The British economy, dislocated by World War I, had been faltering since 1918; the French economy, growing very slowly, was less integrated into world trade. By the mid-1930s, however, the Great Depression had become a global phenomenon. Most economists believed it would be self-correcting: unemployment would cause wages to fall, which would in turn increase the demand for labor. Businesses that had overreached themselves would be liquidated, purging the system of inefficiencies.[4]

By 1932, U.S. voters, if not economists, had lost patience with this view, and Franklin D. Roosevelt won a landslide victory with his promises of a New Deal. Neither his philosophy nor his policies were well-formed at that time, but he moved quickly to establish government relief efforts and win passage of the Social Security Act of 1935. This legislation (discussed briefly in Chapter 18) built on earlier state legislation to provide public assistance to the elderly, indigent mothers and children, and the unemployed. Re-elected in 1936, Roosevelt used his second Inaugural Address to establish his new philosophical touchstone: "We have always known that heedless self-interest was bad morals; we know now that it is bad economics."[5]

In Great Britain, economic events seemed to validate the views of economists like John Maynard Keynes, who had long expressed skepticism regarding the magic of self-interest. Keynes described economics as a moral science.[6] In a small but elegant book entitled *The End of Laissez Faire* published in 1926, he offered a concise reprise of economic doctrines that challenged prevailing views, emphasizing that private and social interests did not always coincide (see epigraph to this chapter).[7] In *Economic Possibilities for our Grandchildren* he wavered a bit, suggesting that avarice should rule until prosperity was more widespread.[8]

But in his enormously influential *General Theory of Employment, Interest and Money*, published in 1936, Keynes rejected the argument that greed could regulate itself. He pictured an economy driven by aggregate demand

and government spending rather than individual decisions. The analytical tools that grew out of the *General Theory* explained how competitive economies could get stuck in low-level equilibrium traps. The cumulative implications seemed eerily consistent with Roosevelt's philosophy.

The Opposite Reaction

While Great Britain and France had already expanded provisions for public welfare, the demands of World War II and its aftermath shoved them, as well as the U.S., farther in that direction. The end of military alliance with the socialist countries and gradual heating up of the Cold War intensified political divisions. This historical shift sharpened the edge of debates over the economics of self-interest. Even before the end of the war the Austrian economist Friedrich von Hayek began to argue that any form of socialism would lead to totalitarianism. His book, *The Road to Serfdom*, gained a particularly wide audience in the U.S., where it was condensed in *Reader's Digest*.[9]

Von Hayek's suspicions regarding abuse of state power proved warranted, especially in the case of Stalinist Russia. But he was overconfident of the efficiency of market economies. He overreached himself most conspicuously in his critique of the very concept of altruism, which he described as a primitive, even atavistic sentiment.[10] His views on this topic were popularized by a Russian émigré who adored his ideas, Ayn Rand, whose most famous novel, *The Fountainhead* (later made into a movie starring Gary Cooper), idealized individualism. However admirable her hero's steadfast commitment to his own artistic vision, his rants against altruism implied that it was a destructive force: "Every major horror of history was committed in the name of an altruistic motive", and "The world is perishing from an orgy of self-sacrificing."[11]

Von Hayek's views remained unpopular within the academy for some time, but he influenced colleagues at both the London School of Economics and the University of Chicago, where he visited as a lecturer. His ideas gradually gained ground. In 1974 he was awarded the Nobel Prize (sharing with an ideological opposite, Gunnar Myrdal). A favorite of Margaret Thatcher and of economic advisors to Ronald Reagan and George H. W. Bush, he remains the hero of many conservative think tanks. Alan Greenspan, Chairman of the Board of Governors of U.S. Federal Reserve Board from 1987 to 2006, has acknowledged Ayn Rand's—and, by implication, von Hayek's—influence on him as a young man.[12]

Von Hayek's philosophical influence is particularly visible in the work of social choice theorist James Buchanan, winner of the 1986 Nobel Prize for economics, who also warns that charity and compassion weaken economic efficiency.[13] Pro-market views were expressed in a far more temperate and persuasive style by University of Chicago's Milton Friedman, who tended to sidestep philosophical debates in the name of "value-free" science. His positivist stance represented a more nuanced critique, labeling moralistic concerns irrelevant to economic analysis.[14] Friedman published influential research on the determinants of consumption, graciously acknowledging both the ideas and the friendship of Margaret Reid.[15] He is probably best known among economists for a monetarist account of the Great Depression that places greater emphasis on government missteps than on market malfunction.[16]

Friedman served as a cheerful, quick-witted spokesman for his cause. In *Capitalism and Freedom*, and later in *Free to Choose* (coauthored with his wife Rose), he accentuated the positive features of individualism. His public persona emerged both from the regular columns he wrote for *Newsweek* between 1966 and 1983 and the PBS television series based on *Free to Choose*.[17] He often advocated policies that could potentially increase individual choice and promote equitable outcomes. His proposal for a negative income tax that would reduce the work disincentives of public assistance contributed to the development of the Earned Income Tax Credit (EITC) in the U.S. His school voucher proposals have increased the scope of school choice, even where they have not been directly adopted. His more libertarian proposals, including legalization of both drugs and prostitution, gained far less political traction.

Friedman's criticisms of social welfare programs were often animated by genuine concern for the poor. He misstepped, however, when he visited Chile to provide economic advice for the military dictatorship of Augusto Pinochet in 1975. His public pronouncements to the effect that social welfare spending would inevitably undermine democracy did not come off well: Chile's socialist president, Salvador Allende, had been democratically elected. His usurpers, advocates of free markets, were hardly advocates of free elections. Friedman wrote Pinochet a personal letter in 1975 advocating "shock therapy" in the form of reductions in government spending. The same term was later applied to the policies recommended for Eastern Europe and the former Soviet Union as they made the transition to capitalism.[18]

The Chilean military regime became notorious for its abuse of human rights, including use of electric shock in torture of political prisoners; Pinochet himself narrowly escaped international prosecution.[19] Ever cheerful, Friedman and his fellow economic advisors insisted that the economic growth their policies had ultimately contributed to the re-establishment of democratic governance in Chile. The privatized Chilean Social Security system became the model for President George W. Bush's campaign to privatize the U.S. Social Security system, a campaign that foundered in the wake of dramatic stock market declines and corporate accounting scandals in 2001.[20]

Friedman's genial tone, combined with his optimism regarding the civilizing effects of economic growth, recalls Adam Smith. But Friedman was careful never to endorse the importance of moral sentiments. In *Capitalism and Freedom*, and later in the *New York Times*, he challenged the very concept of corporate social responsibility: "Few trends could so thoroughly undermine the very foundations of our free society as the acceptance by corporate officials of a responsibility other than to make as much money for their stockholders as possible."[21] Corporate management experts further developed this view, arguing that salaried Chief Executive Officers (CEOs) had little incentive to maximize profits. In the 1980s and 1990s many corporations shifted toward bonus-based compensation schemes that generously rewarded short-term performance, possibly at the expense of long run efficiency.[22] From a libertarian perspective, like von Hayek's, selfishness is good.

Is it good for women as well as men? Von Hayek avoided the question. Oddly enough, so did Ayn Rand—the women in her novels never came close to showing her own level of selfish initiative. Milton Friedman never suggested that women had any less right to individual choice than did men. But for the most part, this generation of libertarians confined their attention to comparisons between the market and the state. Asked if the family represented a realm distinct from both, James Buchanan replied that he had never considered that question and had no opinion to offer on it.[23] His writings describe the pursuit of self-interest in memorably masculine terms. As he put it, the assumption that public servants could be altruistic was tantamount to the assumption that they were "economic eunuchs".[24]

Everyone a Capitalist

Fresher ideas emerged from the efforts of those who sought to reconcile neoclassical individualism with the feminine realm of family life. Adam Smith had first deployed the concept of human capital and Alfred Marshall had embraced its significance, but neither sought to explain the production of human capital in economic terms. Enthusiasm for that task became the hallmark of economists at the University of Chicago. Margaret Reid may have exercised a quiet, indirect influence. She encouraged her colleague Theodore Schultz as he prepared a presidential address to the American Economics Association in 1960 on the benefits of investments in human capital.[25]

Largely ignoring family inputs into the development of children's capabilities, Schultz focused on earnings foregone by "mature students". He conceded the desirability of measuring the value of human capital goods by the same means as physical capital goods—namely adding up the costs of producing them. Unfortunately, he noted, there was no way to distinguish between those expenditures that merely satisfied utility and those that enhanced capabilities, or between "consumption" and "investment". The best alternative, he argued, was to measure human investment in terms of its yield, ignoring its cost of production.[26]

This was a significant departure from historical precedent. Farr had tried to estimate the difference between the value of what a man produced and what he consumed; Dublin and Lotka had tried to determine what lump sum insurance payment could compensate a family for losses resulting from a death (see earlier discussion in Chapter 17). But Schultz sought to measure the value of human capital to the adult individual who had acquired it, and to no one else. Should a man invest in an additional year of education? Only if the net present discounted value of the resulting increase in his future earnings exceeded the cost.

Gary Becker, who earned his Ph.D. at the University of Chicago in 1955 and returned as a faculty member in 1969, initially followed Schultz's lead.

Becker's classic *Human Capital* starts with a broad definition of human capital as "activities that influence future monetary and psychic income by increasing the resources in people."[27] It quickly narrows its focus to adult decisions to acquire education and labor market experience, emphasizing that most human capital accumulation takes the form of "self-investment".[28] The investments people make in themselves are preceded by the investments that families and communities make in them. Parental expenditures of money and time on children have discernable effects on success in school and later in life, a point eloquently made by Arleen Leibowitz in an early volume edited by Schultz.[29]

But the new wave of research on human capital, developed by Jacob Mincer and Reuben Gronau, as well as Becker, initially treated individuals rather than families as the basic unit of analysis. Like Thomas Hobbes, who asked his readers to assume that adult men, like mushrooms, had simply sprung from the earth, early human capital theorists stipulated that individual preferences and endowments should be taken as a given. Like Stanley Jevons, they postulated that individuals always acted to maximize their own utility—or, in more ordinary language, their own happiness. Those who chose to invest in education and to accumulate valuable labor market experience would earn more money than those who did not. Tampering with these outcomes ran the risk of penalizing—and thus discouraging—human capital investment. If every person represents capital, then of course every person is a capitalist.

Here came the familiar refrain. If everyone acted in their own self-interest, society as a whole would gain. Becker emphasized that not everyone, at least initially, was sufficiently enlightened. Some employers might have discriminatory tastes. That is, they might prefer not to hire workers of a different race or sex, even though they were equally productive. This irrational preference would reduce the demand for those workers, lowering their market wages. Others pointed out that the problem could be self-correcting. Any employers interested only in maximizing their profits, unencumbered by discriminatory tastes, would jump at the opportunity to hire less expensive, but equally productive workers.[30] Their greater efficiency would enable them to drive discriminators out of business.

The basic human capital model, developed in more detail by Jacob Mincer, provided a happy opportunity for econometric analysis of large data sets.[31] Individual earnings represented the dependent variable, or outcome to be explained. Measures of self-investment such as years of education and labor market experience represented one set of independent variables, those that represented social virtue. Another set of independent variables, those indicating the sex or race of the individual, capturing the possible effects of discrimination, represented social vice. More complex causalities (such as the possibility that potential earnings might determine labor market experience, or that individuals were unable to gain access to their preferred level of education) were largely set aside.

The human capital model virtuously highlighted its own measure of discrimination. The empirical results consistently showed that women and blacks were paid significantly less than white males, even controlling for differences in their level of human capital. These results, in turn, sparked new efforts to explain why discrimination might prove more persistent than Becker's original formulation had suggested. Becker himself began to shift his attention from individual to family decisions. But the model seemed to suggest that an economy in which wages could be completely explained by differences in education and experience would be entirely fair. It also deflected attention from the costs of creating human capital to the individual benefits of education.

Capitalizing Humans

This deflection gradually exerted effects on macroeconomic theory, evident in the evolution of ideas concerning the valuation of human capital within the national income accounts. As explained in Chapter 17, designers of the accounts explicitly chose to exclude non-market work. Keynes, often pre-occupied with the challenge of financing British wars, raised no concerns about this decision beyond his expressed concerns about slow population growth. But the growing appreciation of human capital raised questions about how it should be valued in macroeconomic terms.

National income accounting—like all accounting—focuses on results rather than motives. Growth in the stock of harvestable timber may represent a growth in capital assets, even if it is not the result of any conscious investment decision. Likewise, parental expenditures on children may represent a productive investment whether or not parents consciously view them in these terms. If education yields a positive rate of return for individuals in the labor market, then public expenditures on education should properly be categorized as investment rather than consumption.

Some consideration of these issues surfaced in a prescient analysis by John Kendrick, *The Formation and Stocks of Total Capital*, published by the National Bureau for Economic Research in 1976. Kendrick adopted a strategy that represented the exact opposite of Schultz and Becker: he focused entirely on the costs of producing human capital, rather than what it would yield. He also emphasized the difference between "tangible" human capital (the actual bodies and brains of working-age adults and "intangible" human capital (the capabilities developed by education and on-the-job training). Kendrick operationalized the tangible part as the "accumulated rearing costs (in constant prices) at age fourteen for each cohort."[32] He included estimates of the depreciation of the tangible human capital stock (also known as "aging"). He also measured "intangible" human capital in terms of costs, tallying total educational expenditures after age fifteen.

Yet Kendrick could not stomach the idea that parental labor was an input into human capital. He defined "accumulated rearing costs" entirely in terms of parental expenditures—the cost of purchasing food and diapers should be included, but not the value of the time devoted to bearing the child, feeding the child or cleaning its rear end. In this respect, Kendrick echoed Dublin and Lotka, even though he was clearly aware of the potential contribution of time use data on hours of non-market work. Indeed, he used such data to estimate the replacement cost of all non-market work, generating expanded estimates of total consumption and Gross National Product.[33] He apparently assumed that non-market work—including the work of parents in general and mothers in particular—could contribute to consumption but not to investment.

Most national income accountants considered Kendrick's efforts to calculate the value of non-market work interesting but uncomfortable. One of the few to take up his banner was macroeconomist Robert Eisner, who also developed estimates of the aggregate value of non-market work.[34] Eisner chose not to include expenditures on children as a component of investment. Invoking Marshallian scruples without much explanation, he stated "the production of human beings themselves would better ... be omitted from income and product accounts."[35] On the other hand, he emphasized that non-market work contributes to the development of "intangible" human capital in the form of enhanced capabilities. In his calculations of national product, he valued the time that parents devote to educating and instructing their children (through activities such as reading aloud) on a par with purchased educational inputs.

Like Kendrick before him, Eisner failed to exercise much immediate influence on the discipline. Most subsequent efforts to assign an aggregate value to human capital adopted Schultz's strategy—valuing it primarily in term of its future yield, rather than its costs of production.[36] Yields can be adjusted to factor in and compensate for the effects of labor market discrimination.[37] Estimates of rates of return call attention to the enormous contribution that investments in human capital can make to economic growth. But they deflect from the question of who pays for such investments—not, in most instances, the individual who captures the benefits. Parents and taxpayers—not wage earners themselves—pay most of the tab for the creation of their tangible and intangible human capital.[38]

The Altruistic Family

Gary Becker was quick to recognize that a coherent theory of human capital required a theory of family, rather than individual decision-making. But families, like societies are aggregations of individuals; a family welfare function suffers from the same conundrum as a social welfare function— how can one person's desires be weighed against those of others? The easiest solution was to treat the family as though it were an individual, the larger self in the pursuit of self-interest.

James Mill had adopted this strategy in the early nineteenth century when he explained that women were politically represented by their fathers, husbands, and brothers and therefore did not require the right to vote. Paul Samuelson reiterated the argument in 1956, suggesting that family members act as a unit because they are bound together by altruism and mutual affection.[39] Becker refined the theory further, invoking evolutionary biology to explain why altruism should prevail in the family, self-interest in the market.[40]

Families seek to maximize their collective happiness. Who defines this happiness? Altruistic household heads love not only their children, but their children's children, encompassing the utility of future generations in a dynastic utility function. One wonders how they factor in the preferences of the unborn, and also how they could know which dynasties will be linked with their own through future marriages. The boundary between family and non-family is hardly fixed.[41] One also wonders what it means when families are essentially discontinued as the result of abandonment, separation or divorce—presumably their altruistic preferences have atrophied.

Becker's confidence in the altruism of the household head sounds unshakeable. Some individuals within the family, so-called rotten kids, may be tempted to act in selfish ways. But an altruistic head that wields sufficient power can induce even spoiled brats to behave in ways that benefit the family as a whole.[42] The possibility that a family head might behave in rotten ways is ruled out, by definition: As Becker puts it, the "head of a family is defined not by sex or age but as that member, if there is one, who transfers general purchasing power to all other members because he cares about their welfare."[43] Historically, women have been designated household heads only in the absence of an adult male. Although he uses gender-neutral terminology, Becker seems to invert the traditional association between femininity and altruism, implying that husbands are altruistic benefactors, wives potential opportunists.[44]

The assumption that families make decisions that are in the best interests of all their members implies that the distribution of resources within families is always efficient. Economists have found many possible applications for such reasoning, arguing, for example, that poor families in India may allocate less food and health care to female than to male children because they depend so heavily on the future income that male children can more effectively provide.[45] The higher mortality of female than male children, however unfortunate, presumably leaves the family unit better off (it is never clear what preferences the dead girls might have had).

Families that successfully maximize their collective welfare respond in predictable ways to changes imposed from outside their boundaries. Any unanticipated increase in the resources available to one family member should lead the family to shift some of their own resources away from that member, neutralizing the change much the same way as government spending can crowd out private investment (the more typical macroeconomic usage of the term). For instance, public provision of school lunches should reduce the amount of food parents feed the child at breakfast, and public provision of higher education should displace the resources that parents would otherwise have spent.

Selfish dynasties that have perfect economic foresight can counteract government fiscal policies. When parents see an increase in government spending that leads to higher national debt, they anticipate that their children will be required to pay higher taxes in the future to finance that debt. In response, they increase the amount of money they save in order to transfer more to their children at a later date, offsetting the impact of increased government spending.[46] Human capital models provide the microeconomic foundation for a distinctly anti-Keynesian approach to macroeconomic analysis.[47] In this conceptual world, selfish families are not only predominant; they are, in a sense, hegemonic. Not even the modern state can neutralize their decisions.

Families, Gender Inequality, and the State

One can disagree with many of Becker's assumptions and still admire his analytical powers. Unlike his neoclassical predecessors, he brings household decision-making into the purview of economic analysis. Unlike his more institutionalist predecessors, such as Margaret Reid and Hazel Kyrk, he develops a theoretical model that predicts responses to shifts in relative prices and incomes. Becker's model clearly explains why families would respond to modern economic development by choosing to raise fewer children and investing more resources in a smaller number, a shift from "quantity to quality" of children.

The human capital approach purports to explain why small differences in the comparative advantage of men and women in childbearing and nursing could have large cumulative effects.[48] Women gain less experience in market work, which reduces their expected wage, which in turn encourages further specialization in household production. When they do work outside the home, women may choose occupations where starting salaries are relatively high but gains to labor force experience are relatively low— reducing the cost of taking time out of paid employment to care for family members.[49] Fertility decline reduces the extent of early specialization, leads to increases in women's participation in market work, which in turn raises their market wages, which induce further shifts in women's allocation of time.

Becker and his fellow-travelers also provide a deft explanation of the role of the state in providing education: parents and children cannot negotiate private binding commitments to exchange resources, but the state can tax one generation of working-age adults to finance education for the younger generation, which can in turn be taxed to provide the older generation with income security in old age. Becker clearly recognizes the role that interest groups play in influencing public policy.[50] Yet he characterizes marriage as a virtually universal contractual arrangement designed to provide income security for mothers and children. He never examines the contractual asymmetries criticized by feminists since the mid-nineteenth century— legal provisions that accord more legal authority and control over household resources to husbands than to wives.[51] Nor does he explore the ways in which women have organized themselves into "interest groups" to challenge patriarchal rules.

Becker's ideas regarding preference formation are also tantalizingly incomplete. On the one hand, he observes that people's experiences can shape their preferences, leading to forms of "addiction". On the other hand, he asserts that individuals have sufficient foresight to anticipate these effects, and therefore, in a sense, choose their own preferences. Likewise, he observes that powerful groups seek to create norms to influence the preferences of others but asserts that individuals being socialized are always aware of the process, explicitly allowing their preferences to be influenced.[52]

In the end, Becker, like his modern neoclassical colleagues, remains confident that individuals know what they want and can get what they want as long as they are free to choose. What a refreshing change from the double standard of self-interest that Marshall and Jevons applied to men but not to women. But Becker's very confidence in choice helps justify gender inequalities. Women are paid less than men because they choose jobs that pay less.[53] Mothers take more responsibility for family care than fathers because they enjoy doing so.[54] Spending on children, like on pets, is merely a form of discretionary spending.[55] If people choose to have children, they should pay the costs of rearing and educating them. If work is provided for free, why count its contributions as part of GDP?

The Third Realm

Women and men try to make good choices. But their range of choice is shaped by social norms and limited by other people's power. Women who know exactly what they want may be unable to get it unless they work with others to change the structures of constraint. Even those who give freely of their love may withdraw it in the long run if they feel that it is neither honored nor reciprocated.

The neoclassical economic tradition celebrates individual decisions, worrying about the effects of any interference with them. Economists who worry more about the unintended consequences of individual decisions, including those working within the Keynesian tradition—insist on the need for social coordination. Most economists continue to interpret this tension in dualistic terms, contrasting the realm of the market with the realm of the state. The increasing importance of human capital dramatizes the realm of family life. Much as we like to think of ourselves as producers, we are, ourselves, produced.

Parents recognize that their own decisions will influence their children's values, norms, and preferences at least to some extent. Likewise, economists should recognize that our institutional arrangements influence what we want as well as what we get. What then should we want? Economists like Milton Friedman and Gary Becker avoid this question, for fear that moral concerns will threaten scientific objectivity.

NOTES TO CHAPTER 19

[1] Peter H. Lindert, *Growing Public. Social Spending and Economic Growth Since the Eighteenth Century* (New York: Cambridge University Press, 2004).

[2] Alfred Marshall, *Principles of Economics*, 8th edn, London: Macmillan, 1962), p. 221.

[3] Arthur C. Pigou, *The Economics of Welfare* (London: Macmillan, 1920); Nahid Aslanbeigui, "Rethinking Pigou's Misogyny", *Eastern Economic Journal* 23:3 (1997), 301–16.

[4] Bradford De Long, *Slouching Toward Utopia*, available at http://www.j-bradforddelong. net/TCEH/slouchingtowardutopia.html, accessed July 15, 2008.

[5] Franklin D. Roosevelt, Second Inaugural Address, January, 1937, accessed on line at http://www.yale.edu/lawweb/avalon/presiden/inaug/froos2.htm, May 27, 2008.

[6] A. B. Atkinson, "Economics as a Moral Science", Inaugural Joseph Rowntree Foundation Lecture, University of York, January 2008, available at www.jrf.org.uk.

[7] John Maynard Keynes, *The End of Laissez-Faire* (Hogarth Press, 1926), section IV.

[8] John Maynard Keynes, *Essays in Persuasion*, first published 1930 (New York: W. W. Norton, 1963), 358–73.

[9] Friedrich von Hayek, *The Road to Serfdom*, first published 1944. Text and documents edited by Bruce Caldwell (Chicago: University of Chicago Press, 2007).

[10] Friedrich von Hayek, *The Fatal Conceit. The Errors of Socialism* (Chicago: University of Chicago Press, 1988).

[11] Ayn Rand, *The Fountainhead*, first published 1943 (New York: Plume, 1993) pp. 715, 717.

[12] Alan Greenspan, *The Age of Turbulence. Adventures in a New World* (New York: Penguin, 2007), pp. 51–3.

[13] James M. Buchanan, "The Samaritan's Dilemma", 71–85 in *Altruism, Morality, and Economic Theory*, Edmund S. Phelps, ed. (New York: Russell Sage, 1975).

[14] Milton Friedman, *Essays in Positive Economics* (Chicago: University of Chicago, 1953).

[15] See his 1976 Nobel Prize autobiography at http://nobelprize.org/nobel_prizes/economics/ laureates/1976/friedman-autobio.html, accessed May 28, 2008.

[16] Milton Friedman and Anna Jacobson Schwartz, *A Monetary History of the United States, 1867–1960*. First published, 1953 (Ann Arbor: University of Michigan Press, 1995).

[17] Justin M. Norton, "Milton Friedman", *San Francisco Chronicle*, November 16, 2006.

[18] See Naomi Klein, *The Shock Doctrine* (New York: Metropolitan, 2007); and Milton Friedman and Rose Friedman, *Two Lucky People: Memoirs* (Chicago: University of Chicago, 1999).

[19] For details on the Pinochet prosecution, see Human Rights Watch, http://www.hrw.org/ campaigns/chile98/index.html, accessed May 28, 2008; See also the report of the Chilean Truth Commission at <http://www.usip.org/library/tc/doc/reports/chile/chile_1993_toc.html>

[20] Barbara T. Dreyfuss, "The Siren of Santiago", *Mother Jones* (March/April 2005), 18–21.

[21] Milton Friedman, *Capitalism and Freedom* (Chicago: University of Chicago Press, 1962) p. 133; "The Social Responsibility of Business is to Increase its Profits", *New York Times Magazine*, September 30, 1970.

[22] John Cassidy, "The Greed Cycle", *The New Yorker*, September 23, 2002.

[23] I pressed James Buchanan on this issue personally at a public lecture he delivered at the Australian National University in 2004. He stated that he had simply never given the matter much thought.

[24] James Buchanan, *Cost and Choice* (Chicago: University of Chicago Press, 1969). Buchanan won the Nobel Prize in 1986 and the phrase "economic eunuch" was credited to him by the award committee (see http://www.nobelprize.org/economics/laureates/1986).

[25] Theodore W. Schultz, "Investment in Human Capital", *American Economic Review* LI:1 (1961), p. 8.

[26] Schultz, "Investment in Human Capital", *American Economic Review* LI:1 (1961), p. 8.

[27] Gary S. Becker, *Human Capital*, 2nd edn. (Chicago: University of Chicago Press, 1975), p. 9.

[28] Becker, *Human Capital*, p. 98.

[29] Arleen Leibowitz, "Home Investments in Children", in *Economics of the Family. Marriage, Children, and Human Capital*, T. W. Schultz, ed. (Chicago: University of Chicago Press, 1973). See also Frank Stafford's published comment on her article in this volume.

[30] Kenneth Arrow, "Models of Job Discrimination", in *Discrimination in Labor Markets*, Orley Ashenfelter and Albert Rees, eds. (Princeton: Princeton University Press, 1973).

[31] Jacob Mincer, *Schooling, Experience, and Earnings* (New York: Columbia University Press, 1974).

[32] John Kendrick, *The Formation and Stocks of Total Capital* (Cambridge, MA: National Bureau of Economic Research, 1976), p. 7.

[33] John Kendrick, "Expanding Imputed Values in the National Income and Product Accounts", *Review of Income and Wealth* 25:4 (1979), 349–63.

[34] Robert Eisner, *The Total Incomes System of Accounts* (Chicago: The University of Chicago Press, 1989).

[35] Eisner, *The Total Incomes System*, p. 16.

[36] Dale W. Jorgenson and Barbara M. Fraumeni, "The Accumulation of Human and Non-Human Capital, 1948–1984", 227–82 in R. E. Lipsey and H. S. Tice, eds, *The Measurement of Savings, Investment and Wealth* (Chicago: University of Chicago Press, 1989).

[37] Robert H. Haveman, Andrew Bershadker, and Jonathan A. Schwabish, *Human Capital in the United States from 1975 to 2000: Patterns of Growth and Utilization* (Kalamazoo, MI: Upjohn, 2002).

[38] Folbre, *Valuing Children: Rethinking the Economics of the Family* (Cambridge MA: Harvard University Press, 2008).

[39] Paul Samuelson, "Social Indifference Curves", *Quarterly Journal of Economics* 190 (1956), p. 122.

[40] Gary S. Becker, "Altruism in the Family and Selfishness in the Market Place", *Economica* 48:1 (1981), 1–15. See also his *Treatise on the Family,* enlarged edition (Cambridge: Harvard University Press, 1991).

[41] Frances Woolley, "Getting the Better of Becker", *Feminist Economics* 2:1 (1996), 114–20.

[42] Jack Hirschleifer, "Shakespeare versus Becker on Altruism: The Importance of Having the Last Word", *Journal of Economic Literature,*" 11 (1977), 500–502.

[43] Becker, *Treatise on the Family*, p. 193.

[44] Edith Kuiper, *The Most Valuable of All Capital* (Amsterdam: Tinbergen Institute, 2001), p. 33.

[45] Mark Rosenzweig and T. Paul Schultz, "Market Opportunities, Genetic Endowments, and Intrafamily Resource Distribution", *American Economic Review* 72 (1982), 803–15. For an early critique of this approach, see Nancy Folbre, "Market Opportunities, Genetic Endowments, and Intrafamily Resource Distribution: A Comment", *American Economic Review*, 74:3 (1984), 518–22. See also Susan Himmelweit et al. "Decision-Making in Households", Ch. 6 in *Households* (The Open University, Social Sciences Third Level Course, 1998).

[46] Robert Barro, "Are Government Bonds Net Wealth?" *Journal of Political Economy* 82 (1974), 1095–117.

[47] For a textbook summary, see William Lord, *Household Dynamics* (New York: Oxford University Press, 2002).

[48] Jacob Mincer, "The Labor Force Participation of Married Women", in H. G. Lewis, ed., *Aspects of Labor Economics* (Princeton: Princeton University Press, 1962); Reuben Gronau, "Leisure, Home Production and Work: The Theory of the Allocation of Time Revisited", *Journal of Political Economy* 85:6 (1977), 1099–123.

[49] Solomon Polachek, "Occupational Self-Selection: A Human Capital Approach to Sex Differences in Occupational Structure", *Review of Economics and Statistics* 63:1 (1981), 60–9; For a critique, see Paula England, "The Failure of Human Capital Theory to Explain Occupational Sex Segregation", *Journal of Human Resources* 17:3 (1982), 358–70.

[50] Gary S. Becker, "A Theory of Competition among Pressure Groups for Political Influence", *The Quarterly Journal of Economics* 98 (1983), 371–400.

[51] For a spirited critique, see Barbara Bergmann, "Becker's Theory of the Family: Preposterous Conclusions", *Feminist Economics* 1:1 (1995), 141–50. Similar criticisms apply to Richard Posner's *Sex and Reason* (Cambridge: Harvard University Press, 1992).

[52] Gary S. Becker, *Accounting for Tastes* (Cambridge: Harvard University Press, 1996), p. 226.

[53] Warren Farrell, *Why Men Earn More* (New York: AMACOM, 2005).

[54] Victor Fuchs, *Women's Quest for Economic Equality* (Cambridge: Harvard University Press, 1988).

[55] M. Luisa Ferreira, Reuben C. Buse, and Jan-Paul Chavas, "Is There a Bias in Computing Household Equivalence Scales," *Review of Income and Wealth* 44 (1998), 183–98. For a detailed critique, see Hilde Bojer and Julie Nelson, "Equivalence Scales and the Welfare of Children: A Comment on, 'Is There Bias in the Economic Literature on Equivalence Scales,'" *Review of Income and Wealth* 45 (1999), 531–4.

CHAPTER 20

Beyond Economic Man

I have a little dream that in 1990–91, which is the next period designated by the United Nations for a census to be held in every country, all women claim unpaid worker as their designation.　　　　Marilyn Waring

At the 1990 meetings of the American Economics Association a group of dissident women formed a network that evolved into the International Association for Feminist Economics (IAFFE). European members organized a meeting in Amsterdam with the title "Out of the Margin" challenging the economic profession's tendency to marginalize women and resist challenges to mainstream approaches.[1] The title of an important collection of feminist economic essays published in 1993 also conveyed a message: *Beyond Economic Man*.[2]

Those essays explain that the man who knows exactly what he wants and how best to get it on his own is a caricature dependent on the women who nurtured him as an infant, care for his children, and promise to care for him in old age. No society based on selfishness could persist, and neither could any society that simply takes altruism as a given. The claim that everyone pursues their own self-interest is circular. What matters is the size and shape of the circle—the boundaries of the self and extent to which its preferences include concern for moral values and the well-being of other people.

The history of men's efforts to claim women as appendage to themselves—whether in the home, the polity, the labor market, or the national income accounts—reveals the impact of economic power on economic theory. As women gained more individual and collective bargaining power, they gradually changed the discipline. Feminist perspectives in economics join a host of other efforts to better understand the ways in which individuals come to identify with, and care for, others. Such forms of solidarity challenge the conventional assumption that self-interest is just another word for selfishness. They also help explain the formation and pursuit of collective interests.

The Waves

Feminist movements, like the business cycle, have always had their ups and downs. Intellectual contributions and political successes have not always moved in concert. By the early twentieth century, women's groups in the U.S. and Britain had coalesced around the demand for suffrage, achieved in 1920 and 1928 respectively. French women, either less focused on individual rights or less successful in acquiring them, did not reach this milestone until 1944.[3]

Feminist intellectuals in France reached into philosophy and literature, but were more effectively excluded from the discourse of economics than their counterparts in the English-speaking world. Simone de Beauvoir's classic, *The Second Sex*, anticipated many of the concerns of the women's movement of the 1960s, but did not reach much of an audience in the United States until similar concerns regarding the treatment of women as "other" were expressed in more practical terms by Betty Friedan in *The Feminine Mystique*.[4]

After 1950, the pace of change in married women's entrance into wage employment picked up, and women gained access to more reliable forms of contraception. These economic and demographic changes gradually and unevenly destabilized conventional gender norms.[5] Other forms of collective mobilization came into play. The emergence of the Civil Rights movement in the U.S. in the early 1960s contributed to the resurgence of the women's movement there.

Passage of laws against overt discrimination in the U.S. and the United Kingdom increased women's access to professional and managerial jobs. These economic gains probably contributed to a significant backlash and intensified class and racial differences among women in the U.S.[6] However, women's increased presence and power within academia fostered the development of Women's Studies programs and women's caucuses within separate disciplines. Feminist theory itself began to be . . . theorized.[7]

Women were slower to enter economics than other social science disciplines and also less likely to assert a gendered perspective. In the 1980s, women were less well-represented in the discipline in the U.S. than they had been in the 1920s, and few economists in the early 1990s acknowledged any awareness of feminist issues.[8] Lack of awareness is not, however, the same as immunity from influence. Pressure from many grass-roots women's organizations, as well as international networking efforts prompted the 1995 United Nations Fourth World Conference on Women in Beijing to call for an end to gender inequality in paid employment and greater recognition of women's work in the home.[9] Also in that year, the first issue of the journal *Feminist Economics* came off the press.

Feminist Economics

Feminist contributions to economics took many different forms, and opinions differ as to which were the most important. One notable feature was attention to the intellectual history of the discipline, reflected in many of the sources cited in preceding chapters. Three other areas of innovation in data collection and research directly challenged the disciplinary bias that is the primary focus of this book—the tendency to view the family as an idealized, moral, feminine, non-economic realm.

Empirical research on the sexual wage differential had long been underway. However, standard human capital models (briefly described in the preceding chapter) generally interpreted women's lower levels of job market experience as an independent variable—looking at their effects, but not their causes. In the 1990s, research began to look more directly at the costs of specializing in care provision. Studies of pay standards revealed that most women's jobs were typically paid less than men's independently of the characteristics of their workers. Jobs that involved care for others seemed especially underpaid.[10] Research also began to show that women who took time out of paid employment to care for a child paid a greater price in lifetime earnings than the standard models could account for.[11] Mary Astell and Poulain de la Barre would not have been surprised by these results (see discussion in Chapter 2).

For decades, most national statistical agencies assumed that all households had one "head" that could only be a female if no adult male family member was present in the home. Political mobilization spearheaded by Congresswoman Patricia Schroeder in the U. S. in the 1980s lead to new wording and definitions based on "householders" and "reference persons".[12] The U.S. Census Bureau also developed a new survey monitoring enforcement of child support responsibilities that increased pressure for legislative change in that area.[13]

During the same time period the World Bank and other multilateral agencies began to develop and field household-based surveys that devoted more attention to the economic contributions of women and children outside of market employment—the Living Standards Measurement Surveys.[14] Economists and other social scientists began to use these data to explore bargaining and inequality within the family.[15] William Thompson, Anna Wheeler, John Stuart Mill, and Harriet Taylor could have predicted their results.

Surveys of time use based on detailed diary data had long been administered by academic researchers, but no national statistical agencies supported such efforts. The New Zealander activist Marilyn Waring revitalized feminist arguments for valuing non-market work with her internationally-recognized book, *If Women Counted*.[16] The little dream she described in the epigraph to this chapter has not yet been realized, but seems underway. In the 1990s many countries, including England, Australia, and Canada, expanded their efforts to collect survey data on time use and the statistical office of the European Union, Eurostat, soon followed suit. In 2001 the U.S. Bureau of Labor Statistics made a commitment to implement the American Time Use Survey (ATUS) on an annual basis.[17] These surveys provide an improved basis for imputation of the total value of family and volunteer work: what it would cost to replace that work were it withdrawn.[18] The ladies of the Association for the Advancement of Women would have been pleased by such an estimate (see discussion in Chapter 17).

Motivations

Economists have been slow to take advantage of new data on time devoted to family work, and continue to largely ignore its implications for measures of economic output or inequality in living standards.[19] The inertial force of habit and tradition helps explain resistance to change. But additional resistance derives from the neoclassical definition of work as an activity performed only for extrinsic rewards, like a wage, or as Stanley Jevons more vividly defined it, "any painful exertion of mind or body undergone partly or wholly with a view to future good."[20] Many activities of family care are performed out of a sense of reciprocity, or for the pleasure making other people happy. By Jevons's definition they should not "count".

This definition, however, does not hold. Individual motives cannot be directly observed, and the distinction between intrinsic and extrinsic motivation does not necessarily coincide with the distinction between market and non-market work. Many people report deriving considerable satisfaction or "process benefits" from paid employment, and intrinsic motivation often affects the productivity of employees.[21] Many activities once confined to families have moved into the market—including child care, health care, and elder care. The once-sharp distinction between activities performed for love or money has lost its edge.[22]

As Margaret Reid pointed out in 1934, work can alternatively be defined as something you could, in principle, pay someone else to do (see discussion in Chapter 17). You can't pay someone to sleep or relax on your behalf; you can pay someone to clean your house, prepare your meals, or look after your child. This definition is somewhat incomplete. For instance, it leaves out studying, which sometimes recalls Jevons's emphasis on "painful exertion," or developing one's skills in other ways, such as getting regular exercise. These activities surely differ from leisure, which is less oriented toward future benefits. Perhaps they require a separate category of their own—self-care as a form of self-investment or personal work.

Most direct care activities, however, are undertaken on behalf of others, often those who cannot care for themselves. As Adam Smith pointed out, moral sentiments help align individual and social interests (see discussion in Chapter 4). As Gary Becker emphasizes, households often act on altruistic preferences (see discussion in Chapter 19). But altruistic preferences, in turn, are affected by the organization of economic institutions such as families and firms.

Economists have traditionally assumed that the boundaries of the self are obvious and clear. The textbook portrait of economic man making decisions

to buy or sell paints him as entirely selfish—with no interdependent preferences. The textbook portrait of an altruistic household head assumes that he
or she knows what all of the household members want and how to maximize
their total happiness.[23] Feminist social scientists have challenged such
assumptions, arguing that the concepts of a static "separative self" and its
inverse, a self with no boundaries whatsoever—reflect androcentric views.[24]

The boundaries of the self—defined as that entity whose interests we
pursue—can expand, contract, and reconfigure as individuals come to care
for and identify with others.[25] Collective action is seldom based on consideration of purely selfish interests. Feminist theory calls attention to men's
collective interests in resisting forms of change that might either restrict
male choices or increase male obligations. It does not imply that gender
represents the only dimension of interpersonal allegiance.

Markets and Non-Markets

The image of a market economy embedded in a non-economic natural and
social environment that can be taken as a given represents the macroeconomic counterpart of the separative self. Economists often describe the
spillover effects of market transactions, such as pollution, as "externalities"
as though they lie outside the economy itself. The reasoning behind taxes or
subsidies that adjust market prices to more accurate measures of social cost is
sound, but the commonly applied phrase "internalize externalities" oddly
evokes both gluttony and lust. From a feminist perspective, the externalities
in question dwarf the little body of the market, which relies on the larger
body of Mother Nature and figuratively suckles at her breast.

The natural assets of our ecosystem and the social wealth of human
capabilities represent assets of far greater value than forms of private capital
that are more easily bought and sold. Estimates of what it would cost to
replace ecological services, were they withdrawn, far exceed the value of
global Gross Domestic Product.[26] Even short-run estimates of the cost of
specific forms of ecological disruption, such as higher ocean levels associated
with global warming, or the loss of pollination services from disappearing
honeybees, make market output look small.[27]

The distinction between market and non-market is linked to distinctions
between private and public, purchase and gift, choice and commitment.

Many important goods and services cannot easily be bought and sold because they are non-excludable in consumption, like the air we breathe or the sunlight we enjoy. If no one can own them, no one can sell them. Some transactions, such as slavery, are prohibited because we agree that the property rights that they entail have perverse consequences. The quality of some goods and services is difficult to judge, and market transactions entail both costs and risks. As a result, most firms develop relationships with their workers and suppliers rather than making decisions every day to buy their services.[28] Individuals choose their sexual partners, and have some control over decisions to become a parent, but families entail obligations and commitments that restrict individual freedom.[29]

The distinction between market and non-market also evokes the distinction between masculine and feminine. Even in advanced capitalist countries like the U.S., Great Britain, and France, men devote significantly more time and effort to market work overall than women do, and within market employment seem more likely to choose jobs on the basis of their pay. Women continue to specialize in forms of work that are not paid on the basis of their market value, because they are not bought and sold in markets. Childrearing and family care are rewarded to some extent by sharing and reciprocity but pay is not—and probably cannot be—provided on the basis of performance.

The Costs of Care

The distinctive characteristics of care work help explain women's economic vulnerability.[30] Care for dependents is costly, and emotional attachments make primary caregivers "prisoners of love" unable or unwilling to threaten withdrawal of their services. Markets can function well where many buyers and many sellers compete to offer the best deal on homogeneous commodities. But care services are often person-specific—substitutability is limited. Their value depends not merely on the work performed but also on a relationship between provider and recipient that develops over time.[31]

Many care services are "non-excludable" in consumption. A mother can end her personal relationship with the father of her children, but it is difficult for her to deny him access to those children unless she is willing to pursue the Medea option—harming her children and therefore herself.

Many of the benefits of care are diffuse, creating public as well as private benefits that are difficult to measure or directly remunerate.[32]

Occupational segregation of women and men remains quite significant, reinforced by gender norms that deem women appropriate for jobs that require service, nurturance, and social interaction.[33] Jobs with a substantial "care" component pay less than other jobs, all else equal, for both men and women.[34] Women may choose traditionally feminine jobs partly because these contribute to their success in finding male partners and raising children.[35]

Family commitments lower women's lifetime earnings. As overt forms of sex discrimination have declined, the "motherhood penalty" has become increasingly salient. In 1991, by one estimate, it accounted for more than 60 percent of the difference in men's and women's earnings in the U.S.[36] The penalty varies considerably across the advanced capitalist economies, shaped in large part by welfare state provisions.[37]

In the U.S. in particular, social policies have been designed to increase women's labor force participation, with little concern for possible reductions in the supply of labor to non-market work including parental care.[38] Public support for parenting is uneven and inconsistent and families maintained by mothers alone suffer high rates of poverty.[39] The difficulties of balancing paid employment with the needs of family members lead to a long total work week, creating stress for all parents, especially single mothers.[40]

Why haven't women responded to the high costs of care by choosing to supply less? In many ways, they have. In the realm of family life, they have done so through declines in average family size, increases in childlessness, and reduced likelihood of living in a married couple household. In the realm of paid employment they have done so by shifts into a variety of new jobs, most notably in professions other than nursing and teaching. Yet women continue to provide more care than men, evidenced by increases in the percentage of children living with mothers alone and a tendency to pursue educational and career paths that are less remunerative than those of men. Care provision represents an important dimension of women's identity as women.

Gender Norms

Cultural constructs such as femininity and masculinity have economic implications. The General Social Survey (GSS), administered on a regular basis in the United States since 1972, asks many questions designed to trace changes in norms regarding women's behavior (with relatively little attention, until recently, to men's behavior). The wording of these questions, as well as responses to them, link femininity and care and reflect the traditional assumption that care represents a moral obligation rather than an economic achievement. For instance, the GSS asks, "Do you strongly agree, agree, disagree, or strongly disagree with the following: It is much better for everyone if the man is the achiever and the woman takes care of the home and family."

Even more consequential is the way this question ignores the counterfactual. What would be better than the existing gender division of responsibilities for care? One possibility is that men and women might more equitably share them. But another is simply that no one takes care of home and family. Women's willingness to withdraw care services may well depend on their perceptions of what might happen if they did. From a game–theoretic perspective, men and women seem engaged in a giant game of Chicken.[41]

Dating and marriage "markets" reinforce gender specialization. Men have much to gain by marrying—and pooling income with—a high-earning woman, but they have something to lose from a reduction in their bargaining power within the home. Women who choose a traditionally male occupation such as plumbing or electrical work may earn more money over their lifetime, but they tend to be ranked as less attractive by men than those who choose a traditionally female occupation such as nursing.[42]

Many women struggle to find ways of improving their economic prospects without undermining their perceived femininity. When they earn more than a potential partner, they often take steps to conceal their economic advantage.[43] Women who earn more than their husbands seem to compensate by performing more housework than might otherwise be predicted.[44] Willingness to opt out of a career for several years in order to assume full-time mothering responsibilities also represents a powerful display of femininity.[45]

Gender identity in general is expensive. Just as femininity imposes costs on women, masculinity imposes costs on men. Men face pressures not to display weakness and, sometimes, to sacrifice their lives in military combat or other dangerous jobs. Intrinsic motivation is central to the work of both mothers and soldiers; neither group is easily paid for performance on a per unit output basis. As a result, the market does not generously reward either type of work. On the other hand, the costs of defying gender norms are also high. Gay, lesbian, bisexual, and transsexual individuals often face significant forms of discrimination that lower their family income.[46]

Gender norms influence individual behavior in ways that often operate below the level of conscious choice. Yet norms depend, for their influence, on a high degree of conformity or compliance. If too many individuals defy them, they lose their force. As the economic costs of compliance increase, nonconformity can reach a tipping point. Consideration of changes in sexual behavior, family behavior, and popular culture, as well as attitudinal surveys suggest that gender norms are, in a sense, undergoing renegotiation.

This renegotiation can be interpreted in the same terms that economist Albert Hirschman prescribed for understanding behavior in firms, organizations and states: choose exit, voice, or loyalty.[47] To "exit" traditional gender norm assignment, men and women can literally change their gender, whether through surgery or demeanor. To remain "loyal" implies a willingness to celebrate the costs of traditional femininity or masculinity, and to insist that they reflect intrinsic benefits. Some evolutionary psychologists suggest that such intrinsic benefits are easily primed, if not biologically determined, by hormonal differences between women and men.[48]

In between these two options, yet not mutually exclusive with either one, lies the voice option: complain, protest, and modify traditional gender norms. Voice is a strategy that can be costly if pursued by isolated individuals; pursued in concert with others, achieving a critical volume, voice can have a dramatic impact. The voice strategy extends to academic discourse: the preceding chapters of this book document a history of feminist efforts to encourage women to consider their collective interests. In particular they show how women have challenged norms urging women toward cooperative altruism and men toward competitive self-interest.

Feminist theory's attention to the tensions between individual and collective interests is embedded in centuries of debate. These tensions illustrate an asymmetry evident in changing gender roles: it is easier for women to claim traditionally masculine rights than to persuade men to assume traditionally feminine obligations. It seems easier to make women more self-interested than to make men more altruistic. Indeed, if the pursuit of self-interest is as hegemonic—and the definition of the self as narrow—as conventional economic theory suggests, modern capitalist society may shift toward a gender-neutral ideal of selfishness. Feminist care theorists are not the only ones who believe that such a shift would be problematic.

Fairness, Reciprocity, and Care

As a core tenet of economic theory, the pursuit of individual self-interest has typically been assumed rather than proved. Since individual utility cannot be directly observed, the presumption that individuals always try to maximize can take a circular form. What is utility? Whatever it is that individuals try to maximize. Still, the theory generates some predictions that can be tested in experimental situations.[49]

A growing body of research suggests that individuals behave less selfishly than has traditionally been supposed. Social norms of fairness and reciprocity appear to have a significant impact on individual decisions.[50] An experiment dubbed the Ultimatum Game provides a particularly vivid example. Subjects are divided into pairs. One member of the pair, Player A, is provided an easily divisible sum of money (such as ten U.S. dimes), and instructed to make a take-it-or-leave-it offer to share part of this sum with Player B. If Player B accepts the offer, both players can retain the agreed upon shares. If Player B rejects the offer, however, all the money must be returned to the experimenter and neither Player A nor Player B enjoys any benefit.

The predictions of standard economic theory are clear: Player A should make the smallest possible offer to Player B (out of ten dimes, only one). Player B should accept this offer, because otherwise he or she will receive absolutely nothing. Most players defy these predictions. In a variety of different settings, with different experimental subjects, with sums of money large and small, Players A and B seem influenced by an egalitarian sharing norm that comes into play when people enjoy a windfall gain. The most common response from Player A is to offer an even split of the money with Player B. If Player A offers a less than even split, a substantial percentage of Player Bs will turn it down, even at considerable cost to themselves. These results hold even if the game is played only once (with no potential for long run gains from cooperation) and even if it is played anonymously.[51]

Few situations in the real world conform to such simple conditions. For the most part, people receive money that they have earned, and, as a result, are much less disposed to share. But the Ultimatum Game calls attention to the impact of social norms of fairness and reciprocity, which are likely to be affected by definitions of productive work. Disapproval of idle slackers helps explain widespread disapproval of public assistance to the non-working poor in the United States. Those who ignore the contributions of family work outside of paid employment are not likely to count mothers raising children on their own among the deserving poor.[52]

While many researchers have documented the positive impact of norms of trust and reciprocity on economic outcomes, few have examined the impact of norms of care and obligation—norms more likely to affect the well-being of dependents. Some experiments do, however, reveal significant differences in men's and women's behavior that seem related to responsibilities for care. Women tend to avoid competitive pay schemes, even when their performance suggests that they would benefit from them.[53] Competition seems to enhance the performance of men more than women. When paid according to a piece rate, men and women perform about equally. In a mixed tournament, however, in which only the winner is paid, the variance in women's performance is much greater and overall, they perform worse than men.[54]

Such gender differences might work to the advantage of women in educational settings, where grades are based on successful completion of tasks similar to a piece rate. But women's predispositions may disadvantage them in competitive work environments or job searches where contenders are ranked against one another. Men tend to be more enthusiastic than women about the positive effects of competitive pressure as a stimulus to effort, but the optimal level of competition may vary among different types of work and different types of workers. These results highlight the importance of institutional design: we should develop work environments and incentive systems that bring out the best in everyone.

Gross National Happiness

Textbook economics tells us that more money is always better than less, because it expands our choice set. Wealth and income are the arbiters of success in our society, which explains why feminists complain that women have less of these than men. But confidence that wealth and income automatically increase happiness is eroding. Surveys have long shown that economic success is unevenly linked to reported measures of subjective well-being—family and friends exert a stronger impact than money income.[55] These results suggest that women's economic disadvantages may have been counterbalanced to some extent by subjective benefits—another insight into the complex effects of gender norms.

Money does have some effect on reported happiness. People living in poverty or lacking a job are less happy than those who have made it to that vague category known as the middle class. Relative income may affect perceptions more strongly than absolute income; age exerts significant influence, suggesting that either physiological changes or modified expectations play an important role.[56] Yet big increases in income beyond a relatively modest threshold have little effect compared to relationships that are largely produced and maintained by the unpaid work of caring for friends and family.

The further comparisons of men's and women's welfare diverge from standard economic measures, the better women fare. Norms of femininity may shield women from competitive stress, encourage collaboration with others, and discourage criminal behavior. Women live longer than men, on average, and tend to report that they are happier.[57] If adoption of masculine norms and values can increase women's earnings, it can also reduce their sense of subjective well-being. Surveys show that women's reported happiness relative to men has been declining over time, even as they have been making economic gains.[58]

From an individual perspective, then, greed does not seem that good. Nor does lust. While people report a strong link between sexual activity and happiness, married individuals report more of both.[59] Higher income does not lead to more sex; here again, relationships seem key. Both male and female college students, in the U.S., report better sexual experiences in relationships than in casual sex.[60] The mere pleasures of the flesh offer a lower rate of return, apparently, that the yield on these when combined with more sustained emotions.

Happiness research offers interesting results. But it sometimes suffers from the same solipsism as research on income. Can we presume that happiness is our most important goal? If it were, we could easily resort to opiates like heroin that send sensations of pleasurable well-being off scale. As the foundation texts of human civilization suggest, our goals could and should be more profound. Our revealed preferences suggest that in fact they are: We devote enormous resources to efforts to better understand and express ourselves through religion, poetry, art, therapy, sports, and music.

The belief that money buys us what we most want encourages behavior that contributes to the accumulation of economic and political power, which in turn, reinforces the power of the belief.[61] Adam Smith suggested as much when he wrote that men's imagination of the pleasures of wealth and greatness, rather than their actual experience of it, "rouses and keeps in continual motion the industry of mankind."[62] Likewise, Thomas Robert Malthus argued that self-love motivated the "noblest exertions of human genius" (see discussion in Chapter 8). Both men valued the wealth of their nation as an end unto itself, the triumph of energetic civilization over hedonistic barbarism. Neither one considered the possibility that the pursuit of short-term self-interest might undermine the long-term sustainability of our natural environment.

From an evolutionary standpoint, maximizing happiness doesn't make much sense. Natural selection does not weed out unhappy individuals, but unsuccessful ones. Likewise with the group selection that drives cultural evolution: economic and military superiority, not collective happiness, separate the winners from the losers. The "dark side of the force", the collective conquest of less powerful groups and the appropriation of their land, their resources, and their labor, helps explain the "rise of the West" and "how the West grew rich."[63] Yet this competitive process also raises the specter of mutually assured destruction through nuclear or biological warfare.

The issue of competition versus cooperation does not boil down to gender differences. Men and women within both dominant and subjugated groups are typically allied. Still, the long history of gender inequality, gradually altered by convergence between men's and women's economic power, offers crucial insights into the evolution of social inequality writ large. Economic organization shapes our perceptions of who we are and what we can do. The causality works the other way as well: we can design social institutions that reward care and cooperation.

Rational and Caring People

Rational economic man is not necessarily selfish, but he doesn't pay much attention to his relationships with others. Feminist economics has never aimed to replace him with his idealized mirror image—irrational loving woman—but to move beyond these polarized stereotypes to develop a broader perspective—economics for humans.[64] Feminist values emerge from opposition to arbitrary inequalities; feminist science delves into the rich experience of women's incomplete empowerment. A feminist economics with roots in both the individualist and socialist traditions can flourish in the new terrain of institutional and behavioral economics.

Adam Smith's interest in the moral sentiments can be restated in modern terms: the precept of "do unto others—male or female—as you would have them do unto you" helps solve coordination problems. Norms of trust and reciprocity have economic consequences, as do norms of care and obligation. Unfortunately these two normative categories are now somewhat at odds: highly gendered and uneven responsibilities for the care of dependents undermine trust and reciprocity between men and women, old and young, rich and poor.

NOTES TO CHAPTER 20

[1] Many of the papers from this conference appeared in Edith Kuiper and Jolande Sap, editors, *Out of the Margin: Feminist Perspectives* (New York: Routledge, 1995).

[2] Marianne A. Ferber and Julie A. Nelson, *Beyond Economic Man: Feminist Theory and Economics* (Chicago: University of Chicago Press, 1993). For a more detailed history of these events, see Marianne A. Ferber and Julie A. Nelson, "Introduction" in *Feminist Economics Today* (Chicago: University of Chicago Press, 2003), 1–31.

[3] Trevor Lloyd, *Suffragettes International: The World-wide Campaign for Women's Rights* (New York: American Heritage Press, 1971).

[4] Simone de Beauvoir, *The Second Sex,* first published 1949 (New York: Knopf, 1971); Betty Friedan, *The Feminine Mystique,* first published 1963 (New York: W.W. Norton, 2001).

[5] George Akerlof, Michael Katz, and Janet Yellen, "An Analysis of Out-of-Wedlock Births in the U.S.," *Quarterly Journal of Economics* 111: 2 (1996), 277–317; Claudia Goldin and Lawrence Katz, "The Power of the Pill: Oral Contraceptives and Women's Career and Marriage Decisions," *Journal of Political Economy* 110:4 (2002), 730–70.

[6] Susan Faludi, *Backlash: The Undeclared War Against American Women,* first published 1991 (Three Rivers Press, 2006); Nancy Folbre and Barnet Wagman, "The Feminization of Inequality: Some New Patterns" *Challenge* (1988), 56–9.

[7] Christie Farnham, *The Impact of Feminist Research in the Academy* (Bloomington: Indiana University Press, 1987); Elizabeth Langland, Walter R. Gove, *A Feminist Perspective in the Academy: The Difference it Makes* (Chicago: University of Chicago Press, 1983).

[8] See survey results described in Randy Albelda, *Economics and Feminism. Disturbances in the Field* (New York: Twayne, 1997).

[9] For the text of this statement see http://www.un.org/womenwatch/daw/beijing/platform/plat1.htm, accessed July 13, 2008.

[10] Paula England, *Comparable Worth: Theories and Evidence* (Edison, NJ: Aldine Transaction, 1992).

[11] Heather Joshi, "The Cash Opportunity Costs of Childbearing: An Approach to Estimation using British Data," *Population Studies* 44 (1990), 41–60; Jane Waldfogel, The Effect of Children on Women's Wages," *American Sociological Review* 62 (1997), 209–17.

[12] Harriet B. Presser, "Decapitating the U.S. Census Bureau's 'Head of Household': Feminist Mobilization in the 1970s," *Feminist Economics* 4:3 (1998), 145–58.

[13] Jocelyn Elise Crowley, "The Gentrification of Child Support Enforcement Services, 1950–1984," *Social Service Review* (2003), 585–604.

[14] M. Grosh and P. Glewwe, "A Guide to Living Standards Measurement Study Surveys and Their Data Sets," LSMS Working Paper no. 120, (Washington: The World Bank, 1995).

[15] Daisy Dwyer and Judith Bruce, eds, *"A Home Divided: Women and Income in the Third World"* (Stanford, CA: Stanford University Press, 1987); Paula England and George Farkas, *Households, Employment, and Gender* (Piscataway, NJ: Aldine, 1984).

[16] Marilyn Waring, *If Women Counted. A New Feminist Economics* (New York: Harper and Row, 1988). Epigraph, p. 319.

[17] For more information on the American Time Use Survey, see http://www.bls.gov/tus/

[18] Katherine Abraham and Christopher Mackie, eds, *Beyond the Market* (Washington, D.C.: National Academy of Science, 2005).

[19] Nancy Folbre, "Inequality and Time Use in the Household," in *Oxford Handbook of Economic Inequality*, Wiemer Salverda, Brian Nolan, and Timothy Smeeding, eds (New York: Oxford University Press, 2008).

[20] Edith Kuiper, *The Most Valuable of All Capital* (Amsterdam: Tinbergen Institute Research Series, 2000), p. 124.

[21] An early analysis of similarities between incentive problems in firm and family is provided in Paula England and George Farkas, *Households, Employment, and Gender*. An early discussion of process benefits can be found in Gregory K. Dow and F. Thomas Juster, "Goods, Time, and Well-being: The Joint Dependence Problem," 397–413 in *Time, Goods, and Well-Being*, F. Thomas Juster and Frank P. Stafford, eds (Survey Research Center, Institute for Social Research, University of Michigan, 1985). For a summary of research on motivation, see Donald E. Campbell, *Incentives. Motivation and the Economics of Information* (New York: Cambridge University Press, 1995).

[22] Nancy Folbre and Julie Nelson "For Love or Money?," *The Journal of Economic Perspectives*, 14:4 (2000), 123–40.

[23] Nancy Folbre and Robert Goodin, "Revealing Altruism," *Review of Social Economy* 62:1 (2004), 1–25.

[24] Paula England, "The Separate Self: Androcentric Bias in Neoclassical Assumptions," in Ferber and Nelson, *Beyond Economic Man*; "Separative and Soluble Selves: Dichotomous Thinking in Economics," in Ferber and Nelson, *Feminist Economics Today*, pp. 33–59; Julie Nelson, "Thinking about Gender and Value," pp. 3–19 in Julie A. Nelson, *Feminism, Objectivity, and Economics* (New York: Routledge, 1996); Nancy Folbre, "Hearts and Spades: Paradigms of Household Economics," *World Development* 14:2 (1986), 245–55.

[25] George A. Akerlof and Rachel E. Kranton, "Economics and Identity," *The Quarterly Journal of Economics* CXV:3 (2000), 715–53; Gary Charness, Luca Rigotti, and Aldo Rustichini, "Individual Behavior and Group Membership," *The American Economic Review* 97:4 (2007), 1340–52.

[26] Robert Costanza, Ralph d'Arge, Rudolf de Groot, Stephen Farber, Monica Grasso, Bruce Hannon, Karin Limburg, Shahid Naeem, Robert V. O'Neill, Jose Paruelo, Robert G. Rankin, Paul Sutton, Marjan van den Belt, "The Value of the World's Ecosystem Services and Natural Capital," *Nature* 387 (1977), 253–9.

[27] William Nordhaus, *A Question of Balance. Weighing the Options on Global Warming Policy* (New Haven: Yale University Press, 2008); P. G. Kevan and T. P. Phillips, "The Economic Impacts of Pollinator Declines: An Approach to Assessing the Consequences. *Conservation Ecology* 5: 1 (2001), available at http://www.consecol.org/vol5/iss1/art8/, accessed July 20, 2008.

[28] Ronald Coase, "The Nature of the Firm," *Economica* 4 (1937), 386–485; Oliver Williamson, *The Economic Institutions of Capitalism: Firms, Markets, Relational Contracting* (New York: Free Press); J. E. Stiglitz, "The Causes and Consequences of the Dependence of Quality on Price." *Journal of Economic Literature* 25 (1987), 1–48.

[29] Robert A. Pollak, "A Transaction Cost Approach to Families and Households," *Journal of Economic Literature* 23 (1985), 581–608; Nancy Folbre, *Valuing Children, Rethinking the Economics of the Family* (Cambridge, MA: Harvard University Press, 2008), Chapter 2.

[30] Nancy Folbre, "Reforming Care," in Janet Gornick, Marcia Meyers, and Erik Olin Wright, eds. *Gender Egalitarianism*, forthcoming, Verso.

[31] Nancy Folbre, "When a Commodity is Not Exactly a Commodity," *Science* 319:5871 (2008), 1769–70.

[32] Paula England and Nancy Folbre, "The Cost of Caring," *Annals of the American Academy of Political and Social Sciences* 561 (1999), 39–51; Nancy Folbre, *Valuing Children*.

[33] Maria Charles and David B. Grusky, *Occupational Ghettos* (Stanford, CA: Stanford University Press, 2004).

[34] Paula England, Michelle Budig, and Nancy Folbre, "Wages of Virtue: The Relative Pay of Care Work," *Social Problems* 49:4 (2002), 455–73.

[35] Lee Badgett and Nancy Folbre "Job Gendering: Occupational Choice and the Labor Market," *Industrial Relations* 42:2 (2003), 270–98.

[36] Jane Waldfogel, "Understanding the 'Family Gap' in Pay for Women with Children," *Journal of Economic Perspectives* 12:1 (1998), 137–56.

[37] Janet Gornick and Marcia Meyers, *Families That Work* (New York: Russell Sage, 2003); Heather Joshi, "The Cash Opportunity Costs of Childbearing: An Approach to Estimation using British Data," *Population Studies* 44 (1990), 41–60; Jane Waldfogel, "The Effect of Children on Women's Wages," *American Sociological Review* 62 (1997), 209–17; Michelle Budig and Paula England., "The Wage Penalty for Motherhood," *American Sociological Review* 66 (2001), 204–25; Shelley Phipps, Peter Burton, and Lynn Lethbridge, "In and Out of the Labour Market: Long-Term Income Consequences of Child-Related Interruptions to Women's Paid Work," *Canadian Journal of Economics* 34 (2001), 411–29.

[38] Nancy Folbre, "Disincentives to Care: A Critique of U.S. Family Policy," Chapter 11, pp. 231–61 in *The Future of the Family*, eds. Daniel Patrick Moynihan, Timothy Smeeding, and Lee Rainwater (New York: Russell Sage Foundation, 2005).

[39] Nancy Folbre, *Valuing Children*.

[40] Jerry A. Jacobs and Kathleen Gerson, *The Time Divide. Work, Family, and Gender Inequality* (Cambridge, MA: Harvard University Press, 2004).

[41] Nancy Folbre and Thomas Weisskopf, "Did Father Know Best? Families, Markets and the Supply of Caring Labor," in *Economics, Values and Organization*, eds. Avner Ben-Ner and Louis Putterman, pp. 171–205 (Cambridge: Cambridge University Press, 1998).

[42] Badgett and Folbre, "Job Gendering."

[43] Alex Williams, "Putting Money on the Table," *New York Times*, September 23, 2007.

[44] Julie Brines, "Economic Dependency, Gender, and the Division of Labor at Home," *American Journal of Sociology* 100:3 (1994), 652–88; Michael Bittman, Paula England, Liana Sayer, Nancy Folbre, and George Matheson, "When Does Gender Trump Money? Bargaining and Time in Household Work," *American Journal of Sociology* 109:1 (2003), 186–214.

[45] Pamela Stone, *Opting Out? Why Women Really Quit Careers and Head Home* (Berkeley: University of California Press, 2007).

[46] Lee Badgett, *Money, Myths, and Change: The Economic Lives of Lesbians and Gay Men* (Chicago: University of Chicago Press, 2001).

[47] Albert O. Hirschman, *Exit, Voice, and Loyalty: Responses to Decline in Firms, Organizations, and States* (Cambridge, MA: Harvard University Press, 1970).

[48] Susan Pinker, *The Sexual Paradox: Men, Women and the Real Gender Gap* (New York: Scribner, 2008); Shelley E. Taylor, *The Tending Instinct* (New York: Holt, 2003).

[49] Daniel Ariely, *Predictably Irrational* (New York: Harper Collins, 2008); Richard H. Thaler and Cass R. Sunstein, *Nudge. Improving Decisions About Health, Wealth, and Happiness* (New Haven: Yale University Press, 2008).

[50] Bruno Frey, *Not Just for the Money. An Economic Theory of Personal Motivation.* (Cheltenham, UK: Edward Elgar, 1997); Herbert Gintis, Samuel Bowles, Robert T. Boyd,

and Ernst Fehr, eds. *Moral Sentiments and Material Interests: The Foundations of Cooperation in Economic Life* (Cambridge, MIT Press, 2006).

[51] Joseph Henrich, Robert Boyd, Samuel Bowles, Colin Camerer, Ernst Fehr, and Herbert Gintis, eds. *Foundations of Human Sociality: Economic Experiments and Ethnographic Evidence from Fifteen Small-Scale Societies* (New York: Oxford University Press, 2004).

[52] Samuel Bowles and Herbert Gintis, "Is Equality Passe?" and Nancy Folbre, "Bad Behavior," *Boston Review*, December/January 1998, available on line at http://bostonreview.net/BR23.6/, accessed January 21, 2009.

[53] Muriel Niederle and Lise Vesterlund, "Do Women Shy Away from Competition? Do Men Compete Too Much?" *Quarterly Journal of Economics* 122:3 (2007), 1067–101.

[54] Uri Gneezy, Muriel Niederle, and Aldo Rustichini, "Performance in Competitive Environments: Gender Differences," *Quarterly Journal of Economics* 118:3 (2003), 1049–74.

[55] Richard Easterlin, "Does Money Buy Happiness," *Public Interest* 3 (1973), 3–10; Robert Lane, "Does Money Buy Happiness," *Public Interest* 113 (1993), 56–65.

[56] For a general discussion of these measures see D. Kahneman, E. Diener, and N. Schwarz, *Well-Being: The Foundations of Hedonic Psychology* (New York: Russell Sage Foundation, 1999); David Blanchflower and Andrew Oswald, "Well-Being Over Time in Britain and the U.S.A." *Journal of Public Economics* 88:7–8 (2004a), 1359–86.

[57] "Global Gender Gaps," Pew Global Attitudes Project, http://pewglobal.org/commentary, accessed August 30, 2007.

[58] Betsey Stevenson and Justin Wolfers, "The Paradox of Declining Female Happiness," Working Paper, Wharton School, University of Pennsylvania, Draft of September 17, 2007, available at http://bpp.wharton.upenss.edu/jworkers/Papers, accessed January 21, 2009.

[59] David G. Blanchflower and Andrew J. Oswald, "Money, Sex, and Happiness: An Empirical Study," *Scandinavian Journal of Economics* 106 (2004b), 393–415.

[60] Elizabeth A. Armstrong, Paula England, and Alison C. K. Fogarty, "Orgasm in College Hookups and Relationships," forthcoming in *Families as They Really Are*, Barbara Risman, ed.

[61] Daniel Gilbert, *Stumbling on Happiness* (New York: Knopf, 2006), p. 219.

[62] Adam Smith, *Theory of Moral Sentiments* (New York: Augustus Kelley, 1966), Book IV, I, 8, p. 263.

[63] Jack Hirshleifer, "The Dark Side of the Force," *Economic Inquiry* XXXII (1994), 1–10; Jared Diamond, *Guns, Germs, and Steel. The Fates of Human Societies* (New York: W. W. Norton, 1997).

[64] Julie Nelson, *Economics for Humans* (Chicago: University of Chicago Press, 2006).

CONCLUSION

Never before, in any society, had the pursuit of wealth been legitimated, much less celebrated for everyone.   Robert Heilbroner

Never before? The pursuit of wealth has not yet been fully legitimated, much less widely celebrated for women. Both women and men living in Great Britain, France, and the United States today have more space to define and pursue their economic and sexual self-interest than they have ever had before. But pursuit of wealth is still considered a distinctly masculine priority. And even as greater material wealth has come into women's reach, doubts about reaching for it at the expense of all else have grown. The great historian of economic ideas, Robert Heilbroner, was right to observe that "the worldly philosophy" of economics was the "child of capitalism."[1] The child is growing up now, in a world very different from that inhabited by her father.

The female pronoun calls attention to gender in a way that the more typical and putatively universal male pronoun does not. Most educated readers know that the word "she" seldom appeared in liberal political theory or classical political economy. But they don't know what a difference that non-appearance made. Recognizing that women might pursue interests inconsistent with their own, the fathers of economics banished them from the realm of social theory. The androcentric blinders they created blinded them for centuries to the relevance of women's unpaid work and the impact of expanded wage employment on family life. These blinders also obscured the ways in which patriarchal rules and norms helped stabilize an emergent capitalist economy.

Most economists have either focused their attention on the market or described non-market institutions like the family and the state as though they operate much as markets do. But the family and the state cannot be described purely as realms of individual choice. Both institutions shape human character, social norms, and individual preferences. Both institutions enforce obligations for the care of dependents. The rise of the welfare state is sometimes described as a vastly inefficient intrusion into the market economy. Yet welfare state spending on education, health, and old age security finance forms of care that were traditionally provided by families, not through markets. And the transfer payments made by governments today remain small compared to the transfers of money and time that take place within families.[2]

The United States ranks among the most affluent capitalist countries in the world. Women now represent about 50 percent of the American paid labor force (although many work in part-time rather than in full-time jobs).[3] Yet about half of all the work performed in the country, measured in terms of hours, is not paid for by anyone. It takes the form of housework, shopping, telephone calls and email, caring for and helping others, and participation in organizational, civic and religious activities.[4] Many individuals go through a stage of their lifecycle in which they live alone. But almost all grow up in families and most grow old—or hope to—with the assistance of families, friends, and neighbors.

If we use the word "capitalism" to describe the economic world we live in, rather than some idealized abstraction of economic texts, we should recognize that capitalism is not equivalent to "the market" but to a complex combination of markets, families, communities, and the state. The economic success of individuals can be defined in terms of their income and wealth. The economic success of families and nations is defined in terms of their ability to sustainably reproduce themselves. Successful social reproduction requires concern for the future not just the present. It requires concern for other people's children, as well as one's own. It requires commitment to the stability of an entire ecosystem, not merely a single nation. The pursuit of individual self-interest can benefit us all only if we define our interests to include not just concern for others, but also moral obligations to them.

The Avenues of Greed and Lust

Most economists proudly claim Adam Smith as the father of their discipline without acknowledging a mother. Despite the criticisms of Smith and his discipline that I have offered here, I believe that he would agree with much of what I say were he alive today. In his world, custom, law, and religion confined markets, and the expansion of markets represented in many ways, a liberating force. In today's world the cultural legitimation of selfish pursuits has gone further than he could have imagined. A man who acknowledged the possible corruption of moral sentiments would surely warn (like Alan Greenspan, post-2008) against overconfidence in self-regulation.

A variety of field experiments show that individuals living in societies lacking opportunities for market exchange behave in particularly selfish and opportunistic ways.[5] Yet experiments also show that men and women are sensitive to small differences in institutional environments. We tend to behave selfishly when we are told that is appropriate, or where we fear that others will take advantage of us if we don't.[6] A recent commentary on financial meltdown updates Karl Polanyi's emphasis on the ways markets are embedded—or disembedded—in society. "Obviously the greater the market pressure to excel in the short term, the greater the need for pressure from outside the market to consider the long term. But that's the problem: There is no longer any serious pressure from outside the market."[7]

It is difficult to determine if we are any more greedy or lustful than we were two centuries ago. We can't measure individual desires and we lack clear standards of comparison for changes over time.[8] Fewer of us now believe in the infinite punishments of Hell, administered by an all-knowing God. If individuals are rational economic actors, they may respond to reductions in the perceived risk and cost of greed and lust by acting more selfishly. On the other hand, if individuals are not (and have never been) very good at balancing the pleasures of the flesh against the tortures of the soul, this may not matter much.

In a lovely variation on a question posed by the Academy of Dijon in 1750, The Templeton Foundation recently invited a range of public intel-lectuals to address the following question: "Does the free market corrode moral character?"[9] John Gray gave the answer that best conforms to the analysis presented in this book: "It depends." It depends on what the term free market means and the context in which that market operates. A market for food may be virtuous as long as helpless individuals are not allowed to starve. A market for labor may be virtuous as long as everyone willing to work can find a job. A market for care may be virtuous as long as it encourages personal commitments and affections. In her paean to the bourgeois virtues, Deirdre McCloskey claims that capitalism can be virtuous, but says little of the particular efforts that might be required to make it so.[10]

The positive effects of capitalist development are most apparent when it undermines feudal and patriarchal property rights or authoritarian regimes. Its negative effects are most apparent when it weakens institutions that enforce moral obligations. Albert Hirschman emphasized the complex and contradictory effects of capitalism long ago, yet hardly mentioned women.[11] The preceding chapters show what a central role gender inequality has played in economic theory and economic practice. Even the most enthusiastic advocates of a market economy felt anxious about the extension of individual rights to women. The significant, if limited, gains that women have made over the last one hundred and fifty years testify to a widening of the avenues for the pursuit of self-interest. One can happily traverse these avenues and still worry where they lead. King Midas rued the power that he gained to turn everything he touched to gold—his food, his drink, and his own daughter.

The gendered history of self-interest illustrates a coordination problem. It is most profitable to be selfish when others are altruistic. Yet even altruists will punish those who don't reciprocate. In the early stages of cultural individualism, men asserted their own rights but reasserted women's obligations for the care of others. After centuries of gradual and uneven effort, women gained the power to assert the same rights as men. They were less successful persuading men to accept greater obligations. Women have continued to assume most of the costs and risks of family care, partly because they fear the consequences of what might happen if they don't. It will always be difficult to agree on the best balance between our own interests and those of others, including future generations. But this is the balance we should seek to find, rather than simply trusting either to God's will or the so-called magic of the market.

NOTES TO CONCLUSION

[1] Robert Heilbroner, *The Worldly Philosophers*, 7th edn (New York: Simon and Schuster, 1999), p. 313. The epigraph to this chapter appears on the same page.

[2] Nancy Folbre, *Valuing Children. Rethinking the Economics of the Family* (Cambridge, MA: Harvard University Press, 2008).

[3] Casey B. Mulligan, "A Milestone for Working Women," *New York Times*, January 14, 2009, available at http://economix.blogs.nytimes.com/tag/gender/, accessed January 25, 2009.

[4] Bureau of Labor Statistics, American Time Use Survey, Table 1. Time Spent in Primary Activities and Percent of Civilian Population Engaging in Each Activity, Averages Per Day, By Sex, 2007 Annual Averages, at http://www.bls.gov/news.release/atus.t01.htm, accessed January 24, 2009.

[5] Joseph Henrich, Robert Boyd, Samuel Bowles, Colin Camerer, Ernst Fehr, and Herbert Gintis, eds, *Foundations of Human Sociality: Economic Experiments and Ethnographic Evidence from Fifteen Small-scale Societies* (New York: Oxford University Press, 2004).

[6] Samuel Bowles, "Policies Designed for Self-Interested Citizens May Undermine 'The Moral Sentiments': Evidence from Economic Experiments," *Science* 320 (20 June 2008) 1605–09.

[7] Michael Lewis and David Einhorn, "The End of the Financial World as We Know It," *New York Times*, January 3, 2009.

[8] Samuel Bowles, "Endogenous Preferences: The Cultural Consequences of Markets and Other Economic Institutions," *Journal of Economic Literature* 36:1 (1998), 75–111.

[9] See the full exchange at www.templeton.org/market/, accessed January 24, 2009.

[10] Deirdre McCloskey, *The Bourgeois Virtues: Ethics for an Age of Commerce* (Chicago: University of Chicago Press, 2006).

[11] Albert O. Hirschman, *Rival Views of Market Society* (New York: Viking, 1986).

BIBLIOGRAPHY

Abraham, Katherine and Christopher Mackie (eds.), 2005. *Beyond the Market, Designing Nonmarket Accounts for the United States*, Washington, D.C.: The National Academies Press.

Abray, Jane, 1975. "Feminism in the French Revolution," *American Historical Review*, 80(1), 43–62.

Akerlof, George, Michael Katz, and Janet Yellen, 1996. "An Analysis of Out-of Wedlock Births in the U.S.," *Quarterly Journal of Economics*, 111 (2), 277–317.

—— Rachel E. Kranton, 2000. "Economics and Identity," *Quarterly Journal of Economics*, 115(3), 715–53.

Albelda, Randy, 1997. *Economics and Feminism. Disturbances in the Field*, New York: Twayne.

Allen, Ruth, 1934. "Review of *Economics of Household Production*," *American Economic Review*, 24, 761–2.

American Rhetoric. "Movie Speech: Wall Street," <http://www.americanrhetoric.com/MovieSpeeches/moviespeechwallstreet.html>, accessed January, 2008.

Anderson, Gosta Esping, 1990. *Three Worlds of Welfare Capitalism*, Princeton: Princeton University Press.

Anderson, Perry, 1974. *Passages from Antiquity to Feudalism*, London: New Left Books.

—— 1979. *Lineages of the Absolutist State*, London: Verso.

Anonymous, 1854. "Occupations of the People," *Westminster Review* 48, reprinted in *Population Problems in the Victorian Age*, Westmead: Gregg International Publishers Limited.

—— 1973. "Proposals for an Improved Census of the Population," *The Edinburgh Review* (March 1829), reprinted in *Population Problems in the Victorian Age*, vol. 1, Westmead: Gregg International Publishers Limited.

Aquinas, Thomas, 1990. *On Faith, Summa Theologiae, Part 2-2, Questions 1–16 of St. Thomas Aquinas*, trans. Mark D. Jordan, Notre Dame, IN: University of Notre Dame Press.

Ariely, Daniel, 2008. *Predictably Irrational*, New York: Harper Collins.

Aristotle, 1935. *Metaphysics, Books X–XIV, Oeconomica and Magna Moralia*, trans. G. Cyril Armstrong, Cambridge, MA: Harvard University Press.

Armstrong, Elizabeth A., Paula England, and Alison C. K. Fogarty, forthcoming. "Orgasm in College Hookups and Relationships," in Barbara Risman (ed.), *Families as They Really Are*, New York: W. W. Norton and Company.

Arrow, Kenneth, 1973. "Models of Job Discrimination," in Orley Ashenfelter and Albert Rees (eds.), *Discrimination in Labor Markets*, Princeton, NJ: Princeton University Press.

Ashcroft, Richard, 1986. *Revolutionary Politics and Locke's Two Treatises of Government*, Princeton: Princeton University Press.

Aslanbeigui, Nahid, 1997. "Rethinking Pigou's Misogyny," *Eastern Economic Journal*, 23(3), 301–16.

Astell, Mary, 1704. "A Prefatory Discourse to Dr. D'Avenant," in Vivien Jones (ed.), *Moderation Truly Stated*, London: Printed by J. L. for Rich. Wilkin at the King's Head in St. Paul's Church Yard, xii.

—— 1990. "The Hardships of the English Laws in Relation to Wives," in Vivien Jones (ed.), *Women in the Eighteenth Century. Constructions of Femininity*, 217.

Atkinson, A. B., 2008. "Economics as a Moral Science," Inaugural Joseph Rowntree Foundation Lecture, University of York, available online at <http://www.jrf.org.uk/publications/economics-moral-science-inaugural-jrf-lecture>.

Ayer, A. J., 1986. *Voltaire*, New York: Random House.

Badgett, Lee, 2001. *Money, Myths, and Change: The Economic Lives of Lesbians and Gay Men*, Chicago, IL: University of Chicago Press.

—— Nancy Folbre, 2003. "Job Gendering: Occupational Choice and the Labor Market, *Industrial Relations*, 42(2), 270–98.

Bailyn, Bernard, 1967. *Ideological Origin of the American Revolution*, Cambridge, MA: Harvard University Press.

—— 1986. *Voyagers to the West*, New York: Random House.

—— 1992. *The Ideological Origins of the American Revolution*, Cambridge, MA: Harvard University Press.

Banks, J. A. and Olive Banks, 1964. *Feminism and Family Planning in Victorian England*, New York: Schocken Books.

Banner, Lois, 1980. *Elizabeth Cady Stanton, A Radical for Woman's Rights*, Boston: Little Brown.

Barber, William J., 1963. *A History of Economic Thought*, New York: Penguin.

Barker-Benfield, G. J., 1976. *The Horrors of the Half-Known Life: Male Attitudes Toward Women and Sexuality in Nineteenth-Century America*, New York: Harper and Row.

Barro, Robert, 1974. "Are Government Bonds Net Wealth?", *Journal of Political Economy*, 82, 1095–117.

Beauvoir, Simone de, 1953. "Must We Burn Sade?" in Marquis de Sade, *The Marquis de Sade. An Essay by Simone de Beauvoir*, New York: Grove Press.

—— 1971. *The Second Sex*, first published 1949, New York: Knopf.

Bebel, August, 1971. *Woman Under Socialism*. Translated from the original German of the 33rd edition by Daniel De Leon, New York: Schocken Books.

Becker, Gary S., 1975. *Human Capital*, second edition, Chicago, IL: University of Chicago Press.

—— 1981. "Altruism in the Family and Selfishness in the Market Place," *Economica*, 48(1), 1–15.

—— 1983. "A Theory of Competition among Pressure Groups for Political Influence," *The Quarterly Journal of Economics* 98, 371–400.

—— 1991. *Treatise on the Family*, enlarged edition, Cambridge, MA: Harvard University Press.

—— 1996 *Accounting for Tastes*, Cambridge, MA: Harvard University Press.

Beecher, Catherine and Harriet Beecher Stowe, 1869. *The American Woman's Home*, New York: J. B. Ford and Company.

Beecher, Jonathan, 1986. *Charles Fourier. The Visionary and His World*, Berkeley, CA: University of California Press.

—— Richard Bienvenu, 1983. *The Utopian Vision of Charles Fourier. Selected Texts on Work, Love, and Passionate Attraction*, Columbia, MO: University of Missouri Press.

Ben Yehuda, N., 1980. "The European Witch Craze of the 14th to the 17th Centuries: A Sociologist's Perspective," *American Journal of Sociology*, 86 (1), 1–31.

Benenson, Harold, 1984. "Victorian Sexual Ideology and Marx's Theory of the Working Class," *International Labor and Working Class History*, 25, 1–23.

Bentham, Jeremy, 1931. *The Theory of Legislation*, (ed.), C. K. Ogden, New York: Harcourt, Brace.

—— 1954. *Jeremy Bentham's Economic Writings*, (ed.), W. Stark, London: Allen and Unwin.

Bergmann, Barbara, 1986. *The Economic Emergence of Women*, New York: Basic Books.

Bergmann, Barbara, 1995. "Becker's Theory of the Family: Preposterous Conclusions," *Feminist Economics*, 1(1), 141–50.

Bestor, Arthur, 1950. *Backwoods Utopias. The Sectarian Origins and the Owenite Phase of Communitarian Socialism in America: 1663–1829*, Philadelphia, PA: University of Pennsylvania Press.

Bittman, Michael, Paula England, Liana Sayer, Nancy Folbre, and George Matheson, 2003. "When Does Gender Trump Money? Bargaining and Time in Household Work", *American Journal of Sociology*, 109(1), 186–214.

Blake, Judith, 1974. "Coercive Pronatalism and American Population Policy," in Robert Parke and Charles E. Westoff (eds.), *Aspects of Population Growth Policy*, Washington, D.C.: Government Printing Office, 85–108.

Blanchflower, David and Andrew Oswald, 2004a. "Well-Being Over Time in Britain and the U.S.A.," *Journal of Public Economics*, 88(7–8), 1359–86.

—— —— 2004b. "Money, Sex, and Happiness: An Empirical Study," *Scandinavian Journal of Economics*, 106, 393–415.

Blanqui, Jerome-Adolphe, 1880. *History of Political Economy in Europe*, New York: G. P. Putnam and Sons.

Blaug, Mark, 1985. *Economic Theory in Retrospect*, Fourth Edition, New York: Cambridge University Press.

Bodichon, Barbara, 1859. *Women and Work*, New York: C. S. Francis.

Bodin, Jean, 1962. *The Six Books of a Commonweal*. A facsimile reprint of the English translation of 1606, Kenneth Douglas McRae (ed.), Cambridge, MA: Harvard University Press.

Bojer, Hilde, and Julie Nelson, 1999. "Equivalence Scales and the Welfare of Children: A Comment on, 'Is There Bias in the Economic Literature on Equivalence Scales,' " *Review of Income and Wealth*, 45, 531–4.

Booth, Arthur John, 1871. *Saint-Simon and Saint-Simonism. A Chapter in the History of Socialism in France*, London: Longmans, Green.

Boralevi, Lea Campos, 1987. "Utilitarianism and Feminism," in Ellen Kennedy and Susan Mendus (eds.), *Women in Western Political Philosophy*, New York: St. Martin's Press, 163.

Borresen, Kari, 1981. *Subordination and Equivalence. The Nature and Role of Woman in Augustine and Thomas Aquinas*, Washington, D.C.: University Press of America.

Boserup, Ester, 1965. *The Conditions of Agricultural Growth*, New York: Aldine.

Boswell, James, 1934. *Boswell's Life of Johnson*, (ed.), George Birkbeck Hill, in six volumes, Oxford: The Clarendon Press.

Boswell, John, 1980. *Christianity, Social Tolerance and Homosexuality. Gay People in Western Europe from the Beginning of the Christian Era to the Fourteenth Century*, Chicago, IL: University of Chicago Press.

Bouton, Cyntha A., 1993. *The Flour War: Gender, Class, and Community in Late Ancient Regime French Society*, State College PA: Pennsylvania State University Press.

Bowles, Samuel, 1998. "Endogenous Preferences: The Cultural Consequences of Markets and Other Economic Institutions," *Journal of Economic Literature*, 36(1), 75–111.

—— 2008. "Policies Designed for Self-Interested Citizens May Undermine 'The Moral Sentiments': Evidence from Economic Experiments," *Science*, 320(20 June), 1605–9.

—— Herbert Gintis, 1998. "Is Equality Passe?" *Boston Review*, December/January, available online at <http://bostonreview.net/BR23.6/>, accessed 21 January, 2009.

Boyer, George R., 1998. "The Historical Background of the Communist Manifesto," *Journal of Economic Perspectives*, 12(4),151–74.

Braudel, Fernand, 1979. *Civilization and Capitalism, 15th–18th Century. Vol. II. The Wheels of Commerce*, trans. Sian Reynolds, New York: Harper and Row.

—— 1992. *The Wheels of Commerce*, Berkeley, CA: University of California Press.

Braunstein, Elissa and Nancy Folbre, 2001. "To Honor or Obey: The Patriarch as Residual Claimant," *Feminist Economics*, 7(1), 25–54.

Breckinridge, Sophonisba B., 1923. "The Home Responsibilities of Women," *Journal of Political Economy*, 31(4), 535.

Brennan, Teresa and Carole Pateman, 1979. " 'Mere Auxiliaries to the Commonwealth': Women and the Origins of Liberalism," *Political Studies*, 27(2), 183–200.

Briggs, Robin, 1977. *Early Modern France, 1560–1715*, New York: Oxford University Press.

Brines, Julie, 1994. "Economic Dependency, Gender, and the Division of Labor at Home, *American Journal of Sociology*, 100(3), 652–88.

Brinton, Crane, 1936. *French Revolutionary Legislation on Illegitimacy, 1789–1804*, Cambridge, MA: Harvard University Press.

Brisbane, Albert, 1840. *Social Destiny of Man, or Association and Reorganization of Industry*, Philadelphia: C. F. Stollmeyer.

Brookes, Barbara, 1980. "The Feminism of Condorcet and Sophie de Grouchy," *Studies on Voltaire and the Eighteenth Century*, 189, 314.

Brown, John, 1765. *On the Female Character and Education*, London: Printed for L. Davis and C. Reymers.

Brown, Kathleen M., 1996. *Good Wives, Nasty Wenches, and Anxious Patriarchs. Gender, Race, and Power in Colonial Virginia*, Chapel Hill, NC: University of North Carolina Press.

Bruce, E., 1995. *Napoleon and Josephine: An Improbable Marriage*, London: Weidenfeld and Nicolson.

Buchanan, James M., 1969. *Cost and Choice*, Chicago, IL: University of Chicago Press.

—— 1975. "The Samaritan's Dilemma," in Edmund S. Phelps (ed.), *Altruism, Morality, and Economic Theory*, New York: Russell Sage, 71–85.

Budig, Michelle and Paula England, 2001. "The Wage Penalty for Motherhood," *American Sociological Review*, 66, 204–25.

Buhle, Mary Jo, 1981. *Women and American Socialism, 1870–1920*, Urbana, IL: University of Illinois Press.

Bunyan, John, 1981. *The Pilgrim's Progress*, first published 1678, New York: Signet.

Bureau of Labor Statistics, 2008. *American Time Use Survey*, available online at <http://www.bls.gov/tus/>.

—— "American Time Use Survey," available online at <http://www.bls.gov/tus/>.

Burke, Edmund, 1955. *Reflections on the Revolution in France*, New York: Liberal Arts Press.

Burrows, Edwin G. and Michael Wallace, 1972. "The Ideology and Psychology of and Psychology of National Liberation," *Perspectives in American History* VI, 167–306.

Butler, Joseph, 1874. "Sermon 3.9," in S. Halifax (ed.), *The Works of Bishop Butler*, vol. 1, Oxford: Clarendon Press.

Butler, Melissa, 1978. "Early Liberal Roots of Feminism: John Locke and the Attack on Patriarchy," *American Political Science Review*, 72, 135–50.

Calder, Jenni, 1977. *The Victorian Home*, London: B. T. Batsford.

Campbell, Donald E., 1995. *Incentives. Motivation and the Economics of Information*, New York: Cambridge University Press.

Campbell, T. D., 1971. *Adam Smith's Science of Morals*, London: George Allen and Unwin Ltd.

Carey, Henry C., 1840. *Principles of Political Economy*, Philadelphia: Lea and Blanchard.

—— 1853. *The Slave Trade. Domestic and Foreign, Why it Exists and How it May be Extinguished*, Philadelphia: Henry Cary Baird Industrial Publisher. Available online at <http://yamaguchy.netfirms.com/7897401/carey/carey_index.html>.

—— 1967. *Harmony of Interests: Agricultural, Manufacturing and Commercial*, reprint of the 1851 edition, New York: A. M. Kelley.

Carlyle, Thomas, 1976. *Past and Present*, London: Vision.

Carsten, F. L. (ed.), 1961. *The New Cambridge Modern History. Vol. V. The Ascendancy of France, 1648–88*, Cambridge: Cambridge University Press.

Carter, Angela, 1978. *The Sadeian Woman and the Ideology of Pornography*, New York: Pantheon Books.

Carter, Susan B., Roger L. Ransom, and Richard Sutch, 2002. "Family Matters: The Life-Cycle Transition and the Unparalleled Antebellum American Fertility Decline," in Timothy W. Guinnane, William A. Sundstrom, and Warren Whatley (eds.), *History Matters: Essays on Economic Growth, Technology, and Demographic Change*, Stanford, CA: Stanford University Press.

Cassidy, John, 2002. "The Greed Cycle," *The New Yorker*, September 23.

Cavendish, Margaret, 1982. Cited in Jerome Nadelhaft, "The Englishwoman's Sexual Civil War, 1650–1740," *Journal of the History of Ideas*, 43(4), 564.

Chambers-Schiller, L. V., 1984. *Liberty, A Better Husband. Single Women in America: The Generations of 1780–1840*, New Haven: Yale University Press.

Chang, Ha-Joon, 2002. *Kicking Away the Ladder: Development Strategy in Historical Perspective*, London: Anthem Press.

Charles, Maria and David B. Grusky, 2004. *Occupational Ghettos*, Stanford, CA: Stanford University Press.

Charness, Gary, Luca Rigotti, and Aldo Rustichini, 2007. "Individual Behavior and Group Membership," *The American Economic Review*, 97(4), 1340–52.

Chase-Lansdale, P. L. L. S. Wakschlag, and J. Brooks-Gunn, 1995. "A Psychological Perspective on the Development of Caring in Children and Youth: The Role of the Family," *Journal of Adolescence, 18*, 515–56.

Chesler, Ellen, 1992. *Woman of Valor. Margaret Sanger and the Birth Control Movement in America*, New York: Simon and Schuster.

Chilean Truth Commission, available online at <http://www.usip.org/library/tc/doc/reports/chile/chile_1993_toc.html>.

Christ, Carol, 1977. "Victorian Masculinity and the Angel in the House," in Martha Vicinus (ed.), *A Widening Sphere. Changing Roles of Victorian Women*, Bloomington: Indiana University Press, 146–62.

Clark, Lorenne and Lynda Lange, 1979. *The Sexism of Social and Political Theory: Women and Reproduction from Plato to Nietzsche*, Toronto: University of Toronto Press.

Clark, Alice, 1967. *Working Life of Women in the Seventeenth Century*, New York: Augustus Kelley.

—— 1992. *Working Life of Women in the Seventeenth Century*, New York: Routledge.

Clark, Christopher, 1990. *The Roots of Rural Capitalism: Western Massachusetts, 1780–1860*, Ithaca, NY: Cornell University Press.

Clark, Christopher, 1995. *The Communitarian Moment: The Radical Challenge of the Northampton Association*, Ithaca, NY: Cornell University Press.

Clark, John P., 1977. *The Philosophical Anarchism of William Godwin*, Princeton: Princeton University Press.

Closson, Carlos C., 1900. "The Real Opportunity of the So-Called Anglo-Saxon Race," *Journal of Political Economy*, 9, 96.

Coase, Ronald, 1937. "The Nature of the Firm," *Economica*, 4, 386–485.

Coats, A. W., 1976. "The Relief of Poverty, Attitudes to Labor, and Economic Change in England, 1660–1782," *International Review of Social History*, 21, 104.

—— 1992. *On the History of American Thought. British and American Economic Essays*, vol. 1, New York: Routledge.

Cobban, Alfred, 1965. *A History of Modern France*, New York: Braziller.

Cole, Margaret, 1961. *The Story of Fabian Socialism*, Stanford: Stanford University Press.

Collet, Clara, 1896. "Female Labour," *Palgrave Dictionary of Political Economy*, vol. 2, London: Macmillan, 49–50.

Condorcet, Antoine-Nicolas de, 1955. *Sketch for a Historical Picture of the Progress of the Human Mind*, trans. June Barraclough, New York: The Noonday Press.

Cook, Richard I., 1974. *Bernard Mandeville*, New York: Twayne Publishers, Inc.

—— 1975. "The Great Leviathan of Lechery: Mandeville's Modest Defence of Publick Stews," in Irwin Primer (ed.), *Mandeville Studies. New Explorations in the Art and Thought of Dr. Bernard Mandeville*, The Hague, Martinus Nijhoff, 23–33.

Corbin, Alain, 1990. *Women for Hire. Prostitution and Sexuality in France after 1850*, trans. Alan Sheridan, Cambridge, MA: Harvard University Press.

Cory, Abby L., 2004. "Wheeler and Thompson's Appeal: The Rhetorical Re-visioning of Gender," *New Hibernia Review*, 8(2), 106–20.

Costanza, Robert, Ralph d'Arge, Rudolf de Groot, Stephen Farber, Monica Grasso, Bruce Hannon, Karin Limburg, Shahid Naeem, Robert V. O'Neill, Jose Paruelo, Robert G. Rankin, Paul Sutton, Marjan van den Belt, 1977. "The Value of the Worlds' Ecosystem Services and Natural Capital," *Nature* 387, 253–9.

Cot, Annie L., 2003. " 'Let There be no Distinction Between the Sexes': Jeremy Bentham on the Status of Women," in Robert Dimand and Chris Nyland (eds.), *The Status of Women in Classical Economic Thought*, Cheltenham UK: Edward Elgar, 165–93.

Cott, Nancy F., 1987. *The Grounding of Modern Feminism*, New Haven, CT: Yale University Press.

—— 1979. "Passionlessness: An Interpretation of Victorian Sexual Ideology, 1790–1850," in Nancy F. Cott and Elizabeth H. Pleck (eds.), *A Heritage of Her Own:*

Toward a New Social History of American Women, New York: Simon and Schuster, 162–81.

—— 1997. *The Grounding of Modern Feminism*, New Haven: Yale University Press.

Cowherd, Raymond, 1956. *The Humanitarians and the Ten Hour Movement in England*, (Publication of the Kress Library of Business and Economics, no. 10), Boston: Baker Library, Harvard Graduate School of Business Administration.

—— 1977. *Political Economists and the English Poor Laws. A Historical Study of the Influence of Classical Economics on the Formation of Social Welfare Policy*, Athens: Ohio University Press.

Cowling, Maurice, 1963. *Mill and Liberalism*, New York: Cambridge University Press.

Crocker, Lester, 1963. *Nature and Culture. Ethical Thought in the French Enlightenment*, Baltimore: The Johns Hopkins University Press.

Crompton, Louis, 1985. *Byron and Greek Love. Homophobia in 19th-Century England*, Berkeley: University of California Press.

Crowley, Jocelyn Elise, 2003. "The Gentrification of Child Support Enforcement Services, 1950–1984, *Social Service Review*, 77(4), 585–604.

Daly, Mary, 1992. *Pure Lust. Elemental Feminist Philosophy*, New York: Harper-Collins.

Darwin, Charles, 1952. *The Descent of Man*, New York: Encyclopedia Britannica, Inc.

Darwin, Frances., 1888. *The Life and Letters of Charles Darwin*, New York: D. Appleton and company.

David, Paul A. and Warren C. Sanderson, 1986. "Rudimentary Contraceptive Methods and the American Transition to Marital Fertility Control," in Stanley L. Engerman and Robert E. Gallman (eds.), *Long-Term Factors in American Economic Growth*, Chicago: University of Chicago Press, 307–90.

Davies, Celia, 1980. "Making Sense of the Census in Britain and the U.S.A.: The Changing Occupational Classification and the Position of Nurses," *Sociological Review*, 28(3), 581–609.

Davis, David Brion, 1975. *The Problem of Slavery in the Age of Revolution, 1770–1823*, Ithaca, NY: Cornell University Press.

Davis, Ralph, 1973. *The Rise of the Atlantic Economies*, Ithaca, New York: Cornell University Press.

De Long, Bradford, 1996. *Slouching Toward Utopia*, available online at <http://www.j-bradford-delong.net/TCEH/slouchingtowardutopia.html>, accessed July 15, 2008.

De Marchi, Neil, 1974. "The Success of Mill's Principles," *History of Political Economy*, 6(2), 119–57.

Deacon, Desley, 1985. "Political Arithmetic: The Nineteenth Century Australian Census and the Construction of the Dependent Woman," *Signs: Journal of Women in Culture and Society*, 11(1), 35.

Delano, Sterling F., 2004. *Brook Farm: The Dark Side of Utopia*, Cambridge: Belknap Press.

Desroche, H., 1971. "Images and Echoes of Owenism in Nineteenth-Century France," in Sidney Pollard and John Salt (eds.), *Robert Owen. Prophet of the Poor*, Lewisburg, PA: Bucknell University Press, 239–84.

Diamond, Jared, 2005. *Guns, Germs and Steel. The Fates of Human Societies*, New York: W. W. Norton and Company.

Dickens, Charles, 1961. *Hard Times*, New York: New American Library.

Diderot, Denis, 1951. "Sur les Femmes," in Diderot, *Oeuvres*, édition établie et annoté par André Billy, Paris: Gallimard, 957.

Diderot, D'Alembert, and a Society of Men of Letters, 1965. *Encyclopedia. Selections*, trans. Nelly S. Hoyt and Thomas Cassirer, New York: The Bobbs-Merrill Company, Inc., 230.

Dimand, Mary Ann, 1995. "The Economics of Charlotte Perkins Gilman," in Mary-Ann Dimand, Robert Dimand, and Evelyn Forget (eds.), *Women of Value: Feminist Essays on the History of Women in Economics*, Aldershot: Edward Elgar.

—— Robert W. Dimand, and Evelyn L. Forget, 1995. *Women of Value: Feminist Essays on the History of Women in Economics*, Aldershot: Edward Elgar.

Dimand, Robert W., 2000. "Nineteenth-Century American Feminist Economics: From Caroline Dall to Charlotte Perkins Gilman," *American Economic Review*, 90(2), 480–4.

—— 2003a. "Women in Nassau Senior's Economic Thought," in Robert Dimand and Chris Nyland (eds.), *The Status of Women in Classical Economic Thought*, Northampton, MA: Edward Elgar, 224–40.

—— 2003b. "An Eighteenth-Century English Feminist Response to Political Economy: Priscilla Wakefield's Reflections," in Robert Dimand and Chris Nyland (eds.), *The Status of Women in Classical Political Economy*, Cheltenham UK: Edward Elgar, 194–205.

—— Mary Ann Dimand, and Evelyn L. Forget (eds.), 2000. *The Biographical Dictionary of Women Economists*, Cheltenham: Edward Elgar.

—— Evelyn Forget, and Chris Nyland, 2004. "Gender in Classical Economics," *Journal of Economic Perspective*, 18(1), 229–40.

DiStefano, Christine, 1991. *Configurations of Masculinity. A Feminist Perspective on Modern Political Theory*, Ithaca NY: Cornell University Press.

Dobb, Maurice, 1963. *Studies in the Development of Capitalism*, New York: International Publishers.

Donovan, Josephine, 1991. *Uncle Tom's Cabin. Evil, Affliction, and Redemptive Love*, Boston: Twayne Publishers.

Dorfman, Joseph, 1969. *The Economic Mind in American Civilization*, New York: Augustus Kelley.

Douglas, Dorothy, 1920. "The Cost of Living for Working Women: A Criticism of Current Theories," *Quarterly Journal of Economics*, 34(2), 209–59.

Douglas, Paul H., 1925. *Wages and the Family*, Chicago, IU: University of Chicago Press.

Dow, Gregory K. and F. Thomas Juster, 1985. "Goods, Time, and Well-being: The Joint Dependence Problem," in F. Thomas Juster and Frank P. Stafford (eds.), *Time, Goods, and Well-Being*, Ann Arbor, MI: Survey Research Center, Institute for Social Research, University of Michigan, 397–413.

Doyle, William, 1988. *Origins of the French Revolution*. Second Edition, New York: Oxford University Press.

Dreyfuss, Barbara T., 2005. "The Siren of Santiago," *Mother Jones*, (March/April), 18–21.

Dublin, Louis I. and Alfred J. Lotka, 1930. *The Money Value of a Man*, New York: Ronald.

Dubois, Ellen Carol, 1978. *Feminism and Suffrage: The Emergence of an Independent Women's Movement in America, 1849–1869*, Ithaca, NY: Cornell University Press.

—— Richard Candida Smith, 2007. *Elizabeth Cady Stanton, Feminist as Thinker. A Reader in Documents and Essays*, New York: New York University Press.

Duby, Georges, 1991. *France in the Middle Ages 987–1460. From Hugh Capet to Joan of Arc*, trans. Juliet Vale, Cambridge, MA: Blackwell.

Duggan, Lisa and Nan D. Hunter, 1995. *Sex Wars: Sexual Dissent and Political Culture*, New York: Routledge.

Dupâquier, Jacques et Michel, 1985. *Histoire de la Démographie. La statistique de la population des origines à 1914*, Paris: Librairie Académique Perrin.

Dupâquier, Jacques, René le Mée, Joseph Goy, Maurice Garden, Hervé le Bras, Bernard Lepetit, Jean-Pierre Poussou, Daniel Courgeau, Jean-Pierre Bardet, Alain Bideau, Jean-Noël Biraben, Jacques Léonard, Bernard Lécuyer, Patrice Bourdelais, Agnès Fine, Martine Segalen, Yves Charbit, André Begin, 1988. *Histoire de la Population Française de 1789 á 1914*, Paris: Presses Universitaire de France.

Dwyer, Daisy and Judith Bruce (eds.), 1987. *A Home Divided: Women and Income in the Third World*, Stanford, CA: Stanford University Press.

Easterlin, Richard, 1973. "Does Money Buy *Happiness*," *Public Interest*, 3, 3–10.

Edgeworth, F. Y., 1922. "Equal Pay to Men and Women for Equal Work," *The Economic Journal*, 32(128), 431–57.

—— 1923. "Women's Wages in Relation to Economic Welfare," *Economic Journal*, 33(132), 487–95.

—— 1967. *Mathematical Psychics. An Essay on the Application of Mathematics to the Moral Sciences*, New York: Augustus M. Kelley.

Eisner, Robert, 1989. *The Total Incomes System of Accounts*, Chicago, IL: The University of Chicago Press.

Ellis, Joseph J., 2002. *Founding Brothers. The Revolutionary Generation*, New York: Vintage.

Ellis, Mrs. Sarah, 1844. *The Mothers of England; Their Influence and Responsibility*, New York: D. Appleton and Company.

Ely, Richard T. and George Ray Wicker, 1904. Elementary Principles of Economics: Together With A Short Sketch of Economic History, New York, Macmillan Company.

Emerson, Ralph Waldo, 1842. "Fourierism and the Socialists," *The Dial*, III, 86–96.

Engels, Frederick, 1958. *The Condition of the Working Class in England*. Translated and edited by W. O. Henderson and W. H. Chaloner, Stanford, CA: Stanford University Press.

Engerman, Stanley, 1994. "Reflections on 'The Standard of Living Debate': New Arguments and New Evidence," in John A. James and Mark Thomas (eds.), *Capitalism in Context: Essays on Economic Development and Cultural Change in Honor of R. M. Hartwell*, Chicago, IL: University of Chicago Press, 50–79.

England, Paula, 1982. "The Failure of Human Capital Theory to Explain Occupational Sex Segregation," *Journal of Human Resources*, 17(3), 358–70.

—— 1992. *Comparable Worth: Theories and Evidence*, Edison, NJ: Aldine Transaction.

—— 1993. "The Separative Self: Androcentric Bias in Neoclassical Assumptions," in Marianne Ferber and Julie Nelson, *Beyond Economic Man*, Chicago, IL: University of Chicago Press, 37–53.

—— 2003. "Separative and Soluble Selves: Dichotomous Thinking in Economics," in Marianne Ferber and Julie Nelson (eds.), *Feminist Economics Today*, 33–59.

—— George Farkas, 1984. *Households, Employment, and Gender*, Piscataway, NJ: Aldine.

———— 1986. *Households, Employment, and Gender. A Social, Economic, and Demographic View*, New York: Aldine Publishers.

—— Nancy Folbre, 1999. "The Cost of Caring," *Annals of the American Academy of Political and Social Sciences*, 561, 39–51.

—— Emily Fitzgibbons Shafer, and Alison C. K. Fogarty, 2007. "Hooking Up and Forming Romantic Relationships on Today's College Campuses," in Michael Kimmel (ed.), *The Gendered Society Reader*, New York: Oxford University Press.

—— Michelle Budig, and Nancy Folbre, 2002. "Wages of Virtue: The Relative Pay of Care Work," *Social Problems*, 49(4), 455–73.

Erickson, Amy Louise, 1999. Entry on Alice Clark in *Encyclopedia of Historians and Historical Writing*, Chicago: Fitzroy Dearborn Publishers.

Everett, Alexander H., 1970. *New Ideas on Population, With Remarks on the Theories of Malthus and Godwin*, first published 1826, New York: Augustus M. Kelley.

Fauré, Christine, 1985. *Democracy Without Women. Feminism and the Rise of Liberal Individualism in France*, trans. Claudia Gorbman and John Berks, Bloomington, IND: Indiana University Press.

Faludi, Susan, 2006. *Backlash: The Undeclared War Against American Women*, first published 1991, New York: Three Rivers Press.

Farnham, Christie, 1987. *The Impact of Feminist Research in the Academy*, Bloomington, IND: Indiana University Press.

Farr, William, 2001. "On the Economic Value of Population" reprinted in *Population and Development Review*, 27, 567.

Farrell, Warren, 2005. *Why Men Earn More*, New York: AMACOM.

Fay, C. R., 1932. *The Corn Laws and Social England*, Cambridge: Cambridge University Press.

Federici, Silvia, 2004. *Caliban and the Witch: Women, The Body, and Primitive Accumulation*, Brooklyn: Autonomedia.

Feinberg, Kenneth, 2006. *What Is Life Worth? The Inside Story of the 9/11 Fund and Its Effort to Compensate the Victims of September 11th*, New York: Public Affairs.

Ferber, Marianne A. and Julie A. Nelson, 1993. *Beyond Economic Man: Feminist Theory and Economics*, Chicago, IL: University of Chicago Press.

—— —— 2003. *Feminist Economics Today*, Chicago, IL: University of Chicago Press.

Ferreira, M. Luisa, Reuben C. Buse, and Jan-Paul Chavas, 1998. "Is There a Bias in Computing Household Equivalence Scales," *Review of Income and Wealth*, 44, 183–98.

Filmer, Sir Robert, 1949. "Observations Upon Aristotle's Politics," in Peter Laslett (ed.), *Patriarcha and Other Political Works*, Oxford: Basil Blackwell.

Fischer, Kirsten, 2002. *Suspect Relations. Sex, Race, and Resistance in Colonial North Carolina*, Ithaca, NY: Cornell University Press.

Fisher, Irving, 1906. *The Nature of Capital and Income*, New York: Macmillan.

Flandrin, Jean-Louis, 1991. *Sex in the Western World. The Development of Attitudes and Behavior*, Philadelphia, PA: Harwood Academic Publishers.

Fleischacker, Samuel, 2002. "Adam Smith," in Steven Nadler (ed.), *A Companion to Early Modern Philosophy*, Malden, MA : *Blackwell* Publishing Ltd., 4.

Flexner, Eleanor, 1971. *Century of Struggle. The Woman's Rights Movement in the United States*, New York: Atheneum.

—— 1972. *Mary Wollstonecraft. A Biography*, New York: Coward, McCann and Geoghegan.

Flubacher, Joseph F., 1950. *The Concept of Ethics in the History of Economics*, New York: Vantage Press.

Fogel, Robert William and Stanley L. Engerman, 1974. *Time on the Cross: The Economics of American Negro Slavery*, New York: Little, Brown.

—— 1989. *Without Consent or Contract. The Rise and Fall of American Slavery*, New York: W. W. Norton and Company.

Folbre, Nancy, 1984. "Market Opportunities, Genetic Endowments, and Intrafamily Resource Distribution: A Comment," *American Economic Review*, 74(3), 518–22.

—— 1985. "The Wealth of Patriarchs: Deerfield, Massachusetts, 1760–1840," *Journal of Interdisciplinary History*, 16(2), 199–220.

—— 1986. "Hearts and Spades: Paradigms of Household Economics," *World Development*, 14(2), 245–55.

—— 1994. *Who Pays for the Kids? Gender and the Structures of Constraint*, New York: Routledge.

—— 1998a. "Bad Behavior," *Boston Review*, December/January, available online at <http://bostonreview.net/BR23.6/folbre.html>, accessed 21 January, 2009.

—— 1998b. "The 'Sphere of Women in Early-Twentieth-Century Economics," in Helene Silverberg (ed.), *Gender and American Social Science*, Princeton, NJ: Princeton University Press, 35–60.

—— 2001. *The Invisible Heart. Economics and Family Values*, New York: The New Press.

—— 2004. "Sleeping Beauty Awakes: Self-Interest, Feminism, and Fertility in the Early Twentieth Century," *Social Research*, 71(2), 343–56.

—— 2005. "Disincentives to Care: A Critique of U.S. Family Policy, Chapter 11, in Daniel Patrick Moynihan, Timothy Smeeding, and Lee Rainwater (eds.), *The Future of the Family*, New York: Russell Sage Foundation, 231–61.

—— 2006. "Chicks, Hawks, and Patriarchal Institutions," in Morris Altman (ed.), *Handbook of Behavioral Economics*, Armonk, NY.: M. E. Sharpe, 499–516.

—— 2008. "Inequality and Time Use in the Household," in Wiemer Salverda, Brian Nolan, and Timothy Smeeding (eds.), *Oxford Handbook of Economic Inequality*, New York: Oxford University Press.

—— 2008a. "When a Commodity is Not Exactly a Commodity," *Science*, 319 (5871), 1769–70.

—— 2008b. *Valuing Children, Rethinking the Economics of the Family*, Cambridge, MA: Harvard University Press.

—— forthcoming. "The Qualities and Inequalities of Care," in Janet Gornick, Marcia Meyers, and Erik Olin Wright (eds.), *Gender Egalitarianism*, London: Verso.

—— Barnet Wagman, 1988. "The Feminization of Inequality: Some New Patterns" *Challenge*, 31(6), 56–9.

—— —— 1993. "Counting Housework: New Estimates of Real Product in the U.S., 1800–1860," *The Journal of Economic History*, 53(2), 275–88.

—— Julie Nelson, 2000. "For Love or Money?", *The Journal of Economic Perspectives*, 14(4), 123–40.

—— Robert Goodin, 2004. "Revealing Altruism," *Review of Social Economy*, 62(1), 1–25.

—— Thomas Weisskopf, 1998. "Did Father Know Best? Families, Markets and the Supply of Caring Labor," in Avner Ben-Ner and Louis Putterman (eds.), *Economics, Values and Organization*, Cambridge: Cambridge University Press, 171–205.

Foner, Eric, 1976. *Tom Paine and Revolutionary America*. New York: Oxford University Press.

Foner, Philip, 1945. *The Complete Writings of Thomas Paine*, New York: Citadel Press. (Available online at <http://www.thomaspaine.org>.)

—— 1979. *Women and the American Labor Movement. From Colonial Times to the Eve of World War I*, New York: Free Press.

Forget, Evelyn, 2001. "Saint-Simonian Feminism," *Feminist Economics*, 7(1), 79–96.

—— 2003a. "The Market for Virtue: Jean-Baptiste Say on Women in the Economy and Society," in Robert Dimand and Chris Nyland (eds.), *The Status of Women in Classical Economic Thought*, Cheltenham UK: Edward Elgar, 206–23.

—— 2003b. "Cultivating Sympathy: Sophie Condorcet's Letters on Sympathy," in Robert Dimand and Chris Nyland (eds.), *The Status of Women in Classical Economic Thought*, Cheltenham: Edward Elgar, 142–64.

Forrest, Alan, 1981. *The French Revolution and the Poor*, New York: St. Martin's Press.

Foucault, Michel, 1979. *Discipline and Punish. The Birth of the Prison*, New York: Vintage Books.

—— 1990. *History of Sexuality: An Introduction*, vol. 1, New York: Vintage Books.

Fourier, Charles, 1996. *The Theory of the Four Movements*, (ed.), Gareth Stedman Jones and Ian Patterson, first published 1808, Cambridge: Cambridge University Press.

Fox-Genovese, Elizabeth, 1976. *The Origins of Physiocracy. Economic Revolution and Social Order in Eighteenth-Century France*, Ithaca NY: Cornell University Press.

Fraad, Harriet, Steven Resnick and Richard Wolff, 1999. *Bringing It all Back Home*, London: Pluto.

Fraser, Antonia, 1985. *The Weaker Vessel*, New York: Vintage.

Frey, Bruno, 1997. *Not Just for the Money. An Economic Theory of Personal Motivation*, Cheltenham, UK: Edward Elgar.

Friedan, Betty, 2001. *The Feminine Mystique*, first published 1963, New York: W. W. Norton and Company.

Friedman, Benjamin M, 2005. *The Moral Consequences of Economic Growth*, New York: Knopf.

Friedman, Milton, 1953. *Essays in Positive Economics*, Chicago, IL: University of Chicago Press.

—— 1962. *Capitalism and Freedom*, Chicago, IL: University of Chicago Press.

—— 1970. "The Social Responsibility of Business is to Increase its Profits," *New York Times Magazine*, September 30.

—— 1976. Nobel Prize autobiography, available online at <http://nobelprize.org/nobel_prizes/economics/laureates/1976/friedman-autobio.html>, accessed 28 May, 2008).

—— Anna Jacobson Schwartz, 1995. *A Monetary History of the United States, 1867–1960*, first published 1953, Ann Arbor, MI: University of Michigan Press.

Fuchs, Victor, 1988. *Women's Quest for Economic Equality*, Cambridge, MA: Harvard University Press.

Gabriel, Mary, 1998. *Notorious Victoria. The Life of Victoria Woodhull, Uncensored*, Chapel Hill, NC: Algonquin Books.

Gay, Peter, 1969. *The Enlightenment: An Interpretation. The Science of Freedom*, New York: W. W. Norton and Company.

Genovese, Eugene D., 1965. *The Political Economy of Slavery: Studies in the Economy and Society of the Slave South*, New York: Vintage.

Geremek, Bronislaw, 1994. *Poverty. A History*, Cambridge, Mass: Blackwell.

Gilbert, Daniel, 2006. *Stumbling on Happiness*, New York: Knopf.

Gilman, Charlotte Perkins, 1966. *Women and Economics*, first published 1898, Carl N. Degler (ed.), New York: Harper and Row.

—— 1972. *The Home: Its Work and Influence*, Chicago, IL: University of Illinois Press.

Gintis, Herbert Samuel Bowles, Robert T. Boyd, and Ernst Fehr (eds.), 2006. *Moral Sentiments and Material Interests: The Foundations of Cooperation in Economic Life*, Cambridge, MA, MIT Press.

Glickman, Lawrence B., 1997. *A Living Wage. American Workers and the Making of Consumer Society*, Ithaca, NY: Cornell University Press.

Gneezy, Uri Muriel Niederle, and Aldo Rustichini, 2003. "Performance in Competitive Environments: Gender Differences," *Quarterly Journal of Economics*, 118 (3), 1049–74.

Godineau, Dominique, 1998. *The Women of Paris and Their French Revolution*, Katherine Streip (trans.), Berkeley, CA: University of California Press.

Godwin, William, 1926. *An Enquiry Concerning Political Justice and Its Influence on General Virtue and Happiness*, (ed.), Raymond A. Preston, New York: Alfred A. Knopf.

Goldin, Claudia and Lawrence Katz, 2002. "The Power of the Pill: Oral Contraceptives and Women's Career and Marriage Decisions," *Journal of Political Economy*, 110(4), 730–70.

Goldsmith, Barbara, 1998. *Other Powers. The Age of Suffrage, Spiritualism, and the Scandalous Victoria Woodhull*, New York: Alfred A. Knopf.

Goleman, Daniel, 1997. *Emotional Intelligence*, New York: Bantam.

Gordon, Barry, 1989. *The Economic Problem in Biblical and Patristic Thought*, New York: E. J. Brill.

Gordon-Reed, Annette, 1998. *Thomas Jefferson and Sally Hemings: An American Controversy*, Charlottesville, VA: University Press of Virginia.

Gornick, Janet and Marcia Meyers, 2003. *Families That Work*, New York: Russell Sage.

—— —— 2005. *Families that Work*, New York: Russell Sage.

Gossett, Thomas F., 1963. *Race. The History of an Idea in America*, Dallas, TX: Southern Methodist University Press.

Grapard, Ulla, 1995. "Robinson Crusoe: The Quintessential Economic Man?" *Feminist Economics*, 1(1), 33–52.

—— 2001. "The Trouble with Women and Economics: A Postmodern Perspective on Charlotte Perkins Gilman," in Stephen Cullenberg, Jack Amariglio, and David Ruccio (eds.), *Postmodernism, Economics, and Knowledge*, New York: Routledge.

Grapard, Ulla, 1992. "Who Can See the Invisible Hand? Or, From the Benevolence of the Butcher's Wife," Paper presented at the First Conference on Feminist Economics, Sponsored by IAFFE, Washington, DC.

Gray, Alexander, 1947. *The Socialist Tradition. Moses to Lenin*, New York: Longmans, Green and Company.

Great Britain Census Office, 1822. *Census of Great Britain*, Population: viz. Enumeration and Parish Registers; According to the Census of M.D. CCC XXI (1822), xxx.

—— 1970a. *Census of England and Wales 1881*, British Parliamentary Papers, Dublin: Irish University Press.

—— 1970b. *Census of Great Britain, 1851, vol. 1. Population*, British Parliamentary Papers, Dublin: Irish University Press.

Great Britain. Poor Law Commissioners, 1834. *Report from his Majesty's Commissioners for Inquiring into the Administration and Practical Operation of the Poor Laws*, London: B. Fellowes, Ludgate St.

Greenspan, Alan, 2007. *The Age of Turbulence. Adventures in a New World*, New York: Penguin.

Greven, Phillip, 1970. *Four Generations: Population, Land and Family in Colonial Andover, Massachusetts*, Ithaca, NY.: Cornell University Press.

Grigg, D. B., 1980. *Population Growth and Agrarian Change: An Historical Perspective*, Cambridge: Cambridge University Press.

Grimke, Sarah, 1988. *Letters on the Equality of the Sexes and Other Essays*, (ed.), Elizabeth Ann Bartless, New Haven, CT: Yale University Press.

Groenewegen, Peter, 1994. "A Neglected Daughter of Adam Smith: Clara Elizabeth Collet (1860–1948)," in Peter Groenewegen (ed.), *Feminism and Political Economy in Victorian England*, Aldershot: Edward Elgar, 147–72.

—— 1994. "Alfred Marshall–Women and Economic Development: Labor, Family, and Race," in Peter Groenewegen (ed.), *Feminism and Political Economy in Victorian England*, Aldershot: Edward Elgar, 79–109.

Grogan, Susan K., 1992 French Socialism and Sexual Difference. Women and the New Society, 1803–44, London: Macmillan.

Gronau, Reuben, 1977. "Leisure, Home Production and Work: The Theory of the Allocation of Time Revisited," *Journal of Political Economy*, 85(6), 1099–123.

Grosh, M. and P. Glewwe, 1995. "A Guide to Living Standards Measurement Study Surveys and Their Data Sets," LSMS Working Paper #120, Washington: The World Bank.

Haac, Oscar (ed.), 1995. *The Correspondence of John Stuart Mill and Auguste Comte*, New York: Transaction Press.

Haakonssen, Knut, 1981. *The Science of a Legislator. The Natural Jurisprudence of David Human and Adam Smith*, New York: Cambridge University Press.

Hakim, Catherine, 1980. "Census Reports as Documentary Evidence: The Census Commentaries, 1801–1951," *Sociological Review*, 28(3), 551–80.

Hamburger, Joseph, 1999. *John Stuart Mill on Liberty and Control*, Princeton, NJ: Princeton University Press.

Hamilton, Alexander, 5 December 1791. *Papers* 10:252, available online at <http://press-pubs.uchicago.edu/founders/documents/v1ch4s31.html>.

Harrison, John F. C., 1969. *Quest for the New Moral World: Robert Owen and the Owenites in Britain and America*, New York: Charles Scribner's Sons.

Harsin, Jill, 1985. *Policing Prostitution in Nineteenth-Century Paris*, Princeton, NJ: Princeton University Press.

Hartman, Mary S., 2004. *The Household and the Making of History*, New York: Cambridge University Press.

Hartsock, Nancy, 1983. *Money, Sex and Power: Toward a Feminist Historical Materialism*, New York: Longman.

Haveman, Robert H., Andrew Bershadker, and Jonathan A. Schwabish, 2002. *Human Capital in the United States from 1975 to 2000: Patterns of Growth and Utilization*, Kalamazoo, MI: Upjohn.

Hayden, Dolores, 1981. *The Grand Domestic Revolution. A History of Feminist Designs for American Homes, Neighborhoods, and Cities*, Cambridge, MA: MI T. Press.

Hayek, F. A. von, 1951. *John Stuart Mill and Harriet Taylor. Their Correspondence and Subsequent Marriage*, Chicago, IL: University of Chicago Press.

—— 1988. *The Fatal Conceit. The Errors of Socialism*, Chicago, IL: University of Chicago Press.

—— 2007. *The Road to Serfdom*, (first published 1944), Bruce Caldwell (ed.), Chicago, IL: University of Chicago Press.

Hazard, Paul, 1973. *European Thought in the Eighteenth Century. From Montesquieu to Lessing*, Gloucester, Mass.: Peter Smith.

Hazlitt, William, 1930. "A Reply to the Essay on Population by the Rev. T. R. Malthus," in P. P. Hower (ed.), *The Complete Works of William Hazlitt*, London: J. M. Dent and Sons, Ltd., 202.

Heather-Bigg, Ada, 1894. "The Wife's Contribution to Family Income," *The Economic Journal* 4, 55.

Hecksher, Eli, 1931. *Mercantilism*, New York: Macmillan.

Heilbroner, Robert L., 1961. *The Worldly Philosophers*, New York: Simon and Schuster.

Heilbroner, Robert L., 1986. *The Worldly Philosophers. The Lives, Times, and Ideas of the Great Economic Thinkers*, New York: Simon and Schuster.

—— 1999. *The Worldly Philosophers*, 7th Edition, New York: Simon and Schuster.

Heiman, Edward, 1923. "The Family Wage Controversy in Germany," *Economic Journal* 33, 509–15.

Henrich, Joseph, Robert Boyd, Samuel Bowles, Colin Camerer, Ernst Fehr, and Herbert Gintis (eds.), 2004. *Foundations of Human Sociality: Economic Experiments and Ethnographic Evidence from Fifteen Small-scale Societies*, New York: Oxford University Press.

Herlihy, David, 1990. *Opera Muliebra. Women and Work in Medieval Europe*, Philadelphia, PA: Temple University Press.

Higginbotham, A. Leon, 1980. *In the Matter of Color*, New York: Oxford University Press.

Higgs, Edward, 1987. "Women, Occupations, and Work in the Nineteenth Century Censuses," *History Workshop*, 23, 59–80.

Hill, Bridget, 1989. *Women, Work, and Sexual Politics in Eighteenth-Century England*, New York: Basil Blackwell.

Hill, Christopher, 1969. *The Pelican History of Britain, Vol. 2: Reformation to Industrial Revolution*, Harmondsworth, England: Penguin Books.

—— 1982. *Century of Revolution, 1603–1714*, New York: W. W. Norton and Company.

Himes, Norman, 1937. "Jeremy Bentham and the Genesis of English Neo-Malthusianism," *Economic History*, 3(2), 267.

Himmelfarb, Gertrude, 1974. *On Liberty and Liberalism: The Case of John Stuart Mill*, New York: Alfred A. Knopf.

—— 1984. *The Idea of Poverty. England in the Early Industrial Age*, New York: Alfred A. Knopf.

—— 1995. *The Demoralization of Society. From Victorian Virtues to Modern Values*, New York: Alfred A. Knopf.

—— 2001. "The Idea of Compassion: The British vs. the French Enlightenment," *The Public Interest*, 145, 9.

—— 2004. *The Roads to Modernity: The British, French, and American Enlightenments*, New York: Knopf.

Himmelweit, Susan, et al, 1998. *Households*, Milton Keynes, England: The Open University.

Hirschleifer, Jack, 1977. "Shakespeare versus Becker on Altruism: The Importance of Having the Last Word," *Journal of Economic Literature*, 11, 500–2.

Hirschman, Albert O., 1970. *Exit, Voice, and Loyalty: Responses to Decline in Firms, Organizations, and States*, Cambridge, MA: Harvard University Press.

—— 1977. *The Passions and the Interests: Political Arguments for Capitalism Before its Triumph*, Princeton, NJ: Princeton University Press.

—— Albert O., 1986. *Rival Views of Market Society*, New York: Viking.

Hirshleifer, Jack, 1994. "The Dark Side of the Force," *Economic Inquiry*, 32, 1–10.

Historical Statistics of the U.S. Colonial Times to 1970. Part I, Washington: Bureau of the Census.

Hobbes, Thomas, 1978. *Man and Citizen*, Bernard Gert (ed.), Gloucester, Mass: Peter Smith.

—— 1986. *Leviathan*, C. B. MacPherson (ed.), Harmondsworth, England: Penguin.

Hobsbawm, E. J., 1962. *The Age of Revolution, 1789–1848*, New York: The World Publishing Company.

Hoffman, Philip T., 1996. *Growth in a Traditional Society. The French Countryside 1450–1815*. Princeton, NJ: Princeton University Press.

Holcombe, Lee, 1973. *Victorian Ladies at Work*, Newton Abbot, Devon: David and Charles.

—— 1977. "Victorian Wives and Property," in Martha Vicinus (ed.), *A Widening Sphere. Changing Roles of Victorian Women*, Bloomington, IND: Indiana University Press, 3–28.

Hollander, Samuel, 1997. *Malthus*, London: University of Toronto Press.

Holloway, Mark, 1951. *Heavens on Earth. Utopian Communities in America 1680–1880*, London: Turnstile Press.

Horne, Thomas A., 1978. *The Social Thought of Bernard Mandeville. Virtue and Commerce in Early Eighteenth-Century England*, New York: Columbia University Press.

Houghton, Walter E., 1957. *The Victorian Frame of Mind, 1830–1870*, New Haven, CT: Yale University Press.

Hufton, Olwen H., 1974. *The Poor of Eighteenth-Century France 1750–1789*, Oxford: The Clarendon Press.

—— 1992. *Women and the Limits of Citizenship in the French Revolution*, Toronto: University of Toronto Press.

Huizinga, Johan, 1954. *The Waning of the Middle Ages*, trans. F. Hopman, New York: Doubleday.

Human Rights Watch. "The Pinochet Prosecution," available online at <http://www.hrw.org/campaigns/chile98/index.html>, accessed 28 May, 2008.

Hume, David, 1882. *A Treatise on Human Nature and Dialogues Concerning Natural Religion*, London: Longmans, Green, and Company.

Hume, David, 1966. *An Enquiry Concerning the Principles of Morals*, reprinted from the edition of 1777 with an introductory note by John B. Stewart, La Salle, IL: Open Court.

Humphries, Jane, 1990. "Enclosures, Common Rights, and Women: The Proletarianization of Families in the late Eighteenth and Early Nineteenth Centuries," *The Journal of Economic History*, 50(1), 17–42.

Hundert, E. J., 1995. "Bernard Mandeville and the Enlightenment's Maxims of Modernity," *Journal of the History of Ideas*, 56(4), 580.

Hunt, E. K., 1979. *History of Economic Thought: A Critical Perspective*, Belmont, California: Wadsworth Publishing Company.

Hunt, Felicity, 1986. "Opportunities Lost and Gained: Mechanization and Women's Work in the London Bookbinding and Printing Trades," in Angela V. John (ed.), *Unequal Opportunities. Women's Employment in England 1800–1918*, New York: Basil Blackwell, 71–94.

Hunt, Lynn, 1990. "The Unstable Boundaries of the French Revolution," in Michelle Perrot (ed.), *A History of Private Life. From the Fires of Revolution to the Great War*, Cambridge, MA: The Belknap Press of Harvard University Press, 15.

—— 1993. *The Family Romance of the French Revolution*, Berkeley, CA: University of California Press.

Hutchins, B. L. and A. Harrison, 1966. *A History of Factory Legislation*, first published 1903, New York: Augustus M, Kelley.

Hutchinson, E. P., 1967. *The Population Debate. The Development of Conflicting Theories Up to 1900*, Boston, MA: Houghton Mifflin Company.

Huzel, James, 1969. "Malthus, the Poor Law, and Population in Early Nineteenth-Century England," *Economic History Review*, 22(3), 430–51.

—— 1980. "The Demographic Impact of the Old Poor Law: More Reflections on Malthus," *Economic History Review*, 33(3), 367–81.

—— 2006. *The Popularization of Malthus in Early 19th Century England*, Burlington, VT: Ashgate.

Inglis, Brian, 1971. *Poverty and the Industrial Revolution*, London: Hodder and Stoughton.

Ireland, Thomas R., 1998. "Compensable Nonmarket Services in Wrongful Death Litigation: Legal Definitions and Measurement Standards," *Journal of Legal Economics*, 7(2), 15–34.

Isaac, Rhys, 2004. *Landon Carter's Uneasy Kingdom: Revolution and Rebellion on a Virginia Plantation*, New York: Oxford.

Jacobs, Jerry A. and Kathleen Gerson, 2004. *The Time Divide. Work, Family, and Gender Inequality*, Cambridge, MA: Harvard University Press.

James, Patricia, 2006. *Population Malthus*, New York: Routledge.

Jevons, William Stanley, 1965. *The Theory of Political Economy*, New York: Augustus M. Kelley.

—— 1972. *Papers and Correspondence of William Stanley Jevons*, Volume I, London: Macmillan.

John Templeton Foundation, 2009. "Does the free market corrode moral character?" available online at <http://www.templeton.org/market/>, accessed 24 January, 2009.

John, Angela V., 1986. *Unequal Opportunities. Women's Employment in England 1800–1918*, New York: Basil Blackwell.

Johnson, E. A. J., 1965. *Predecessors of Adam Smith*, New York: Augustus Kelley.

Johnson, E. D. H., 1969. *Charles Dickens: An Introduction to His Novels*, New York: Random House.

Johnson, Elizabeth A., 1992. *She Who Is. The Mystery of God in Feminist Theological Discourse*, New York: Crossroad.

Johnson, Samuel, 1755. *A Dictionary of the English Language*, London: W. Strahan.

Johnston, Carolyn, 1992. *Sexual Power. Feminism and the Family in America*, Tuscaloosa, AL: University of Alabama Press.

Jorgensen, Dale W. and Barbara M. Fraumeni, 1989. "The Accumulation of Human and Non-Human Capital, 1948–1984," in R. E. Lipsey and H. S. Tice (eds.), *The Measurement of Savings, Investment and Wealth*, Chicago, IL: University of Chicago Press, 227–82.

Joshi, Heather, 1990. "The Cash Opportunity Costs of Childbearing: An Approach to Estimation using British Data," *Population Studies*, 44, 41–60.

Kahneman, D., E. Diener, and N. Schwarz, 1999. *Well-Being: The Foundations of Hedonic Psychology*, New York: Russell Sage Foundation.

Kamm, Josephine, 1977. *John Stuart Mill in Love*, London: Gordon and Cremonesi.

Kaplan, Stephen L., 1976. *Bread, Politics, and Political Economy*, The Hague, Netherlands: Martinus Nijhoff.

Kelly, Linda, 1987. *Women of the French Revolution*, London: Hamish Hamilton Ltd.

Kendrick, John, 1976. *The Formation and Stocks of Total Capital*, Cambridge, MA: National Bureau of Economic Research.

—— 1979. "Expanding Imputed Values in the National Income and Product Accounts," *Review of Income and Wealth*, 25(4), 349–63.

Kennedy, David M., 1970. *Birth Control in America. The Career of Margaret Sanger*, New Haven, CT: Yale University Press.

—— 1973. *Birth Control in America. The Career of Margaret Sanger*, New Haven, CT: Yale University Press.

Kerber, Linda, 1986. *Women of the Republic: Intellect and Ideology in Revolutionary America*, New York: W. W. Norton and Company.

—— 1989. "Women and Individualism in American History," *Massachusetts Review*, 589–609.

Kessler-Harris, Alice, 1990. *A Woman's Wage. Historical Meanings and Social Consequences*, Lexington, KY: University of Kentucky.

Kevan, P. G., and T. P. Phillips, 2001. "The Economic Impacts of Pollinator Declines: An Approach to Assessing the Consequences," *Conservation Ecology*, 5 (1), available at <http://www.consecol.org/vol5/iss1/art8/>, accessed 20 July, 2008.

Keynes, John Maynard, 1926. *The End of Laissez-Faire*, London: Hogarth Press.

—— 1963. *Essays in Persuasion*, first published 1930, New York: W. W. Norton and Company.

King, Gregory, 1936. *Two Tracts. Natural and Political Observations and Conclusions Upon the State and Condition of England: Of the Naval Trade of England Around 1688 and the National Profit then Arising Thereby*, George E. Barnett (ed.), Baltimore, MD: Johns Hopkins University Press.

King, Willford I., Wesley G. Mitchell, Frederick Macaulay, and Oswald W. Knauth, 1921. *Income in the United States, Its Amount and Distribution*, New York: Harcourt, Brace, and Co.

Kinnaird, Joan, 1979. "Mary Astell and the Conservative Contribution to English Feminism," *The Journal of British Studies*, 19(1), 53–75.

Kneeland, Hildegarde, 1934. "Review of *Economics of Household Production*," *Journal of Home Economics*, 26, 525.

Kolmerten, Carol A., 1993. "Women's Experiences in the American Owenite Communities," in Wendy E. Chmielewski, Louis J. Kern, and Marlyn Klee-Hartzell (eds.), *Women in Spiritual and Communitarian Societies in the U.S*, Syracuse NY: Syracuse University Press, 38–51.

Komlos, John, 1989. "Thinking About the Industrial Revolution," *The Journal of European Economic History*, 18(1), 191–206.

Koven, Seth and Sonya Michel, 1993. *Mothers of a New World. Maternalist Politics and the Origins of Welfare States*, New York: Routledge.

Kraditor, Aileen, 1968. *Up from the Pedestal. Selected Writings in the History of American Feminism*, Chicago, IL: Quadrangle Books.

—— 1971. *The Ideas of the Woman Suffrage Movement, 1890–1920*, New York: Anchor Books.

Krouse, Richard W., 1982. "Patriarchal Liberalism and Beyond: From John Stuart Mill to Harriet Taylor," in Jean Bethke Elshtain (ed.), *The Family in Political Thought*, Chicago, IL: University of Chicago Press, 145–72.

Kuiper, Edith, 2000. *The Most Valuable of All Capital*, Amsterdam: Tinbergen Institute Research Series.

—— 2001. *The Most Valuable of All Capital*, Amsterdam: Tinbergen Institute.

—— 2003. "The Construction of Masculine Identity in Adam Smith's Theory of Moral Sentiments," in D. Barker and E. Kuiper, (eds.), *Toward a Feminist Philosophy of Economics*, New York: Routledge, 145–60.

—— Jolande Sap (eds.), 1995. *Out of the Margin: Feminist Perspectives*, New York: Routledge.

Kulikoff, Alan, 1989. "The Transition to Capitalism in Rural America," *William and Mary Quarterly*, 3rd Ser., (46), 120–44.

Kussmaul, Ann, 1981. *Servants in Husbandry in Early Modern England*, New York: Cambridge University Press.

Kuznets, Simon, 1941. *National Income and Its Composition, 1919–1938*. Assisted by Lillian Epstein and Elizabeth Jencks, New York: National Bureau of Economics Research.

Kyrk, Hazel, 1929. *Economic Problems of the Family*, New York: Harper and Brothers Publishers.

Laidler, Harry W., 1927. *A History of Socialist Thought*, New York: Thomas Y. Crowell.

—— 1933. *A History of Socialist Thought*, New York: Thomas Y. Crowell.

Landes, David, 1983. *Revolution in Time. Clocks and the Making of the Modern World*, Cambridge, MA: The Belknap Press.

Landes, Joan, 1982. "Hegel's Conception of the Family," in Jean Bethke Elshtain (ed.), *The Family in Political Thought*, Amherst, MA: The University of Massachusetts Press, 125–144.

Lane, Robert, 1993. "Does Money Buy Happiness," *Public Interest*, 113, 56–65.

Lange, Lynda, 1981. "Rousseau and Modern Feminism," *Social Theory and Practice*, 7, 245–77.

Langer, Gary, 1987. *The Coming of Age of Political Economy, 1815–1825*, New York: Greenwood Press.

Langland, Elizabeth Walter R. Gove, 1983. *A Feminist Perspective in the Academy: The Difference it Makes*, Chicago, IL: University of Chicago Press.

Laslett, Peter, 1965. *The World We Have Lost. England Before the Industrial Age*, New York: Charles Scribner's Sons.

—— 1989. *The World We Have Lost*, New York: Routledge.

Le Goff, Jacques, 1988. *Your Money or Your Life. Economy and Religion in the Middle Ages*, New York, Basic Books.

Leach, William, 1980. *True Love and Perfect Union. The Feminist Reform of Sex and Society*, New York: Basic Books, Inc.

Lecky, William Edward Hartpole, 1869. *History of European Morals from Augustus to Charlemagne*, New York: D. Appleton and Company.

Leibowitz, Arleen, 1973. "Home Investments in Children," in T. W. Schultz (ed.), *Economics of the Family. Marriage, Children, and Human Capital*, Chicago, IL: University of Chicago Press.

Lerner, Gerda, 1986. *The Creation of Patriarchy*, New York: Oxford University Press.

—— 1998. *The Feminist Thought of Sarah Grimke*, New York: Oxford University Press.

Letwin, William, 1963. *The Origins of Scientific Economics. English Economic Thought 1660–1776*, Westport, CT: Greenwood Press Publishers.

Levine, David, 1977. *Family Formation in an Age of Nascent Capitalism*, New York: Academic Press.

Levy, David M., 2001. *How the Dismal Science Got Its Name: Classical Economics & the Ur-Text of Racial Politics*, Ann Arbor, MI: University of Michigan Press.

—— 2003. "Taking Harriet Martineau's Economics Seriously," in Robert Dimand and Chris Nyland (eds.), *The Status of Women in Classical Economic Thought*, Northampton, MA: Edward Elgar, 262–84.

Lewis, Jane, 1980. *The Politics of Motherhood. Child and Maternal Welfare in England, 1900–1939*, London: Croom Helm.

—— 1984. *Women in England 1870–1950: Sexual Divisions and Social Change*, Sussex: Wheatsheaf.

Lewis, Michael and David Einhorn, 2009. "The End of the Financial World as We Know It," *New York Times*, January 3.

Liggio, Leonard P., 1977. "Charles Dunoyer and French Classical Liberalism," *Journal of Libertarian Studies* 1(3), 153–78.

Lindert, Peter, 1994. "Unequal Living Standards," in Roderick Floud and Donald McCloskey (eds.), *The Economic History of Britain Since 1700, Second Edition, Vol. 1: 1700–1860*, Cambridge: Cambridge University Press, 357–86.

—— 2004. *Growing Public. Social Spending and Economic Growth Since the Eighteenth Century*, New York: Cambridge University Press.

Lloyd, Trevor, 1971. *Suffragettes International: The World-wide Campaign for Women's Rights*, New York: American Heritage Press.

Locke, Don, 1980. *A Fantasy of Reason. The Life and Thought of William Godwin*, Boston, MA: Routledge and Kegan Paul.

Locke, John, 1967. *Two Treatises of Government*, Peter Laslett (ed.), Cambridge, MA: Cambridge University Press.

Logan, Deborah A., 2007. "The Redemption of a Heretic: Harriet Martineau and Anglo-American Abolitionism in Pre-Civil War America," in Kathryn Kish

Sklar and James Brewer (eds.), *Women's Rights and Transatlantic Antislavery in the Era of Emancipation*, New Haven, CT: Yale University Press, 242–65.

Lord, William, 2002. *Household Dynamics*, New York: Oxford University Press.

Lowenthal, Ester, 1911. *The Ricardian Socialists*, New York: Longmans, Green.

MacFarlane, Alan, 1986. *Marriage and Love in England 1300–1840*, New York: Basil Blackwell.

Macintyre, Alasdair, 1984. *After Virtue. A Study in Moral Theory*. Notre Dame, IN.: University of Notre Dame Press.

Mack, Mary P., 1963. *Jeremy Bentham, 1748–1792*, New York: Columbia University Press.

Maclachlan, Fiona, 1999. "The Ricardo-Malthus Debate on Underconsumption: A Case Study in Economic Conversation," *History of Political Economy*, 31(3), 563–74.

Malthus, Thomas Robert, 1836. *Principles of Political Economy*, London: W. Pickering.

—— 1932. *Observations on the Effects of the Corn Laws, and of a Rise or Fall in the Price of Corn on the Agriculture and General Wealth of the Country*, Baltimore, MA: Johns Hopkins University Press.

—— 1965. *An Essay on the Principle of Population as it Affects the Future Improvement of Society with Remarks on the Speculations of Mr. Godwin, Mr. Condorcet and Other Writers*, New York: Augustus M. Kelley.

—— 1990. *Essay on the Principle of Population*, The version published in 1803, with the variora of 1806, 1807, 1817 and 1826, (ed.), Patricia James, New York: Cambridge University Press.

Mandeville, Bernard, 1709. *The Virgin Unmask'd: or Female Dialogues betwixt an Elderly Maiden Lady and her Niece, on Several Diverting Discourses of the Times*, London: J. Morphero.

—— 1924a. *A Modest Defense of Public Stews: or, an Essay Upon Whoring*, London: A. Bussy.

—— 1924b. *The Fable of the Bees; or Private Vices, Publick Benefits*, Vols. I and II, Oxford: Clarendon Press.

Manuel, Frank E., 1962. *The Prophets of Paris*, Cambridge, MA: Harvard University Press.

—— Fritzie P. Manuel, 1979. *Utopian Thought in the Western World*, Cambridge, MA: Harvard University Press.

Marcet, Jane, 1817. *Conversations on Political Economy*, London: Longman.

Marilley, Suzanne M., 1996. *Woman Suffrage and the Origins of Liberal Feminism in the U.S., 1820–1920*, Cambridge, MA.: Harvard University Press.

Marshall, Alfred, 1907. "The Social Possibilities of Economic Chivalry," *The Economic Journal*, 17, 7–17.

—— 1962. *Principles of Economics*, first published 1890, 8th edition, London: Macmillan.

—— 1966. *Memorials of Alfred Marshall*, (ed.), A. C. Pigou, New York: Augustus M. Kelley.

Martineau, Harriet, 1839. *The Martyr Age of the United States*, Boston: Weeks, Jordan and Company.

—— 1859. "Female Industry," *Edinburgh Review* 222, 300.

—— 1869. *Biographical Sketches, 1852–1868*, 2nd edition, London: Leypoldt and Holt.

—— 1879, *Autobiography*, with Memorials by Maria Weston Chapman, 4th ed., Boston: Houghton, Osgood and Co, vol. 2, 562–74.

—— 1985. "The Political Non-Existence of Women," in Gayle Graham Yates (ed.), *Harriet Martineau on Women*, New Brunswick: Rutgers University Press.

Marx, Karl, 1977. *Capital*, Vol. 1. Ben Fowkes (trans.), New York: Vintage Books.

—— Frederick Engels, 1972*a*. "Manifesto of the Communist Party," in Robert Tucker (ed.), *The Marx-Engels Reader*, New York: W. W. Norton and Company.

—— —— 1972*b*. "The German Ideology," in Robert Tucker (ed.), *The Marx-Engels Reader*, New York: W. W. Norton and Company, 124.

Massachusetts Bureau of Labor Statistics, 1876–77. *The Census of Massachusetts: 1875*, Boston: Albert J. Wright.

—— 1889. *Twentieth Annual Report of the Bureau of the Statistics of Labor*, Boston, MA: Wright and Potter Printing Company.

May, Elaine Tyler, 1980. *Great Expectations. Marriage and Divorce in Post-Victorian America*, Chicago, IL: University of Chicago Press.

May, Martha, 1985. "Bread Before Roses: American Workingmen, Labor Unions and the Family Wage," in Ruth Milkman (ed.), *Women, Work and Protest. A Century of U.S. Women's Labor History*, Boston, MA: Routledge and Kegan Paul, 2.

Mazlish, Bruce, 1975. *James and John Stuart Mill. Father and Son in the Nineteenth Century*, New York: Basic Books.

McCaffery, Edward J., 1997. *Taxing Women*, Chicago, IL: University of Chicago Press.

McCann, Carole R., 1994. *Birth Control Politics in the United States, 1916–1945*, Ithaca: Cornell University Press.

McCloskey, Deirdre, 2007. *The Bourgeois Virtues: Ethics for an Age of Commerce*, Chicago, IL: University of Chicago Press.

McKibben, Bill, 2007. *Deep Economy, The Wealth of Communities and the Durable Future*, New York: Times Books.

McLaren, Angus, 1978. *Birth Control in Nineteenth-Century England*, London: Croom Helm.

—— 1983. *Sexuality and Social Order. The Debate over the Fertility of Women and Workers in France, 1770–1920*, New York: Holmes and Meier.

McLellan, David, 1973. *Karl Marx. His Life and Thought*, New York: Harper and Row.

McMillan, James F., 2000. *France and Women, 1789–1914*, New York: Routledge.

McPherson, C. B., 1962. *The Political Theory of Possessive Individualism: Hobbes to Locke*, New York: Oxford University Press.

McWilliams-Tullberg, Rita, 1977. "Women and Degrees at Cambridge University, 1862–1897," in Martha Vicinus (ed.), *A Widening Sphere. Changing Roles of Victorian Women*, Bloomington, IND: Indiana University Press, 117–45.

Merrill, Michael, 1995. "Putting 'Capitalism' in its Place: A Review of Recent Literature," *The William and Mary Quarterly*, 3rd Series, Vol. 52(2), 315–26.

Middleton, Christopher, 1979. "The Sexual Division of Labor in Feudal England," *New Left Review*, No. 113/114, 105–54.

Mill, James, 1963. *Elements of Political Economy*, 3rd edition, Revised and Corrected, New York: Augustus Kelley.

—— 1983. "Article on Government," reprinted in Susan Groag Bell and Karen M. Offen (eds.), *Women, the Family and Freedom*, Stanford, CA: Stanford University Press.

Mill, John Stuart, 1859. *Dissertations and Discussions*, London: John D. Parker.

—— 1952. *Autobiography*, New York: Oxford University Press.

—— 1965. *Principles of Political Economy with Some of Their Applications to Social Philosophy*, Books I and II, based on the 7th edition, London: Routledge and Kegan Paul.

—— 1970. *The Subjection of Women*, with an introduction by Wendell Carr, Cambridge, MA: MIT. Press.

—— 1983. "Speech Before the House of Commons," 20 May 1867, reprinted in Susan Groag Bell and Karen M. Offen (eds.), *Women, the Family and Freedom*, Stanford, CA: Stanford University Press, 486.

Mincer, Jacob, 1962. "The Labor Force Participation of Married Women," in H. G. Lewis (ed.), *Aspects of Labor Economics*, Princeton, NJ: Princeton University Press.

—— 1974. *Schooling, Experience, and Earnings*, New York: Columbia University Press.

Mitchell, B. R., 1988. *British Historical Statistics*, New York: Cambridge University Press.

—— 1998. *International Historical Statistics, Europe, 1750–1993*, 4th edition, New York: Stockton Press.

Mokyr, Joel, 2002. "The Factory System," in Joel Mokyr, *Gifts of Athena. Historical Origins of the Knowledge Economy*, Princeton, NJ: Princeton University Press, 120–61.

Montesquieu, Charles de Secondat, 1952. *The Spirit of Laws*, Chicago IL: Encyclopedia Britannica, Inc.

—— 1973. *Persian Letters*, trans. C. J. Betts, New York: Penguin.

Morton, A. L., 1969. *The Life and Ideas of Robert Owen*, New York: International Publishers.

Moses, Claire Goldberg, 1984. *French Feminism in the Nineteenth Century*, Albany, NY: State University of New York Press.

—— 1993. "Difference in Historical Perspective," in Claire Goldberg Moses and Leslie Wahl Rabine (eds.), *Feminism, Socialism, and French Romanticism*, Bloomington, IND: Indiana University Press, 17–84.

Muller, Jerry Z., 2002. *The Mind and the Market. Capitalism in Western Thought*, New York: Anchor Books.

Mulligan, Casey B., 2009. "A Milestone for Working Women," *New York Times*, 14 January, available online at <http://economix.blogs.nytimes.com/2009/01/14/a-milestone-for-women-workers/>, accessed 25 January, 2009.

Munroe, James Phinney, 1923. *A Life of Francis Amasa Walker*, New York: Henry Holt and Company.

Murray, Margaret, 1971. *The Witch Cult in Western Europe*, Oxford: Clarendon Press.

Nardinelli, Clark, 1990. *Child Labor and the Industrial Revolution*, Bloomington, IND: Indiana University Press.

Nelson, Julie, 1996. "Thinking about Gender and Value," in Julie A. Nelson, *Feminism, Objectivity, and Economics*, New York: Routledge, 3–19.

—— 2006. *Economics for Humans*, Chicago, IL: University of Chicago Press.

Nelson, Robert H., 2001. *Economics as Religion. From Samuelson to Chicago and Beyond*, University Park, PA: Pennsylvania State University Press.

Newhauser, Richard, 2000. *The Early History of Greed. The Sin of Avarice in Early Medieval Thought and Literature*, New York: Cambridge University Press.

Newman, Lance, 2003. "Thoreau's Natural Community and Utopian Socialism," *American Literature*, 75(3), 530.

Nibley, Hugh, 1989. *Approaching Zion, The Collected Works of Hugh Nibley*, Vol. 9, Salt Lake City, UT: Deseret Books.

Niederle, Muriel and Lise Vesterlund, 2007. "Do Women Shy Away from Competition? Do Men Compete Too Much?" *Quarterly Journal of Economics*, 122(3), 1067–101.

Noble, David F., 1922. *A World Without Women. The Christian Clerical Culture of Western Science*, New York: Alfred A. Knopf.

—— 1993. *A World Without Women. The Christian Clerical Culture of Western Science*, New York: Oxford University Press.

Noonan, J. T., 1965. *Contraception. A History of its Treatment by the Catholic Theologians and Canonists*, Cambridge, MA: Harvard University Press.

Nordhaus, William, 2008. *A Question of Balance. Weighing the Options on Global Warming Policy*, New Haven, CT: Yale University Press.

Norris, Floyd, 2002. "Greenspan Coins a New Phrase," *New York Times*, 17 July.

North, Douglas and R. P. Thomas, 1973. *The Rise of the Western World: A New Economic History*, Cambridge: Cambridge University Press.

Norton, Justin M., 2006 "Milton Friedman," *San Francisco Chronicle*, 16 November.

Norton, Mary Beth, 1980. *Liberty's Daughters: The Revolutionary Experience of American Women, 1750–1800*, Boston MA: Little, Brown.

Nove, Alex, 1983. *The Economics of Feasible Socialism*, Boston: Allen and Unwin.

Nown, Graham, 1986. *Mrs. Beeton. 150 Years of Cookery and Household Management*, London: Ward Lock Ltd.

Noyes, John Humphrey, 1961. *History of American Socialisms*, first published 1870, New York: Hillary House Publishers.

Nuttall, A. D., 1984. *Pope's Essay on Man*, London: George Allen and Unwin.

Nye, John Vincent, 1991. "The Myth of Free Trade Britain and Fortress France: Tariffs and Trade in the Nineteenth Century," *Journal of Economic History*, 51 (1), 23–46.

Nyland, Chris, 1993*a*. "Poulain de la Barre and the Rationalist Analysis of the Status of Women," *History of Economics Review*, 19, 18–33.

—— 1993*b*. "John Locke and the Social Position of Women," *History of Political Economy*, 25(1), 39–63.

—— Tom Heenan, 2003. "William Thompson and Anna Doyle Wheeler: A Marriage of Minds on Jeremy Bentham's Doorstep," in Robert Dimand and Chris Nyland (eds.), *The Status of Women in Classical Economic Thought*, Cheltenham UK: Edward Elgar, 241–61.

O'Brien, Mary, 1981. *The Politics of Reproduction*, Boston, MA: Routledge and Kegan Paul.

Owen, Robert, 1817. *A New View of Society: or, Essays on the Formation of the Human Character, Preparatory to the Development of a Plan for Gradually Ameliorating the Condition of Mankind*, 3rd edition, London: R. and A. Taylor.

—— 1836. *The Book of the New Moral World, Containing the Rational System of Society*, London: Effingham Wilson, Royal Exchange.

Owen, Robert, 1840. *Socialism or the Rational System of Society*, London: Effingham Wilson.

—— 1969. "The Revolution in the Mind and Practice of the Human Race," in A. L. Morton, *The Life and Ideas of Robert Owen*, New York: International Publishers.

Pankhurst, Richard, 1954. *William Thompson, Pioneer Socialist*, London: Pluto Press.

—— 1957. *The Saint Simonians Mill and Carlyle*, London: Lalibela Books.

Parent-Duchâtelet, Alexandre, 1981. *La Prostitution á Paris au XIXieme Siecle*, first published 1836, Paris: Editions de Seuil.

Pateman, Carol, 1988. *The Sexual Contract*, Stanford, CA: Stanford University Press.

—— 1989. *The Disorder of Women. Democracy, Feminism, and Political Theory*, Stanford, CA: Stanford University Press.

Patmore, Coventry, 1937. *The Angel in the House*, Vol. 1, *The Betrothal*, Boston, MA: Tickner and Fields.

Pearson, Karl, 1901. *The Ethic of Free Thought*, London: Adam and Charles Black.

Pedersen, Susan, 1993. *Family, Dependence, and the Origins of the Welfare State. Britain and France 1914–1945*, New York: Cambridge University Press.

Perry, Ruth, 1986. *The Celebrated Mary Astell. An Early English Feminist*, Chicago, IL: The University of Chicago Press.

Petty, Sir William, 1963. *The Economic Writings of Sir William Petty Together with the Observations Upon the Bills of Mortality more probably by Captain John Graunt*, New York: Augustus M. Kelley.

Pew Research Center, 2003. "Global Gender Gaps," Pew Global Attitudes Project, available online at <http://pewglobal.org/commentary/display.php?AnalysisID=71>, accessed 30 August, 2007.

Phipps, Shelley, Peter Burton, and Lynn Lethbridge, 2001. "In and Out of the Labour Market: Long-Term Income Consequences of Child-Related Interruptions to Women's Paid Work," *Canadian Journal of Economics*, 34, 411–29.

Pigou, Arthur C., 1920. *The Economics of Welfare*, London: Macmillan.

Pinchbeck, Ivy, 1969. *Women Workers and the Industrial Revolution, 1750–1850*, London: Frank Cass.

Pinker, Susan, 2008. *The Sexual Paradox: Men, Women and the Real Gender Gap*, New York: Scribner.

Place, Francis, 1967. *Illustrations and Proofs of the Principle of Population*, with critical and textual notes by Norman Himes, New York: Augustus Kelley Publishers.

Pocock, J. G. A., 1985. *Virtue, Commerce, and History. Essays on Political Thought and History, Chiefly in the Eighteenth Century*, New York: Cambridge University Press.

Podmore, Frank, 1907. *Robert Owen. A Biography*, New York: D. Appleton and Company.

Polachek, Solomon, 1981. "Occupational Self-Selection: A Human Capital Approach to Sex Differences in Occupational Structure," *Review of Economics and Statistics*, 63(1), 60–9.

Polanyi, Karl, 1944. *The Great Transformation*, Boston, MA: Beacon Press.

Pollak, Robert A., 1985. "A Transaction Cost Approach to Families and Households," *Journal of Economic Literature*, 23(2), 581–608.

Pope, Alexander, 1865. "Essay on Man," in *The Poems of Alexander Pope*. Bungay, Suffolk: Methuen and Company Ltd.

Porter, Roy, 1982. "Mixed Feelings: The Enlightenment and Sexuality in Eighteenth-Century Britain," in Paul-Gabriel Boucé (ed.), *Sexuality in Eighteenth-Century Britain*, Manchester: Manchester University Press.

Porter, Theodore M., 2004. *Karl Pearson. The Scientific Life in a Statistical Age*, Princeton NJ: Princeton University Press.

Posner, Richard, 1992. *Sex and Reason*, Cambridge, MA: Harvard University Press.

Poulain de la Barre, François, 1990. *The Equality of the Sexes*, Desmond M. Clarke (trans.), New York: Manchester University Press.

Presser, Harriet B., 1998. "Decapitating the U.S. Census Bureau's 'Head of Household': Feminist Mobilization in the 1970s," *Feminist Economics*, 4 (3),145–58.

Price, Richard, 1784. *Observations on the Importance of the American Revolution*, London, available online at <http://www.constitution.org/price/price_6.htm>.

Pujol, Michèle, 1984. "Gender and Class in Marshall's Principles of Economics," *Cambridge Journal of Economics*, 8, 217–34.

—— 1992. *Feminism and Anti-Feminism in Early Economic Thought*, Aldershot, UK: Edward Elgar.

—— 1995. "The Feminist Thought of Harriet Taylor," in R. W. Dimand and E. L. Forget (eds.), *Women of Value. Feminist Essays on the History of Women in Economics*, Aldershot, UK: Edward Elgar, 82–102.

Quaife, G. R., 1979. *Wanton Wenches and Wayward Wives: Peasants and Illicit Sex in Early Seventeenth Century England*, New Brunswick, NJ: Rutgers University Press.

Raeder, Linda C., 2002. *John Stuart Mill and the Religion of Humanity*, Columbia, MO: University of Missouri Press.

Rand, Ayn, 1993. *The Fountainhead*, first published 1943, New York: Plume.

Rathbone, Eleanor, 1917. "The Remuneration of Women's Services," *The Economic Journal*, 27, 54–68.

Rathbone, Eleanor, 1924. *The Disinherited Family*, London: Edward Arnold and Company.

Reid, Margaret, 1934. *Economics of Household Production*, New York: John Wiley and Sons.

Reisman, David, 1990. *Alfred Marshall's Mission*, New York: St. Martin's Press.

Rendall, Jane, 1978. *The Origins of the Scottish Enlightenment*. New York: St. Martin's Press.

—— 1985. *The Origins of Modern Feminism: Women in Britain, France and the United States 1780–1860*, Chicago, IL: Lyceum Books.

—— 1987. "Virtue and Commerce: Women in the Making of Adam Smith's Political Economy," in *Women in Western Political Philosophy*, Ellen Kennedy and Susan Mendus (eds.), New York: St. Martin's Press.

Residents of Hull House, 1970. *Hull House Maps and Papers*, first published 1895, New York: Arno Press.

Resneck, Samuel, 1935. "The Social History of an American Depression, 1837–1843," *American Historical Review*, 40, 662–87.

Reuther, Rosemay Radford, 1990. "The Liberation of Christology from Patriarchy," in Ann Wages (ed.), *Feminist Theology: A Reader*, London: SPCK, 138–48.

Ricardo, David, 1962. *The Principles of Political Economy and Taxation*, New York: E. P. Dutton.

—— 1966. *On the Principles of Political Economy and Taxation. The Works and Correspondence of David Ricardo, Volume I*, (ed.), Piero Sraffa, Cambridge, MA: The University Press, For the Royal Economic Society.

Richardson, J. H., 1924. "The Family Allowance System," *Economic Journal*, 35, 373–86.

Robespierre, Maximilien, 1965. "Republic of Virtue," in Richard W. Lyman and Lewis W. Spitz (eds.), *Major Crises in Western Civilization*, vol. 2, New York: Harcourt, Brace, and World, 71–2.

Robinson, E. A. G., 1964. "John Maynard Keynes 1883–1946," in Robert Lekachman (ed.), *Keynes' General Theory. Reports of Three Decades*, New York: St. Martin's Press.

Roemer, John, 1988. *Free to Lose. An Introduction to Marxist Economic Philosophy*, Cambridge, MA: Harvard University Press.

Ronsin, Francis, 1980. *La grève des ventres. Propagande néo-malthusienne et baisse de la natalité en France 19e–20e siècles*, Paris: Éditions Aubier Montaigne.

Roosevelt, Franklin D., 1937. *Second Inaugural Address*, available online at <http://www.yale.edu/lawweb/avalon/presiden/inaug/froos2.htm>, accessed 27 May, 2008.

Roosevelt, Theodore, 1906. Interviewed in "Mr. Roosevelt's Views on Race Suicide," *Ladies Home Journal*, February, 21.

—— 1917. *The Foes of Our Own Household* (New York: George Doran.

Rose, June, 1992. *Marie Stopes and the Sexual Revolution*, Boston: Faber and Faber.

Rosen, Ruth, 1982. *The Lost Sisterhood. Prostitution in America, 1900–1918*, Baltimore, MA: Johns Hopkins University Press.

Rosenberg, Nathan and L. E. Birdzall, Jr., 1986. *How the West Grew Rich. The Economic Transformation of the Industrial World*, New York: Basic Books.

Rosenzweig, Mark and T. Paul Schultz, 1982. "Market Opportunities, Genetic Endowments, and Intrafamily Resource Distribution," *American Economic Review*, 72, 803–15.

Rossiaud, Jacques, 1988. *Medieval Prostitution*, trans. Lydia G. Cochrane, New York: Basil Blackwell.

Rossiter, Margaret W., 1982. *Women Scientists in America. Struggles and Strategies to 1940*, Baltimore, MA: Johns Hopkins University Press.

Rothenberg, Winifred Barr, 1992. *From Market-Places to a Market Economy: The Transformation of Rural Massachusetts, 1750–1850*, Chicago, IL: University of Chicago Press.

Rousseau, Jean-Jacques, 1968. *Politics and the Arts: A Letter to M. D'Alembert on the Theatre*, trans. A. Bloom, Ithaca, NY: Cornell University Press.

—— 1994a. *Discourse on Political Economy and the Social Contract*, trans. Christopher Betts, New York: Oxford University Press.

—— 1994b. *Discourse on the Origin of Inequality*, New York: Oxford University Press.

Rowntree, B. Seebohm and Frank D. Stuart, 1921. *The Responsibility of Women Workers for Dependants*, Oxford: Clarendon Press.

Ruskin, John, 1985. *Unto This Last and Other Writings*, New York: Penguin.

Ryan, Mary P., 1975. *Womanhood in America. From Colonial Times to the Present*, New York: New Viewpoints.

Ryan, John, 1920. *A Living Wage*, (first published 1906), New York: The Macmillan Company.

Safire, William, 1986. "Ode to Greed," *New York Times*, 5 January, 1986, section 4, 19.

Sahakian, William S. and Mabel Lewis Sahakian, 1975. *John Locke*, Boston, MA: Twayne Publishers.

Saint-Simon, Henri de, 1964. "First Extract from the 'Organizer,' " in Felix Markham (ed.), *Social Organization, The Science of Man and Other Writings*, first published 1819, New York: Harper Torchbooks, 72–3.

Samuelson, Paul, 1956. "Social Indifference Curves," *Quarterly Journal of Economics*, 190, 1–22.

Sanger, Margaret, 1920. *Woman and the New Race*, New York: Brentano's.

—— 1922. *Pivot of Civilization*, New York: Brentano's.

—— 1931. *My Fight for Birth Control*, Elmsford, New York: Maxwell Reprint Company.

Sanger, William, 1939. *The History of Prostitution. Its Extent, Causes and Effects Throughout the World*, New York: Eugenics Publishing Company.

Sargent, Lydia (ed.), 1981. *Women and Revolution*, Boston, MA: South End Press.

Savile, George, Marquis of Halifax, 1990. "The Lady's New Year's Gift: or, Advice to a Daughter," in Vivien Jones (ed.), *Women in the Eighteenth Century. Constructions of Femininity*, New York: Routledge), 18.

Schabas, Margaret, 1990. *A World Ruled by Number. William Stanley Jevons and the Rise of Mathematical Economics*, Princeton, NJ: Princeton University Press.

Schloesser, Pauline, 2002. *The Fair Sex. White Women and Racial Patriarchy in the Early American Republic*, New York: New York University Press.

Schochet, Gordon J., 1975. *Patriarchalism in Political Thought: The Authoritarian Family and Political Speculation and Attitudes, Especially in 17th Century England*, Oxford: Blackwell.

Schultz, Theodore W., 1961. "Investment in Human Capital," *American Economic Review* 51(1), 8.

Schumpeter, Joseph A., 1950. *Capitalism, Socialism and Democracy*, 3rd edition (first published 1942), New York: Harper Torchbooks.

—— 1954. *History of Economic Analysis*, New York: Oxford University Press.

Scott, Joan Wallach, 1988. *Gender and the Politics of History*, New York: Columbia University Press.

—— 1997. *Only Paradoxes to Offer. French Feminists and the Rights of Man*, Cambridge, MA: Harvard University Press.

Searle, G. R., 2005. *A New England. Peace and War 1886–1918*, New York: Oxford University Press.

Seccombe, Wally, 1992. *A Millenium of Family Change: Feudalism to Capitalism in Northwestern Europe*, New York: Verso.

—— 1993. *Weathering the Storm. Working-Class Families from the Industrial Revolution to the Fertility Decline*, New York: Verso.

Seiz, Janet A. and Michele A. Pujol, 2000. "Harriet Taylor Mill," *American Economic Review*, 90(2), 476–9.

Sellers, Charles, 1991. *The Market Revolution. Jacksonian America, 1815–1846*, New York: Oxford University Press.

Sen, Amartya, 1999. *Commodities and Capabilities*, London: Oxford University Press.

Seymour-Jones, Carole, 1992. *Beatrice Webb*, Chicago, IL: Ivan Dee.

Shaftesbury, Anthony Ashley Cooper, Earl of, 1963. *Characteristics of Men, Manners, Opinions, Times, etc.*, (ed.), John M. Robertson, Gloucester, MA.: Peter Smith.

Shah, Sumitra, 2006. "Sexual Division of Labor in Adam Smith's Work," *The History of Economic Thought*, 28(2), 221–41.

Shakespeare,William, 1976. *Coriolanus*, Philip Brockbank (ed.), New York: Harper and Row.

Shammas, Carole, 1994. "Re-Assessing the Married Women's Property Acts," *Journal of Women's History*, 6(1), 9–29.

Shaw, George Bernard, 1928. *The Intelligent Woman's Guide to Socialism and Capitalism*, New York: Brentano's.

Shelley, Percy, 1947. "Queen Mab," in Thomas Hutchinson (ed.), *The Complete Poetical Works of Percy Bysshe Shelley*, London: Oxford University Press, 780.

Sherr, Lynn (ed.), 1995. *Failure is Impossible. Susan B. Anthony in Her Own Words*, New York: Random House.

Shonkoff, Jack P. and Deborah Phillips, 2000. *From Neurons to Neighborhoods: The Science of Early Child Development*, Washington, D.C.: National Academy Press.

Siegel, Reva B., 1994. "Home as Work: The First Woman's Rights Claims concerning Wives' Household Labor, 1850–1880," *Yale Law Journal*, 103, 1073–217.

Simons, Henry, 1938. *Personal Income Taxation. The Definition of Income as a Problem of Fiscal Policy*, Chicago, IL: University of Chicago Press.

Simonton, Deborah, 1998. *A History of European Women's Work. 1700 to the Present*, New York: Routledge.

Sismondi, J.C. L. Simonde de, 1966. *Political Economy* (1815), New York: A. M. Kelley.

Skinner, Quentin, 1988. "Meaning and Understanding in the History of Ideas," in James Tully (ed.), *Meaning and Context. Quentin Skinner and His Critics*, Princeton, NJ: Princeton University Press, 29–67.

Sklar, Katherine Kish, 1973. *Catherine Beecher. A Study in American Domesticity*, New Haven, CT: Yale University Press.

Skocpol, Theda, 1993. *Protecting Soldiers and Mothers. The Politics of Social Provision in the United States, 1870s–1920*, Cambridge, MA: Harvard University Press.

Smart, William, 1895. *Studies in Economics*, London: Macmillan and Company.

—— 1899. *The Distribution of Income*, New York: The Macmillan Company.

Smith, Adam, 1911. *The Theory of Moral Sentiments*, with a biographical and critical memoir of the author by Dugald Stewart, London: G. Bell and Sons, Ltd.

—— 1976. *An Inquiry in the Nature and Causes of the Wealth of Nations*, Oxford: Clarendon Press.

Smith, Daniel S., 1973. "Family Limitation, Sexual Control and Domestic Feminism in Victorian America," *Feminist Studies*, 1(3–4), 40–57.

Smith, Richard Cándida, 2007. "Stanton on Self and Community," in Ellen Carol DuBois and Richard Candida Smith (eds.), *Elizabeth Cady Stanton. Feminist as Thinker. A Reader in Documents and Essays*, New York: New York University Press, 66–81.

Solow, Robert, 1987. "What Do We Know that Francis Amasa Walker Didn't?", *History of Political Economy*, 19(2), 183–90.

Soloway, Richard Allen, 1982. *Birth Control and the Population Question in England, 1877–1930*, Chapel Hill, NC: University of North Carolina Press.

Spencer, Herbert, 1910. *The Principles of Ethics*, New York: D. Appleton.

Spengler, Joseph, 1965. French Predecessors of Malthus. A Study in Eighteenth Century Wage and Population Theory, New York: Octagon.

Stanton, Elizabeth Cady, 1868a. "Reasons Why Some Marriages are Unhappy," *The Revolution*, October 15.

—— 1868b. *The Revolution*, December 24.

—— 1899. "The Equilibrium of Sex," *Commonwealth*, 6 (June 24), 12–13.

—— 1993. *Eighty Years and More. Reminiscences 1815–1897*, Boston, MA: Northeastern University Press.

—— 1997. "The Subjection of Women," in Ann D. Gordon (ed.), *The Selected Papers of Elizabeth Cady Stanton and Susan B. Anthony*, New Brunswick: Rutgers University Press, 626.

—— 2007. "Has Christianity Benefited Woman," in Ellen Dubois and Richard Smith (eds.), *Elizabeth Cady Stanton*, New York: New York University Press, 249.

—— Susan B. Anthony, and Matilda Jocelyn Gage, 1882. *History of Woman Suffrage*, Volumes 1–3, New York: Fowler and Wells.

Staveren, Irene van, 2003. "Feminist Fiction and Feminist Economics," in Drucilla K. Barker and Edith Kuiper (eds.), *Toward a Feminist Philosophy of Economics*, New York: Routledge, 56–69.

Stevenson, Betsey and Justin Wolfers, 2007. "The Paradox of Declining Female Happiness," Working Paper, Wharton School, University of Pennsylvania, Draft of 17 September, 2007, available online at <http://bpp.wharton.upenn.edu/bet-seys/papers/Paradox%20of%20declining%20female%20happiness.pdf>, accessed 21 January, 2009.

Stiglitz, Joseph E., 1987. "The Causes and Consequences of the Dependence of Quality on Price," *Journal of Economic Literature*, 25, 1–48.

Stone, Lawrence, 1977. *The Family, Sex, and Marriage in England, 1500–1800*, New York: Harper and Row.

Stone, Pamela, 2007. *Opting Out? Why Women Really Quit Careers and Head Home*, Berkeley, CA: University of California Press.

Stopes, Marie, 1932. *Married Love. A New Contribution to the Solution of Sex Difficulties*, New York: Eugenics Publishing Company.

Stowe, Harriet Beecher, 1852. *Uncle Tom's Cabin; or Life Among the Lowly*, Boston, MA: John P. Jewett.

Sumption, Jonathan, 1978. *The Albigensian Crusade*, London: Faber.

Taussig, Frank W., 1916. "Minimum Wages for Women," *Quarterly Journal of Economics*, 30(3), 411–42.

Tawney, R. H., 1926. *Religion and the Rise of Capitalism*, London: John Murray.

Taylor, Alan, 2001. *The People of British America, 1700–1750*, Foreign Policy Research Institute, available online at <www.fpri.org/orbis/> accessed 10 January, 2006, 1 (based on chapters 8 and 14 in Alan Taylor, *American Colonies*, New York: Viking Penguin).

Taylor, Barbara, 1983. *Eve and the New Jerusalem. Socialism and Feminism in the Nineteenth Century*, New York: Pantheon.

Taylor, Harriet, 1970. "The Enfranchisement of Women," in John Stuart Mill and Harriet Taylor, *Essays on Sex Equality*, (ed.), Alice Rossi, Chicago, IL: University of Chicago.

Taylor, Shelley E., 2003. *The Tending Instinct*, New York: Holt.

Thaler, Richard H. and Cass R. Sunstein, 2008. *Nudge. Improving Decisions About Health, Wealth, and Happiness*, New Haven, CT: Yale University Press.

The New English Bible, 1970. Oxford University Press and Cambridge University Press.

Thomas, Keith, 1958. "Women and the Civil War Sects," *Past and Present*, 13, 42–62.

Thompson, E. P., 1963. *The Making of the English Working Class*, New York: Vintage Books.

—— 1971. "The Moral Economy of the English Crowd," *Past and Present*, 50(1), 76–136.

Thompson, Flora McDonald, 1900. "The Servant Question," *Cosmopolitan*, 28 (March), 521–8.

Thompson, William, 1825. *Appeal of One Half the Human Race, Women, Against the Pretensions of the Other Half, Men, to Retain Them in Political, and Thence in Civil and Domestic Slavery*, London: Printed for Longman, Hurst, Rees, Orme, Brown, and Green.

—— 1827. *Labor Rewarded*, London: Hunt and Clarke.

Thomson, Dorothy Lampen, 1973. *Adam Smith's Daughters*, New York: Exposition Press.

Tomalin, Claire, 1992. *The Life and Death of Mary Wollstonecraft*, New York: Penguin.

Topalov, Christian, 1999. "Une révolution dans les représentations du travail: L'émergence de la catégorie statistique de 'population active' au XIXe siècle en France, en Grande-Bretagne et aux Etats-Unis," *Revue Française de Sociologie*, 40 (3), 445–73.

Toqueville, Alexis de, 1951. *Democracy in America*, Vol. II, New York: Alfred A. Knopf.

Tronto, Joan, 1987. "Beyond Gender Difference to a Theory of Care," *Signs: Journal of Women in Culture and Society* 12(4), 644–63.

—— 1993. *Moral Boundaries: A Political Argument for an Ethics of Care*, New York: Routledge.

Trumbach, Randolph, 1992. "Sex, Gender, and Sexual Identity in Modern Culture: Male Sodomy and Female Prostitution in Enlightenment London," in John C. Fout (ed.), *Forbidden History*, Chicago, IL: University of Chicago Press, 89–106.

Tuana, Nancy, 1993. *The Less Noble Sex. Scientific, Religious, and Philosophical Conceptions of Women's Nature*, Bloomington, IND: Indiana University Press.

Tucker, Josiah, 1993. *Instructions for Travelers*, in *The Collected Works of Josiah Tucker*, with a new introduction by Jeffery Stern (6 vols.), London: Routledge.

U.S. Women's Bureau, 1921. *State Laws Affecting Working Women*, Bulletin No. 16, Washington: Government Printing Office.

United Nations Fourth World Conference on Women, 1995. "Platform for Action," available online at <http://www.un.org/womenwatch/daw/beijing/platform/plat1.htm>, accessed 13 July, 2008.

United States Senate, Memorial of Mary F. Eastman, Henrietta L. T. Woolcott, and others, officers of the Association for the Advancement of Women, praying that the tenth census may contain a just enumeration of women as laborers and producers, *Senate Miscellaneous Documents*, 45th Congress, 2nd Session, Vol. 2, No. 84 (Serial Set, 1786).

Ure, Andrew, 1967. *The Philosophy of Manufactures*, New York: Augustus M. Kelley.

Valenze, Deborah, 1995. *The First Industrial Woman*, New York: Oxford University Press.

Velzen, Susan van, 2003. "Hazel Kyrk and the Ethics of Consumption," in Drucilla K. Barker and Edith Kuiper (eds.), *Toward a Feminist Philosophy of Economics*, New York: Routledge, 38–55.

Veret, Jeanne-Désirée, 1993. "Improvement of the Destiny of Women and the People through a New Household Organization," Claire Goldberg Moses and Leslie Wahl Rabine (eds.), *Feminism, Socialism, and French Romanticism*, Bloomington, IND: Indiana University Press, 290.

Vickrey, William, 1947. *Agenda for Progressive Taxation*, New York: The Ronald Press Company.

Vogel, Lise, 1983. *Marxism and the Oppression of Women*, New Brunswick: Rutgers University Press.

Voltaire, Francois, 1971. *Philosophical Dictionary*, New York: Penguin Books.

Wagman, Barnet and Nancy Folbre, 1996. "Household Services and Economic Growth in the U.S., 1870–1930," *Feminist Economics*, 2(1), 43–66.

Wahrman, Dror, 2001. "The English Problem of Identity in the American Revolution," *The American Historical Review*, 106(4).

Waldfogel, Jane, 1997. "The Effect of Children on Women's Wages," *American Sociological Review*, 62, 209–17.

—— 1998. "Understanding the 'Family Gap' in Pay for Women with Children," *Journal of Economic Perspectives*, 12(1), 137–56.

Walker, Frances, 1896. "Restriction of Immigration," *Atlantic Monthly*, 25 (June), 822–29.

Wallerstein, Immanuel, 1974. *The Modern World System. Capitalist Agriculture and the Origins of the European World Economy in the Sixteenth Century*, New York: Academic Press.

Waring, Marilyn, 1988. *If Women Counted. A New Feminist Economics*, New York: Harper and Row.

Waterman, A. M. C., 1991. *Revolution, Economics, and Religion. Christian Political Economy, 1798–1833*, New York: Cambridge University Press.

—— 1997. "Recycling Old Ideas: Economics Among the Humanities," *Research in the History of Economic Thought and Methodology*, 15, 237–49.

—— 2001. "The Beginning of 'Boundaries': The Sudden Separation of Economics from Christian Theology," in G. Erreygers (ed.), *Economics and Interdisciplinary Research*, New York: Routledge, 41–63.

Waterman, A. M. C., 2004. *Political Economy and Christian Theology Since the Enlightenment. Essays in Intellectual History*, New York: Palgrave Macmillan.

—— 2008. "The English School of Political Economy," in The *New Palgrave Dictionary of Economics*, 2nd edition, New York: Palgrave Macmillan.

Webb, Beatrice, 1919. *The Wages of Men and Women: Should They be Equal?*, London: The Fabian Society.

—— 1948. *Our Partnership*, London: Longmans, Green.

—— 1982. *The Diary of Beatrice Webb, Vol. l, 1873–1892. Glitter Around and Darkness Within*, (ed.), Norman and Jeanne McKenzie, Cambridge: Harvard University Press.

Webb, Sidney, 1907. *The Decline in the Birth Rate*, London: The Fabian Society.

Weber, Max, 1956. *The Protestant Ethic and the Spirit of Capitalism*, (first published 1930), New York: Charles Scribner's Sons.

Wellman, Judith, 2004. *The Road to Seneca Falls. Elizabeth Cady Stanton and the First Woman's Rights Convention*, Chicago, IL: University of Illinois Press.

Wells, H. G., 1906. *Socialism and the Family*, London: A. C. Fifield.

—— 1919. *New Worlds for Old*, New York: MacMillan.

—— 1931. *The Work, Wealth, and Happiness of Mankind*, New York: Doubleday, Doran.

White, Michael V., 1994. "Following Strange Gods: Women in Jevon's Political Economy," in Peter Groenewegen (ed.), *Feminism and Political Economy in Victorian England*, Aldershot: Edward Elgar, 46–78.

Williams, Alex, 2007. "Putting Money on the Table," *New York Times*, 23 September.

Williams, David, 1971. "The Politics of Feminism in the French Enlightenment," in Peter Hughes and David Williams (eds.), *The Varied Pattern: Studies in the 18th Century*, Toronto: A. M. Hakkert, Ltd, 337.

Williamson, Oliver, 1985. *The Economic Institutions of Capitalism: Firms, Markets, Relational Contracting*, New York: Free Press.

Winch, Donald, 1987. *Malthus*, New York: Oxford University Press.

—— 1993. "Robert Malthus: Christian Moral Scientist, Arch-Demoralizer or Implicit Secular Utilitarian," *Utilitas*, 5(2), 239–53.

Wollstonecraft, Mary, 1992. *A Vindication of the Rights of Woman*, (ed.), Miriam Brody, New York: Penguin Books.

Wood, Gordon S., 1993. *The Radicalism of the American Revolution*, New York: Knopf.

Woolley, Frances, 1996. "Getting the Better of Becker," *Feminist Economics*, 2(1), 114–20.

Wordsworth, William, 1969. "Humanity," in Thomas Hutchinson (ed.), *Poetical Works*, New York: Oxford University Press, 393.

Wright, Carroll, 1900. *The History and Growth of the U.S. Census*, Washington, D.C.: Government Printing Office.

Yates, Gail (ed.), 1985. *Harriet Martineau*, New Brunswick: Rutgers University Press.

Yeo, Eileen, 1971. "Robert Owen and Radical Culture," in Sidney Pollard and John Salt (eds.), *Robert Owen, Prophet of the Poor*, Lewisburg, PA: Bucknell University Press.

Zelizer, Viviana A., 1985. *Pricing the Priceless Child. The Changing Social Value of Children*, New York: Basic Books.

GENERAL INDEX